CompTIA®
Project+®
Study Guide
Exam PK0-005
Third Edition

Kim Heldman, MBA, PMP

SYBEX®
A Wiley Brand

Published by John Wiley & Sons, Inc., Hoboken, New Jersey.
Published simultaneously in Canada and the United Kingdom.

ISBN:978- 1-119-89245-8
ISBN:978- 1-119-89246-5(ebk.)
ISBN:978- 1-119-89247-2(ebk.)

For general information on our other products and services or for technical support, please contact our Customer Care Department within the United States at (800) 762-2974, outside the United States at (317) 572-3993 or fax (317)572- 4002.

Wiley also publishes its books in a variety of electronic formats. Some content that appears in print may not be available in electronic formats. For more information about Wiley products, visit our web site at www.wiley.com.

Library of Congress Control Number: 2022936876

Cover image: © Jeremy Woodhouse/Getty Images
Cover design: Wiley

Printed and bound by CPI Group (UK) Ltd, Croydon, CR0 4YY

C004283_170822

In loving memory of my father, Lt. Col. David L. Taylor, who was an exemplary leader

Acknowledgments

Thank you for buying the third edition of *CompTIA Project+ Study Guide: Exam PK0-005* to help you study and prepare for the CompTIA Project+ exam. I believe this book is a good introduction to the in-depth world of project management and certification and will open up many opportunities for you.

I would like to thank all the great team members at Wiley who were part of this project: Kenyon Brown, senior acquisitions editor; David Clark, development editor; Barath Kumar Rajasekaran, production editor; and all those behind the scenes who helped make this book a success. They are terrific to work with, as always, and I appreciate their keen eyes and insightful ideas and suggestions.

Special thanks go to Vanina Mangano for her work as technical editor. I appreciate her diligence and great suggestions that helped make the content stronger.

And a thank-you, as always, goes to my husband and family for understanding my crazy schedule while working on the book. And Dad, this one is for you. I learned my leadership and organizational skills from the best!

About the Author

Kim Heldman, MBA, PMP® is the CIO/Sr. Manager Information Technology for the Regional Transportation District in Denver, Colorado. Kim directs IT resource planning, budgeting, project prioritization, and strategic and tactical planning. She directs and oversees IT design and development, enterprise resource planning systems, IT infrastructure, application development, cybersecurity, IT program management, intelligent transportation systems, data center operations, and more.

Kim oversees a portfolio of projects ranging from small in scope and budget to multimillion-dollar, multiyear projects. She has more than 25 years of experience in information technology project management. Kim has served in an executive leadership role for more than 18 years and is regarded as a strategic visionary with an innate ability to collaborate with diverse groups and organizations, instill hope, improve morale, and lead her teams in achieving goals they never thought possible.

Kim is also the author of *PMP® Project Management Professional Exam Study Guide, 10th Edition, 2021, John Wiley & Sons* and *Project Management JumpStart, 3rd Edition, 2021, John Wiley & Sons* and coauthor of several other project management books. Kim has also published several articles and is currently working on a leadership book.

Kim continues to write on project management best practices and leadership topics, and she speaks at conferences and events. You can contact Kim at Kim.Heldman@gmail.com. She personally answers all her email.

About the Technical Editor

Vanina Mangano is a program management leader within Google LLC where she leads a team of program managers within the Ads organization. She devotes time to furthering the project management profession through her volunteer work at the Project Management Institute; currently, she serves as an advisory member within PMI's Standards Insight Team, helping to shape the standards roadmap.

Contents at a Glance

Introduction   *xxi*

Assessment Test   *xxx*

Chapter 1   Introducing the Project   1

Chapter 2   Understanding IT Fundamentals   33

Chapter 3   Creating the Project Charter   71

Chapter 4   Planning the Project   107

Chapter 5   Creating the Project Schedule   153

Chapter 6   Resource Planning and Management   195

Chapter 7   Defining the Project Budget and Risk Plans   239

Chapter 8   Communicating the Plan   283

Chapter 9   Processing Change Requests   329

Chapter 10   Managing Quality and Closing Out the Project   363

Appendix   Answers to Review Questions   399

Index   *417*

Contents

Introduction   *xxi*

Assessment Test   *xxx*

Chapter   1   Introducing the Project   **1**

Defining the Project   2
  Identifying the Project   2
  Programs and Portfolios   3
  Understanding Operations   4
  Using the PMBOK® Guide   5
Project Life Cycle Phases   5
  Discovery Phase   6
  Initiating Phase   6
  Planning Phase   7
  The Executing Phase   9
  The Closing Phase   10
Performing the Discovery/Concept Preparation Phase   10
  How Projects Come About   11
  Creating the Business Case and Selecting Projects   13
  Determining Benefits and Rewards   14
  Examining Existing Artifacts   21
Project Selection Methods   23
  Decision Models   24
  Expert Judgment   25
Summary   25
Exam Essentials   26
Key Terms   27
Review Questions   28

Chapter   2   Understanding IT Fundamentals   **33**

Understanding the Role of the Project Manager   34
  Leadership   35
  Communication   35
  Problem Solving   36
  Negotiating   36
  Organization and Time Management   37
Factors That Influence Project Management Activities   38
  Environmental, Social, and Governance (ESG) Factors   38
  Compliance and Privacy Considerations   40
Information Technology Fundamentals   46
  Infrastructure   46

Cloud Models	51
Software	55
Financial Systems	60
Summary	62
Exam Essentials	64
Key Terms	65
Review Questions	67

Chapter 3   Creating the Project Charter   71

Identifying and Assessing Stakeholder Roles and Responsibilities	72
The Customer and End Users	73
The Project Sponsor	74
The Project Manager	75
The Senior Management Team	76
The Business Analyst	76
The Subject Matter Experts	76
The Project Management Office	77
The Program Manager	77
The IT Team	78
The Stakeholder Register	79
Assessing Stakeholders	80
Creating the Preliminary Scope Statement	83
Understanding the Need	84
Documenting the Preliminary Scope Definition	85
Creating the Project Charter	85
Purpose or Justification for the Project	86
Objectives	86
Project Description	87
Key Deliverables	87
High-Level List of Requirements	87
High-Level Milestones	87
Preapproved Budget	88
High-Level Assumptions	88
High-Level Constraints	88
Overall Risks	89
Other Contents	89
Project Success Criteria	89
Formal Approval	90
Creating the Records Management Plan	90
Determining Access Requirements	92
Holding the Kickoff Meeting	93
Summary	98

		Exam Essentials	99
		Key Terms	101
		Review Questions	102
Chapter	**4**	**Planning the Project**	**107**
		Defining the Planning Phase	108
		Documenting the Scope Management Plan	109
		Writing the Scope Statement	110
		Project Objectives	111
		Project and Product Description	111
		Success Criteria and Key Performance Indicators	111
		Key Deliverables	112
		Exclusions from Scope	112
		Time and Cost Estimates	112
		Assumptions	113
		Constraints	113
		Approval of the Scope Statement	118
		Documenting the Requirements	119
		Requirement Categories	119
		The Requirements Document	121
		Determining a Project Methodology	122
		Projects in Control (PRINCE2)	124
		DevOps	124
		Development Life Cycle Methodologies	125
		Using the Waterfall Methodology	125
		Using Agile Methodologies	126
		Scrum	127
		Kanban	127
		Scrumban	129
		Lean	129
		Extreme Programming	130
		Feature-Driven Development	132
		Dynamic Systems Development Method	132
		Agile Unified Process	133
		Hybrid	133
		Summary of Project Life Cycles	134
		Selecting a Methodology	136
		Determining Scope on Agile Projects	138
		Agile Team Members	139
		Determine a Solutions Design	140
		Summary	143
		Exam Essentials	145
		Key Terms	146
		Review Questions	148

Chapter   5   Creating the Project Schedule   **153**

Creating the Work Breakdown Structure   154
   Decomposing the Major Deliverables   155
   Guidelines for Creating a WBS   156
   Benefits of the WBS   157
   WBS Dictionary   158
   Scope Baseline   158
Documenting the Project Management Plan   159
Schedule Planning   160
Defining Tasks   161
Task Sequencing   162
   Types of Dependencies   162
   Logical Relationships   163
   Creating a Network Diagram   164
Assigning Resources   164
Determining Task Durations   165
   Defining Duration   165
   Estimating Techniques   165
Developing the Project Schedule   167
   Milestones   168
   Program Evaluation and Review Technique   169
   Gantt Charts   170
   The Critical Path Method   170
   Duration Compression   172
   Resource Loading   173
   Project Scheduling Software   175
   Setting the Baseline and Obtaining Approval   175
   Quality Gates   176
   Establishing Governance Gates   176
Scheduling Techniques Using Agile Methodologies   177
   Estimating Techniques Using Agile   177
   Burndown Chart   178
   Story Points and Velocity   179
   Kanban Board   180
   Scrum Board   181
   Agile Release Planning   182
Summary   185
Exam Essentials   186
Key Terms   188
Review Questions   190

Chapter	6	**Resource Planning and Management**	**195**
		Understanding Organizational Structures	196
		The Functional Organization	196
		The Matrix Organization	198
		The Projectized Organization	200
		Determining Resource Needs	201
		Resource Overallocation	203
		Interproject Work	203
		Resource Life Cycle	204
		Personnel Management	206
		Team Composition	206
		Selecting Team Members	206
		Roles and Responsibilities	208
		Organization Charts and Position Descriptions	208
		Matrix-Based Charts	209
		Building and Managing a Cohesive Team	211
		Trust Building	212
		Monitoring Team Performance	212
		Conflict Management	216
		Managing Conflict	216
		Project Kickoff Part Two	219
		Procurement Planning	220
		Statement of Work	221
		Vendor Solicitation	222
		Vendor Selection Criteria	223
		Types of Contracts	226
		Vendor-Related Documents	228
		Summary	230
		Exam Essentials	232
		Key Terms	233
		Review Questions	235
Chapter	7	**Defining the Project Budget and Risk Plans**	**239**
		Understanding Information Security Concepts	240
		Corporate IT Security Policies	240
		Categorizing Security Policies	242
		Estimating Costs	245
		Cost-Estimating Techniques	245
		Estimating Tips	249
		Creating the Project Budget	250
		Creating the Project Budget	251
		Cost Baseline	253
		Expenditure Tracking and Reporting	254

Budget Burndown Chart	255
Earned Value Management	256
Expenditure Reporting	260
Risk Planning	260
Risk Identification	261
Risk Analysis	263
Preparing Risk Responses	267
Risk Monitoring	270
Summary	272
Exam Essentials	273
Key Terms	275
Review Questions	277

Chapter 8   Communicating the Plan   283

Communications Planning	284
Exchanging Information	285
Listening	287
Methods of Communicating	288
Assessing the Forms of Communication	288
Written and Verbal Communication	289
Communication Methods and Tools	289
The Communication Plan	292
Communicating with Project Team Members	293
Communicating on an Agile Team	294
Factors That Influence Communications	297
Communication Triggers	299
Holding Effective Meetings	302
Meeting Types	302
Preparing for Meetings	305
Communication Platforms	307
Collaboration Tools	307
Meeting Tools	309
Reporting Project Information	310
Project Status Reports	310
Project Dashboard	311
Charts	311
Establishing Communication Channels	313
Maintaining Communication Records	313
Controlling Communications	315
Managing Stakeholder Expectations and Communication Needs	316
Summary	321
Exam Essentials	322
Key Terms	323
Review Questions	325

Chapter   9   Processing Change Requests   **329**

Executing Phase Activities   330
Reviewing the Project Management Plan   331
Managing Vendors   332
    Contract Change Control   333
    Paying Vendors   334
Implementing Change Control Systems   335
    Create and Submit the Change Request   336
    Documenting Changes in the Change Control Log
      and Conducting a Preliminary Review   336
    Conducting Impact Assessments   337
    Documenting Change Recommendations   338
    Determining Decision-Makers   339
    Managing the Change Control Board   339
    Documenting Approval Status in the Change Control Log   340
    Communicating Change Status   340
    Updating the Project Management Plan   341
    Implementing the Change   341
    Validating the Change and Perform a Quality Check   342
    Communicating Change Deployment   342
    Other Change Requests   342
Project Change Management   342
Implementing Organizational Change   343
    Types of Organizational Change   343
    Implementing Organizational Change   344
Operational Change Control on an IT Project   347
    IT Infrastructure Control   347
    Software Change Control   348
    Other IT Change Processes   349
Agile Frameworks   349
    Scaling Frameworks   350
Projects in Control (PRINCE2)   351
Summary   353
Exam Essentials   354
Key Terms   355
Review Questions   357

Chapter   10   Managing Quality and Closing Out the Project   **363**

Controlling Quality   364
    Inspecting and Testing   364
    Using Quality Charts   366
    Common Causes of Variances   372
    Taking Action on Quality Control   373

Managing Issues	374
Roles and Responsibilities	374
Issue Tracking	374
Resolution Plan	375
Resolution Techniques	376
Outcome Documentation	376
Action Items	376
Using Performance Measures	377
Key Performance Indicators	377
Balanced Scorecard	379
Key Objectives and Results	379
Cost and Schedule Performance	379
Project Endings	380
Characteristics of Closing	380
Types of Project Endings	380
Steps in Closing Out a Project	382
Verification and Validation of Deliverables	382
Obtaining Sign-Off	383
Developing a Transition Plan and Operational Handoff	383
Removing Access	384
Releasing Team Members	384
Closing Out the Contract	384
Archiving Documentation	385
Documenting Lessons Learned and Project Evaluation	385
Project Closure Meeting	388
Project Closeout Report	388
Rewards and Celebrations	389
Postimplementation Support and Warranty Period	389
Summary	390
Exam Essentials	391
Key Terms	393
Review Questions	394
Appendix **Answers to Review Questions**	**399**
Chapter 1: Introducing the Project	400
Chapter 2: Understanding IT Fundamentals	401
Chapter 3: Creating the Project Charter	403
Chapter 4: Planning the Project	404
Chapter 5: Creating the Project Schedule	406
Chapter 6: Resource Planning and Management	408
Chapter 7: Defining the Project Budget and Risk Plans	409
Chapter 8: Communicating the Plan	411
Chapter 9: Processing Change Requests	413
Chapter 10: Managing Quality and Closing Out the Project	414
Index	*417*

Introduction

Have you ever wondered how the pyramids were built? Or the Eiffel Tower? How did someone have the organizational skills to put all those people together and create such magnificent structures? Coming forward to recent times—how is Microsoft capable of putting together *millions* of lines of code for its latest operating system? The answer to all of these is project management.

The CompTIA Project+ exam will test your knowledge of the concepts and processes involved in project management. There are several project management methodologies you can follow, each with their own processes and procedures, but at the foundation of each one are sound project management principles and techniques. CompTIA Project+ is vendor neutral. It acknowledges other methodologies such as those published by the Project Management Institute® and PRINCE2® but doesn't follow them precisely.

In this edition of *CompTIA Project+ Study Guide*, you'll find plenty of discussion of project management concepts such as defining the requirements, creating the project charter document, creating the scope document, planning the project, assessing and managing risk, and closing out the project. You'll also find exam questions in categories such as information technology fundamentals, agile processes, team building and personnel management, quality management, status reporting, and more, and these are discussed as well.

The Project+ certification is centered on information technology (IT) projects. My job-related experience is in IT, and many of the examples in this book are drawn from real-life situations, but the names and scenarios have been changed to protect the guilty.

Where should you go beyond taking your Project+ test? If you find you're interested in all things project management, you should enroll in a good university-level class that takes you through the meatier stages of project management. This book and this test only touch the surface of project management techniques. You'll find there is much more to learn and that it's possible to make a career of managing projects.

 Make certain to study all the questions and answers in the assessment test and at the end of each chapter. Then head over to the online test bank at www.wiley.com/go/sybextestprep and take the two practice exams included with your purchase of this book. The Project+ exam is designed to test your knowledge of a concept or idea, so use this book to learn the objective behind the question.

What Is the Project+ Certification?

CompTIA's mission is to create tests and certifications that aren't company-specific. For example, you can take a server test that deals with the elements of servers and server operation but doesn't ask you specifics about Dell, HP, or IBM equipment. CompTIA got its start with what is now an industry standard, the A+ exam. This test is designed to examine your understanding of the workings of a PC and its associated connection to a network. There are other tests as well: Network+, Linux+, Cloud+, CySA+, and many others.

Why Become Project+ Certified?

Certification in project management has increasingly become a requirement for those interested in full-time careers in this field. It improves your credibility with stakeholders and customers. Becoming certified demonstrates your intent to learn the processes associated with project management and provides you with opportunities for positions and advancements that may not otherwise be possible.

Here are some reasons to consider the Project+ test and this study guide:

Demonstrates Proof of Professional Achievement   Certification demonstrates to current and potential employers that you are knowledgeable and well-grounded in project management practices and have taken the initiative to prove your knowledge in this area.

Increases Your Marketability   If you take a moment to browse job postings for project management positions, you'll often find that certification is either highly desirable or required. The CompTIA Project+ certification will help you stand out from other candidates and demonstrate that you have the skills and knowledge to fulfill the duties required of a project manager.

Provides Opportunity for Advancement   You may find that your Project+ certification is just what you need to get that next step up the ladder. People who study and pass certification tests prove, if nothing else, that they have the tenacity to get through a difficult subject and to demonstrate their understanding by testing on the subject.

Provides a Prerequisite for Advanced Project Management Training   If you're considering a project management career, the Project+ exam is a great way to start. Studying for this exam gives you a foundation in project management. After passing the exam, you should consider obtaining the Certified Associate Project Management (CAPM®) or Project Management Professional (PMP®) certification through the Project Management Institute (PMI). This study guide follows the principles and processes outlined by PMI and is a great introduction to its certifications.

Raises Customer Confidence Because It Raises Your Confidence   Customers who know you're certified in project management and who hear you speak and act with confidence are more confident in the company you represent. If you're able, for example, to identify and describe the four categories of risks to prepare for on a project, your customer gains confidence in you.

How to Become Project+ Certified

First, study the topics and processes outlined in this book, make certain to answer all the end-of-chapter questions, and then take the bonus exams found here: www.wiley.com/go/sybextestprep.

Then go to the CompTIA website (www.comptia.org) to find the list of testing sites where the exam is currently conducted.

 Prices and testing centers are subject to change at any time. Please visit CompTIA's website for the most up-to-date information: www.comptia.org.

If you take the test in person, you'll need a driver's license and one other form of ID when you arrive at the testing center. No calculators, computers, cell phones, or other electronic devices are allowed in the testing area. CompTIA also offers an online test option. You're allowed 90 minutes to take the exam, and there are a maximum of 95 multiple-choice and drag-and-drop questions. You must score a 710 (on a scale of 100–900) to pass. There are no prerequisites for this exam. You'll be notified of your grade as soon as you finish the test.

Who Should Buy This Book?

You should buy this book if you're interested in project management and want to learn more about the topic. The Project+ exam is an ideal way to introduce yourself to project management concepts and techniques, and this book will immerse you in the basics of those techniques.

If you've never taken a certification test before, you'll find that the Project+ exam is a pleasant way to get your feet wet. The test isn't overly complicated or riddled with trick questions; it simply covers the basics of project management. Once you pass the exam and gain confidence in your project management knowledge and skills, you'll be ready to progress to other certifications and be eager to learn the more in-depth topics involved in project management.

What Does This Book Cover?

This book follows the CompTIA Project+ exam blueprint and is divided into chapters that cover major topic areas. Each section is explained in sufficient detail to become a Project+ certified professional. Certain areas have been expanded upon, which are important concepts to know. However, they do not map directly to an exam objective.

You will learn the following information in this book:

Chapter 1: Introducing the Project provides a high-level overview of project management, introducing the basic terminology of project management, an understanding of the project phases, and how the Discovery/Concept phase is conducted.

Chapter 2: Understanding IT Fundamentals outlines information technology concepts, including understanding the basic concepts of infrastructure, cloud models, and software; understanding development life cycles; using project selection criteria; and understanding project team roles.

Chapter 3: Creating the Project Charter begins with a discussion of the Initiating phase. It then examines the elements of the project charter, how to identify and assess stakeholders, creating a records management system, and developing information security procedures, and concludes with an overview of the kickoff meeting.

Chapter 4: Planning the Project moves into project planning, beginning with documenting the project scope statement, understanding project influences and constraints, documenting the requirements, and defining requirements on an agile project.

Chapter 5: Creating the Project Schedule extends planning to creation of a detailed project schedule. It starts with an explanation of the work breakdown structure and how that is developed, then covers the entire schedule planning process, beginning with identifying and sequencing the tasks to be performed and allocating resources. You'll learn how to calculate task durations and the critical path through them, as well as determine milestones and set a baseline and obtain approval. Finally, you'll see how to prepare and conduct sprint planning for agile projects.

Chapter 6: Resource Planning and Management is where you'll learn about organizational structures, determining resource needs, personnel management, team structure on agile projects, conflict resolution, and procurement and vendor selection techniques.

Chapter 7: Defining the Project Budget and Risk Plans covers cost estimating and cost budgeting and the risk activities and strategies for your project. You'll learn the basic techniques of estimating and then tracking costs, along with risk analysis and planning.

Chapter 8: Communicating the Plan covers the role of communication—with stakeholders, team members, and others—in project management. You'll learn what information needs to be communicated and how to do so most effectively. You'll learn about communication tools as well as factors that influence communication, and we'll end with agile communication methods.

Chapter 9: Processing Change Requests outlines the activities in the Executing phase. It shows how to deal with changing project requirements and how to set up a change control system. It also looks at the types of organizational change that can affect a project, operational change control for an IT project, and how to manage vendor performance.

Chapter 10: Managing Quality and Closing Out the Project looks at quality management concepts, testing, performance charts, and performance measures. It also reviews the steps a project manager will take in closing out a project, including validating deliverables and creating a transition plan.

Many of the examples used to demonstrate practical application of the material in this book focus on IT projects. However, the techniques and concepts discussed here can be applied to projects in any industry.

Interactive Online Learning Environment and Test Bank

The interactive online learning environment that accompanies the Project+ exam certification guide provides a test bank and study tools to help you prepare for the exam. By using these tools, you can increase your chances of passing the exam on your first try.

The online section includes the following:

Sample Tests   Sample tests are provided in the book and online. In the book you'll find the assessment test at the end of this introduction, and the chapter tests that include the review questions at the end of each chapter. Online, there are two bonus practice exams that simulate the actual test. Use these questions to test your knowledge of the study guide material. The online test bank runs on multiple devices.

Flashcards   The online flashcard bank includes more than 300 flashcards to ensure that you're ready for the exam. Questions are provided in digital flashcard format (a question followed by a single correct answer). You can use the flashcards to reinforce your learning and provide last-minute test prep before the exam. And no worries—armed with the review questions, practice exams, and flashcards, you'll be prepared when exam day comes!

Other Study Tools   A glossary of key terms from this book and their definitions are available as a fully searchable PDF.

Go to www.wiley.com/go/sybextestprep to register and gain access to this interactive online learning environment and test bank with study tools.

How to Use This Book

If you want a solid foundation for preparing for the CompTIA Project+ exam, then look no further. I've spent hundreds of hours writing this book and online materials with the intention of helping you pass the exam as well as helping you learn about the exciting field of project management.

This book is loaded with valuable information, and you will get the most out of your study time if you understand why the book is organized the way it is.

To maximize your benefit from this book, I recommend the following study method:

1. Take the assessment test that's provided at the end of this introduction. (The answers are at the end of the test.) It's okay if you don't know any of the answers; that's why you bought this book! Carefully read over the explanations for any question you get wrong and note the chapters in which the material is covered. This information should help you plan your study strategy.

2. Study each chapter carefully, making sure you fully understand the information and the test objectives listed at the beginning of each one. Pay close attention to any chapter that includes material covered in questions you missed.

3. Answer all the review questions at the end of each chapter. (The answers appear in the Appendix.) Note the questions that confuse you and study the topics they cover again until the concepts are crystal clear. Do not just skim these questions. Make sure you fully comprehend the reason for each correct answer. Remember that these will not be the exact questions you will find on the exam, but they're written to help you understand the chapter material and ultimately pass the exam.

4. Take the bonus exams that are exclusive to this book. You can find them at www.sybex.com/go/sybextestprep.

5. Test yourself using all the flashcards, which are also found at the URL mentioned previously.

Set aside the same time period every day to study and select a comfortable and quiet place to do so. I'm confident that if you work hard to understand the concepts presented, you'll be surprised at how quickly you learn this material. Studying for the CompTIA exam is a lot like getting in shape—if you don't go to the gym every day, it's not going to happen.

Tips for Taking the Project+ Exam

Here are some general tips for taking your exam successfully:

- Bring two forms of ID with you. One must be a photo ID, such as a driver's license. The other can be a major credit card or a passport. Both forms must have a signature.

- Arrive early at the exam center so that you can relax and review your study materials.

- Read the questions carefully. Don't be tempted to jump to an early conclusion. Make sure you know exactly what the question is asking.

- Don't leave any unanswered questions. Unanswered questions are scored against you.

- There will be questions with multiple correct responses. When there is more than one correct answer, there will be a statement at the end of the question instructing you to select the proper number of correct responses, such as "Choose two."

- When answering multiple-choice questions you're not sure about, use a process of elimination to eliminate the incorrect responses first. This will improve your odds if you need to make an educated guess.

- For the latest pricing on the exam and updates to the registration procedures, refer to the CompTIA site at www.comptia.org.

The Exam Objectives

Behind every certification exam, there are exam objectives. The objectives are competency areas that cover specific topics of project management. The introductory section of each chapter in this book lists the objectives that are discussed in the chapter.

 Exam objectives are subject to change at any time without prior notice and at CompTIA's sole discretion. Please visit the Certification page of CompTIA's website (www.comptia.org) for the most current listing of Project+ exam objectives.

The Project+ exam will test you on four domains:

- 1.0 Project Management Concepts
- 2.0 Project Life Cycle Phases
- 3.0 Tools and Documentation
- 4.0 Basics of IT and Governance

Project+ Exam Map

The following objective map will allow you to find the chapter in this book that covers each objective for the exam.

1.0 Project Management Concepts

Exam Objective	Chapters
1.1 Explain the basic characteristics of a project and various methodologies and frameworks used in IT projects	1, 4, 9
1.2 Compare and contrast agile vs. waterfall concepts	4, 6, 8
1.3 Given a scenario, apply the change control process throughout the project life cycle	9
1.4 Given a scenario, perform risk management activities	7, 10
1.5 Given a scenario, perform issue management activities	10
1.6 Given a scenario, apply schedule development and management activities and techniques	5, 7

Exam Objective	Chapters
1.7 Compare and contrast quality management concepts and performance management concepts	10
1.8 Compare and contrast communication management concepts	8
1.9 Given a scenario, apply effective meeting management techniques	8
1.10 Given a scenario, perform basic activities related to team and resource management	2, 3, 4, 6
1.11 Explain important project procurement and vendor selection concepts	6

2.0 Project Life Cycle Phases

Exam Objective	Chapters
2.1 Explain the value of artifacts in the discovery/concept preparation phase for a project	1, 7
2.2 Given a scenario, perform activities during the project initiation phase	3, 4, 6
2.3 Given a scenario, perform activities during the project planning phase	4, 5, 6, 7, 8, 10
2.4 Given a scenario, perform activities during the project execution phase	6, 8, 9
2.5 Explain the importance of activities performed during the closing phase	10

3.0 Tools and Documentation

Exam Objective	Chapters
3.1 Given a scenario, use the appropriate tools throughout the project life cycle	5, 6, 7, 8, 9, 10
3.2 Compare and contrast various project management productivity tools	8
3.3 Given a scenario, analyze quality and performance charts to inform project decisions	5, 8, 10

4.0 Basics of IT and Governance

Exam Objective	Chapter
4.1 Summarize basic environmental, social, and governance (ESG) factors related to project management activities	2
4.2 Explain relevant information security concepts impacting project management concepts	7
4.3 Explain relevant compliance and privacy considerations impacting project management	2
4.4 Summarize basic IT concepts relevant to IT project management	2
4.5 Explain operational change-control processes during an IT project	9

How to Contact the Publisher

If you believe you've found a mistake in this book, please bring it to our attention. At John Wiley & Sons, we understand how important it is to provide our customers with accurate content, but even with our best efforts an error may occur. In order to submit your possible errata, please email it to our Customer Service Team at wileysupport@wiley.com with the subject line "Possible Book Errata Submission."

Assessment Test

1. In this type of organization, the project manager shares responsibility for team member assignments and performance evaluations with the functional manager.

   A. Functional

   B. Projectized

   C. Hierarchical

   D. Matrix

2. These are units of measures agreed upon by the agile team that are used to estimate the amount of work it takes to complete a user story.

   A. Story point

   B. Epic point

   C. Velocity

   D. Parametric estimate

3. The information you gather in the preliminary scope definition will serve as a basis for which of the following documents?

   A. Scope management plan

   B. Communication plan

   C. Project charter

   D. Stakeholder register

4. David is working on a project where oral health information will be exchanged during the testing of the system. Which of the following is true regarding this question? (Choose two.)

   A. Oral health information is PHII and should follow the standards and laws associated with protecting this data.

   B. PHII is a form of PII.

   C. Oral health information is not PHII and does not need to follow the standards and laws associated with protecting this data.

   D. PHII is a form of SPII.

5. Who is responsible for assembling the project's team members?

   A. Project sponsor

   B. Project stakeholders

   C. Project customer

   D. Project manager

6. Which of these terms describes a critical path task?

   A. Hard logic

   B. Zero float

   C. Critical task

   D. Mandatory task

7. You're the project manager on a project where the scope has expanded. The change has been approved by the change control board (CCB). What steps must you take to acknowledge the new scope? (Choose two.)

A. Update the project management plan.

B. Update the SOW.

C. Communicate the change to stakeholders and team members.

D. Submit a change request.

E. Log the request on the change request log.

8. Which of the following are project management life cycle phases according to CompTIA? (Choose three.)

A. Scheduling

B. Planning

C. Executing

D. Monitoring and Controlling

E. Documenting

F. Budgeting

G. Closing

9. Risk analysis includes all of the following except for which one?

A. Identifying risk

B. Determining a risk response plan

C. Determining an order-of-magnitude estimate for responses

D. Determining probability and impact and assigning a risk score

10. Which of the following describes the responsibilities of the project sponsor?

A. Provides or obtains financial resources

B. Monitors the delivery of major milestones

C. Runs interference and removes roadblocks

D. Provides the project manager with authority to manage the project

E. All of the above

11. Which cost-estimating technique relies on estimating work packages and then rolling up these estimates to come up with a total cost estimate?

A. Top-down

B. Parametric

C. Bottom-up

D. Analogous

12. Fishbone diagrams, Pareto diagrams, decision tress, run charts, and control charts are examples of which of the following?

   A. Examples of various project management tools used to plan the work of the project

   B. Examples of various quality control tools used to examine the quality of work

   C. Examples of various scope management tools to control the quality of deliverables

   D. Examples of various scope management tools used to control scope creep

13. Your project requires a resource with specialized knowledge of a specific business process. The resource will work with the project team during the development of this functionality. What type of resources are these?

   A. Internal resources

   B. Functional/extended resources

   C. Core resources

   D. Benched resources

14. Which of these statements describes an assumption?

   A. Our senior web developer will be available to work on this project.

   B. The electrical capacity at the site of the project event may not be adequate.

   C. The project's due date is June 27.

   D. There's a potential for server administrator to receive a promotion during the course of this project.

15. All of the following are factors that influence communication methods except which one?

   A. Language barriers

   B. Technological barriers

   C. Task completion

   D. Cultural differences

   E. Intra-organizational differences

   F. A, B, D

   G. All of the above

16. Why is it important to comply with laws and regulations such as HIPPA, PIPEDA, GDPR, and CCPA when working as a project manager? (Choose all that apply.)

   A. Failure to comply may result in sanctions to the organization.

   B. Failure to comply may result in reputational damage to the organization.

   C. Failure to comply may result in financial penalties to the organization.

   D. Failure to comply may result in punitive damages to the organization.

   E. All of the above.

17. This tool is often used in the vendor selection process to pick a winning bidder.

   A. Weighted scoring model

   B. Bidder conference

   C. RFQ

   D. SOW

18. The network communication model is a visual depiction of what?

   A. Lines of communication

   B. Participant model

   C. Communication model

   D. Participant communication model

19. Environmental, social, and governance factors that influence project management activities also include all of the following except which one?

   A. Project impact to local and global environment

   B. Awareness of compliance and privacy considerations

   C. Project impact to company brand value

   D. Awareness of company vision, mission statement, and values

   E. Awareness of applicable regulations and standards

20. Which of the following project documents created in the Closing phase describes what went well and what didn't go well on the project?

   A. Project close report

   B. Stakeholder feedback report

   C. Lessons learned

   D. Post-project review

21. This chart shows the remaining time and work effort for an iteration or sprint.

   A. Run chart

   B. Gantt chart

   C. Scrum board

   D. Burndown chart

22. This is the approved, expected cost of the project.

   A. Expenditure budget

   B. Expenditure baseline

   C. Cost budget

   D. Cost baseline

23. This document authorizes the project to begin.

    A. Business case

    B. Project concept document

    C. Project charter

    D. Preliminary scope statement

24. Your project has expected cash inflows of $1.2 million in year 1, $2.4 million in year 2, and $4.6 million in year 3. The project pays for itself in 23 months. Which cash flow technique was used to determine this?

    A. IRR

    B. NPV

    C. Discounted cash flow

    D. Payback period

25. Which cost-estimating technique relies on estimating work packages and then rolling up these estimates to come up with a total cost estimate?

    A. Top-down

    B. Parametric

    C. Bottom-up

    D. Analogous

26. A well-written change request should include which of the following components?

    A. A description of the type of change requested

    B. The amount of time the change will take to implement

    C. The cost of the change

    D. How to update the affected project planning documents

    E. All of the above

27. "Install an Interactive Voice Response System that will increase customer response time by an average of 15 seconds and decrease the number of customer service interactions by 30 percent" is an example of which of the following elements of scope statement?

    A. Requirements

    B. Objectives

    C. Project description

    D. Milestone

28. Which of these can convey that you've achieved the completion of an interim key deliverable?

    A. Completion criteria

    B. Milestone

    C. Success criteria

    D. Project sign-off document

29. You are working for an organization and just learned that another organization with more power and influence is taking over your organization at the first of the year and they will set strategy and make all business decisions going forward. What does this describe?

A. Business merger

B. Business de-merger

C. Business venture

D. Business acquisition

30. All of the following are types of stakeholder analysis except for which one?

A. Salience model

B. Stakeholder register

C. Power/interest grid

D. Prioritization matrix

31. From the following list of options, select three of the five common stages of development that project teams progress through. (Choose three.)

A. Forming

B. Acquiring

C. Storming

D. Collaborating

E. Negotiating

F. Norming

G. Compromising

32. Which of the following are stand-alone PII data elements, also known as SPII?

A. Name, mother's maiden name, criminal history

B. Date of birth and place of birth

C. Employment information and educational information

D. Vehicle registration number and cell phone number

E. Fingerprints, driver's license number, and street address

33. This estimating technique uses the most likely, optimistic, and pessimistic estimates to come up with an average cost or duration estimate.

A. Analogous estimate

B. Bottom-up estimate

C. Parametric estimate

D. Three-point estimate

34. Which option describes an example of asynchronous communications?

   A. Face-to-face conversation

   B. Phone call

   C. Email

   D. Instant message

35. Which of these statements describes an assumption?

   A. Our senior web developer will be available to work on this project.

   B. The electrical capacity in the data center needs upgrading prior to the implementation of the servers.

   C. The project's due date is June 27.

   D. The budget for this project is $125,000.

36. This is often added to the project schedule to provide extra time to account for risks or unforeseen issues that may cause tasks to take longer than the original estimate.

   A. Quality gate

   B. Buffer

   C. Milestone

   D. Governance gate

37. Which of the following is not true regarding cost estimating?

   A. Cost estimates are provided by team members.

   B. Cost estimate accuracy depends on the technique used to determine the estimate.

   C. Cost estimates have a quality factor built into them.

   D. Cost estimates are inputs to the project budget and used to determine the total project cost.

38. Which of these is not an example of a project selection method?

   A. Cost–benefit analysis

   B. Expert judgment

   C. Top-down estimating

   D. Scoring model

39. This is how you will know the user story requirements were met satisfactorily at the end of the sprint.

   A. Acceptance criteria

   B. KPIs

   C. Metrics

   D. EVM

40. This chart or diagram is a type of histogram that rank-orders data by frequency over time.

    A. Run chart

    B. Scatter diagram

    C. Fishbone diagram

    D. Pareto chart

41. One of your project activities requires following a specific procedure, inspecting the results, and signing off on an inspection before it can be included in the final deliverable. What type of dependency does this describe?

    A. External

    B. Discretionary

    C. Mandatory

    D. Logical

42. All of following are the most common elements in a three-tier, multitier architecture except for which one?

    A. Networking layer

    B. Application layer

    C. Processing layer

    D. Presentation layer

43. This is the final, approved version of the project schedule. All of the following are true regarding this description except for which of the following?

    A. It will prevent future schedule risk.

    B. It's approved by the stakeholders, sponsor, and functional managers.

    C. It's used to monitor project progress throughout the remainder of the project.

    D. This describes a schedule baseline.

44. According to CompTIA exam objectives, writing code and making changes to code involve all of the following environments except for which one?

    A. Beta stage

    B. Development

    C. Production

    D. Infrastructure

45. All of the following represent a category of contract most commonly used in procurement except for which one?

    A. Time-and-materials

    B. Cost-reimbursable

    C. Fixed-price

    D. Requests for proposal

46. Risk analysis includes all of the following except for which one?

   A. Identifying risk

   B. Determining a risk response plan

   C. Determining an order-of-magnitude estimate for responses

   D. Determining probability and impact and assigning a risk score

47. These performance measurements are defined when you create the project management plan and are monitored and tracked during the Executing phase to determine whether the project is meeting its goals.

   A. ROI

   B. Balanced score card

   C. IRR

   D. KPI

48. In this organizational structure, you report to the director of project management, and your team members report to their areas of responsibility (accounting, human resources, and IT). You will have complete control of the project team members' time and assignments once the project is underway. Which type of organization does this describe?

   A. Projectized

   B. Functional

   C. Hierarchical

   D. Matrix

49. Your project sponsor told you that the due date for the project is a key to its success and there is no chance of the date changing. What is this known as?

   A. A constraint

   B. An influence

   C. A deliverable

   D. A management directive

50. All of the following are meeting types according to CompTIA exam objectives except for which one?

   A. Decisive

   B. Cooperative

   C. Informative

   D. Collaborative

51. This is a temporary way of resolving conflict and is considered a lose-lose technique. It emphasizes the areas of agreement over the areas of disagreement.

   A. Smoothing

   B. Forcing

   C. Avoiding

   D. Collaborating

52. Which of following describe secondary storage? (Choose two.)

   A. SAN.

   B. Flash drive.

   C. NAS.

   D. RAM.

   E. It's also known as external memory.

53. All of the following describe types of project endings except for which one?

   A. Integration

   B. Starvation

   C. Addition

   D. Extinction

   E. Attrition

54. You need to perform a background check on a potential contract employee. Which of the following IT policies outlines the procedures for this check?

   A. Physical security policy

   B. Digital security policy

   C. Data security policy

   D. Operational security policy

55. Project managers may spend up to 90 percent of their time doing which of the following?

   A. Negotiating

   B. Managing scope

   C. Managing the project team

   D. Communicating

56. In which cloud service model does the cloud service provider have the most control?

   A. PaaS

   B. IaaS

   C. SaaS

   D. XaaS

57. This project management methodology divides up projects into stages that are logically organized. It has seven guiding principles and seven stages.

   A. Scrum

   B. Kanban

   C. PRINCE2

   D. Disciplined Agile

58. This person is responsible for time and duration estimates for tasks, cost estimates, status updates, and dependencies. Which of the following does this describe?

    A. Project manager

    B. Stakeholder

    C. Scheduler

    D. Project team member

59. When taking over an incomplete project, what item should be of most interest to the new project manager?

    A. Project concept statement

    B. Project charter

    C. Project scope statement

    D. Project plan

60. All of the following are examples of records that are managed by a records management system except for which one?

    A. Board report

    B. Employee user access policy

    C. Draft of network diagrams

    D. Resignation letter

61. In project management, the process of taking high-level project requirements and breaking them down into the tasks that will generate the deliverables is called what?

    A. Analyzing

    B. Decomposing

    C. Process flow diagram

    D. Break down

62. Some team members on your team are driving each other crazy. They have different ways of organizing the tasks they are both assigned to, and the disparity in styles is causing them to bicker. Which of the following describes this situation?

    A. This is a constraint that's bringing about conflict on the team.

    B. This should be escalated to the project sponsor.

    C. This is a common cause of conflict.

    D. This is a team formation stage that will pass as they get to know each other better.

63. Your organization is part of a network of researchers who need to share data and experimental results. Which cloud deployment model is the best solution for this scenario?

    A. Public cloud

    B. Private cloud

    C. Hybrid cloud

    D. Community cloud

64. This is a deliverables-oriented hierarchy that defines the work of the project.

   A. Scope document

   B. Scope management plan

   C. Work breakdown structure

   D. Project plan

65. Removable media is a security risk for all organizations. You are working with IT to create a policy that includes encryption procedures for removable media. Which policy are the procedures for removable media contained in?

   A. Physical security policy

   B. Digital security policy

   C. Data security policy

   D. Operational security policy

66. Your organization has recently discovered that PII data has been exposed. What is this known as?

   A. Cybersecurity hack

   B. PII data disclosure

   C. Breach of confidentiality

   D. Data confidentiality exposure

67. Your team has experienced issues in the past in having all IT team members engaged and involved on the project. The server team is notoriously left out of the loop until the last minute and then they have to scramble to get things ready for deployment. Which of the following team structures would help eliminate this issue?

   A. Project team

   B. Scrum team

   C. DevSecOps team

   D. Architect team

68. What is the best way to prevent scope creep?

   A. Make sure the requirements are thoroughly defined and documented.

   B. Put a statement in the charter that no additions to the project will be allowed once it's underway.

   C. Alert the sponsor that you will not be taking any change requests after the project starts.

   D. Inform stakeholders when they sign the project scope statement that no changes will be accepted after the scope statement is published.

69. You're the project manager for a small project that is in the Closing phase. You prepare closure documents and take them to the project sponsor for sign-off. The project sponsor says that the documents are not needed because the project is so small. What should you tell the sponsor?

A. You're sorry to have bothered them and will close the project without sign-off.

B. You explain the sponsor is the one who needs to sign off on the documents, showing that the project is officially closed.

C. You offer to have a stakeholder sign off in the sponsor's place.

D. You offer to sign off on the documents yourself.

70. Which of following software manages documents, records, and data in electronic format for an organization?

A. ERP

B. CRM

C. EDRMS

D. CMS

71. Your subject matter expert tells you that they estimate the time needed to complete their task is 40 hours. The task starts on Thursday, January 20 at 8 a.m. The team works eight-hour days, and they do not work weekends. Which day will the task end?

A. January 24

B. January 25

C. January 27

D. January 26

72. Your project sponsor has expressed their need to have real-time project information at their fingertips. Which of the following is the best way to meet this need?

A. By creating a project dashboard with scope, cost, and time elements

B. By updating the project status report on a daily basis

C. By sending an email every morning to the sponsor describing the current project status

D. By meeting face-to-face with the sponsor every day to update them on status

73. Luke is starting out in his project management career. He has project education but no hands-on experience. He is assigned to a project where he will be working with customer data, including full name, address, email address, phone number, and date of birth. What type of data is this known as?

A. PHI

B. Linkable data

C. SPII

D. Secure data

74. What key meeting is held after the project charter is signed and/or at the beginning of the Executing project management life cycle phase?

A. Project kickoff

B. Project review

C. Project overview

D. Project status meeting

75. These important stakeholders are responsible for meeting the organizational goals and for providing team members from their departments to work on the project.

A. Project champions

B. SMEs

C. PMO

D. Senior management

76. When using an agile methodology, this serves as a placeholder for ideas that are not yet fully formed but that capture the essence of the idea. They are later broken down into user stories. What is this element called?

A. Milestone

B. Preview

C. Backlog

D. Epic

77. All of the following are types of testing used on information technology projects to determine if the system operates as expected except for which one?

A. Progression

B. Smoke

C. End-to-end

D. Stress

E. User acceptance

78. These important stakeholders are responsible for designing solutions for the technology enterprise.

A. QA

B. SMEs

C. Architect

D. Engineers

79. What are the two types of charts that you might utilize to display the project schedule? (Choose two.)

A. Run chart

B. Gantt chart

C. Milestone chart

D. CPM

E. Histogram

80. Which of the following is the focus of HIPAA specifically?

   A. Protecting and safekeeping standards and regulations associated with personal data

   B. Protecting and safekeeping standards and regulations associated with linkable data

   C. Protecting and safekeeping SPII

   D. Protecting and safekeeping ePHI

81. This person is responsible for removing obstacles so that the team can perform their work, assisting the product owner in defining backlog items, and educating the team on agile processes.

   A. Project manager

   B. Scrum master

   C. Functional manager

   D. Subject matter expert

82. Demonstrating competency, respect, honesty, integrity, openness, and doing what you say you'll do is an example of which of the following?

   A. Team building

   B. Managing team resources

   C. Demonstrating leadership skills

   D. Trust building

83. These gates are used as approval points in the project.

   A. Quality gates

   B. Approval gates

   C. Governance gates

   D. Milestone gates

Answers to Assessment Test

1. D. Project managers share authority with functional managers in a matrix organization. For more information, please see Chapter 6.

2. A. Story points are used to measure the amount of work it takes to complete a user story. Velocity is the amount of time it takes to complete story points. Parametric estimates involve multiplying the rate times the amount of work. Epic points don't exist. For more information, please see Chapter 5.

3. C. The information gathered in the preliminary scope definition, such as project goals, the reason for the project, description of the project, and high-level deliverables needed, will serve as a basis for the project charter. For more information, please see Chapter 3.

4. A, B. Oral health information is PHII data, which is a form of PII. For more information, please see Chapter 2.

5. D. The project manager assembles the team members for the project. The project manager may get input from the sponsor, stakeholders, or customers, but it is the project manager who decides what the formation of the team should be. For more information, please see Chapter 2.

6. B. Tasks with zero float are critical path tasks, and if delayed, they will cause the delay of the project completion date. For more information, please see Chapter 5.

7. A, C. Any time there's a significant change to the project, the project management plan must be updated, and the stakeholders notified of the change. Options D and E would have been done before the approval by the CCB. Options A and C occur after an approval. For more information, please see Chapter 9.

8. B, C, G. Discovery/Concept, Initiating, Planning, Executing, and Closing are the five project management life cycle phases outlined by CompTIA. For more information, please see Chapter 1.

9. C. Determining an order-of-magnitude estimate is used for cost or duration estimating, not risk analysis. For more information, please see Chapter 7.

10. E. A project sponsor is responsible for obtaining financial resources for the project, monitoring the progress of the project, and handling escalations from the project manager. For more information, please see Chapter 3.

11. C. The bottom-up cost-estimating method is the most precise because you begin your estimating at the activities in the work package and roll them up for a total estimate. For more information, please see Chapter 5.

12. B. The tools described in this question are used during the Executing phase of the project to monitor quality and assure it meets expectations. It also helps in determining corrective actions needed to get the project back on track. For more information, please see Chapter 10.

13. B. Functional/extended resources are those needed for specific tasks or short periods of time on the project. They may also be stakeholders or subject matter experts who lend expertise to the project. For more information, please see Chapter 6.

14. A. Assumptions are those things we believe to be true for planning purposes. Options B and D describe risks, while option C describes a constraint. For more information, please see Chapter 4.

15. C. Task completion is a communication trigger. The remaining options are examples of factors that influence communications. For more information, please see Chapter 8.

16. E. All of the options are true. For more information, please see Chapter 2.

17. A. A weighted scoring model is a tool that weights evaluation criteria and provides a way to score vendor responses. Bidder conferences, IFB, and SOW are all used during vendor solicitation. For more information, please see Chapter 6.

18. A. Lines of communication describe how many lines of communication exist between participants. The network communication model is a visual depiction of the lines of communication. For more information, please see Chapter 8.

19. B. Compliance and privacy considerations are not part of the ESG factors; however, they can influence and have an impact on the project. For more information, please see Chapter 2.

20. C. Lessons learned describe what went well and what didn't go well on the project. Lessons learned are included in the project close report, the postmortem report, and the post-project review. For more information, please see Chapter 10.

21. D. Burndown charts show the remaining time and work effort for an iteration or sprint. For more information, please see Chapter 5.

22. D. The cost baseline is the approved, expected cost of the project. For more information, please see Chapter 7.

23. C. The project charter authorizes the project to begin. For more information, please see Chapter 3.

24. D. Payback period is a technique that calculates the expected cash inflows over time to determine how many periods it will take to recover the original investment. IRR calculates the internal rate of return, NPV determines the net present value, and discounted cash flows determine the amount of the cash flows in today's dollars. For more information, please see Chapter 1.

25. C. The bottom-up cost-estimating method is the most precise because you begin your estimating at the activities in the work package and roll them up for a total estimate. For more information, please see Chapter 5.

26. E. All of the options are elements of a change request. For more information, please see Chapter 9.

27. B. Objectives are specific and measurable. Project descriptions describe the key characteristics of the product, service, or result of the project. These are characteristics, but the clue in this question is the quantifiable results you're looking for at the conclusion of the project. The project description describes the project as a whole, and milestones describe major deliverables or accomplishments for the project. For more information, please see Chapter 4.

28. B. Milestones often signal that you've completed one of the key deliverables on the project. For more information, please see Chapter 5.

29. D. This question describes a business acquisition. Companies that are acquiring others have the power and influence to make decisions. A business merger is a mutually agreeable arrangement where power is shared among the entities. For more information, please see Chapter 9.

30. B. The stakeholder register is where the information about the stakeholders, including analysis details, are documented. For more information, please see Chapter 3.

31. A, C, F. The five stages of team development are forming, storming, norming, performing, and adjourning. For more information, please see Chapter 6.

32. E. Options A through D are examples of personally identifiable information that are considered linkable but not sensitive. Sensitive personally identifiable information consists of data elements that, on their own, can identify or trace an individual and could cause them harm, inconvenience, or embarrassment if used inappropriately. Option E consists of two pieces of SPII, fingerprints, and driver's license number. Street address is not SPII as a stand-alone element, but since it's linked to fingerprints and driver's license number, it is sensitive data. For more information, please see Chapter 2.

33. D. The three-point estimating technique averages the most likely, optimistic, and pessimistic estimates to determine an overall cost or duration estimate. For more information, please see Chapter 5.

34. C. Asynchronous communication does not happen in real time and does not require an immediate response. All the other options describe synchronous communication, which is for scenarios requiring immediate responses. For more information, please see Chapter 8.

35. A. Assumptions are those things we believe to be true for planning purposes. The other options describe a constraint. For more information, please see Chapter 3.

36. B. A buffer is added to the schedule to provide extra time to account for risks or unforeseen issues that may cause tasks to take longer than the original estimate. For more information, please see Chapter 5.

37. C. Cost estimates do not have a quality factor built into them. They are provided by team members, and the accuracy of the estimate depends on the estimating technique used. All the estimates are used as inputs to the budget to come up with the total project cost. For more information, please see Chapter 7.

38. C. Cost–benefit analysis, expert judgment, and scoring model are all project selection techniques. Top-down estimating is a type of cost estimating technique. For more information, please see Chapter 1.

39. A. Acceptance criteria describe how to determine whether the deliverables are complete and meet the user story requirements. For more information, please see Chapter 4.

40. D. A Pareto diagram rank-orders data by frequency over time. For more information, please see Chapter 10.

41. B. Discretionary dependencies are often process- or procedure-driven. This question describes a discretionary dependency. For more information, please see Chapter 5.

42. A. The Networking layer is not part of the three-tier architecture. For more information, please see Chapter 2.

43. A. The schedule baseline is the final, approved version of the schedule and is signed by the stakeholders, sponsor, and functional managers. Having a schedule baseline will not prevent future schedule risk. For more information, please see Chapter 5.

44. D. Development is where code is written, beta stage is where the code is tested, and production is where the finalized code resides. Infrastructure is what hosts these environments. For more information, please see Chapter 9.

45. D. The three categories of contracts most often used to procure goods and services are time-and-materials, cost-reimbursable, and fixed-price. Requests for proposal are not contracts. For more information, please see Chapter 6.

46. C. Determining an order-of-magnitude estimate is used for cost or duration estimating and for risk response planning, not risk analysis. For more information, please see Chapter 7.

47. D. Key performance indicators (KPIs) are measurable elements of project success defined when you create the project management plan and measure and monitor it throughout the Executing phase. For more information, please see Chapter 10.

48. A. This describes a projectized organization because the project manager works in a division whose sole responsibility is project management, and once the team members are assigned to the project, the project manager has the authority to hold them accountable to their tasks and activities. For more information, please see Chapter 6.

49. A. This describes a constraint. Constraints dictate or restrict the actions of the project team. For more information, please see Chapter 4.

50. B. The three meeting types are decisive, informative, and collaborative. For more information, please see Chapter 8.

51. A. Smoothing is a lose-lose conflict resolution technique. It is a temporary way to resolve conflict. Avoiding can also be a lose-lose conflict technique, but it isn't temporary in nature and doesn't emphasize anything because one of the parties leaves the discussions. For more information, please see Chapter 6.

52. B, E. Options A, C, and D are types of primary storage. For more information, please see Chapter 2.

53. E. Integration occurs when resources are distributed to other areas of the organization, and addition occurs when projects evolve into ongoing operations. Starvation is a project ending caused by resources being cut off from the project. Extinction occurs when the project work is completed and is accepted by the stakeholders. For more information, please see Chapter 10.

54. D. Background check procedures are included in the operational security policy. For more information, please see Chapter 7.

55. D. Project managers may spend up to 90 percent of their time communicating. For more information, please see Chapter 3.

56. C. The software-as-a-service (SaaS) model is where the service provider has the most control over the environment. For more information, please see Chapter 2.

57. C. This question describes the PRINCE2 methodology. For more information, please see Chapter 9.

58. D. The project team members are responsible for the tasks listed in the question. For more information, please see Chapter 3.

59. C. The project's scope statement should be of most interest to the new project manager. The scope statement describes the product description, key deliverables, success and acceptance criteria, exclusions, assumptions, and constraints. For more information, please see Chapter 4.

60. C. Drafts are not records until they are approved and distributed. For more information, please see Chapter 3.

61. B. Decomposition is the process of analyzing the requirements of the project in such a way that you reduce the requirements down to the steps and tasks needed to produce them. For more information, please see Chapter 5.

62. C. This situation describes varying work styles that are a common cause of conflict. Competing resource demands and constraints are also common causes of conflict. Conflicts are anything that restrict or dictate the actions of the project team. And issues like this should almost never have to be escalated to the project sponsor. For more information, please see Chapter 6.

63. D. A community cloud is for a community of consumers who have similar needs. It's a form of private cloud with more than one tenant. For more information, please see Chapter 2.

64. C. The WBS is a deliverables-oriented hierarchy that defines all the project work and is completed after the scope management plan and scope statement are completed. For more information, please see Chapter 5.

65. A. The physical security policy includes instructions for access to facilities, how to secure removable media, and how to secure mobile devices. For more information, please see Chapter 7.

66. C. This is known as a breach of confidentiality. It could have come about as a cybersecurity hacking incident, but the question doesn't state how the data was exposed. For more information, please see Chapter 2.

67. C. The DevSecOps team is one team consisting of team members with program development skills, cybersecurity skills, and operations skills. This framework ensures that all team members are aware of project tasks and increases collaboration and communication among team members, along with delivering products faster and with more fidelity. For more information, please see Chapter 4.

68. A. The best way to avoid scope creep is to make sure the project's requirements have been thoroughly defined and documented. For more information, please see Chapter 4.

69. B. The sponsor is the one who must sign off on the completion of the project, whether successful or unsuccessful. Just as the sponsor is authorized to expend resources to bring forth the project's deliverables, the sponsor must also close the project and sign off. For more information, please see Chapter 10.

70. C. EDRMS stands for electronic document and record management systems and is responsible for managing electronic documents, records, and more. ERP stands for enterprise resource planning. CRM is a customer relationship management system. CMS is a content management system. For more information, please see Chapter 2.

71. D. The task begins on January 20, which is day 1. The team does not work weekends, so the completion date, based on an eight-hour workday, is January 26. For more information, please see Chapter 5.

72. A. The best way to provide this information is to create a dashboard that provides real-time, updated information in a succinct and easy-to-read format. For more information, please see Chapter 8.

73. B. This question describes linkable data. On its own, this is not SPII but when linked with SPII, all the data becomes SPII. For more information, please see Chapter 2.

74. A. The project kickoff meeting is held after the project charter is signed and/or during the Executing process. It serves to introduce team members, review the goals and objectives of the project, review stakeholder expectations, and review roles and responsibilities for team members. For more information, please see Chapter 3.

75. D. The senior management team is responsible for meeting organizational goals and the project manager will work with them to assign resources from their departments to the project. The project champion encourages the organization to get behind the project, the subject matter experts lend expertise to the project and perform the work of the project, and the project management office provides guidance on project management processes as well as overseeing project work. For more information, please see Chapter 3.

76. D. Epics are placeholders that contain big ideas that are not yet fully formed that are broken down into user stories as the project progresses. For more information, please see Chapter 5.

77. A. Testing is used to determine if the system operates as expected and to ensure all the functions, calculations, and features perform as planned. Progression is not a type of test. For more information, please see Chapter 10.

78. C. IT architects design solutions and services for the enterprise, business applications, infrastructure, and more. Quality assurance technicians ensure that the project works as designed, subject matter experts lend expertise to the project and perform the work of the project, and engineers write code and develop applications. For more information, please see Chapter 3.

79. B, C. Gantt charts and milestone charts are the most commonly used formats to display a project schedule. For more information, please see Chapter 5.

80. D. The Health Insurance Portability and Accountability Act provides regulations regarding the safekeeping of electronic protected health information (ePHI). For more information, please see Chapter 2.

81. B. The Scrum master is responsible for removing obstacles that are getting in the way of the team performing the work. They work with the product owner to help define backlog items, and they educate team members on the agile process. For more information, please see Chapter 4.

82. D. This is an example of trust building. As a project manager, you must do what you say you'll do and demonstrate the traits stated in the question. For more information, please see Chapter 6.

83. C. Governance gates are used as approval points along the project. Quality gates are used to determine if the work meets quality standards. CompTIA does not recognize approval gates or milestone gates. For more information, please see Chapter 5.

Chapter

1

Introducing the Project

THE COMPTIA PROJECT+ EXAM TOPICS COVERED IN THIS CHAPTER INCLUDE:

✓ **1.0 Project Management Concepts**

✓ **1.1 Explain the basic characteristics of a project and various methodologies and frameworks used in IT projects**

  ▪ Characteristics of a project

✓ **2.0 Project Life Cycle Phases**

✓ **2.1 Explain the value of artifacts in the discovery/concept preparation phase for a project**

  ▪ Business case or business objective

  ▪ Prequalified vendor

  ▪ Predetermined client

  ▪ Preexisting contracts

  ▪ Financial concepts

Your decision to take the CompTIA Project+ exam is an important step in your career aspirations. Certification is important for project managers because many employers look for this certification in addition to real-life experience and formal education from job applicants. This book is designed to provide you with the necessary concepts to prepare for the Project+ exam. Some of the material here will be based on information documented in *A Guide to the Project Management Body of Knowledge (PMBOK® Guide)* published by the Project Management Institute (PMI®) along with the Agile Practice Guide®. This book will include tips on how to prepare for the exam, as well as examples and real-world scenarios to illustrate the concepts.

This chapter will cover the definitions and characteristics of a project, provide a high-level overview of project management, describe the difference between a program and a portfolio, and explain the Discovery phase, the first phase in the project management life cycle.

Defining the Project

Projects exist to bring about or fulfill the goals of the organization. Most projects benefit from the application of a set of processes and standards known as *project management*. Let's start with some fundamental questions.

- What makes a new assignment a project?
- How do you know if you are working on a project?
- What distinguishes a project from an operational activity?

Projects involve a team of people, and so do day-to-day business activities. They both involve following a process or a plan, and they both result in activities that help reach a goal. So, what is so different about a project? Let's explore all of these questions in the following sections.

Identifying the Project

A *project* is a temporary endeavor that has definite beginning and ending dates, and it results in a unique product, service, or result. A project is considered a success when the goals it sets out to accomplish are fulfilled and the stakeholders are satisfied with the results.

Projects also bring about a product, service, or result that never existed before. This may include creating tangible goods, implementing software, writing a book, planning and executing an employee appreciation event, constructing a building, and more. There is no limit to what can be considered a project as long as it fits the following criteria:

Unique   A project is typically undertaken to meet a specific business objective. It involves doing something new, which means that the end result should be a unique product or service. These products may be marketed to others, may be used internally, may provide support for ongoing operations, and so on.

Temporary   Projects have definite start and end dates. The time it takes to complete the work of the project can vary in overall length from a few weeks to several years, but there is always a start date and an end date.

Reason or Purpose   A project comes about to fulfill a purpose. This might include introducing a new product, fulfilling a business objective or strategic goal, satisfying a social need, and any number of other reasons. It's important to document and communicate the purpose and reasons for the project so that team members remain focused on achieving the goals of the project.

Stakeholder Satisfaction   A project starts once it's been identified, the objectives have been outlined in the project charter, and appropriate stakeholders have approved the project plan. A project ends when those goals have been met to the satisfaction of the stakeholders.

Once you've identified the project, you'll validate it and then write the project charter and obtain approval for the charter. We'll talk in more detail about the project charter in Chapter 3, "Creating the Project Charter."

Programs and Portfolios

Projects are sometimes managed as part of a program or portfolio. A *program* is a group of related projects that are managed together using coordinated processes and techniques. The collective management of a group of projects can bring about benefits that wouldn't be achievable if the projects were managed separately. Each project within the program has a project manager. The project managers report to a program manager, who is responsible for all the projects within their program.

Portfolios are collections of programs, subportfolios, and projects that support strategic business goals or objectives. Unlike programs, portfolios may consist of projects that are not related.

Here's an example to help clarify the difference between programs and portfolios. Let's say your company is in the construction business. The organization has several business units: retail construction, single-family residential buildings, and multifamily residential buildings. Individually, each of the business units may comprise a program. For example, retail construction is a program because all the projects within this program exist to create new retail-oriented buildings. This is not the same as single-family home construction (a different program), which is not the same as multifamily residential construction (a different program). Collectively, the programs and projects within all of these business units make up the portfolio. Other projects and programs may exist within this portfolio as well, such as parking structures, landscaping, and so on.

Programs and projects within a portfolio are not necessarily related to one another in a direct way. And projects may independently exist within the portfolio (in other words, the project isn't related to a program but belongs to the portfolio). However, the overall objective of any program or project in a portfolio is to meet the strategic objectives of the portfolio, which in turn should meet the strategic objectives of the business unit or corporation.

Understanding Operations

Operations are ongoing and repetitive. They don't have a beginning date or an ending date, unless you're starting a new operation or retiring an old one. Operations typically involve ongoing functions that support the production of goods or services. Projects, on the other hand, come about to meet a specific, unique result and then conclude.

It's important to understand that projects and operations go hand in hand in many cases. For example, perhaps you've been assigned to research and implement state-of-the-art equipment for a shoe manufacturing plant. Once the implementation of the equipment is complete, the project is concluded. A handoff to the operations team occurs, and the everyday tasks the equipment and staff perform become an ongoing operation.

Don't be confused by the term *service* regarding the definition of a project. Providing janitorial services on a contract is operations; providing contract Java programmers for 18 months to work on an IT project is a project.

Let's look at the definition of two more terms. *Project management* brings together a set of tools and techniques—performed by people—to describe, organize, and monitor the work of project activities. *Project managers* (PMs) are the people responsible for applying these tools to the various project activities. Their primary purpose is to integrate all the components of the project and bring it to a successful conclusion. Managing a project involves many skills, including dealing with competing needs for your resources, obtaining adequate budget dollars, identifying risks, managing to the project requirements, interacting with stakeholders, staying on schedule, and ensuring a quality product.

I'll spend the remainder of this book describing the tools and techniques you'll use to accomplish the goals of the project, including the key concepts you'll need to know for the exam. Many of the standards surrounding these techniques are documented in the *PMBOK® Guide*.

Using the *PMBOK® Guide*

Project management standards are documented in *A Guide to the Project Management Body of Knowledge* (*PMBOK® Guide*), published by the Project Management Institute (PMI®). PMI® is the de facto standard in project management worldwide. It's a large organization with nearly 700,000 members from multiple countries around the globe.

In addition to publishing the *PMBOK® Guide*, PMI® manages two certification exams for individual project managers: the Certified Associate in Project Management (CAPM)® and the Project Management Professional (PMP)®. The *PMBOK® Guide* is the primary basis for the exam portion of the CAPM® and PMP® certifications.

CompTIA Project+ exam objectives borrow some concepts from the *PMBOK® Guide* and the *Agile Practice Guide*. Throughout this book, I'll reference these guides to explain well-known project management and agile practices.

The material you will study to prepare for the Project+ exam is an excellent foundation on which to build your project management knowledge. Once you've obtained your Project+ certification and gain some experience, you might decide to study and sit for the CAPM® or PMP® certification exams.

Project Life Cycle Phases

Project management is performed in a series of phases that are executed to apply knowledge, skills, tools, and techniques to the project activities to meet the project requirements. According to CompTIA, these processes have been organized into five phases: Discovery/Concept, Initiating, Planning, Executing, and Closing.

These phases are tightly linked. Outputs from one group usually become inputs to another group. The groups may overlap, or you may find that you have to repeat a set of processes within a phase. For example, as you begin executing the work of the project, you may find that changes need to be made to the project management plan. That means you may have to repeat some of the processes found in the Planning phase and then re-perform the Executing phase activities once the changes to the plan are made. This is known as an *iterative* approach.

These phases are the foundation of project management. You need to understand each phase, its characteristics, and how it contributes to delivering the final product, service, or result of the project.

I will reference a lot of new concepts in the phases described in this section. Rest assured I will cover each of these topics in more detail throughout the remainder of the book.

Discovery Phase

The *Discovery/Concept Preparation phase* is the first phase in in the project management life cycle. The purpose of this phase is to determine whether the project is worthwhile. This is where a business case is created. The *business case* is a written document or report that helps executive management and key stakeholders determine the benefits and rewards of the project. It documents the business need or justification for the project and will often include high-level details about estimated budgets and timelines for completing the project. We will talk more in depth about the business case later in this chapter.

The Discovery phase also examines several elements that could help speed up the execution of the project. These activities may include working with prequalified vendors, working with predetermined clients, taking advantage of preexisting contracts, and utilizing financial concepts.

Initiating Phase

Initiation is the formal authorization for a new project to begin or for an existing project to continue into the next phase.

The *Initiating* phase includes all the activities that lead up to the final authorization to begin the project. This process can be formal or informal, depending on the organization. The key activities in the Initiating phase according to the CompTIA Project+ objectives are as follows:

- Creating the preliminary scope statement
- Creating the project charter
- Identifying and assessing stakeholders
- Developing a responsibility assignment matrix (RAM)
- Establishing accepted communication channels
- Developing a records management plan
- Defining access requirements
- Reviewing existing artifacts
- Determining solution design
- Conducting the project kickoff

 Make certain you understand the key activities of each of the project life cycle phases for the exam.

Planning Phase

In the *Planning* phase, the project goals, objectives, and deliverables are refined and broken down into manageable units of work. Project managers create time and cost estimates and determine resource requirements for each activity. Planning involves several other critical areas of project management, such as communication, risk, human resources, quality, and procurement.

Some of the key activities in the Planning process group are as follows:

- Develop a detailed project scope statement
- Develop a project schedule
- Determine budget considerations
- Develop a quality assurance plan
- Develop a communication plan
- Assess and assign project resources
- Perform an initial risk assessment
- Assess the resource pool and assign project resources
- Develop a project management plan
- Train project team members
- Define units of work
- Develop a transition plan/release plan

 The Planning phase is unquestionably one of the most critical elements of managing a project. It's possible that a project manager will spend as much time planning the project as performing the work of the project (sometimes more).

The Planning phase contains many processes that all generally lead to the creation of plans or documents that are used throughout the project to ensure that goals of the project are being met. Table 1.1 shows many of the documents that CompTIA highlights in their objectives along with their purpose and the phase where they are typically produced. You will learn about each of the project management documents shown here, and more, throughout the remainder of the book.

TABLE 1.1   Project management documents

Document name	Document description	Phase
Business case	Justification for the project.	Discovery
Preliminary scope statement	Project objectives are defined; business problem the project will address is stated.	Initiating
Project charter	Authorizes the project to begin.	Initiating
Responsibility assign-ment matrix (RAM)	Defines stakeholder responsibilities. Incorporates the use of a RACI* chart.	Initiating
Communication plan	Documents the types of information needs the stakeholders have, when the information should be distributed, and how the information will be delivered.	Planning
Project schedule	Determines the start and finish dates for project activities and assigns resources to the activities.	Planning
Scope statement	Documents the product description, key deliverables, success and acceptance criteria, key performance indicators, exclusions, assumptions, and constraints.	Planning
Project management plan	Consists of all the project planning documents such as charter, scope statement, schedule, and more.	Planning
Issue log	A list of issues, containing list numbers, descrip-tions, and owners.	Executing
Change log	Describes change requests and their disposition for the project.	Executing
Risk register	A list of risks and their descriptions.	Executing
Status report	A report to stakeholders on the status of the project deliverables, schedule, risks, issues, and more.	Executing
Dashboard information	An electronic reporting tool that lets users choose elements of the project to monitor project health and status.	Executing
Meeting agenda/ meeting minutes	Meeting agendas describe the items to be discussed and addressed at upcoming meetings, and minutes recap what was discussed and the decisions made at the meeting.	Executing

Document name	Document description	Phase
Project closeout report	Reports on the final closeout of all phases of the project.	Closing

* RACI is a way to define responsibilities on the project and stands for responsible, accountable, consult, and inform.

 NOTE   All the documents in this table will be discussed throughout the remainder of this book.

The Executing Phase

The *Executing* phase is where the work of the project is performed and monitored for adherence to the project management plan. This includes coordinating all the project members and project resources assigned to the project, reporting on status, updating project documents, managing change, and more.

The key activities in the Executing process are as follows:

- Producing and verifying deliverables
- Implementing change management
- Managing vendors
- Tracking and reporting project results
- Updating project elements such as budget, risk, and timelines
- Managing conflict
- Monitoring the risks and issues log
- Performing quality assurance/governance activities such as coordinating phase gate reviews
- Monitoring the budget
- Conducting project meetings and updates

Deliverables are produced and verified during this process. If they do not conform to expectations, change requests are created or corrective actions are taken to ensure the deliverables adhere to specifications.

Resource management is important during the Executing processes. You'll build the project team during this process, make certain resources are utilized appropriately, and perform team building activities. This process also includes working with vendors and contractors who are external to the organization.

The Closing Phase

The primary purpose of the *Closing* phase is to validate deliverables and document the formal acceptance of the project work. Once that's complete, a handoff occurs whereby the completed product or result of the project is turned over to the organization for ongoing maintenance and support.

The Closing phase includes validating deliverables, signing off on the project, archiving project documents, handing off the product to the organization, releasing project team members, and reviewing lessons learned.

The key activities in the Closing process are as follows:

- Validating deliverables
- Closing contracts
- Removing access
- Releasing resources
- Holding the project closure meeting
- Writing the project closeout report
- Obtaining feedback and lesson learned
- Project sign-off
- Handing off the product to the organization
- Evaluating the project
- Archiving project documents
- Rewards and celebration

Closing is the phase that is most often skipped in project management. Although some of these activities may seem fairly straightforward, several elements of this process group deserve close attention, and we will cover them in Chapter 10, "Managing Quality and Closing Out the Project."

Performing the Discovery/Concept Preparation Phase

The Discovery/Concept Preparation phase is the first phase in the project management life cycle. This phase entails preparing a business case to determine the merits of the project. You'll also examine existing contracts, vendors, and clients to help prepare future project documents, and/or to kick-start the work of the project.

Before we dive into the business case specifics, let's cover some of the needs and demands that bring about projects.

How Projects Come About

Projects come about for many reasons. Some organizations exist to generate profits and may create projects specifically designed to meet this goal. Other organizations exist to provide services to others with no regard for profits. They may bring about projects to enhance their ability to meet the demand for their services. No matter what the reason for bringing about a project, most of them will fall into one of the seven needs or demands described next:

Market Demand   The demands of the marketplace can drive the need for a project. For example, the pandemic of 2020-2021 changed the way consumers purchased goods. This in turn changed the way many organizations do business and brought about the need for changes to delivery logistics, new vehicles, new equipment, updated technology, and a host of other changes that each would qualify as a project.

Organizational Need   Organizational needs often bring about projects that involve technology solutions. For example, your organization's accounting system may be out-dated and its reporting functions too complicated for the average user. A request is made for a new system to help the organization become more efficient and give all users the ability to easily create reports.

Customer Request   Customer requests can generate an endless supply of potential projects. For example, perhaps the discussions at a recent customer focus group brought about the idea for a new product offering.

Technological Advance   Technology needs are sometimes a chicken-and-egg scenario. Is it the technology that drives the business to think it needs a new product or service, or does the business need drive the development of the new technology? Both scenarios exist, and both bring about the need for new projects. For example, your CEO reads an article on their recent flight about all the benefits of a new, modern customer relation-ship management platform. They decide they want this new platform that's capable of tracking all customer interactions, including monitoring social media posts about the organization, and thus a project is born.

Legal Requirement   Local, state, and federal regulations change during every legislative session and may drive the need for a new project. For example, a city may pass an ordi-nance allowing photos of red-light violations at busy intersections. The new equipment must then be procured and installed. Federal regulations requiring the encryption and secure storage of private data may bring about the need for a project to fulfill these requirements.

🌐 Real World Scenario

Assessing the Impact of Regulations and Legal Requirements

Projects often have legislative, regulatory, or other third-party restrictions imposed upon their processes or project outputs. For example, suppose you are managing a project that will create a new technology system for a company managing stock portfolios. You can imagine that this company is heavily regulated by the Securities and Exchange Commission (SEC) and that your new system, in turn, will encounter several regulatory guidelines that you must follow. The security aspect of your new system is especially pertinent. You must be able to assure the SEC and your shareholders that the system is secure.

It's important that project managers recognize the need to investigate specific industry regulations and requirements and to communicate these requirements and their associated impacts on the project scope and project plan to the stakeholders. Here are a few examples of the many external considerations you need to account for when implementing a technology-based project:

Legal and Regulatory Conditions   Know the statutes covering the type of activity your deliverable involves. For example, if you collect information about customers, make certain you are complying with privacy laws. Also, you may face government reporting and documentation requirements or public-disclosure rules.

Licensing Terms   Understand when trademark, copyright, and intellectual property issues should be considered.

Industry Standards   Industry standards exist in almost every aspect of business. Pharmaceutical companies, car manufacturers, food services, and so on all have industry standards that describe best practices for preparing, manufacturing, shipping, and any number of other elements of their business.

Considerations for industry standards in your organization must be accounted for in the project plan and budget.

Ecological Impacts   Many organizations today are actively involved in mitigating the ecological impacts of their business. They may implement ecologically friendly equipment, adopt new processes, and follow mandates and guidelines designed to protect the environment. Each of these scenarios can bring about the need for a project.

Social Need   Social needs or demands can bring about projects in a variety of ways. For example, a small developing country may have the need for safe, clean drinking water, so a project is initiated to purchase and install a filtering system. Another example may include bringing about a project to develop a vaccine for a new flu virus that's predicted to hit the nation.

The needs or demands that bring about a project are usually documented in the business case.

Creating the Business Case and Selecting Projects

Organizations have many reasons for bringing about a project. Most don't have the resources or time to execute every project that's requested. Typically, there is a formal process for requesting projects and that happens during the Discovery phase of a project life cycle. Validating a project is a two-step process. The first step in validating a project and in the Discovery phase is creating a business case explaining the justification for the project. The second step is analyzing the project stakeholders. Let's dive into the business case next.

Writing and Validating the Business Case

The purpose of the business case is to document the business need for the project and determine whether the investment in the project is worthwhile. It is a written document that describes the justification for the project, it includes financial analysis that will help determine the benefits and rewards of performing the project, and it will often include high-level details regarding estimated budgets and timelines for completing the project. Ideally, the project requestor should create the business case. They have a vested interest in implementing the project and can best articulate why the project is important to the organization. In reality, the project manager or business analyst might assist in creating this document. Once the business case is written, the first step in validating the project is complete. Let's take a look at the elements of the business case:

Description   This section describes the project, including the business need or demand that's driving the project. This should include a list of high-level deliverables and desired outcomes. This section should also include the impacts to the organization if the project is not implemented.

Justification   The justification section describes the benefits to the organization for undertaking the project. These may include tangible and intangible benefits. An example of a tangible benefit is increasing revenues or decreasing expenses. An intangible benefit could be a boost in the organization's reputation or social media standing.

Alignment to the Strategic Plan   Alignment to the strategic plan describes how the project and its outcomes will align to the organization's overall strategic plan. If the reason for the project doesn't support the strategic plan, there's really no reason to undertake the project.

Stakeholders   *Stakeholders* are anyone who has a vested interest in the project. Stakeholders can include individuals as well as organizations.

Analysis of the Problem or Opportunity   This section describes the problem or opportunity the project presents. This section can also include a gap analysis describing how this problem or opportunity currently impacts the organization and how the project might bring about different results once it's implemented.

High-Level Risk Analysis   Known risks and a description of the risks should be documented in the business case. As the project progresses, more risks will be identified and managed during the course of the project.

Alternative Solutions   This should include a high-level description of costs, the feasibility of implementing each alternative, the expected results of each alternative solution, and a description of any impacts to the organization as a result of this solution. (Cost-benefit, payback, and other financial analyses are generally included in this section of the business case.) It's best to limit alternative analysis to the top two or three solutions. Otherwise, the alternatives can become watered down and it becomes difficult to distinguish significant differences among the solutions.

Recommended Solution   This section details the recommended solution. This should include a summary of the analysis performed to determine the solution, a description of the high-level risks associated with the solution, a description of the constraints and assumptions, and a high-level plan documenting the major milestones, high-level timeline, and project dependencies. A brief description of the roles and responsibilities of key stakeholders should be noted here as well.

Feasibility Study Results   A *feasibility study* is undertaken before the business case is written and may come about for several reasons. Feasibility studies can determine whether the project is doable and likely to succeed. They examine the viability of the product, service, or result of the project. They may also examine technical issues related to the project and determine whether it's feasible, reliable, and easily assimilated into the organization's existing infrastructure. Not all business cases will or should include a feasibility study. Feasibility studies are usually conducted when the proposed project is highly complex, has a high potential for risk, or is a new type of project the organization has never undertaken before. Feasibility studies may be conducted as separate projects or as a pre-project phase. It's best to treat this activity as a project when the outcome is uncertain.

Identifying and Analyzing Stakeholders

Stakeholders are anyone who has a vested interest in the project. Stakeholders can include individuals as well as organizations, and both the project sponsor and the project manager are considered stakeholders. The project sponsor is the executive in the organization who authorizes the project to begin and is someone who has the ability and authority to assign funds and resources to the project. Stakeholder roles should be identified and analyzed. This is step 2 in validating a project. We will discuss this more in depth in Chapter 3.

Determining Benefits and Rewards

Alternative solutions, as described in the previous section, should include an analysis of the benefits and rewards of the varying solutions. This is typically done using financial analysis.

These financial methods are also used in selecting among competing projects and determining which projects should move forward and which should be deferred.

Financial and Performance Analysis

Financial analysis is a means to compare the benefits obtained from project requests by evaluating them using the same criteria. There are several financial and performance methods that evaluate benefits and rewards that we will look at next.

Cost-Benefit Analysis

A *cost-benefit analysis* compares the cost to produce the product or service to the financial gain (or benefit) the organization stands to make as a result of executing the project. You should include development costs of the product or service, marketing costs, technology costs, and ongoing support, if applicable, when calculating total costs.

Let's say your proposed project involves developing and marketing a new product. The total costs are projected at $3 million. Based on market research, it appears the demand for this product will be high and that projected revenues will exceed the developing and marketing costs and continue to produce revenues into the future. In this case, the cost-benefit analysis is positive and is a strong indicator you should select this project provided the business case justifies it as well.

The cost-benefit model is a good choice if the project selection decision is based on how quickly the project investment will be recouped from either decreased expenses or increased revenue. The weakness of using a cost-benefit analysis is that it does not account for other important factors, such as strategic value. The project that pays for itself in the shortest time is not necessarily the project that is most critical to the organization.

Scoring Model

A *scoring model* has a predefined list of criteria against which each alternative solution or project is rated. Each criterion is given both a scoring range and a weighting factor. The weighting factor accounts for the difference in importance of the various criteria. Weights are determined by the organization. In the example shown in Table 1.2, I've used a range from 1 to 5, where 5 is the most important.

Scoring models can include financial data, as well as items such as market value, organizational expertise to complete the project, innovation, and fit with corporate culture. Scoring models have a combination of objective and subjective criteria. The final score for an individual project request is obtained by calculating the rating and weighting factor of each criterion. Some companies have a minimum standard for the scoring model. If this minimum standard is not obtained, the project will be eliminated from the selection process. A benefit of the scoring model is that you can place a heavier weight on a criterion that is of more importance. Using a high weighting factor for innovation may produce an outcome where a project with a two-year time frame to pay back the cost of the project may be selected over a project that will recoup all costs in six months. The weakness of a scoring model is that the ranking it produces is only as valuable as the criteria and weighting system the ranking is based on. Developing a good scoring model is a complex process that requires a lot of interdepartmental input at the executive level. Table 1.2 shows an example weighted scoring model to determine between alternative solution 1 and 2 presented in the business case.

TABLE 1.2   Weighted scoring model

Criteria	Weight	Alt 1 score	Alt 1 total	Alt 2 score	Alt 2 total
Profit potential	5	4	20	3	15
Decrease in time to produce	2	5	10	4	8
Marketability	3	5	15	4	12
Weighted score	-	-	45	-	35

Alternative 1 has the highest score and should become the recommended solution. This model can be used to choose among projects as well. Instead of alternatives, you would evaluate projects. The project with the highest score should be chosen to move forward.

Payback Period

The *payback period* is a cash flow technique that identifies the length of time it takes for the organization to recover all the costs of producing the project. It compares the initial investment to the expected cash inflows over the life of the project and determines how many time periods elapse before the project pays for itself. Payback period is the least precise of all the cash flow techniques discussed in this section.

You can also use payback period for projects that don't have expected cash inflows. For example, you might install a new call-handling system that generates efficiencies in your call center operations by allowing the call center to grow over the next few years without having to add staff. The cost avoidance of hiring additional staff can be used in place of the expected cash inflows to calculate payback period.

Let's look at an example. One alternative solution in the business case has an initial investment of $425,00. The project is expected to generate cash inflows of $175,000 in year 1 and $250,000 in year 2. Payback period is calculated this way:

Initial investment = $425,000

Cash inflows = $175,000 year 1, $250,000 year 2

$425,000 (initial investment) − $175,000 (year 1 inflows) = $250,000 remaining balance

$250,000 (year 1 remaining balance) − $250,000 (year 2 inflows) = $0

Payback in this example is reached in two years. You will generally have to do a few more calculations than I've shown here to determine payback. You may find that you need to divide the yearly inflows by 12 to calculate the number of months it will take for payback. You will compare this payback period to other alternatives or projects and generally choose the one with the shortest payback period.

Gustave Eiffel

The extraordinary engineer Gustave Eiffel put up the majority of the money required to build the Eiffel tower, nearly $2 million, himself. This was quite a sum in 1889, and his investment paid off. Tourism revenues exceeded the cost of constructing the tower in a little more than one year. That's a payback period any project manager would love to see. And Eiffel didn't stop there. He was wise enough to negotiate a contract for tourism revenues from the tower for the next 20 years.

Cash Flow Techniques

Cash flow techniques provide data on the overall financials of the alternative solutions or projects. Each of these techniques rely on the concept of the time value of money. Money received in the future is worth less than money received today, so the lender needs to account for this loss. For example, if I asked to borrow $5,000 from you today and promised to pay you back two years from now, you would likely expect me to pay interest in addition to the principal. The reason is that inflation will eat away at the value of the $5,000 over time and it won't have the buying power two years from today that it has now. You also don't have the use of the money during that time. The interest charge attempts to make up for the devaluing of the money over time and your inability to use the funds. This can have significant paybacks for an investor if the returns are high and/or the funds are invested over a long period of time.

If you charged me 5 percent interest to borrow the money, we can determine what the $5,000 is worth in today's dollars by using the future value formula:

$$FV = PV(1+i)^n$$

This says that the future value equals the present value multiplied by 1 plus the interest rate raised to the power of the payback/investment period.

Let's plug in our numbers:

$$FV = 5,000(1.05)^2$$

$$FV = 5,000(1.1025)$$

$$FV = \$5512.50$$

The $5,000 I borrowed from you is worth $5,512.50 in today's dollars.

Entire books have been dedicated to financial evaluation, so here you'll get a brief overview of some of the common cash flow techniques: discounted cash flow, net present value, ROI, and internal rate of return.

Cost of Capital

The *cost of capital* can be used interchangeably with interest rates in any of these formulas. The cost of capital is the rate of return the organization might earn if they chose to invest in something other than the project. The alternative investment must have risk that is similar to that of the project.

Discounted Cash Flow

The *discounted cash flow* technique compares the value of the future worth of the project's expected cash flows to today's dollars, known as present value. Present value is the opposite of future value. In our example previously, you might ask, how much is $5,512.50 two years from now worth today using a 5 percent interest rate? The answer is $5,000. Here is the formula:

$$PV = FV / (1 + i)^n$$

This says present value equals the future value divided by 1 plus the cost of capital raised to the power of the investment period.

Table 1.3 shows an example of two projects with their expected inflows and the PV for each year. Sum the total of the years to come up with net present value (NPV) and then choose the one with the highest NPV.

TABLE 1.3 Discounted cash flow

Project A year	Inflows	PV	Project B year	Inflows	PV
1	25,000	26,250	1	30,000	31,500
2	55,000	60,638	2	35,000	38,588
3	40,000	46,304	3	52,000	60,195
Discounted cash flow		$133,192			$130,283

Typically, alternative solutions or projects with the highest discounted cash flows are chosen over those with lower discounted cash flows.

Net Present Value

Net present value (NPV) is a cash flow technique that takes into account the differences in the value of money over time by calculating the revenues or cash flows the organization expects to receive over the life of the project in today's dollars. You will use the PV formula to calculate each year of revenues as shown in Table 1.3 and compare them to other alternatives or projects. Each period's resulting sum in present-day dollars is added together, and that sum is then subtracted from the initial investment to come up with an overall value for the project. The rule for NPV is that if NPV is greater than 0, you should accept the project. If it's less than 0, you should reject the project.

Table 1.4 compares Project A to Project B. Project A's initial investment is $72,000. Project B's initial investment is $83,000. I'm using a 5 percent cost of capital and rounding up the PV results.

TABLE 1.4   Net present value

Project A year	Inflows	PV	Project B year	Inflows	PV
1	25,000	26,250	1	30,000	31,500
2	55,000	60,638	2	35,000	38,588
3	40,000	46,304	3	52,000	60,195
Total		$133,192			$130,283
Less investment		72,000			83,000
NPV		61,192			47,283

In this example, Project A should be chosen because it has the highest NPV.

The difference between NPV and discounted cash flows is that NPV subtracts the total cash flow in today's dollars from the initial project investment. Discounted cash flow totals the value of each period's expected cash flow to come up with a total value for the project in today's terms.

Return on Investment (ROI)

Return on investment (ROI) measures the profitability of an investment and is often used to compare one investment to another. It measures the expected returns of the investment as compared to its costs and is displayed as a percentage.

ROI is calculated this way:

$$ROI = (\text{Current Value or Gain from the Investment} - \text{Cost of Investment}) /$$
$$\text{Cost of the Investment}$$

Current value of the investment is the worth or value of the investment in today's dollars. Let's assume the current value of our investment is $75,000, our cost was $55,000.

$$75,000(\text{value}) - 55,000(\text{cost}) = 20,000$$

$$20,000 / 55,000 = .36$$

If you multiply the fraction times 100, you'll see that ROI is 36 percent.

ROI does not take timeframes into account. When comparing one ROI to another, you'll need to annualize the returns so that you can compare them accurately. ROI in the formula above is over a one-year investment period. Perhaps the second alternative we are comparing to has an ROI of 52 percent over a two-year time period. You would need to divide 52 by the two-year investment period to come up with an annualized ROI of 26 percent per year. This alternative when annualized has a lower ROI than the first. You should choose the first alternative with a 36 percent ROI.

Higher ROI values produce more benefits than lower ROI values. However, higher values typically come with greater risk. The risks should be taken into account when choosing among alternative solutions or projects. Some organizations may have a high tolerance for risk and will jump in without thinking twice. Other organizations may have a low tolerance and while the ROI value is appealing, they may not be willing to risk other losses or consequences if the project does not produce the expected results. Projects with negative ROI values should not proceed.

Internal Rate of Return

Internal rate of return (IRR) is the discount rate when the present value of the cash inflows equals the original investment. IRR states the profitability of an investment as an average percent over the life of the investment. The general rule is that projects with higher IRR values are considered better than projects with lower IRR values.

Current State vs. Future State

Current state versus future state is a form of performance analysis that examines business processes, compares alternative projects, helps diagram change, and much more. This analysis is not necessarily based on financial analysis. It compares the organization today to the anticipated future state if the project/change/business process is undertaken. This can include a host of ideas too numerous to list. Perhaps the organization is considering automating a process that is currently performed manually. The first step is to document the current state: what do we do, how do we do it, what are the pain points, what are the processes, how are we performing this function, and so on. The next step is to imagine the future state: what are the opportunities if we automate, what efficiencies will come about, what are the benefits and improvements the organization might realize, what problem will be solved, and so on.

 Current state vs. future state is also known as "as is—to be."

You'll want to engage key team members and subject matter experts in this activity. That includes those who have a solid understanding of the current state and the pain points they are causing. In my experience, the people experiencing the pain generally have the best ideas for improvements. They have a vested interest in the outcome because their work life will be easier as a result.

Each of these states should be documented in detail. For example, start by documenting each step of the manual process and describe the problem, issue, or opportunity. Use techniques such as interviewing subject matter experts and observing the process, focus group meetings, surveys, and so on to gather information and document the current state. You could use flowcharts, mind maps, sticky notes on a whiteboard, and other tools to perform this activity.

Next examine the pain points, bottlenecks, and gaps in the process. What is causing the bottleneck? Are there steps missing in the process, or perhaps too many steps? Answers to these questions and more will help you prepare the future state.

Now that you understand the current state, including bottlenecks, gaps, and pain points, get your subject matter experts together again to define the future state. What opportunities are there to improve these bottlenecks? How can we eliminate or reduce gaps and pain points? What new goals and experiences can we define that will improve the process? This part of the exercise is free flowing and more subjective than documenting the current state. You want your team members to think outside the box. Again, you could use several tools to help you in this process. Let the creativity flow and don't shut down ideas out of hand. One seemingly goofy idea may lead to a brilliant solution.

Examining Existing Artifacts

There are any number of existing artifacts that can assist with writing the business case, the project charter, and many other project documents. Artifacts in project management are typically documents that are created during the life of the project such as project charter, scope statement, risk log, schedule, budget, lessons learned, and so on. They may also include evidence, physical elements, and information. These artifacts can also be referred to as historical data. Examining these artifacts before embarking on the project can save you time and alert you to risks or other situations that you might not think about this early in the project. The idea is to review a previous project of similar scope and complexity and see if there were issues that surfaced during the project, or if there were contentious stakeholders, if the project finished on schedule, if unexpected expenses came up, and so on. If you know this information before getting too far into the Planning phase of the project, you can prepare yourself and the project team for the unexpected.

Make certain you are examining artifacts from previous projects that are similar in scope and complexity to the project you are undertaking.

 **Real World Scenario**

The Data Center Upgrade

Long ago I worked on a project upgrading our organization's data center. The upgrades were completed, and the project was closed successfully. A couple of weeks later, bright and early on a Monday morning, my deputy walked down to the data center to check on things and saw water coming out from under the locked door of the room. I immediately got a phone call and joined him in the basement. The entire room was flooded. Fortunately, the equipment was on raised flooring and the water hadn't reached that far yet. After much investigation, we found the source of the problem. One of the racks was placed too close to a copper water pipe. Vibration from the rack rubbed a small hole in the pipe, which leaked water onto the floor all weekend. When the plumber finished splicing the pipe, I kept the small piece with the hole in it as an artifact to remind me to account for risks and out-of-the-ordinary situations on future projects.

According to the CompTIA exam objectives, artifacts may also include a prequalified vendor list, predetermined clients, and preexisting contracts. These documents are also beneficial in preparing for your project. For example, if you know that you'll need contract resources with specific skills to assist with the project work, you can examine your organization's *prequalified vendor list* to find a contractor with these skills. Prequalified vendor lists are prepared by the contract and procurement department in your organization. This is a list of vendors that have already been vetted by the organization, and it includes the vendor, the goods and materials, and services they offer and the pricing for each. The vendors typically need to complete a review process, defined by the procurement department, to be included on this list. Once the procurement department approves the information and certifies the vendor, they are added to the prequalified list. Then, you are able to work with the vendors rather than having to go through the normal procurement processes. We'll look more in depth at the procurement process in Chapter 6, "Resource Planning and Management."

Predetermined clients are typically partner companies that have been certified by a large organization to work with their product or service. For example, Workday® is an enterprise finance, human resource, and planning system based in the cloud. Workday engages with certified partners who are able to implement their system in your organization and configure the system for your needs. Much like a prequalified vendor, you will choose from among the software company's predetermined client list (the vendor's certified partners) to assist you with the project work.

Preexisting contracts are active contracts in place in the organization that you can utilize to procure resources for your project. These can range from services contracts to materials contracts and much more. As stated earlier, rather than having to complete a sometimes lengthy procurement process, you can use an existing contract and save a good deal of time and effort. We will talk more in depth about specific contract types in Chapter 6.

Project Selection Methods

After the business case is created, you'll need some method to decide how you or the project selection committee will choose among competing projects.

Project selection methods are used to determine which proposed projects should receive approval and move forward. Project selection may take place using formal documented guidelines, or it may be informal, requiring only the approval of a certain level of management.

Typically, a selection board or committee made up of senior members of the organization will perform project selection. Large organizations may have selection committees at the division or department level. Committees should include representatives from all departments such as information technology, sales, marketing, finance, and customer service.

A project selection committee uses a set of criteria to evaluate and select proposed projects such as the weighted scoring model and/or financial analysis we discussed in the "Determining Benefits and Rewards" section of this chapter. The selection method needs to be applied consistently across all projects to ensure the company is making the best decision in terms of strategic fit as well as the best use of limited resources.

 Selection criteria should always consider the alignment of project goals to the organization's mission, vision, and values.

Project selection methods will vary depending on the mission of the organization, the people serving on the selection committee, the criteria used, and the project itself. These methods could also include examining factors such as market share, financial benefits, return on investment, customer satisfaction, and public perception. The exact criteria vary, but selection methods usually involve a combination of decision models and expert judgment.

Decision Models

A *decision model* is a formal method of project selection that helps selection committees decide among competing projects. Requests for projects can span a large spectrum of needs, and it can be difficult to determine a priority without a means of comparison. Is an online order entry application for the sales team more important than the addition of online help for the customer-support team? While both of these projects could benefit the organization, there may not be adequate budget or staffing to complete both requests, so a decision must be made to approve one request and deny the other. Your committee must make an "apples-to-apples" comparison of the two requests or the decision will be subjective and they may not choose the most beneficial project. A decision model uses a fixed set of criteria agreed on by the project selection committee to evaluate the project requests. By using the same model to evaluate each project request, the selection committee has a common ground on which to compare the projects and make the most objective decision. You can use a variety of decision models that range from a basic ranking matrix, such as the weighted scoring model shown in Table 1.2, to elaborate mathematical models.

There are two primary categories of decision models: benefit measurement methods and constrained-optimization models. We discussed the benefit measurement methods in the earlier section "Determining Benefits and Rewards." You may recall these methods include the following:

- Cost-benefit analysis
- Scoring models
- Payback period
- Discounted cash flow
- Net present value
- Internal rate of return
- Return on investment

Any of these methods may be used as selection criteria by the committee for choosing and ranking competing projects.

Constrained optimization models are the second type of decision model. They are mathematical models, some of which are very complicated. They are typically used when comparing highly complex projects and require a detailed understanding of statistics and other mathematical concepts. A discussion of these models is beyond the scope of this book.

 Benefit measurement methods are the most commonly used decision model.

Expert Judgment

Expert judgment relies on the expertise of stakeholders, subject matter experts, or those who have previous experience to help reach a decision regarding project selection. Typically, expert judgment is used in conjunction with one of the decision models discussed previously.

Companies with an informal project selection process may use expert judgment to make project selection decisions and not consider financial analysis. Although using only expert judgment can simplify the project selection process, there are dangers in relying on this single technique. It is not likely that the project selection committee members are authorities on each of the proposed projects. Without access to comparative data or financial analysis, a project approval decision may be made based solely on who has the best slide presentation or who is the best speaker.

Political influence is a part of expert judgment. An executive with a great deal of influence may convince the selection committee to approve a particular project (generally one in which they have a vested interest). (Did I say that out loud?)

Let's not forget one of the most important selection factors: the CEO said so! You might be snickering a little at this one, but I can tell you from first-hand experience there is no amount of financial analysis that can dissuade a CEO who has made up their mind that their pet project is moving forward.

Once your selection committee has selected and approved a project or projects, the project manager will move forward with the initiating phase of the project. We'll cover this in Chapter 3.

Summary

A project is a temporary endeavor that produces a unique product service or result. It has definitive start and finish dates. Project management is the application of tools and techniques to organize the project activities to successfully meet the project goals. A project manager is responsible for project integration and applying the tools and techniques of project management to bring about a successful conclusion to the project.

Programs are a collection or group of related projects that are managed together using coordinated processes and techniques. The collective management of a group of projects can bring about benefits that wouldn't be achievable if the projects were managed separately.

Portfolios are collections of programs, subportfolios, and projects that support strategic business goals or objectives. Portfolios may consist of projects that are not related.

The project life cycle phases are Discovery/Concept, Initiating, Planning, Executing, and Closing. Discovery is where the business case is created, and the project is justified. Initiating is where the preliminary scope statement and project charter are created. Planning consists of preparing for the work of the project. Executing is where the work of the project is performed, monitored, and tracked. Closing is the most often skipped process. This is where project closeout occurs and contracts are closed, team members released, and more.

A project comes about as a result of needs or demands, including market demand, organizational need, customer request, technological advance, legal requirement, ecological impact, and social need.

The business case documents the business need for the project and determines whether the investment in the project is worthwhile. There are several financial analysis techniques you can use to determine the benefits and rewards of the project, including cost-benefit analysis, scoring model, payback period, discounted cash flow, net present value, return on investment, internal rate of return, and current state versus future state.

Existing artifacts can assist you with writing the business case and other project documents and can alert you to risks or issues that may occur during the project.

Project selection methods involve the use of decision models, such as the financial analysis used in the business case, weighted scoring models, current state versus future state, and expert judgment.

Exam Essentials

Be able to define a project.   A project brings about a unique product, service, or result and has definite beginning and ending dates.

Be able to identify the difference between a project and ongoing operations.   A project is a temporary endeavor to create a unique product or service. Operational work is ongoing and repetitive.

Be able to define a program and a portfolio.   A program is a group of related projects managed to gain benefits that couldn't be realized if they were managed independently. Portfolios are collections of programs and projects that support strategic business goals or objectives. Programs and projects within the portfolio may not be related to one another.

Be able to name the life cycle phases of a project and their primary purpose.   The phases are Discovery/Concept, Initiating, Planning, Executing, and Closing. Discovery is where the business case is created and the project is justified. Initiating is where the preliminary scope statement and project charter are created. Planning consists of preparing for the work of the project. Executing is where the work of the project is performed, monitored, and tracked. Closing is where project closeout occurs and contracts are closed, team members released, and more.

Understand the needs and demands that bring about a project.   The needs and demands that bring about a project include market demand, organizational need, customer request, technological advance, legal requirement, ecological impacts, and social need.

Understand the purpose of a business case.   A business case documents the business need for the project and determines whether the investment in the project is worthwhile.

Be able to describe the two steps involved in validating a project.   Validating a project involves writing and reviewing the business case and analyzing the stakeholders.

Be able to identify commonly used business case justification and project selection methods.   The most common project selection methods are cost-benefit analysis, scoring model, payback period, discounted cash flow, net present value, return on investment, internal rate of return, and current state versus future state Understand what skills are needed to manage a project beyond technical knowledge of the product.

Key Terms

Before you take the exam, be certain you are familiar with the following terms:

A Guide to the Project Management Body of Knowledge (PMBOK® Guide)	operations
business case	payback period
Closing	Planning
constrained optimization models	portfolio
cost of capital	predetermined clients
cost-benefit analysis	prequalified vendor list
decision model	program
discounted cash flow	project
Discovery/concept preparation phase	project management
Executing	Project Management Institute (PMI®)
expert judgment	project manager
feasibility study	project selection methods
Initiating	return on investment (ROI)
internal rate of return (IRR)	scoring model
Iterative	stakeholder
net present value (NPV)	

Review Questions

1. What is the definition of a project? (Choose two.)

   A. A group of interrelated activities that create a unique benefit to the organization

   B. A set of processes repeated multiple times to produce the same result

   C. A temporary endeavor undertaken to create a unique product, service, or result

   D. A process used to generate profit, improve market share, or adhere to legal requirements

   E. A time-constrained activity used to bring about unique results that align with the organization's goals

2. What is the definition of operations?

   A. Activities that have a definitive start and end date

   B. Activities that are ongoing that support the organization's business

   C. Activities that are unique to the organization and are temporary in nature

   D. Activities that are time bound

3. What is the term for a group of related projects managed in a coordinated fashion?

   A. Life cycle

   B. Phase

   C. Process group

   D. Program

4. Which of the following are true regarding project portfolios? (Choose two.)

   A. The independent projects in the portfolio may not have anything in common.

   B. The programs in the portfolio are related to one another.

   C. The programs and projects within the portfolio support the strategic goals of the portfolio.

   D. An organization has only one portfolio.

   E. Portfolios consist of programs and do not contain stand-alone projects.

5. Which of the following make up the life cycle phases according to the CompTIA exam objectives?

   A. Initiating, Planning, Executing, Closing

   B. Discovery/Concept, Initiating, Planning, Executing, Closing

   C. Discovery/Concept, Planning, Executing, Monitoring and Controlling, Closing

   D. Initiating, Planning, Executing, Monitoring and Controlling, Closing

6. You receive a request from customer service to purchase and implement a customer management system for the service-support staff. What type of need or demand does this describe?

   A. Organizational need

   B. Market demand

   C. Legal requirement

   D. Technological advance

7. Your project stakeholder is working on the business case. They ask you for some assistance. You suggest to them that the business case should include which of the following?

   A. Feasibility study

   B. Alignment to the strategic plan

   C. Justification

   D. Alternative solutions

   E. All of the above

8. Preexisting contracts, prequalified vendors, and project documents such as the scope statement, schedule, risk log, and lessons learned are known as which of the following? (Choose two.)

   A. Vestige

   B. Relic

   C. Historical information

   D. Artifacts

9. Your project has expected cash inflows of $1.2 million in year 1, $2 million in year 2, and $4.4 million in year 3, for a total of $7.6 million in today's dollars. Which technique was used to determine this?

   A. Discounted cash flow

   B. IRR

   C. NPV

   D. Cost-benefit analysis

10. Your selection committee wants to compare the profitability of three projects against each other to determine which should move forward. The projects do not have equal timelines. You are using this formula:

   (Current Value or Gain from the Investment − Cost of Investment) / (Cost of the Investment)

   Which of the following are true regarding this question? (Choose two.)

   A. This is the formula for discounted cash flows.

   B. This is the formula for ROI.

   C. You'll need to annualize the returns since each project has a different time period.

   D. This is the formula for NPV.

   E. The returns are calculated by year and the total return for each project should be used for comparison.

11. The idea behind most cash flow techniques is that money today is worth more than money in the future. What is this known as?

   A. Present value of money

   B. Future value of money

   C. Time value of money

   D. Discounted value of future money

12. Federico, the director of the marketing department, has approached you with an idea for a project. He has prepared a draft business case and included two alternative solutions. What should this section of the business case contain?

   A. High-level description of the costs

   B. Feasibility of implementing each alternative

   C. Expected results of each solution

   D. Description of the impacts of the alternative to the organization

   E. A, B, C

   F. A, B, C, D

13. Your project has projected revenues of $500,000 in year 1 and $700,000 in year 2. Your initial investment was $850,000. What is the payback period?

   A. 21 months

   B. 20 months

   C. 2 years

   D. 18 months

14. You've been given an idea for a project by an executive in your organization. After writing the business case, you submit it to the executive for review. After reading the business case, they determine that the project poses a significant amount of risk to the organization. What do you recommend next?

   A. Proceed to the project selection committee.

   B. Reject the project based on the analysis.

   C. Proceed to writing the project plan.

   D. Perform a feasibility study.

15. Your selection committee has approved a project that requires specialized skills that are not available in the organization. This project has a tight timeline and you are looking for ways to get resources on board as quickly as possible. Which of the following will help you speed up the procurement of resources? (Choose two.)

   A. Preexisting contract

   B. Predetermined clients

   C. Prequalified vendor list

   D. Predetermined selection process

16. Which of the following are used as project selection methods?

    A. Cash flow techniques

    B. Constrained optimization models

    C. Expert judgment

    D. Decision models

    E. A, D

    F. A, B, D

    G. A, B, C, D

17. Your project involves implementing a software platform to manage the organization's general ledger, budget, and financial information. The company you have engaged with recommended three implementation firms for you to choose from in helping to configure the system. What is this known as?

    A. Predetermined clients

    B. Predetermined vendor list

    C. Prequalified clients

    D. Prequalified vendor list

18. Your project has expected cash inflows of $7.8 million in today's dollars. The project's initial investment is $9.2 million. Which of the following is true?

    A. The discounted cash flows are lower than the initial investment, so this project should be rejected.

    B. The discounted cash flows are lower than the initial investment, so this project should be accepted.

    C. NPV is less than 0, so this project should be rejected.

    D. NPV is greater than 0, so this project should be accepted.

19. Which of the following are the steps required to validate a project? (Choose two.)

    A. Analyze the feasibility.

    B. Justify the project.

    C. Align it to the strategic plan.

    D. Create the business case.

    E. Identify and analyze stakeholders.

20. Your selection committee is reviewing two projects that will attempt to improve the efficiency of your current procurement process. They have engaged key team members and subject matter experts to compare two projects. This team is charged with analyzing the current process and determining how this might change or improve, and how it will change, if the project were implemented. What is this technique called? (Choose three.)

A. As is—to be

B. Current state versus future state

C. Project selection methodology

D. Alignment to the strategic plan

E. Justification

F. Performance analysis

Chapter

2

Understanding IT Fundamentals

THE COMPTIA PROJECT+ EXAM TOPICS COVERED IN THIS CHAPTER INCLUDE:

✓ **1.0 Project Management Concepts**

- **1.10 Given a scenario, perform basic activities related to team and resource management**
  - Roles and responsibilities

✓ **4.0 Basics of IT and Governance**

- **4.1 Summarize basic environmental, social, and governance (ESG) factors related to project management activities**
  - Project impact to the local and global environment
  - Awareness of applicable regulations and standards
  - Awareness of company vision, mission statements, and values
  - Project impact to company brand value

- **4.3 Explain relevant compliance and privacy considerations impacting project management**
  - Data confidentiality
  - Legal and regulatory impacts
  - Country-, state-, province-specific privacy regulations
  - Awareness of industry- or organization-specific compliance concerns impacting a project

- **4.4 Summarize basic IT concepts relevant to IT project management**
  - Infrastructure
  - Cloud models
  - Software

In this chapter, we will look at factors that influence project management such as environmental, social, and governance endeavors, as well as privacy and confidentiality concerns. We will also cover some fundamental concepts of information technology. The focus of the CompTIA Project + exam is on technology-related projects, so you'll need a basic understanding of the information technology functions. Many IT departments have a project management function within their department. It's important for a project manager to understand how the various functions of information technology work together to implement projects with a technology component. First, we'll start by describing the role of the project manager. Hang on tight, there is a lot of information packed into this chapter. Grab your favorite beverage and read on.

Understanding the Role of the Project Manager

You'll recall from Chapter 1, "Introducing the Project," that the project manager is the person responsible for integrating all the components and artifacts of a project and applying the various tools and techniques of project management to bring about a successful conclusion to the project. The project manager's role is diverse and includes activities such as managing the team; managing communication; defining scope; managing risk; managing budgets; managing time; managing quality assurance; planning; negotiating; solving problems; and more.

Good soft skills are as critical to the success of a project as good technical skills. Technical skills help when applying a concept or working on programming code, for example. Soft skills are typically the behaviors we exhibit when interacting with others and tend to be more inter-relational. In this section we'll look at some of the important soft skills a good project manager should possess. You'll examine many of the technical and soft skills needed as they relate to the project management processes in the coming chapters as well.

You probably already use some of these skills in your day-to-day work activities. Here's a partial list:

- Leadership
- Communicating
- Listening

- Organizational skills
- Time management
- Planning
- Problem solving
- Consensus building
- Resolving conflict
- Negotiating
- Team building

Let's examine a few of these skills in a little more detail.

Leadership

A project manager must also be a good leader. Leaders understand how to rally people around a vision and motivate them to achieve amazing results. They set strategic goals, establish direction, and inspire and motivate others. Strong leaders also know how to align and encourage diverse groups of people with varying backgrounds and experience to work together to accomplish the goals of the project.

Leaders possess a passion for their work and for life. They are persistent and diligent in attaining their goals. And they aren't shy about using opportunities that present themselves to better their team members, to better the project results, or to accomplish the organization's mission. Leaders are found at all levels of the organization and aren't necessarily synonymous with people in executive positions. We've all known our share of executive staff members who couldn't lead a team down the hall, let alone through the complex maze of project management. It's great for you to possess all the technical skills you can acquire as a project manager. But it's even better if you are also a strong leader who others trust and are willing to follow.

Communication

Most project managers will tell you they spend most of their day communicating. PMI® suggests that project managers spend up to 90 percent of their time in the act of communicating. It is by far the number-one key to project success. Even the most detailed project plan can fail without adequate communication. And of all the communication skills in your tool bag, listening is the most important. Ideally, you have finely honed your leadership skills and have gained the trust of your team members. When they trust you, they'll tell you things they wouldn't have otherwise. As the project manager, you want to know everything that has the potential to affect the project outcomes or anything that may impact your team members.

Project managers must develop a communication strategy for the project that includes the following critical components:

- What you want to communicate
- How often you'll communicate

- The audience receiving the communication
- The medium used for communicating
- Monitoring the outcome of the communication

Keeping these components in mind and developing a comprehensive communication plan early in the project will help prevent misunderstanding and conflict as the project progresses.

 We'll discuss communication in more detail in Chapter 8, "Communicating the Plan."

Problem Solving

There is no such thing as a project that doesn't have problems. Projects always have problems. Some are just more serious than others.

Recognizing the warning signs of trouble as soon as they occur will help simplify the process of resolving problems and help mitigate expensive consequences. Many times, warning signs come about during communications with your stakeholders, team members, vendors, and others. Pay close attention not only to what your team members are saying but also to how they're saying it. Body language plays a bigger part in communication than words do. Learn to read the real meaning behind what your team member is saying and when to ask clarifying questions to get the heart of the issue on the table.

Negotiating

Negotiation is the process of obtaining mutually acceptable agreements with individuals or groups. Like communication and problem-solving skills, this skill is used throughout the life of the project.

You'll get a good amount of practice with this skill by negotiating with other managers for human resources to work on the project. If you will be procuring goods or services from an outside vendor, you will likely be involved in negotiating a contract or other form of procurement document. Some project team members may negotiate specific job assignments. Project stakeholders may change the project objectives, which drives negotiations regarding the schedule, the budget, or both. As you execute the project, change requests often involve complex negotiations as various stakeholders propose conflicting requests. There is no lack of opportunity for you to use negotiating skills during the life of a project.

 Real World Scenario

Negotiating with the Business Unit

You're working on a project for the human resources department in your company. They'd like to streamline the recruitment process and set up a website for applicants to view the job descriptions and apply online. The hiring managers also need a streamlined way to quickly review résumés and applications and arrange for interviews with qualified candidates. You've gotten past the initial project request steps, and you're now in the process of determining the details of the requirements for the project.

You set up a meeting with the director of human resources. At the meeting you ask them two things. First, you want to know whether you can use someone from the business unit to assist you in understanding the business process flows. You make it clear that the assigned individual must be a subject matter expert (SME) in the business process. Second, you ask whether you can have this individual full-time for one week. You suggest the name of someone whom you think will perform well as a business SME.

The director is surprised that you require so much time from one of their people. You explain that in order to create a website that fully meets the business needs, you must first understand how the business process works today and how it can be improved.

After some discussion back and forth, the two of you come to an agreement that you can have three days of the SMEs' time and that you'll use two different business SMEs, splitting their efforts accordingly so that neither one has to fully dedicate their time to the business flow discovery process.

Organization and Time Management

As stated earlier in this chapter, the project manager oversees all aspects of the work involved in meeting the project goals. The ongoing responsibilities of a typical project manager include tracking schedules and budgets and providing updates on their status, conducting regular team meetings, reviewing team member reports, tracking vendor progress, communicating with stakeholders, meeting individually with team members, preparing formal presentations, managing change requests, and much more. This requires excellent organizational skills and the ability to manage your time effectively. I've found that most project managers are good time managers as well, but if you struggle in this area, I strongly recommend taking a class or two on this topic.

Meetings consume valuable project time, so make certain they are necessary and effective. Effective meetings don't just happen—they result from good planning. Whether you conduct a formal team meeting or an individual session, you should define the purpose of the meeting and develop an agenda of the topics to be discussed or covered. It's good practice to make certain each agenda item has a time limit in order to keep the meeting moving and to finish on time. In my experience, the only thing worse than team members coming late to a scheduled meeting is a meeting that goes past its allotted time frame.

Clear documentation is critical to project success, and you'll want a system that allows you to put your hands on these documents at a moment's notice. Technology comes to the rescue here. There are numerous options available that will allow you to store, edit, share, and archive project documents. Find one that works for you and keep it up-to-date.

Factors That Influence Project Management Activities

Several factors influence project management activities. We'll look at both influences on the project and influences the project may have on others. In this section we'll examine three areas—environmental, social, and governance factors—and compliance and privacy considerations.

Environmental, Social, and Governance (ESG) Factors

Environmental, social, and governance (ESG) factors may have a significant impact on your project, and this requires either the project manager, or a subject matter expert, to know and understand these factors. Conversely, the project you are undertaking may itself have an impact on the ESG factors and may affect the organization's reputation if not taken into consideration.

Environmental Factors

Environmental factors refer to the impacts your project may have to the environment. For example, your project may entail building a new facility near a local river. You'll need to consider the precautions that need to be exercised during the construction phase to protect the river from debris. You'll also need to consider the function of this facility and ongoing maintenance and how that may affect the environment. If there are potential impacts, you'll need to take steps to mitigate them. Your organization could suffer reputational loss if environmental factors are not considered and managed.

Social Factors

Social factors in this context primarily include the interactions and relationships among the stakeholders, including project team members, and potential customers. For example, consider the changes that may come about to your employees' daily work life as a result of the project. Will some groups of employees be favored over others? Will some employees have to go to extra effort to perform the same functions they are performing today? Perhaps some employees may lose their job due to automation. Examine impacts to your customers as well. Will the project make it more difficult for customers to interact with the organization? Will this project change the way customers view the goodwill of the organization? Be certain to consider factors such as fairness and equity as well, and how the project may change or influence stakeholders and customers.

Governance Factors

Governance factors refer to the way the project itself will be governed and how that governance will occur within the context of the overall organization. Project governance includes reporting and monitoring of project performance, communication of changes, accountability to the budget, transparency, and many other issues. As the project manager, make certain you are aware of the governance factors that impact projects in your organization.

Other ESG Factors

According to the CompTIA exam objectives, several factors come into play under the ESG heading, including these:

- Awareness of company vision, mission statement, and values
- Project impact on company brand value
- Project impact on local and global environment
- Awareness of applicable regulations and standards

Let's look briefly at each of these factors next.

Company Vision, Mission Statement, and Values   As you learned in Chapter 1, one component of the business case involves examining the alignment of the project to the company's vision, mission, and values. All employees of the organization should have a solid understanding of these factors, and most importantly, so should the project manager. For example, if your organization's mission involves transporting materials and goods, a project that concerns developing a new manufacturing process wouldn't make a lot of sense because it doesn't align with the organization's mission. Remember also that your selection committee should always have the company vision, mission, and values in mind and ensure the project they are selecting aligns with them.

Impact to Company Brand Value   This factor is self-evident. Be sure to examine the project's outcome and its impact on the company brand value and reputation. You may have a project that will significantly improve brand value, and that's a good thing. However, consider the impact of negative comments or social media pressure if the project hurts or hinders the brand value of the organization.

Impact to Local and Global Environment   I discussed this earlier in this section when describing environmental impacts the project might pose. Be certain to consider not only local impacts but global environmental impacts as well.

Awareness of Regulations and Standards   Regulations and standards exist in almost all industries. It is important to understand how these regulations can impact your project and what actions you need to take to ensure you are complying with them. For example, I work in the transportation industry, which is heavily regulated by the federal government. Our projects must include plans to comply with these regulations. If regulations are violated, the government could withhold funding, impart fines, issue sanctions, and more.

 ESG factors should be examined by the project selection committee and used as part of the selection criteria. Consider modifying your business case template to include a section devoted to ESG factors.

Compliance and Privacy Considerations

Compliance and privacy considerations, much like ESG factors, can have an impact on your project and/or on the organization. According to the CompTIA exam objectives, considerations such as data confidentiality, legal and regulatory impacts, privacy regulations, and awareness of industry-related issues should be examined. We'll look at each of these areas next.

Data Confidentiality

Data confidentiality involves protecting sensitive data and data types in order to protect individual identities and personal information relating to those individuals. Data confidentiality is serious business, and project managers must understand what this entails and ensure that projects and systems are implemented in accordance with regulations. There are two types of data confidentiality we'll examine in this section: personally identifiable information (PII) and personal health information (PHI).

Personally Identifiable Information (PII)

The National Institute of Standards and Technology (NIST) in the United States is a widely recognized federal agency that has created frameworks, processes, and controls to help the federal government protect information and information systems. These standards are not only used in government, but in private sectors across many industries as well. NIST has published the "Guide to Protecting the Confidentiality of Personally Identifiable Information," which can be found here: https://nvlpubs.nist.gov/nistpubs/Legacy/SP/nistspecialpublication800-122.pdf.

NIST defines *personally identifiable information (PII)* as:

> . . .any information about an individual maintained by an agency, including (1) any information that can be used to distinguish or trace an individual's identity such as name, social security number, date and place of birth, mother's maiden name, or biometric records; and (2) any other information that is linked or linkable to an individual such as medical, educational, financial, and employment information.

Information that is directly associated with an individual, such as those data elements listed in Table 2.1, are used to "distinguish or trace an individual's identity" as described in the NIST Guide. Distinguishing an individual in this case is to identify an individual. Tracing makes determinations about an individual's status or activities in a way that can be used to identify them. The examples in Table 2.1 are stand-alone data elements that are considered *sensitive personally identifiable data elements (SPII)*. SPII is a subset of PII. Any of these SPII data elements on their own could identify an individual and cause them great harm or potential embarrassment if used inappropriately.

In section 2.2 of the NIST Guide, you'll see a list of example information that may be considered PII. I've summarized them in two tables. Table 2.1 shows examples of stand-alone sensitive personally identifiable information. We'll look at Table 2.2 after this one.

TABLE 2.1 Examples of stand-alone sensitive PII data

Social Security number	Passport number	Driver's license number
Taxpayer identification number	Patient identification number	Financial account or credit card number
Alien registration number	Biometric identifiers (fingerprints, retina scans, voice signature, etc.)	Facial geometry

Linkable data is also personally identifiable data but, on its own, is not sensitive data. However, when you combine linkable data with any of the data elements shown in Table 2.1, it becomes sensitive personally identifiable information. Table 2.2 shows examples of linkable data as noted in the NIST Guide.

TABLE 2.2 Examples of linkable data

Name, full name	Maiden name, mother's maiden name	Alias
Street address	Email address	Internet Protocol (IP) or Media Access Control (MAC) address
Telephone numbers	Vehicle registration number, title number	Personally owned property identification numbers/information
Date of birth	Place of birth	Religion
Race	Financial information	Family members
Weight	Activities	Geographical indicators
Employment information	Medical information	Educational information
Zip code	Age range	Criminal history

Context is important when you're using these data elements and determining whether they are sensitive. Whenever the data may cause substantial harm to an individual, may embarrass them or harm their reputation, or cause them to be treated unfairly, you are likely dealing with SPII.

Linkable information on its own is often easy to find. For example, do a simple search of your local jurisdiction's records to find criminal history data, land ownership, business ownership, and more. On its own, this is not sensitive data. However, if you are collecting a name, zip code, and credit card number, for example, you are now handling sensitive data and need to be aware of the regulations and processes concerned with processing and storing this data.

Protected Health Information (PHI)

Personal health information (PHI), also known as *protected health information,* is a form of PII data. As the name implies, this data refers to the individual's health information. PHI is a nested definition that includes individually identifiable health information (IIHI), which in turn includes the definition of health information. You can refer to the "Special Publication 800-66 Revision 1," published by NIST, to get the full definition for each of these terms.

I recommend you know this about PHI and its health information received orally or in recorded form about an individual's past, present, and future health or mental condition. This information may also include the healthcare the individual received, and payment for that healthcare. As you can imagine, this is highly sensitive data and should be safeguarded.

The Health Insurance Portability and Accountability Act of 1996 (HIPAA) was introduced to provide regulations regarding the safekeeping of electronic protected health information (ePHI). HIPAA regulations generally apply to covered healthcare providers, health plans, healthcare clearinghouses, and Medicare prescription drug sponsors. HIPAA sets out to define how organizations are ensuring there are adequate controls for ePHI, developing compliance strategies, developing a risk management program, and creating documentation to demonstrate compliance with the HIPPA Security Rule.

 As the project manager, it is your responsibility to know and understand the rules and regulations that apply to PII data. There could be significant fines and consequences for not adhering to proper handling of sensitive personally identifiable information.

Remember that PHI (and ePHI) is a form of PII data, and many countries have developed their own standards and regulations for controlling, storing, and transmitting PII data. As stated earlier, in the United States, NIST has published the "Guide to Protecting the Confidentiality of Personally Identifiable Information" as well as many other publications on data privacy issues. Canada has developed the Personal Information Protection and Electronic Documents Act (PIPEDA) and the Privacy Act. The European Union (EU) established the General Data Protection Regulation (GDPR). All organizations that engage in business in the EU must comply with GDPR, whether or not the business itself resides in the EU. Simply doing business in the EU requires compliance with GDPR standards. GDPR regulations are more restrictive than the NIST standards. For example, GDPR describes IP addresses, cookies, and radio frequency identification tags as sensitive personal data. Many other countries have similar acts and directives.

Keep in mind that regions within countries may have different definitions of personally identifiable information and different laws and regulations regarding how you store, handle, share, archive, and delete this information. For example, the state of California in the United States has additional privacy standards, above and beyond NIST standards, as published in the California Consumer Privacy Act (CCPA).

It's important that as the project manager, you ensure the project team is aware of these directives and how the regulations should be incorporated into the project. For example, perhaps your organization is implementing a world-class human resources system that contains much of the information described earlier in this section regarding PII and SPII. Let's say the organization has offices, and employees, in several countries. You'll need to ensure that the system can accommodate all of the privacy regulations pertaining to all the countries where your organization performs business.

Breach of Confidentiality

An organization that handles PII must ensure they are following all regulations for the local, regional, national, and global marketplaces where they conduct business. It is advisable to work closely with legal counsel who have expertise within these jurisdictions to ensure that your project, and your organization, are well advised on the law. In addition, the organization should develop policies and procedures for handling PII, and provide mandatory education, training, and awareness for employees who work with this data. If you have an upcoming project that entails processing PII, make certain to obtain training before embarking on the project.

A breach of confidentiality occurs when PII is exposed to people or organizations that should not have access to the information. Breaches may carry significant fines, penalties, reputational damage, and more. There are numerous examples and types of harm that can come to individuals and to organizations because of a breach of their data. These may include but are not limited to financial harm, social impacts, identity theft, discrimination, emotional distress, administrative burdens, loss of reputation, and so on.

The potential impacts of a breach of confidentiality should be analyzed when dealing with PII. According to NIST, there are three impact levels for a breach: low, moderate, and high. All three impact levels involve the loss of confidentiality, integrity, or availability. Low impact levels have a limited effect on the organization or individual. Moderate impact levels may have serious adverse effects on the organization, including its operations or assets, or may involve serious adverse effects to an individual. High impact levels have severe or catastrophic adverse effects to the organization or individuals. The organization should define these levels in their policies and procedures. The project team should be aware of these impact levels and prepare mitigation plans as needed.

When working on a project, think about the context of the project and the data it will process or collect. Perhaps your project is intended to collect data on consumer behaviors and involves understanding elements such as the income, age, and zip codes of your consumers. Rather than collecting data on each individual, you could consider aggregating the data by using income ranges by zip code, identifying age ranges rather than specific ages, or obscuring the data so that names are not associated with income levels, for example.

Anonymizing the data is a way to take what once was identifiable information and deidentify it so that it's generalized and less precise. This might also include deleting portions of the record or using average values for a group of data.

Information technology projects often involve sensitive data. For example, if you're implementing that new world-class human resources system we talked about previously, there will be weeks of testing needed to ensure the system is performing properly and verifying that your company data has been uploaded correctly. However, you don't want to give all project team members the ability to see employee Social Security numbers or salaries, for example, so you could manage sensitive data by scrambling it, obscuring all but the last two digits of the salary and Social Security number, and so on. Obviously, someone will have to verify Social Security numbers and other sensitive information, but these specific testing scenarios should be assigned to those in the organization who already have these responsibilities such as payroll clerks.

Legal and Regulatory Impacts

We talked about legal and regulatory impacts in Chapter 1 in the section "How Projects Come About." Legal and regulatory impacts may drive the need for a new project, as explained in that chapter. You should also be aware of how legal and regulatory impacts may affect the project you are working on. For example, your organization might be developing a new drug that will eventually require Food and Drug Administration (FDA) approval before it can be distributed. Therefore, you will need to ensure that FDA regulations and policies are strictly adhered to during the project life cycle. The transportation industry is required to abide by a host of regulations defined by the Federal Transit Administration (FTA). There are many examples of legal and regulatory impacts, too many to detail in this book, that could impact your project. Virtually every industry has standards, regulations, and sometimes laws that dictate how business, or business processes, should be performed. Make certain you are aware of those regulations for your industry. If you don't know, ask your subject matter experts or someone on the legal team.

Just as PII regulations can vary by region, so can legal and regulatory requirements. Make certain you are familiar with country, state, province, and regional regulations that could impact your project.

Privacy Regulations

Privacy regulations pertain to classifications or types of data as we've discussed throughout this section. For example, HIPPA, PIPEDA, GDPR, CCPA, and so on. Make certain you are aware of the privacy regulations that pertain to the types and classifications of data you may be dealing with on your project. Failure to follow these regulations can result in punitive, reputational, and significant financial penalties to the organization.

Awareness of Other Compliance Concerns

Legal and regulatory impacts are not the only compliance issues you should consider when undertaking your project. Many industries have their own standards and regulations they abide by to ensure consumers know their products or services are safe. These are not necessarily laws, but generally accepted standards. Often, individuals and organizations come together collaboratively to form consortiums or organizations to establish standards. For example, Underwriters Laboratories (UL) has established UL Standards that exist to assess products, test components, evaluate products, and more. You can read more about them at UL.com.

The International Organization for Standardization (ISO) has developed standards for a wide range of products, energy efficiency, environmental concerns, and more. They are made up of over 250 committees responsible for developing the standards in their area of expertise.

Information technology has a host of standards. For example, sending an electronic message requires specific standards for addressing, formatting, and transmitting the message so that receivers can open and read the email. Weights and measures, money, and time are other examples of standards. I'm sure you can think of many on your own.

As I've emphasized throughout this section, you as the project manager need to be aware of the industry, organizational, or specific compliance concerns that may impact the project.

 **Real World Scenario**

New Wine

Wine making dates to the beginning of time. Grapes are the primary ingredient in wine, although it is possible to make wine from other fruits. Wines take on the flavors and characteristics of the soil and climate in the region where the grapes are grown. This is an important distinction for a winery. In France, for example, where the grapes are grown tells the consumer something about the wine itself. They can discern this by looking at the AOC designation on the bottle. AOC stands for Appellation d'Origine Contrôlée (AOC). This certification process came about in the early 1900s to fight fraud. AOC sets standards about the wine process, including everything from growing the grapes, to pressing the grapes, to bottling the wine. The AOC label will tell you the region and other special classifications about the wine. For example, a Burgundy wine comes from the Burgundy region in France. If your winery does not have an AOC classification, they may not state that the wine is produced in Burgundy. The United States uses a similar designation called an Appellation of Origin, which tells you the region where the grapes were grown. Many countries have similar certifications. If you were working on a project for a winery that wanted to obtain one of these prestigious certificates, you'd need to ensure your project adheres to the standards, laws, and processes defined by these organizations.

Information Technology Fundamentals

Information technology (IT) involves the use of computers and computer networks to create, store, process, and transmit electronic information. IT has evolved over time and encompasses a vast array of technology, machinery, networks, infrastructure, cloud models, software, and more. Organizations may have an IT department, or they may contract out this service. Or perhaps they utilize a cloud provider. Regardless of how the technology is supported in the organization, it's important for project managers to understand some of the basics of IT and the elements involved in supporting technology. Many projects involve technology in one way or another. I can't begin to tell you how many times in my career that non-IT departments undertake a project and have no thought or concern for notifying IT. They believe they can work with their vendor and simply stand up the new software program they need for their business unit . . . until the vendor begins asking about the infrastructure the software program will reside on and who will build the interfaces needed from other systems to bring data into their system. Then IT gets the call, and it becomes our emergency. But I digress. As a project manager, you are very likely going to work on projects that involve IT elements. It is to your benefit to understand some of the basics of IT so that when words like *infrastructure*, *cloud*, and *multitiered architecture* start flying, you understand what they mean.

It is beyond the scope of this book to perform a deep dive into the world of IT. For purposes of the exam, we'll take a high-level look at three areas within IT that are involved in implementing projects with technology components: infrastructure, cloud models, and software.

Infrastructure

Infrastructure consists of all the hardware, software, servers, networks, data centers, and more that comprise and support IT activities for an organization. Infrastructure enables the organization to provide IT services to its employees and customers. You can think of infrastructure as the highway upon which information and services travel. These roads provide the foundation to get information and services from one entity to another. Infrastructure might reside in a data center on-premises, on the cloud, or a combination thereof. (We'll cover cloud in the next section.)

Several components of infrastructure are outlined in the CompTIA exam objectives. We'll look at each of them next.

Computing Services

Computing services refers to the infrastructure that provides computing capability to the organization or its customers. Computing services may include servers, networking, databases, storage, software, and more. Computing services is the foundation for making technology work. For example, you may have a fantastic software program that improves productivity for the organization's employees. Without this software, it would take them hours, rather than minutes, to complete their tasks. However, the software won't work without the server it resides on. The server can't make the software accessible to the users without the network. And without the databases to store the information created in the software, it's useless. All these elements work together to provide technology solutions to the organization. Computing services may reside in a data center on-premises, or they may reside in the cloud, or a combination of both.

Multitiered Architecture

Multitiered architecture refers to physically separating technology functions into their own modules. This architecture defines how a technology system is constructed. Three-tier architecture is the most common form of multitiered architecture. It consists of a presentation tier, a processing tier, and a data tier. Let's take a closer look at each of these tiers.

The presentation tier collects and displays the information the user needs to interact with the system. Web pages are an example of the presentation tier. The web page provides a way for the user to input data, such as adding items to their shopping carts, and displays the results of the input.

The application tier is where the information collected from the presentation tier is processed. For example, the prices for the items in the shopping cart are summed and taxes and shipping charges are added. The total is then displayed back to the user using the presentation tier. The application tier is also known as the middle tier.

The data tier is where the information that was collected and processed is stored. For example, you'll need to enter your name and address when checking out so that the company knows where to ship your package. This information, and more, is stored in the data tier.

These tiers are developed and operate as independent modules. This allows for ease of maintenance because they are separate modules, typically on separate platforms. For example, if the database tier needs maintenance, the IT team can perform it on that tier without impacting the presentation or processing tiers.

Networking and Connectivity

A computer *network* is the collection of devices connected to each other using cables or wireless communication to enable the sharing and exchange of data and services. There are a multitude of examples that networking supports such as text messages, video calls, video streaming, file sharing, device sharing such as printers and scanners, software sharing, and much more. The two primary devices used in networking are routers and switches.

Wired networks use physical cables to transport information between devices. These devices when connected to the network are referred to as nodes. Wireless networks use radio waves to transport data and services. Wired networks are generally faster and more secure than wireless networks, whereas wireless networks allow the user to be mobile and provide more flexibility than their wired counterparts.

There are several types of networks that can be constructed for different purposes. Two of the most common networks are *local area networks (LAN)* and *wide area networks (WAN)*. A LAN is a network used in a specific location such as a school or a business. The LAN connects the technology and devices used by the organization to each other so they can share information, utilize software and services, and communicate with each other. A WAN is a network that covers a larger area and may be used by businesses that have more than one location. This allows the employees at the Main Street location to communicate with and share resources with employees at the Bloom Street location, for example.

> Be aware there are several other types of networks, including metropolitan area networks (MANs), global area networks (GANs), personal area networks (PANs), and more. As you can imagine, a MAN may cover a city, or a metropolitan area. A MAN is made up of a series of LANs and potentially WANs that are interconnected. A GAN connects networks including LANs, WANs, MANs, and others from around the world. The Internet is an example of a GAN. An example of a PAN is when you connect your cellphone to your car via Bluetooth.

Storage

Computer storage may take many forms. It is typically a hardware device where digital data and content are stored and accessed by users or programs. The information may be stored permanently or temporarily. Storage devices on technology equipment consist of primary storage and secondary storage.

Primary Storage

Primary storage is the storage the computer itself uses to operate and perform. It's also known as internal memory. The central programming unit (CPU) is the brain of the computer. It's responsible for processing instructions that make the computer perform basic functions such as running the operating system, running applications, and processing data. The CPU requires storage, also known as memory, to temporarily store instructions or results. Two types of memory the CPU relies on are random access memory (RAM) and read-only memory (ROM).

The CPU uses RAM as short-term, temporary storage. It's used to run applications and process data. For example, I'm writing this chapter in Microsoft Word. The Word program is loaded using RAM and the words I type are temporarily saved into RAM until I formally save the file onto my hard drive. When I close Word, the RAM is cleared and freed up for another application. RAM is volatile, meaning all information in RAM is lost when you shut down the computer or lose power. That's why you should save your work often, although Microsoft Office products do have a feature that autosaves your documents and allows you to recover them should they be accidentally lost.

The information stored in ROM is read-only. The computer cannot write data or information to ROM. It's used primarily for firmware updates. For example, a gaming console contains ROM that allows you to play multiple games (designed for that console) on the same console. ROM is nonvolatile storage that retains data even if the device does not have power.

Secondary Storage

Secondary storage devices may include hard drives, flash drives, optical drives, DVDs, memory cards, virtual drives, and more. Secondary storage is also known as external memory, even though it may be internal to the computer or device, or external. For example, laptop devices come with hard drives installed within the laptop chassis. However, you can also purchase external hard drives that connect to the computer via a USB port to back up your data or provide more storage space. Secondary storage devices are nonvolatile. The data is retained on the device until it's deleted or overwritten by the user or a program.

 Storage is also called memory. Volatile memory is lost when the device is shut down or loses power. Nonvolatile memory is retained until it's deleted or overwritten, even when the device has no power. Primary storage is also known as internal memory and can be volatile, like RAM, or nonvolatile, like ROM. Secondary storage is also known as external memory and is nonvolatile.

Networks use secondary storage as well. These generally fall into two categories: network attached storage (NAS) and storage area networks (SANs). NAS is software that resides on dedicated hardware that performs two functions: data storage requests and file sharing requests. NAS provides a centralized location for data and files that multiple devices can access at the same time. NAS units are used extensively in many businesses and are generally inexpensive to implement.

SAN storage is used for data and provides data reliability. Databases (described later in this section) typically reside on a SAN. SAN systems can be complex, spread out over large geographical expanses and connected using specialized communications environments such as fiber-optic cabling. These are often multimillion-dollar deployments. A SAN provides fast access to data, and it is highly scalable, meaning you can easily expand and add to it, but it requires knowledgeable staff with specific skills and experience to set up and maintain.

 NAS and SANs are similar. They both manage data and files in a central location and make the information available to multiple devices at once. NAS storage is typically less expensive than SAN and is generally easier to use than a SAN. A NAS is easy to set up and administer but can become congested and tends to lag when too many calls are made for the same information. A SAN provides fast access to data and is highly scalable but requires extensive knowledge and experience to set up and maintain.

Data Warehouse

A *data warehouse* is a system that collects, organizes, centralizes, and manages data. Data is aggregated from the organization's databases and other sources and is used and analyzed by managers and executives to make decisions about the business. Analysis can be conducted on this data using business intelligence, and it can also display the results in various formats such as reports, charts, graphs, and text. A data warehouse is highly organized and makes finding and analyzing data fast, accurate, and efficient. It is designed to analyze large amounts of data and is also used for artificial intelligence and machine learning. A data warehouse can analyze large amounts of data quickly without creating a degradation of service. It gives executives access to up-to-date information that allows them to make meaningful decisions quickly. A data warehouse may reside in a data center on-premises or on the cloud.

Documentation

Documentation is an important part of IT as well as project management. We will discuss documentation in many different forms as we progress through the book. In the case of infrastructure, it's important that your documentation is recorded, accurate, and kept up-to-date. In my experience, a lack of documentation leads to mistakes, increased costs, and loss of productivity. When an IT technician needs to start from ground zero to troubleshoot an issue or make a change to the infrastructure, it will dramatically increase the time needed to fulfill the task. It will also likely lead to mistakes. One small change here, a little tweak there, and the downstream implications can be devastating.

Documentation can take many forms. You could start with an inventory of hardware and software. Most devices, including laptops, servers, printers, and so on, should have an ID tag affixed to it. The ID tag should be recorded on a spreadsheet or an inventory software program and should include the type of equipment it is and which employee or organization is responsible for it. It should also document the location of the equipment, such as office number, data center location, building location, and more. While you're busy recording information, be sure to capture serial numbers, deployment dates, and other pertinent information for the equipment.

Documentation should include diagrams of how the infrastructure is constructed. This should include servers, routers, and network segments at a minimum.

Software information should include the purchase date, license codes, vendor information such as contact numbers, system requirements, and so on.

Change logs are a form of documentation that should capture any changes made to the infrastructure, including updates to software, when patches were applied and what version, new equipment, retired equipment, changes to applications, and more.

The idea is if your organization lost key members of the IT department, you'd want new employees or contractors to be able to walk in and begin supporting the organization or troubleshooting issues as soon as possible. Most IT professionals understand the problems a lack of documentation can cause, but it tends to be the last task many of them perform. I've known new hires who came into an organization and discovered that little to no documentation for the service they are supposed to support existed. They immediately resigned. They didn't want to get tasked with multiple late nights and weekends having to figure out the system before they can even troubleshoot the problem that caused the outage.

Cloud Models

Cloud computing allows for the sharing of software, information, data, and services to computers and technology devices on demand. Information, software, and more are stored in the cloud and the Internet is used to exchange the information and services with other devices. Cloud computing services are the infrastructure component of the cloud. As you learned in the "Infrastructure" section of this chapter, computing services may include servers, networking, databases, storage, software, and more.

Cloud models generally eliminate the need for an organization to have a large data center on-site processing programming code, serving up software and providing other services, or storing massive amounts of data. You may be familiar with some aspects of the cloud in the form of OneDrive, DropBox, or Google Drive. These services allow you to store your data, pictures, and videos on their servers and databases in the cloud and access them from anywhere you have an Internet connection. Likewise, there are many programming services hosted on the cloud that allow you to subscribe to the software and have full use of it without having to download a large program to your personal device.

 The publication "The NIST Definition of Cloud Computing," found at https://nvlpubs.nist.gov/nistpubs/legacy/sp/nistspecialpublication800-145.pdf, defines the characteristics of the cloud as it exists today.

Organizations may use the cloud for server time, network storage, data storage, and more. The cloud customer can provision these services as needed. This is known as on-demand self-service. Cloud providers have full-time staff members who monitor every facet of their networks, servers, and data centers. However, these administrators don't necessarily need to get involved with a consumer's cloud service unless there are problems. The cloud is more automated than conventional on-premises data center operations. This reduces the burden of administration and maintenance duties for the IT team and frees up their time to perform other functions.

Cloud infrastructure consists of two layers: the physical layer, which consists of the hardware resources needed to support the cloud services, and the abstraction layer, which consists of the software used to enable the cloud to perform its function. Cloud providers use what NIST calls resource pooling. *Resource pooling* allows the cloud provider to use the same resources to serve multiple consumers using a multitenant model. You can think of a multitenant model as a condominium building with varying types and sizes of units. Each unit is purchased or leased by an individual (or organization), and the keys to each unit are unique. Your neighbor can't use their key to open the door to your unit. Multitenant models work in a similar way. You pay for the types of resources that you need, such as processing power, memory, network bandwidth, storage, and more. Unlike a condominium, however, if you suddenly need more space or power (or less as the case may be), the cloud provider can provision this to you automatically. Too bad the condominium can't flex and provide you with that extra guest bedroom when the relatives come for the holidays.

This is the ability to respond to a consumers need for more (or less) memory, power, and more is known as *rapid elasticity*. This means the cloud environment can grow or shrink at any time, based on the needs of the customer. In the on-premises environment, the system administrator is responsible for standing up new servers. Let's imagine the application development team is working on a new program and they need server space to host the application. They contact the system administrator and inform them of their requirements. The administrator informs the development team that they'll need to order new hardware, install it, and burn it in, and it will likely take eight weeks to complete. Rapid elasticity automatically makes a server available on the cloud.

Cloud providers charge for their services using a measured service model that's based on consumer usage. As you can guess, the more you use, the more you pay. They may charge using metering such as pay-per-use or charge-per-use, or based on storage, processing power, network bandwidth, or even active user accounts.

Cloud Service Models

According to NIST, there are four types of cloud service models: software as a service, platform as a service, infrastructure as a service, and anything as a service. These service models can be offered as stand-alone services or in combination. Let's look at each next.

Software as a Service (SaaS)   *Software as a service (SaaS)* is a model whereby a cloud consumer can access application(s) on demand that have been developed and run on a cloud infrastructure. The software is stored on multiple data centers on the cloud and can be accessed from any Internet-connected device such as a laptop, tablet, or smartphone. There are no hardware, maintenance, or updates for the consumer's IT team to manage related to the software because it's accessible to everyone with an Internet connection. The SaaS consumer does not control any aspect of this model, including the underlying infrastructure, the software, operating systems, or storage. They have limited ability to configure the application settings, depending on the SaaS service provider. Some examples of SaaS include Salesforce, Microsoft Office 365, Google Workspace, and Netflix.

Platform as a Service (PaaS)   *Platform as a service (PaaS)* is a software model that allows application developers to build applications in the cloud. They can build and deploy their applications, or applications they have acquired, onto the cloud infrastructure using software tools supplied by the PaaS solution provider. These solutions are typically easy to scale and are user friendly. This allows developers to start from a jumping-off point, rather than starting from scratch, when developing applications.

The PaaS provider supports the various languages, libraries, services, and tools that the application needs. The developers will use these tools to develop their applications. This obviously requires a good deal of training and experience.

In this model, the cloud consumer only controls the application, not the underlying infrastructure such as the network, servers, or storage. The underlying infrastructure is managed and controlled by the PaaS provider.

Examples of PaaS providers include Amazon Web Services (AWS), Google App Engine, and Microsoft Azure.

Infrastructure as a Service (IaaS) *Infrastructure as a service (IaaS)* is a software model that allows the cloud consumer to provision servers, storage, networking, operating systems, and other computing resources on demand. This in turn provides the consumer with the ability to deploy and run software, operating systems, and applications on this infrastructure. IaaS eliminates the need to have large data centers on-premises to support the organization's technology needs.

PaaS is often created on an IaaS platform. This frees up the organization to focus on development and reduces or eliminates the need for system administrators. Anyone who has ever spent the night in a data center babysitting a sick server can understand the joy of having this nightmare managed by someone else.

In the IaaS model, the consumer does not control the underlying infrastructure, but they do have control over the operating systems, applications deployed on IaaS, storage, and potentially other components such as firewalls, depending on the IaaS service provider.

Examples of IaaS include Azure, AWS, and Rackspace. I hear you thinking, "Azure and AWS were mentioned as examples of PaaS." And you are correct. Both Azure and AWS, along with other service providers, supply all the cloud offerings to its customers, SaaS, IaaS, and PaaS, depending on your needs. Companies like Rackspace offer IaaS services in which you can use public cloud deployments from AWS, Azure, and others. (We'll cover public cloud deployments in the next section.)

Your organization may choose one cloud model, or all three models, depending on their needs. When managing infrastructure on-premises, you are responsible for all aspects of support, from implementation to maintenance to upgrades. Depending on the cloud service you use, your organization may have limited to no responsibility for maintenance. Table 2.3 compares who controls the various elements of IaaS, PaaS, and SaaS. For example, the consumer has more control in the IaaS model than the SaaS model. This is a summarized table to give you an idea of the amount of control you as a consumer have under each model.

TABLE 2.3 Comparison of cloud model controls

	SaaS	PaaS	IaaS
Applications	P	C	C
Data	P	C	C
Operating system	P	P	C
Underlying infrastructure	P	P	P
Storage	P	P	P
Networking	P	P	P

* C = Consumer, P = Service Provider

Anything as a Service (XaaS)   *Anything as a service (XaaS)* (sometimes referred to as "everything as a service") can be any IT function that is converted to a cloud model for use by the organization. It works by providing a platform where users can access Iaas, PaaS, and SaaS providers as well as their on-premises services. There are any number of services you can access with XaaS, including analytics as a service, desktop as a service, database as a service, authentication as a service, and much more. XaaS slims down the need for costly hardware and infrastructure on-premises, along with the full-time resources needed to maintain them. XaaS can be any IT service or function that operates on a cloud model.

You should be aware of some of the cons of the "as a service" models. They can be costly, depending on the services you require; you do not have control over maintenance windows; you may experience performance issues; outages can occur although they are usually rare; and security issues can surface, such as hack attempts or exposure of PII data. As an example, while writing this chapter, the Ultimate Kronos Group incurred a ransomware attack on their Kronos Private Cloud. This incident affected staff management, time keeping, and payroll processing functions for thousands of organizations and will likely take weeks, if not months, to resolve. In the meantime, organizations will need to revert to manual timekeeping and payroll processing until the system comes back online. Again, this is a rare occurrence but should be considered when examining these models for use in your organization.

Cloud Deployment Models

There are several ways customers can use cloud resources. For example, organizations may have a private cloud that only their employees and affiliates can access, or an educational institution may have a public cloud that allows anyone anywhere to access information or services kept there. According to NIST, there are four cloud deployment models. We'll look at each next.

Private Cloud   *Private cloud* is used exclusively by a single organization. This organization may have multiple consumers, which are typically the employees within the business units of the organization, or it may consist of a group of organizations that are legally associated with one another. Only employees or affiliates granted access by the organization may use this cloud. The organization may own, manage, and operate this deployment, or they may enlist the services of a third party, or a combination of both. A private cloud may exist on- or off-premises.

Community Cloud   *Community cloud* is used by a community of customers who have similar needs. It's a form of private cloud but involves more than one organization (or tenant). This allows organizations to share resources and information across those organizations. For example, government agencies often have information that needs to be shared across agencies. Specific research institutions may have information that benefits other researchers who work elsewhere. By pooling information via a community cloud, both sets of researchers can have access to the information. The information is only accessible to the tenants on the community cloud. A community cloud might be owned and managed by one of the tenants, a third party, or some combination thereof. A community cloud may exist on- or off-premises.

Public Cloud A *public cloud* is a model offered by a third party and is intended for use by anyone. Third parties may charge for using the cloud, or governments, educational institutions, and others may offer some of the information or services on the public cloud for free. A public cloud exists on the cloud provider's premises.

Hybrid Cloud A *hybrid cloud* is some combination of private, community, or public cloud. For example, perhaps you are an educational institution and have an on-premises private cloud consisting of a data center but wish to share this information with the general public. You can combine the private cloud with a public cloud to accomplish this task. Combining deployments allows organizations to share data and applications with other organizations or the public, or both. Hybrid clouds use proprietary technology that enables the communication and exchange of data and services between the cloud models.

CompTIA offers two cloud-specific certifications for those who may be interested in this technology:

Cloud+ www.comptia.org/certifications/cloud

Cloud Essentials+ www.comptia.org/certifications/cloud-essentials

Software

IT departments are responsible for the implementation, support, and maintenance of a host of software applications. Software allows businesses to perform numerous functions in an automated fashion, such as accounting, human resources, procurement, inventory, order fulfillment, and much more. These applications may exist on-premises or on the cloud. Even though the software may be hosted on the cloud, IT resources may still be required. For example, tasks such as developing interfaces between systems and maintaining configurations on the software need to be performed by the organization's IT staff or third-party contractors.

The CompTIA exam objectives list several types of software that we'll look at in this section, including enterprise resource planning, customer relationship management, databases, electronic document and record management systems, content management systems, and financial systems.

Enterprise Resource Planning

Enterprise resource planning (ERP) systems help companies coordinate their back-office business activities, such as accounting, procurement, human resources, and more. The idea is that one system provides functionality across the organizational functions and data can be easily shared, compared, and reported on. For example, before you can issue a purchase order, you need to ensure there are funds in the account. Checking on the funds is typically an automated process, and the purchase order is rejected if there are not sufficient funds. If you had a stand-alone system that manages procurements and a different stand-alone system that manages accounting functions, the IT team would have to write an interface to connect the two systems so that the funds check could be performed. An ERP system is self-contained, and these functions are seamless because the data and the functionality reside on one system.

ERP systems are typically modular, and you are not required to purchase all the modules available. Perhaps you need accounting, procurement, and human resources functions but have no need for a real estate module or an inventory module. You only purchase or license the modules you need.

The two primary functions that almost all ERP providers offer are financial and human resources. The offerings within these modules can vary. For example, some ERP vendors provide payroll functions in the finance module and others include this in the human resources module. ERP implementations are major projects and consume a lot of IT and business resources. You'll need to conduct an in-depth requirements analysis to determine the needs for your organization and use that criterion to choose an ERP vendor. The remainder of this book will cover all the essentials of managing a project of this nature.

As a rule of thumb, ERP systems have dedicated staff who are highly trained in the system. Additionally, the modules within the system have unique characteristics that require specialized skills. It can sometimes be difficult to find staff with ERP expertise. These are complex systems that require a lot of time to learn and maintain, and people with these skills are in high demand.

For the exam, remember that ERP systems allow organizations to coordinate their back-office functions within a single system. They are large, complex implementations that involve a significant amount of IT and business resources. They typically take a year or longer to implement (even on the cloud), and prices generally start in the multimillions of dollars.

Customer Relationship Management

Customer relationship management (CRM) software helps businesses manage their relationships and interactions with their customers and future customers. CRMs aggregate data about the customer in one place and provide an efficient and practical way for the organization to interact with their customer. Let's say a customer purchased a new appliance from your company. The sales team had the initial interaction with this customer and recorded this in the CRM. Sometime later, the customer has a service question. They contact the service center via your website and the technician who responds to the chat can see the customer record in the system. The technician sees the appliance that was purchased, the date, model number, and other pertinent information that was recorded by the sales team. The interaction with the service team is also recorded in the customer record. Whenever this customer contacts the organization for any reason, the representative or technician who assists them can see the complete history of this customer since the inception of the relationship. Contact might be in the form of a phone call, email, website, social media, and so on.

Future customer interactions can be captured as well. Perhaps you have a potential customer who enquires about a specific appliance. They don't purchase today, but they want to know some specifications and features. Their name and contact information is recorded, just as though they were a customer, and future contact from this customer can be viewed by anyone in the organization. Let's say this customer walks into the showroom. The salesperson can look them up on the CRM, see what they previously asked about, and guide them in their purchase decision.

CRMs are typically cloud-based systems which allow for real-time updates to customer information. For example, multinational organizations may have call centers in several countries across the globe. When the CRM is hosted in the cloud, anyone within the organization with Internet access (and access rights to the CRM) can access the system and see real-time updates about their customers. Salesforce is one of the leading cloud-based software companies in this space.

It's important that you choose a CRM solution and implementer who can help you determine the types of information you want to collect and report on about your customers. Data for data's sake can be difficult to discern and not helpful to the organization. As a project manager of this type of implementation, you'll want to ensure proper requirements gathering is performed, including a deep understanding of the reporting needs the business and executives expect from this system. In the case of our appliance store example, the CRM could provide reports regarding the units sold, the most popular models, and information like the most common frequently asked questions or service repair. If the executives see a trend in a certain type of service call, they can examine the manufacturing process and determine if changes can be made to reduce the number of calls for this issue.

Databases

A *database* is a collection of data that is stored electronically in a computer system that can be easily accessed by other computer systems and by humans. Databases may consist of structured or unstructured data. Let's look at a brief description of each.

Structured Data   *Structured data* is organized in meaningful ways so that it can be easily retrieved and modified. It is defined in a consistent manner, according to a predefined data model, and can be analyzed and processed by programs and systems. Back in the old days, before databases, businesses used to keep their information on paper in file cabinets. Within the cabinets, there were file folders that were clearly labeled and easily identified by staff. When a customer called the business with a question or issue, the staff member could walk to the file cabinet and pull that customer's file and find all the information pertaining to them in that file. Structured data is similar to this. Some of the PII data I described earlier such as name, age, Social Security number, and so on are examples of structured data.

Unstructured Data   *Unstructured data* does not adhere to a data model. It doesn't have identifiable rules or structure and isn't easily stored or processed. Unstructured data is sometimes called a "blob" of data. This type of data is not useful in a relational database. It also requires a significant amount of storage space (resulting in higher costs), it's difficult to search, and it can't be indexed easily. Some examples of unstructured data include videos, web pages, images, emails, and more.

A *relational database (RDBMS)* is a collection of structured information that is related to each other. The data sets within this database can be linked to other data sets and allow the users to easily manage and process the data. Data in a relational database is organized using rows and columns, much like what a spreadsheet might look like. The rows represent the record, and the columns represent the attributes or fields. Typically, rows contain specific data elements whereas columns represent categories of data. Table 2.4 shows an example database containing model numbers for the appliance business we discussed earlier.

TABLE 2.4   Example database entries for model numbers

CustomerID	LastName	FirstName	ApplianceType	ModelNumber
C100204	Jenkins	Thomas	Refrigerator	WH00098324
C100205	Welch	Sandra	Microwave	SB000679321

Table 2.5 shows the purchase date and warranty period for the appliance purchases. On its own, it doesn't seem very useful; it would be great if there were a way to relate the purchase date and warranty information to the customer and the appliance that was purchased. And there is. We can use a unique key to relate the data in Table 2.4 to the data in Table 2.5. The CustomerID in this example is what's called the primary key. When this primary key (Table 2.4) is added to another table (Table 2.5), it becomes the foreign key in the new table. This primary/foreign key can then be used to relate the tables to one another. In this example, we see that Sandra Welch purchased a microwave on August 20, 2022, and she has a 6-month warranty that will expire in February 2023.

TABLE 2.5   Example database entries for purchase date

CustomerID	PurchaseDate	WarrantyPeriodExpirationDate
C100204	2022.12.10	2023.12.11
C100205	2022.08.20	2022.02.23

Relational databases have been around for well over 30 years. New database technologies are continually emerging. However, it takes industry a very long time to catch up to new technology because companies don't have the funding or time to shift to new technology quickly. Some experts argue that relational databases will always have a place in technology. No matter where you stand on the debate, relational databases are the most popular type of databases and are likely here for a long time to come.

Electronic Document and Record Management Systems

Earlier in this section I talked about the days before databases and technology when documents were created on paper and stored in file drawers. As you can imagine, if you didn't have an effective filing system your documents could end up in the wrong file folder, or the wrong drawer, or the wrong cabinet, and never be found again until someone stumbled on them accidentally. In today's work environment, most documents are created and stored electronically. After they are created, they may end up getting printed so that signatures can be obtained in ink, but they are typically scanned and stored electronically for safekeeping.

An *electronic document and record management system (EDRMS)* is a software system that manages electronic documents, records, and data from creation to disposal. An EDRMS stores your organization's documents electronically. This makes it easy and convenient for appropriate users to access the information, and it takes up a lot less room than a basement full of filing cabinets. An EDRMS gives administrators the ability to limit who can access documents. For example, someone in the real estate department may have no need to access documents used in the service operations department. Permissions can be set to eliminate this scenario. An EDRMS also provides a way to track and monitor who accessed the documents, who modified them, when they were created, when they were deleted, and more.

Consider a court case, for example. There are documents that are used in discovery, documents that detail the court proceedings, documents presented in court, and more. In situations like this, date and time stamps, signatures, and other relevant data must be safeguarded and maintained in a way that ensures the documents are genuine and have not been tampered with. One of the features of an EDRMS is the ability to perform compliance audits on the information so that you can verify the data has been managed appropriately.

Content Management Systems (CMS)

A *content management system (CMS)* is software that provides a way for users with little to no technical knowledge to create a website and manage, modify, share, and upload content to the website. The CMS manages various types of content such as blogs, music, images, videos, online training courses, forums, and more.

Most content management systems are made up of two components: the content management application and the content delivery application. The content management application, as its name implies, allows the users to add, edit, and manage the content they intend to post to the website. This information is stored in a database within the CMS. The delivery application publishes the content and makes it visible on the website.

It is possible to create websites without a CMS, but you'll need to know some programming code to accomplish this. Websites can be built using Hypertext Markup Language (HTML). HTML provides the building blocks and structure for the documents you intend to post. Cascading Style Sheet (CSS) is a design language that helps you define the visual appearance of the web page. You can define things such as text, font size, colors, and much more. All the style information is contained in the CSS. Each web page on the website may have a different CSS.

There are several CMS providers, including WordPress, Drupal, Textpattern, and many others.

Financial Systems

Financial systems manage the accounting and budgeting aspects of a business. They may be part of an ERP, discussed earlier in this section, or stand-alone systems. Financial systems may include different modules such as general ledgers, accounts payable, accounts receivable, forecasting, budgeting, reporting, and more. These systems allow decision-makers to analyze and take actions based on the financial information and reporting contained in the system. It also provides a means to report on the status of the organization's financial standing to stakeholders, shareholders, executives, and so on.

Keep in mind that financial accounting and budgeting are two different functions. Financial accounting concerns recording and interpreting the monetary transactions of the organization. Much of this information is shared with stakeholders via annual reports using information from the system such as income statements, cash flow, and balance sheets. For example, shareholders are interested in where the organization stands in terms of profit and loss, and they can read about this in the annual report. Accounting typically concerns what has already transpired. Financial accounting is highly accurate. All monies need to be accounted for and the books must balance.

Budgeting looks at what we should do, or what might happen in the future. It's a prediction of the amount of income we think the organization will generate and how that should be spread among the various needs of the organization over the coming time period. It also attempts to predict the expenses the organization may face. Budgeting is a planning tool and, more importantly to all the project managers out there, determines the amount of money we can use for planned and unplanned projects for the coming time period. Budgeting is not as precise as accounting but does need to be within reasonable limits.

Accounting Looks to the Past; Budgeting Looks to the Future

Implementing software is often a complex, time-consuming project. It requires careful attention to requirements, lengthy testing periods, and excellent communication. Software projects are typically intended to improve and/or automate processes, improve efficiencies, improve reporting, increase collaboration, and more. I have been involved in dozens of software implementation projects during my career. Here are some of the keys to a successful implementation, based on my experience.

- Accurate requirements

- Involvement of the right resources from across the organization

- Defining of the critical milestones

- Comprehensive testing

- Rigorous communication

- Risk management

- Change management

- Lessons learned

We will cover all of these keys to success in the remainder of this book.

 **Real World Scenario**

The ERP Implementation

The Widget organization is looking to consolidate over 50 stand-alone systems that manage every aspect of their business into one ERP system. This will allow inventory information to be easily exchanged with operations and all financial, budget, procurement, inventory, and human resources information will be in the same system.

You are an experienced project manager and understand the complexity of an implementation of this nature. You also have worked on a similar ERP implementation in the past that was successful.

You set a meeting with the executives to discuss the idea of freeing up subject matter experts from their departments to work on this project near full time. The benefit of their expertise, experience, and insights will be invaluable for this project, and you provide them with several examples of how this will benefit them. One example you share from a past project showed that the subject matter experts from the payroll department spotted some miscalculations for payroll for the delivery drivers who worked shifts around the clock. Catching this error in the testing phase enabled the vendor to correct it in a timely manner and kept the project from exceeding the timeline. You also make sure to mention the embarrassment and reputational damage the company would have experienced if this error had made it to production. You recommend backfilling these key positions with contractors to fulfill the employee's day-to-day functions so their work doesn't lag behind. They agree to the suggestion, and you set about working with procurement to hire contract positions.

Next we'll begin a case study that will continue throughout the remainder of the book. The case study will outline the concepts you've learned in the chapter and walk you through a simulated project based on a fictitious business.

Real World Scenario

Main Street Office Move

Your organization is moving all their offices to a new, centralized location. Currently, there are staff members in three different buildings located throughout the city. You are the project manager and will coordinate, communicate, and manage all aspects of the project.

Your project sponsor is Emma Anderson. She is the chief information officer and wrote the business case for this project. Emma sent you a copy of the business case to review. You picked out a few key points on first reading, including that the move will be completed by December 31 and that there should be minimal disruption to employees. The data center will be downsized significantly. The IT team is moving infrastructure services to the cloud as part of this project. They will be using an IaaS vendor to host most of the servers, databases, and applications the organization uses.

The cost-benefit to the organization is significant because the new building is energy efficient and, more importantly, all employees are collocated so there is no need to travel between locations for meetings. This will save on fuel costs, reduce the size of the fleet, and increase productivity. The IaaS platform will provide efficiencies to the IT staff by moving ordinary maintenance items to the platform vendor. The staff members who ordinarily patched servers, upgraded operating systems, and more will be freed up to work on other important projects for IT.

Your first step is to set up a meeting with Emma to discover the objectives for this project and begin a rough draft of the project charter.

Summary

Project managers are individuals charged with overseeing every aspect of a given project from start to finish. A project manager needs not only technical knowledge of the product or service being produced by the project but also a wide range of general management skills. Key general management skills include leadership, communication, problem-solving, negotiation, organization, and time management.

There are many factors that influence project management activities. Environmental, social, and governance (ESG) factors cover many aspects the project manager may need to examine to ensure that the project is in compliance and will not damage an organization's reputation. ESG factors also include awareness of company vision, mission statement, and values; impact on the company brand value; impact on local and global environment; and awareness of applicable regulations and standards.

Compliance and privacy considerations should be examined on every project. Data confidentiality involves protecting sensitive data that could reveal the identities of individuals. NIST has developed several frameworks, processes, and controls to protect personal information. PII is information about an individual that can be used to trace their identity, including SPII and linkable data. SPII is data that can be used on its own to identify an individual. SPII might include Social Security number or passport number, and linkable data may include full name or street address. PHI is personal health information about an individual and includes ePHI, which are health records kept in electronic format.

Many industries have legal and regulatory requirements that must be followed. Make certain to ask subject matter experts in your organization about these requirements for your project. Don't forget industry-specific regulations or those related to information technology projects.

Information technology (IT) involves the use of computers and computer networks to create, store, process, and transmit electronic information. Infrastructure consists of all the hardware, software, servers, networks, data centers, and more that comprise and support IT activities for an organization. Infrastructure enables the organization to provide IT services to its employees and customers. Computing services refer to the infrastructure that provides computing capability to the organization and may include servers, networking, databases, storage, software, and more. Multitiered architecture refers to physically separating technology functions into their own modules. This architecture defines how a technology system is constructed. Three-tier architecture is the most common form of multitiered architecture. It consists of a presentation tier, a processing tier, and a data tier.

A computer network is the collection of devices connected to each other using cables or wireless communication to enable the sharing and exchange of data and services. There are several types of networks that can be constructed for different purposes. Two of the most common networks are local area networks (LANs) and wide area networks (WANs).

Computer storage may take many forms. It is typically a hardware device where digital data and content are stored and accessed by users or programs. Primary storage is the storage the computer itself uses to operate and perform. It is also known as internal memory. The CPU uses two types of memory: RAM and ROM. Secondary storage devices may include hard drives, flash drives, optical drives, DVDs, memory cards, virtual drives, and more. Secondary storage is also known as external memory.

A data warehouse is a system that collects, organizes, centralizes, and manages data. Data is aggregated from the organization's databases and other sources and is used and analyzed by managers and executives to make decisions about the business.

Infrastructure should be documented. This may include inventories, serial numbers, drawings, change logs, and more.

Cloud computing allows for the sharing of software, information, data, and services to computers and technology devices on demand. Information, software, and more are stored in the cloud and the Internet is used to exchange the information and services with other devices. Resource pooling allows the cloud provider to use the same resources to serve multiple consumers using a multitenant model. Rapid elasticity means the cloud environment can grow or shrink at any time, based on the needs of the customer.

There are several cloud service models, including SaaS, PaaS, IaaS, and XaaS. Cloud deployment models include private cloud, community cloud, public cloud, and hybrid cloud. A private cloud is used exclusively by a single organization or entity. A community cloud serves multiple customers who have similar needs. A public cloud is accessible by anyone. A hybrid cloud is the combination of one or more of these models.

Software is a large part of an IT department. ERP systems help companies coordinate their back-office business activities such as accounting, procurement, human resources, and more. CRM software helps businesses manage their relationships and interactions with their customers and future customers. CRMs aggregate data about the customer in one place and provide an efficient and practical way for the organization to interact with their customer. A database is a collection of data that is stored electronically in a computer system that can be easily accessed by other computer systems and by humans. An EDRMS is a software system that manages electronic documents, records, and data from creation to disposal. CMS software provides a way for users with little to no technical knowledge to create a website and manage, modify, share, and upload content to the website. Financial systems manage the accounting and budgeting aspects of a business. They may be part of an ERP or a stand-alone systems.

Exam Essentials

Be able to define the role of a project manager.   A project manager's core function is project integration. A project manager leads the project team and oversees all the work required to complete the project goals to the satisfaction of the stakeholders.

Understand what skills are needed to manage a project beyond technical knowledge of the product.   Key general management skills include leadership, communication, problem-solving, negotiation, organization, and time management.

Be able to define ESG factors that influence project management activities.   ESG stands for environmental, social, and governance factors that may influence project management activities. Compliance and privacy considerations as well as legal and regulatory requirements are part of ESG factors.

Be able to define PII and SPII data.   PII is personally identifiable information that may be used to distinguish or trace an individual's identity. SPII data is a subset of PII and on its own has the potential to cause harm, inconvenience, embarrass, or cause harm to an individual's reputation. PII data becomes SPII data when it's linked with SPII data. PHI is personal health information and is a form of PII.

Understand legal and regulatory impacts.   Legal and regulatory impacts must be defined and accounted for when performing project management. Make certain to ask subject matter experts in your organization about these requirements for your project. Don't forget industry-specific regulations or those related to information technology projects.

Be able to define information technology.   IT involves the use of computers and computer networks to create, store, process, and transmit electronic information.

Be able to define IT infrastructure.   Infrastructure consists of all the hardware, software, servers, networks, data centers, and more that comprise and support IT activities for an organization. Infrastructure enables the organization to provide IT services to its employees and customers.

Understand the two most common types of computer networks.   A computer network is the collection of devices connected to each other using cables or wireless communication to enable the sharing and exchange of data and services. A LAN is a local area network used in a specific location such as a school or a business. The LAN connects the technology and devices used by the organization to each other so they can share information, utilize software and services, and communicate with each other. A WAN is a network that covers a larger area and may be used by businesses that have more than one location.

Be able to describe computer storage.   Computer storage is a hardware device where digital data and content are stored and accessed by users or programs. It consists of primary storage, also known as internal memory, such as RAM and ROM; and secondary storage, also known as external memory, such as hard drives, flash drives, memory cards, and more.

Be able to define a data warehouse.   A data warehouse is a system that collects, organizes, centralizes, and manages data that is used and analyzed by managers and executives to make decisions about the business.

Understand cloud computing.   Cloud computing allows for the sharing of software, information, data, and services to computers and technology devices on demand.

Understand cloud service models.   There are four primary cloud service models: SaaS, PaaS, IaaS, and XaaS.

Be able to name four software systems common to IT.   Four systems are ERP, CRM, EDRMS, and CMS.

Key Terms

Before you take the exam, be certain you are familiar with the following terms:

anything as a service (XaaS)	local area networks (LAN)
cloud computing	multitiered architecture
community cloud	network
computer storage	personal health information (PHI)

computing services

content management system (CMS)

customer relationship management (CRM)

data confidentiality

data warehouse

database

electronic document and record management system (EDRMS)

Enterprise resource planning (ERP)

environmental, social, and governance (ESG) factors

financial systems

hybrid cloud

information technology (IT)

infrastructure

infrastructure as a service (IaaS)

personally identifiable information (PII)

platform as a service (PaaS)

primary storage

private cloud

protected health information (PHI)

public cloud

rapid elasticity

relational database (RDBMS)

resource pooling

secondary storage

sensitive personally identifiable data elements (SPII)

software as a service (SaaS)

structured data

unstructured data

wide area networks (WAN)

Review Questions

1. Which of the following general management skills consumes up to 90 percent of a project manager's time?

   A. Programming

   B. Communicating

   C. Leading

   D. Problem solving

2. Which general management skill concerns obtaining mutually acceptable agreements with individuals or groups?

   A. Leadership

   B. Problem solving

   C. Negotiating

   D. Communicating

3. All of the following are true regarding ESG except which one?

   A. It's imperative the project manager understands ESG as it relates to the project so that regulations, standards, and guidelines are followed.

   B. S in ESG stands for social.

   C. Awareness of applicable regulations and standards are an ESG factor.

   D. PII is an ESG factor that relates to the social factor.

   E. Project impact to company brand value is an ESG factor.

4. You work for a company that is growing rapidly. The company's leadership wants to install a system that will allow both current and future customers to interact with the company to learn more about the company's products and to obtain support. What kind of a system will you recommend be implemented?

   A. CMS

   B. ERP

   C. CRM

   D. IaaS

5. Your company currently has a large data center that consists of hundreds of servers and a host of enterprise applications such as large databases. Corporate stakeholders want to get away from the costs of maintaining a data center but also want to continue their operations in much the same way as they currently do. You know that a cloud solution is the way to go. Which cloud environment should you pursue?

   A. PaaS

   B. IaaS

   C. XaaS

   D. SaaS

6. A database that consists of tables and relationships can be considered which kind of data?

    A. Structured

    B. Unstructured

    C. Flat

    D. Unregulated

7. Which of the following data sources are considered SPII? (Choose two.)

    A. First name

    B. Social Security number (SSN)

    C. City

    D. Political party

    E. Driver's license number

8. Which of the following is an example of linkable data becoming SPII?

    A. When the link connects an individual's name to a corporate website

    B. When an individual's name is linked to their Taxpayer Identification Number (TIN)

    C. When the IP address of an individual's cable modem is shown

    D. When an individual is shown to live within a specific zip code

9. Why are you required to stand far back from the pharmacy counter when you are waiting to talk to a customer service person about refilling a prescription?

    A. It is PHI data and is required by HIPAA.

    B. It is not a requirement, but it is a good idea in a place where there are so many sick people.

    C. It is required by PIPEDA.

    D. It is required by GDPR.

10. Suppose that you work for a company that has several campuses located in different locations in the city. Which network will connect them together?

    A. LAN

    B. SAN

    C. WAN

    D. GAN

11. In a multitiered architecture, which tier helps the user interact with the system?

    A. Presentation

    B. Processing

    C. Data

    D. Application

12. Suppose that you work for a company that has gone through a rapid growth cycle and now has several one-off systems for activities like the company's finances, manufacturing, and human resources. The leaders of the company want to have a system that brings these activities together. What kind of system will you recommend?

A. Cloud

B. LAN

C. ERP

D. SAN

13. A user you support has worked for hours on a spreadsheet document. A sudden power outage to the building causes their computer to power down. When the power comes back, they cannot find the spreadsheet they've been working on. Why is this? (Choose two.)

A. The user was working on the document in RAM memory. When the computer went down, everything in RAM was erased.

B. There must have been a glitch in the computer's memory when the power went down. Thus, the user cannot restore it.

C. The user neglected to save the document to the computer's hard drive.

D. When the power went down and came back up, there was a power glitch in the computer's ROM.

14. What is the purpose of a data warehouse?

A. To bring all the company's unstructured data together in a central location

B. To bring various data sources together for the purpose of analysis and decision-making

C. To handle an extremely large data environment

D. To separate the data's physical location from other applications

15. Who is responsible for documenting the various systems, applications, databases, and other computing infrastructure the company owns?

A. Risk management

B. Human resources

C. The Procurement department

D. Information technology

16. Your company has decided to use an application that was developed by a cloud provider and hosted on the cloud. The executives like this because someone else is responsible for the development and support of the application. What kind of cloud does this describe?

A. XaaS

B. IaaS

C. SaaS

D. PaaS

17. In the multitenant model of cloud computing, providers that offer their services to a variety of customers can utilize which of the following?

   A. Single-source computing

   B. Resource pooling

   C. Multitiered architecture

   D. CMS

18. In the United States, which organization is responsible for publishing rules that control personally identifiable information standards (PII)?

   A. GDPR

   B. HIPAA

   C. EPHI

   D. NIST

19. All of the following are examples of secondary storage except which one?

   A. NAS

   B. SAN

   C. Flash drive

   D. RAM

20. Your organization was hacked and PII data was exposed. All of the following are true except which one?

   A. This is a breach of confidentiality.

   B. Significant fines could be imposed on the organization as a result of exposing this data.

   C. This could cause emotional distress to those individuals who were impacted by the exposure.

   D. According to NIST, there are four levels of impact that can affect the organization.

Chapter

3

Creating the Project Charter

THE COMPTIA PROJECT+ EXAM TOPICS COVERED IN THIS CHAPTER INCLUDE:

✓ **1.0 Project Management Concepts**

- ■ **1.10 Given a scenario, perform basic activities related to team and resource management**

✓ **2.0 Project Life Cycle Phases**

- ■ **2.2 Given a scenario, perform activities during the project initiation phase**

This chapter will kick off the Initiating phase of the project. Initiating is the second phase of the project management life cycle. It involves developing the project charter, identifying and assessing stakeholders, reviewing existing artifacts, developing a records management plan, and more.

This chapter will examine stakeholders and their roles and responsibilities. Stakeholders are integral to any project, and a good project manager should understand the roles of each key player on the project. We will then examine how a preliminary scope statement and a project charter are constructed. A preliminary scope statement defines the objectives of the project and explains the business reason the project is trying to solve. The project charter officially recognizes a project has begun.

Then we will look at developing a records management plan along with defining access control requirements. Finally, we will look at performing an official kickoff meeting with the stakeholders.

Identifying and Assessing Stakeholder Roles and Responsibilities

Throughout the life of your project, you will interact with an important group of people: your stakeholders. Gaining stakeholder buy-in is critical for the success of your project. Let's talk a bit about who they are, what they want, and your role as the project manager in engaging with them.

 Remember from Chapter 1, "Introducing the Project," that identifying and analyzing stakeholders is one of two steps in validating a project. The other is preparing a business case.

A stakeholder is a person or an organization that has a vested interest in your project. In other words, they have something to gain or lose as a result of performing the project. As you would expect, most of your stakeholders are concerned about the needs of their own departments (or organizations) first. They'll be looking to you as the project manager to help them understand how they'll benefit from this project. If you are successful at winning the confidence and support of the project's key stakeholders, it will go a long way toward assuring the success of the project overall.

The general management skills discussed in Chapter 1 will come in handy when dealing with your stakeholders, particularly your communication and negotiation skills. Individual stakeholders may have different priorities regarding your project, and you may have to do some negotiating with your stakeholder groups to bring them to a consensus regarding the end goal of the project. Building consensus among a group with diverse viewpoints starts with up-front negotiation during the initial phases of the project and continues with ongoing communication throughout the life of the project.

Stakeholders are the people and organizations you will work with to determine project requirements. The expertise they bring from their respective business areas helps the project manager and project team when defining requirements, reviewing deliverables, and assuring the end product or result meets quality standards. Stakeholders provide direction throughout the life of the project and review and approve the final end product, service, or result.

Identifying stakeholders can occur in a number of ways. Review past project artifacts to see what types of stakeholders were involved on past projects of a similar nature to the one you're undertaking. Ask subject matter experts and business associates. Use a brainstorming technique with project team members and key stakeholders you've already identified to see who might be missing. Examine org charts and ask which business processes might be impacted as a result of the project to help find stakeholders that may not be obvious. The remainder of this section will identify some of the key stakeholders on your project. Let's start with the customer.

Don't forget to identify important stakeholders. It could be a project killer. Leaving out an important stakeholder and their requirements, or not considering a stakeholder whose business processes are impacted as result of your project, could spell disaster.

The Customer and End Users

The *customer* is the recipient of the product or service created by the project. A customer is often a group or an organization rather than a single person. Customers can be internal or external to the organization. IT projects involve people known as *end users*. End users are people or organizations that will use the system you are developing. End users may be customers as well if you are selling your applications or systems to others. If you are implementing new software internal to the organization such as an ERP system, end users are those people who will access the system to perform business functions. It is critical to get buy-in of key end user groups for the system you're implementing. If they don't like the system and believe it's cumbersome or involves too many steps to perform a task, they will complain from the day of implementation until you replace it with a new system. Ask me how I know.

The Project Sponsor

The project *sponsor* is usually an executive in the organization who has the authority to assign money and resources to the project. The sponsor is responsible for approving and signing the project charter. The project manager may write this document, but the sponsor is the person who should sign it.

The sponsor may also serve as a *champion* for the project within the organization. The sponsor is an adviser to the project manager and acts as the tie-breaker decision-maker when consensus can't be reached among the stakeholders. One of the primary duties of a project manager is keeping the project sponsor informed of current project status, including conflicts or potential risks.

 A project champion is usually the project sponsor or one of your key stakeholders. They spread the great news about the benefits of the project and act as a cheerleader of sorts, generating enthusiasm and support for the project.

The project sponsor/champion typically has the following responsibilities:

- Provide or obtain financial resources
- Approve and sign the project charter
- Approve the project baseline
- Help define and approve the high-level requirements
- Define the business case and justification for the project
- Authorize assignment of human resources to the project
- Assign the project manager and describe their level of authority
- Serve as final decision-maker for all project issues
- Negotiate support from key stakeholders
- Communicate or market the benefits of the project
- Monitor and control delivery of major milestones
- Run interference and remove roadblocks

 The *project baseline* includes the approved schedule, cost, scope, and quality plans and documents. The project baseline is then used to measure performance as the project progresses. You can refer to the project baseline at any time to determine whether you are on schedule, within scope, within budget, and whether the quality standards are on target.

The Project Manager

Chapter 1 talked about the project manager in detail. You will recall that this is the person responsible for managing the work associated with the project. The following is a brief list of the project manager's responsibilities and is not all-inclusive. Each of these items will be discussed in more detail in the remaining chapters of this book.

Managing the Project Team   The *project team* consists of members from inside and sometimes outside the organization. You will not always have the ability to choose your project team. Often, other managers will assign resources to your team.

Communicating with Stakeholders and Project Team Members   Keeping the sponsor, stakeholders, and team members up-to-date on current project status, issues, and other information is a key responsibility of the project manager. Communicating starts the moment a project idea is formulated and continues through to final close-out and approval of the project.

Managing Scope   Scope describes the goals, deliverables, and requirements of the project. The project manager will capture and document scope, along with help from the stakeholders and team members, and will monitor and manage project scope using change-control processes.

Managing Risk   Risks are events that may occur that would impact the project, either positively or negatively, and generally have consequences if they occur. Risks are identified, managed, tracked, and monitored by the project manager.

Managing the Project Budget   Project managers are responsible for monitoring and tracking project costs and alerting the sponsor as soon as possible if costs are higher than expected or the project is running through funds faster than anticipated.

Managing the Schedule   Most project sponsors and executive-level stakeholders love the saying "on time and on budget" and will often chant this phrase in project meetings. Along with managing the budget, you are also responsible for managing the schedule and assuring that key deliverables are performed on time.

Managing Quality Assurance   It isn't enough to deliver on time and on budget. You will also be responsible for assuring the quality of the deliverables and making certain they meet quality standards and are fit for use.

Project Artifacts   Project *artifacts* are the documents, templates, agendas, diagrams, and other work products used in managing the project. The project charter is an artifact. The project manager is responsible for maintaining and archiving the artifacts of the project.

The project manager is responsible for many aspects of the project. The most important include making sure stakeholders are satisfied with the deliverables and end product, service, or result of the project; integrating the work of the project; and communicating with stakeholders.

 It's your responsibility as the project manager to manage stakeholder expectations throughout the project.

The Senior Management Team

Senior managers are those executives in the organization who can make or break a project. They are responsible for meeting organizational goals and keeping shareholders, board members, constituents, and others happy. They may prioritize projects and authorize spending. They will also be the ones to approve releasing team members from their departments to work on the project. Senior managers wield a lot of power, and you'll want to know who they are, what they need, and what motivates them.

The Business Analyst

The *business analyst* is responsible for gathering and documenting requirements for the project. They are often involved in the intake process for a project and may also assist with the business case. The business analyst applies their knowledge and skills to derive and document project requirements, including interviewing stakeholders and facilitating the implementation of the requirements into the final product or result of the project. Business analysts are specifically trained in obtaining requirements by asking pointed questions, probing issues and problems, and recommending potential solutions, all to help encourage stakeholders to be forthcoming with their requirements.

The Subject Matter Experts

Project team members are the *subject matter experts (SMEs)* who will be performing the work associated with the project. SMEs are the people who have specific knowledge and experience working at their jobs. For example, if you're replacing your organization's financial system, you'll want experts from each area of accounting involved on the project. As the project manager, you are not expected to know all the intricacies of accounts payable, but the SME is, and they will assist you and the team with the system functions, configurations, and implementation.

If your SMEs are coming from another department in the organization, the managers who assign those resources are critical stakeholders. You need to establish a good relationship with those managers and brush up on your negotiation skills because normally, more than one project manager is competing for the same resource pool. It's a good idea to document your agreements with the manager regarding the amount of time the resource will be available for your project, as well as the deliverables they're accountable for, to prevent future misunderstandings.

Project team members may be assigned to the project either full-time or part-time. Most projects have a combination of dedicated and part-time resources. If you have part-time resources, you need to understand their obligations outside the project and make certain they are not overallocated.

Project team members are responsible for several activities on the project. One of their most important duties is providing deliverables according to the schedule. A partial list of other duties may include the following:

- Knowledge and expertise in their line of business

- Time and duration estimates for the tasks they are working on

- Cost estimates for deliverables or other project work purchased from outside the organization

- Status updates on the progress of their tasks

- Dependencies related to their tasks

The Project Management Office

Many organizations have a *project management office (PMO)* in place that manages projects, programs, and portfolios. The PMO provides guidance to project managers and helps present a consistent, reliable approach to managing projects across the organization. PMOs are responsible for maintaining standards, processes, procedures, and templates related to the management of projects. They are responsible for identifying the various projects across the organization and including them within a program, where appropriate, to capitalize on the collective benefits of all the projects within the program.

Some of the functions a PMO may provide are as follows:

- Project management standards and processes

- Tools, templates, and artifacts to help manage projects consistently

- Setting of deliverables

- Governance process for managing projects and setting of priorities

- Key performance indicators and metrics

- Standards of performance, including consequences of nonperformance

- Coordination of resources among projects

The Program Manager

You'll recall from Chapter 1 that programs are a grouping of related projects that are managed together to capitalize on benefits that couldn't be achieved if the projects were managed separately. The managers of these programs are known as *program managers*, ironically enough. The project managers who manage individual projects within a program report to the program managers. This makes them a stakeholder in your project, and it also makes them your boss. They will have a vested interest in the management of the project, so be on your best behavior and keep them informed.

The IT Team

The IT team will have a variety of team members on the project, depending on the nature of the project and the deliverables. The CompTIA exam objectives identifies three roles in IT you should know about: architects, developers (or engineers), and testers/quality assurance (QA) specialists. Let's look at each:

Architect   An IT *architect* is responsible for designing technology solutions and services for business applications, infrastructure, networks, storage, cloud solutions, security, and more. There are several types of architects, such as infrastructure architects, enterprise architects, solutions architects, security architects, cloud architects, and more. Those architects with a specific focus in their title, such as infrastructure architect, are responsible for designing solutions for their area of expertise. Enterprise architects focus on the entire enterprise, not just one system, service, or solution. They work closely with business managers and SMEs to determine strategies, processes, and overarching designs for technology systems. They also develop frameworks and guidelines for adding to or modifying the existing enterprise as well as adding new technology to the environment.

Developers/Engineers   *Developers*, sometimes called *engineers*, are the team members responsible for writing programming code, documenting code, developing applications, maintaining and modifying applications, and more. They work closely with the end users to understand requirements and functionality, and with the testing/quality assurance team to determine whether the program functions as designed. Developers also work with other IT team members to ensure proper configuration of the hardware, storage, and networking needs for the applications or systems they are developing.

Testers/Quality Assurance (QA)   *Quality assurance (QA)* for IT is a process used to ensure the requirements for the system or application are met and function as designed. The project team members, IT team members, and end users are all responsible for ensuring quality standards and criteria are met. QA for software applications and systems is typically achieved using testing methodologies. There are several methods used in testing, including smoke testing, unit testing, integration testing, end-to-end testing, regression testing, and user acceptance testing. We will cover testing in more depth in Chapter 10, "Managing Quality and Closing Out the Project."

A complete list of stakeholders varies by project and by organization. The larger and more complex your project is, the more stakeholders you will have. Sometimes you will have far more stakeholders than you want or need, especially on high-profile projects. I recommend you define who you think the stakeholders are on the project and review the list with your project sponsor. The project sponsor is often in a better position to identify those stakeholders who are influential people in the organization. These types of stakeholders can make or break your project, and your sponsor can assist you in identifying their needs.

Unfortunately, some stakeholders may not support your project for any number of reasons. They may not like the person who requested the project, they may not like the goal of the project, it might create major change in their business unit, it might change their operational procedures, and so on. A project that creates a major impact on operational procedures may be viewed as a threat. In fact, any project that brings about a major change in the organization can cause fear and generate resistance.

The key is to get to know your stakeholders as soon as possible. Set up individual meetings or interviews early on to understand their perspectives and concerns about the project. Their concerns aren't going to go away and the issues they raise will become more and more difficult to resolve as the project progresses. Take the time to meet with them regularly. This will help you to set and clarify expectations and help them see the benefits of moving forward with the project.

As you can see, your project team members and stakeholders represent a wide range of functional areas and a diverse set of wants and needs relative to your project. To keep track of everyone, you may want to develop a stakeholder register.

The Stakeholder Register

If you have a large project with multiple stakeholders, it may be appropriate to create a stakeholder register to help you keep track of everyone. The matrix can be a simple roster with name and contact information or may include more details such as the stakeholder's level of influence in the organization. You can use a simple spreadsheet to create the matrix. It should include a list of all the project stakeholders with the following information for each one:

- Name
- Department
- Contact information
- Role on the project
- Needs, concerns, and interests regarding the project
- Level of involvement on the project
- Level of influence over the project
- Notes for your own reference about future interactions with this stakeholder, political issues to be aware of, or individual quirks you want to remember about this stakeholder

Since project stakeholders can move on and off the project at different times, it's important that the project manager reviews and updates the matrix periodically.

Real World Scenario

The Enterprise Resource Planning Implementation

Your organization is considering implementing an enterprise resource planning (ERP) system. This system will handle all the back-office functions for your organization, including procurement, human resources, materials inventory, fleet management, budgeting, and accounting. Currently, your organization has 14 disparate systems that handle these functions.

Identifying your stakeholders for this project turns out to be a daunting task. Within each of the departments, there are executives with their own ideas regarding the system requirements, and there are also functional managers who are much closer to their processes and business unit functions on a day-in and day-out basis. For the most part, their requirements match those of the executives, but you are having some difficulty reconciling the day-to-day processing requirements with some functionality the executives have requested.

Project success or failure can rest on any one of these stakeholders. As the project manager, your best course of action is to meet individually with each stakeholder and understand their individual requirements and concerns about the project. Next, you'll document those requirements and concerns and then bring the key stakeholders together to discuss where they agree and gain consensus regarding the differences.

Assessing Stakeholders

Stakeholder analysis involves assessing which stakeholders' interests should be considered throughout the project. Those with the most influence will also have the most impact, so you need to know who they are. During stakeholder assessment, you'll want to identify the influences stakeholders have on the project and understand their expectations, needs, and desires.

You can start the assessment by examining the customers of the organization and documenting their wants and needs. What expectation might they have because of the project? Also search out those with specific industry experience and expertise on similar projects. Use the brainstorming technique with team members and others to derive as much information as you can about the stakeholders involved on the project and what they know of their behaviors and influence from their experience on past projects. Discuss the culture of the organization and how stakeholders adapt to and work within that culture and how that might impact the project.

My favorite technique is interviewing the stakeholders. Ask them directly what their interests are on the project. Here is a list of some questions you might include in your interviewing process:

- What is your interest in the project?

- What are your expectations regarding the project outcomes?

- What do you anticipate will be your level of involvement with the project?

- What is your knowledge level of the project and of any skills or information needed to produce a successful project outcome?

- What contributions are you anticipating making to the project?

- How will the project impact your organization both positively in the form of benefits or negatively in the terms of consequences or impacts? What are those benefits and/ or impacts?

- Are there other stakeholders who have expectations of this project that conflict with yours?

The information you're gathering by asking these questions is known as *stakeholder analysis*. You have identified the stakeholders and created a stakeholder register with their basic information. Now, you'll want to add their interests and needs to this register and indicate, based on your interviews, the potential impact their needs or interests may have on the project. I recommend using a simple high-medium-low indicator for potential impacts. You could ask the stakeholder, as part of your interviewing process, what level of impact they think these needs or desires have on the project. This will give you an idea of the importance of their expectations. As the project manager, you will have to sift through this information and make judgment calls based on the overall objectives of the project. Not every stakeholder's interests will carry the highest impact. You can add additional columns to the stakeholder register to record needs and interests and potential impacts using the high-medium-low score.

Exam Spotlight

Stakeholder identification and assessment should occur as early as possible in the project and continue throughout its life.

Another form of assessment is categorizing stakeholders in terms of the power and influence they have in the organization. Influence and power are indicators of how much one stakeholder's opinion or decision will have on others in the organization and how it will affect your project. For example, in every organization I've ever worked in, the chief financial officer (CFO) wields a lot of power and control. (You know the old saying, "They who own the gold make the rules.") If the CFO says no, it will likely have a ripple effect throughout the organization and your project. The CFO by virtue of their position and standing in the organization has the authority to say no. Because of this standing, they also have influence over most company decisions. This is what is meant by power and influence.

This is one of the things you probably can't or shouldn't ask the stakeholders directly about. Some stakeholders have inflated opinions of their influence in the organization, and others may think they have little influence when in reality they wield a lot of influence. Deriving this information may require a bit of undercover work on your part as project manager. If you've worked in the organization for any length of time, you probably have a good feel for the influence certain stakeholders may possess. If you've identified stakeholders on your project that you don't know well, you might want to conduct a brainstorming session with a few key, trusted individuals who can help you identify the level of influence the stakeholders have in the organization. I advise that you don't make this information available to everyone on the project. This is information you need to know as project manager but that could potentially damage relationships if it were published.

One of the ways you can analyze or classify stakeholders' power and influence is using a power/interest grid, a power/influence grid, or an impact/influence grid. Each of these grids uses two factors to identify the power, authority, interest, or influence level the stakeholder has on the project. For example, the power/interest grid plots power on one axis of the graph and interest on the other. They are most useful on small projects where it's easier to identify the relationship between the stakeholder and the project. Figure 3.1 shows a sample power/interest grid.

FIGURE 3.1 Example of a power/interest grid

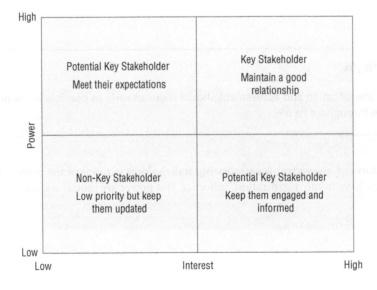

Stakeholder cubes are another method for analyzing stakeholders. This model uses some of the same elements described in the power/interest grid, along with others such as attitudes, influence-level designations, power-level designations, or any combination of elements associated with power, influence, and the abilities of the stakeholders to impact, change, or influence the project. This cube is displayed as a 3D model.

A salience model is yet another way to categorize and analyze stakeholders. This model uses three elements: power, urgency, and legitimacy. Power refers to their ability to influence the project outcomes as we've discussed throughout this section. Urgency may seem strange here, but it refers to stakeholders who may have a significant investment or interest in the outcomes of the project (meaning they will require a lot of attention and likely need a lot of handholding throughout the project), how attentive you'll need to be, and whether their participation or needs are time sensitive and/or time bound. Legitimacy means they have a legitimate need to participate in or receive the benefits from the project. This model is very helpful when you have a large number of stakeholders and/or a significant amount of interaction among the large community of stakeholders. The Salience model is displayed as a Venn diagram. Each element (power, urgency, legitimacy) is represented in a circle, and the intersection of the three circles shows the strongest influences of the stakeholder at a glance.

Stakeholders who only exhibit one of these three categories (power, legitimacy, or urgency) will not likely have a big impact on the project and your engagement with them will be limited. If stakeholders overlap in two of the areas, power and legitimacy for example, or all three, they are more likely to exert influence on the project and may need extra care and attention in ensuring their needs are met.

The Salience model was developed by Ronald K. Mitchell, Bradley R. Agle, and Donna J. Wood and presented in an article published in *The Academy of Management Review* published in 1997. You can reference the article here:

www.jstor.org/stable/259247?seq=22#metadata_info_tab_contents

This is a complex model with multiple attributes and classifications. I recommend reviewing the article cited if you are interested in learning more about the Salience model.

You may also classify stakeholders in a simple spreadsheet using prioritization indicators for their level of influence, political power, interest levels, and more. A scale such as high-medium-low can be assigned for each category, or you could use a weighted scoring model like the one we discussed in Chapter 2, "Understanding IT Fundamentals."

Creating the Preliminary Scope Statement

The preliminary scope statement is the first artifact you'll create once the business case is approved. The purpose of the *preliminary scope statement* is to describe the objectives and the reason for the project. It may also include a rough order of magnitude timeline, deliverables, resources, preliminary budget, high-level risks, benefits, assumptions, and constraints.

All the elements in the preliminary scope statement are included in the project charter and the project scope statement. We will cover these elements in detail later in this chapter and in Chapter 4, "Planning the Project."

You'll recall that the business objectives and reason for the project were documented in the business case. You should review the information contained there and update both the objectives and the reasons for the project and add any new information that's appropriate. The business case describes enough of the project need and objectives to determine whether a project is warranted. The preliminary scope statement goes into more detail on the objectives of the project.

Objectives should be clear, measurable, and actionable. Objectives are the actions needed to achieve a goal. For example, the goal of the project might be to collect and store all customer information in one central place. The objective of the project might be to implement a customer relationship management system within 18 months that reduces customer agent response times by 10 percent. You'll need to meet with the project requestor and key stakeholders in order to understand the business problem they are trying to solve with this project and ensure that the objective has been documented accurately.

Understanding the Need

The preliminary scope statement describes the major characteristics of the product or service of the project and the relationship between the business need and the product or service requested. You must make certain the problem or need that generated the project request is clearly defined and understood. This entails meeting with the person requesting the project to clarify the project objectives and understand what problem they're trying to solve. If the problem is unclear, the solution may be off target, so it's critical that you understand the problem before moving on to defining deliverables and requirements.

 Problems can arise when project requests are proposed in the form of a solution. It is not uncommon for customers to come to you with a specific request and a software solution they've already discovered that satisfies the request. You may be thinking this is great news because there is no need to tie up your calendar with a lot of requirements-gathering meetings. The problem is your customer may not be asking for the right solution. As a project manager, you need to make certain that the problem has been identified before the solution is proposed.

Asking questions of the project requestor is one of the best ways to understand the need and the problem they are trying to solve. Let's say you get a request for a new billing system. The first thing you should do is meet with the person making the request to get more information. Why do they need a new billing system? What functionality is missing from the existing system? What business need or opportunity do they believe this new system will solve? These kinds of questions will help you understand what is behind the request. If your project requestor is concerned about the number of customer calls related to general billing questions, the best solution might not be a new system but rather a clearer explanation of the charges. If they are interested in a new look and feel for the bill, you may be dealing with requirements that range from reformatting the current bill data to rewriting the website. Numerous business needs may cause your customer to want a "new billing system," but many of them may have nothing to do with developing an entirely new application. That is why a good project manager asks questions to uncover what is behind a request. Lack of up-front clarification and problem definition has been the downfall of numerous projects. Do not assume that a customer-requested solution is always the best solution until you understand the business need.

Documenting the Preliminary Scope Definition

Once you understand the answers to the questions posed in the previous section, you should have a good grasp of the objectives of the project. You can document the reason for the project, state the problem you're trying to solve, and provide a high-level description of some of the deliverables needed to make the project a success. This information will serve as a basis for the project charter, which you'll learn about in the next section, and for the scope statement, which we'll cover in Chapter 4.

Creating the Project Charter

The result of the Initiating process is the *project charter*. This document provides formal approval for the project to begin and authorizes the project manager to apply resources to the project. The project sponsor is the one who publishes, signs, and approves the project charter. Publishing the charter is a major milestone because it is the first official document of your approved project.

The project sponsor is the person who authorizes and approves the project charter. The project manager or the person who requested the project is typically the one who writes the project charter and makes certain it's distributed to all the key stakeholders, but the sponsor is the one who approves it.

Organizational standards may drive the specific format of the project charter and the information it contains. As a project manager, you should check with the PMO to determine whether there is a template or a required format for the project charter.

The following are the key elements that should be included in your project charter. Chapter 1, "Introducing the Project," talked about the purpose or justification for the project. This is documented in the business case and can easily be copied into the project charter. The next section will cover the remaining elements:

- Purpose or justification for the project
- Project objectives
- Project description
- Key deliverables
- High-level list of requirements
- High-level milestones
- Preapproved budget
- High-level assumptions
- High-level constraints
- Overall risks
- Name of the project manager and their authority level
- Name of the sponsor
- List of key stakeholders
- Project success criteria

Purpose or Justification for the Project

This section describes the benefit the organization hopes to receive as a result of implementing the project. These may include tangible and intangible benefits. Increasing revenues or decreasing expenses is an example of a tangible benefit. Increasing the organization's reputational or social media standing is an example of an intangible benefit.

Objectives

The charter documents the objectives of the project. A project charter needs to include a clear statement as to what end result the project will produce and how success will be measured. Objectives must be clear and stated in such a manner that the end result is easily measured against the objective. Instead of stating "Build a new highway," the goal should include measurable outcomes like "Build a new highway between City A and City B that has three lanes in both directions by June 30."

Working with the sponsor to document quantifiable and measurable goals is key to the project success. It gives the customer, sponsor, key stakeholders, project manager, and team members the same common understanding of the end result of the project.

Project Description

The *project description* documents the key characteristics of the product, service, or result that will be created by the project. The project description also documents the relationship between the product being created and the business need that drove the project request. This description needs to contain enough detail to be the foundation for the Planning process group, which begins once the charter is signed.

The project description in the charter starts out at a high level, and more details are added once you develop the project scope statement, which is discussed in Chapter 4.

Key Deliverables

Deliverables are measurable outcomes or results or are specific items that must be produced in order to consider the project complete. Deliverables are tangible and are easily measured and verified. For example, let's say your project involves manufacturing a new garden cart. One of the components of the cart is wheels. Because of the design of your cart, the wheels must be 12 inches in diameter. This is a tangible, verifiable deliverable that must be met in order for the project to be a success.

Getting the deliverables and the requirements correct are critical to the success of your project. No matter how well you apply your project management skills, if the wrong deliverables are produced or the project is managed to the wrong objectives, you will have an unsuccessful project on your hands (and will probably need to update your résumé).

High-Level List of Requirements

Requirements describe the characteristics of the deliverables that must be met in order to satisfy the needs of the project. Requirements might also describe results or outcomes that must be produced in order to satisfy a contract, specification, standard, or other project document (typically, the scope statement). Requirements quantify and prioritize the wants, needs, and expectations of the project sponsor and stakeholders.

The project charter contains a high-level look at the requirements. As you progress in the planning of the project, more information will become known, and the requirements will become much more detailed. I will talk more about requirements in Chapter 4.

High-Level Milestones

Milestones are major events in a project that are used to measure progress. They may also mark when key deliverables are completed and approved. Milestones are also used as checkpoints during the project to determine whether the project is on schedule.

Preapproved Budget

The detailed project budget is prepared later during the Planning processes. But for the purposes of the project charter, you need to have a high-level estimate of the project's costs. You can use historical information from past projects that are similar in size, scope, and complexity to the current project. Or you may ask your vendor community to help you with some high-level estimates for the project.

High-Level Assumptions

Assumptions are events, actions, concepts, or ideas you believe to be true and plan for. For example, you may have a resource need for the project with a highly specialized skill. Someone with this skill set resides in your maintenance department, and since you've worked with both the functional manager and this resource on past projects, you assume they'll be available for this project. You can make assumptions about many elements of the project, including resource availability, funding, weather, timing of other related events, availability of vendors, and so on. It's important to always document and validate your project assumptions.

 Real World Scenario

Planning a School Building Repair

You have been assigned a project that requires repairs to the roof of a school building and replacement of the air-conditioning and airflow cleaning systems. The heavy-duty equipment for these systems will be staged in the parking lot. The old equipment will come off the roof and remain in the parking lot until the disposal crew picks it up. The new equipment will be dropped off in the parking lot, and a crane will lift it to the roof when the workers are ready. You scheduled this project to begin on June 15 because all the students and faculty are gone for the summer. You list this assumption in the project charter. During the kickoff meeting, one of your stakeholders informs you that the school building is occupied during the summer. A neighboring community college uses the building (and the parking lot) to hold classes. You will add the community college as a stakeholder on the project and devise an alternative solution for equipment staging as you develop other planning documents.

High-Level Constraints

Constraints are anything that either restricts or dictates the actions of the project team. For example, you may have a hard due date that can't be moved. If you're developing a trade show event that occurs on September 25, this date is a constraint on the project because you can't move it. Budgets, technology, scope, quality, and direct orders from upper management are all examples of constraints.

 The term *triple constraint* is one you'll hear often in project management circles. The triple constraints are time, scope, and cost, all of which affect quality.

Overall Risks

Risks pose either opportunities or threats to the project. Most of the time, we think of risks as having negative impacts and consequences.

You should include a list of high-level risks in the project charter. These may cover a wide range of possibilities, including budget risks, scheduling risks, project management process risks, political risks, legal risks, management risks, and so on. The difference between a risk and a constraint is that a constraint is a limitation that currently exists. A risk is a potential future event that could impact the project. Beginning the project with a hard due date of September 25 is a constraint. The potential for a vendor missing an important delivery on September 15 is a risk.

Other Contents

Other elements you should describe in your charter include the name and authority level of the project manager, the name of the project sponsor, a reference to the stakeholder register, and any team members you've committed ahead of time to serve on the project team.

Project Success Criteria

Last but not least, the project charter should outline the criteria for project approval. These *success criteria* will be used to determine whether the deliverables and the final product, service, or result of the project are acceptable and satisfactory. Think of this as the definition for a successful project. Remember that a project is successful when the stakeholders are satisfied. Therefore, it's critical that you ask the project sponsor and key stakeholders which criteria indicate a successful project for them. There are hundreds of examples, but the most important are those your stakeholders want fulfilled by project completion.

The following is a sample list of acceptance criteria:

- Delivered on time
- Delivered within budget
- Fit for use
- Adheres to regulations
- Quality criteria

- Performance criteria
- Increased profits
- Increased productivity
- Reduced waste

These criteria will be used to determine whether the deliverables and the final product, service, or result of the project are acceptable and satisfactory. This section of the project charter should also describe the process that stakeholders will use to indicate their acceptance of the deliverables. It's a good idea to make this a formal acceptance process with signatures.

Formal Approval

The project sponsor should review and sign the project charter. This sign-off provides the project manager with the authority to move forward, and it serves as the official notification of the start of the project. This approval is usually required prior to the release of purchase orders or the commitment to provide resources to support the project.

Exam Spotlight

It may seem the business case, preliminary scope statement, and project charter are redundant, but they each have their purpose. The business case contains enough information to determine whether the project should proceed. The preliminary scope statement defines the objectives and business needs of the project in more detail. The project charter authorizes the project to begin. In practice, your organization may not use all three of these documents, but for the exam, know the purpose of each.

Issuing the project charter and defining the preliminary scope statement moves the project from the Initiating phase into the Planning phase. Make certain all stakeholders receive a copy of the charter or can access it from your project repository. It is also a good idea to schedule a meeting to review the charter, review the next steps, and address any questions or concerns they may have. This is a good time to examine the records management plan you'll use for the project. Let's look at this next.

Creating the Records Management Plan

A *record* is data or documents used to conduct and perform business such as a contract, personnel records, PII, financial records, project charter, project management plan, and much more. It's essential that the organization ensures that employees understand the definition of a record and that they are trained on proper records management. In my experience, a lack of definition can lead to confusion and employees will end up saving everything, even sticky notes (for the record, these are not records). Many documents we handle throughout the course of our workday do not fit the definition of a record. For example, a draft board report that's circulated to management for review and approval is not a record. Once the report is approved and published to the board of directors, it is a record. Make certain the project team is aware of the definition of a record and that project management records are managed appropriately.

A *records management plan* describes the policies and standards the organization has defined for the life cycle of data and records, starting with their creation, use, maintenance, and archival or disposal. The records management life cycle is typically managed using a *records management system*. These software systems have the records management life cycle functionality built in and enable customizations that fit the organization's needs.

The records management plan should document the following:

- Definition of a record
- List of records liaisons by department
- Location where records are stored (both physical and electronic)
- Classification of records
- Retention schedule
- Disposition procedures

The classification of records is important because different types of records will have different retention schedules. Classification will depend on the organization and type of business it conducts. For example, health records will have much different classifications than construction records. Two types of records common to most organizations are human resource records and financial records. The records management plan should describe how these records are classified.

Retention schedules define how long a record should be kept. Be careful here because there could be laws and regulations that dictate how long a record should be retained. For example, the U.S. federal government has established laws pertaining to personnel records. For example, job application and résumés should be retained for one year after the hire date (for all applicants), whereas payroll records should be retained for three years.

Records related to a project will have varying retention schedules depending on the project type. Projects using federal funds will have certain retention schedules outlined by the government. If your project entails other legal or regulatory activities such as environmental or health, there will be retention periods defined by law that must be met.

Disposition of records will depend on the retention schedule and the classification of the record. For example, PII data should be shredded. Documents or records that are not sensitive could be deleted. Proper maintenance and care of the records management system, including disposition of records according to the retention schedule, will prevent an overabundance of information and a continual increase in storage needs and costs.

Determining Access Requirements

Organizations may have multiple systems performing various business functions such as enterprise resource planning systems, customer relationship management systems, a records management system, and many more. The organization needs a way of determining who has access to these systems and what functions they can perform within the system. For example, the records management system we talked about in the last section may contain sensitive information or employee records that shouldn't be shared with the entire employee population. Access controls should be in place to limit access to only those who need to know. How access controls are determined should be documented in a policy. Many organizations require a senior manager of the business unit who owns the system to grant access permissions. For example, the senior manager of human resources will determine which roles have access to recruiting records, performance reviews, and so on.

Access requirements are usually based on user roles. For example, a payroll clerk will have access to payroll information but an accounts receivable clerk will not. Permission should be based on the lowest level of access needed to perform the job. This is known as the *principle of least privilege*. As an example, a manager should have the ability to view performance appraisals for the employees who report to them, but not for all employees in the organization. The principle of least privilege helps protect the organization from cyberattacks. The idea is perhaps someone in the facilities department is targeted by a cyberattack and the bad actors are looking for access to the organization's banking information. Certain employees in facilities should only have access to the financial accounts associated with their department, not the entire organization, and certainly not the company's banking information.

Exam Spotlight

The principle of least privilege helps protect the organization's critical data from cyberattacks.

Access controls restrict access to systems, functions within the system, and/or data within the system, and more. As an example, all employees have access to the human resources system to enter their time worked, view paycheck stubs, and more while privileged access to payroll data, medical information, and other sensitive information is only given to those whose role requires it. Access controls are set up in the software itself, or in another system IT uses to provision access to organizational programs, by system administrators. Access controls are used for systems as well as humans. For example, a backup system has access to data to replicate it and store it somewhere else for safekeeping, but it wouldn't have access to change configuration settings in the system it's backing up.

When a user logs in to a system, authentication occurs to ensure the requestor has permission to access the system. Once authentication occurs, access controls will determine authorization within the system and then grant access to the functions assigned to the role or user.

Access requirements should be audited and reviewed on a periodic basis. If an employee changes positions within the company, they should not necessarily retain the same access rights to systems they had previously in the new role. Audits will ensure users and systems only have the access they need for their role. Be certain to consider access requirements for IT projects and include this information in your project documentation.

Holding the Kickoff Meeting

Once the project charter is signed and approved, your next task is to hold a project kickoff meeting. This meeting should include the sponsor, project team members, and stakeholders. The goal is to ensure everyone understands the purpose and objectives of the project and for them to understand their role on the project. At this meeting, you'll discuss the objectives of the project, the project description, the high-level milestones, and the general project approach. The project charter and the project scope statement, covered in Chapter 4, are the two documents you'll come back to when stakeholders try to steer you or the team in a different direction than what was originally outlined. I'm not saying that stakeholders would ever do this on purpose but trying to sneak in one more feature or making this "one little change" tends to make its way into most projects I've worked on. These documents are your safety net and the way to keep out-of-control requests at bay. The project sponsor signs the charter, and the key stakeholders on the project sign the project scope statement. So, they can't say they didn't know!

The project kickoff meeting is the best way to formally introduce team members and stakeholders and convey the same message to everyone at the same time. You may not know all of your team members, and you may not even have had the opportunity to interview them for the positions they will fill, depending on how they were selected (or appointed) to work on the project.

The tone that you set at the project kickoff meeting can make or break your relationship with the team. An ideal project kickoff session is a combination of serious business and fun. Your goal is to get the team aligned around the project goals and to get the team members comfortable with each other.

There are many ways to structure a kickoff meeting. Create an agenda for this meeting and distribute it to the attendees ahead of time. Here are some of the key agenda items you might choose to include:

Welcome   It is a good idea to start the meeting by welcoming the team members and letting them know that you are looking forward to working with them. The welcome also gives you an opportunity to set the stage for the rest of the day. Take a few minutes to run through what participants can expect out of the meeting and what activities they will be involved in during the course of the project.

Introductions   A typical introduction format may include the person's functional area, brief background, and role in the project. The project manager should start the process to set an example of the appropriate length and detail. Put some thought into the information you want team members to share so that the time invested is worthwhile.

Project Sponsor and Key Stakeholders   Invite the project sponsor, the customer, and any other executive stakeholders who are key to the project. It's important that the team members know them and hear their goals and expectations for the project firsthand. These people may not be able to stay for the whole session, but do your best to get them to at least make an appearance and say a few words to the team.

You may need to do some coaching here, so spend time prior to the session communicating with the executive stakeholders regarding the message they should deliver. If your sponsor happens to be a dynamic speaker, you might want to schedule them for a little more time to get the troops excited about the project they are working on.

Project Overview   You'll start out this section with the project goals and objectives. You should also summarize the key deliverables for each of the project phases, as well as the high-level schedule and budget. This overview will help team members get the big picture and understand how they fit on the project. It also helps set the foundation regarding the purpose and goals for the project.

Stakeholder Expectations   This section is a natural segue from the previous section. Along with explaining the objectives, schedule, and budget, it's important that the team understands the stakeholder expectations for the project. Explain the reasons for the project deadline or budget constraints if they exist. Make certain team members are aware of any quality concerns, regulatory and legal issues, or market announcements that are tied to this project.

Roles and Responsibilities   Start this section with a description of your roles and responsibilities for the project. Many of the team members may not know you or be familiar with your management style, so this is your chance to communicate how you will be managing the project and your expectations for how the team will function.

Depending on the size of the project, you may want to review the roles and responsibilities for each key team member or skill area. Let them know your expectations regarding project management procedures, reporting and escalation of issues, team meeting schedules, what you expect in terms of individual progress reports, and how they will be asked to provide input into project progress reports.

Question and Answer   One of the most important agenda items for the kickoff session is the time you allocate for team members to ask questions. This engages them on the project and is the ideal opportunity to clarify questions regarding goals, deliverables, expectations, and more.

In some cases, you may not know all the project team members until later in the project. If that's the case, it's a good idea to conduct another kickoff meeting with all team members once they are assigned. It's not uncommon to conduct one kickoff meeting after signing the project charter and another once all team members are assigned during the Executing phase of the project.

 The timing of the kickoff meeting isn't as important as actually holding a kickoff meeting. It should occur early on in the project, ideally after the project charter is signed.

This chapter concludes the Initiating phase of the project management life cycle. The next chapter will begin the Planning phase.

 **Real World Scenario**

Main Street Office Move

After you reviewed the business case, you identified one more key stakeholder and will confirm this with Emma. The stakeholder is Alden Lewis, the director of facilities. He will oversee the physical move components of the project such as furniture and equipment, as well as ensure the new building is properly configured.

When you meet with Emma, you will ask who she believes the key stakeholders are on this project and document them in your stakeholder register. You'll perform stakeholder analysis to understand the level of power and potential impacts these stakeholders may have on the project.

You've started a rough draft of the project charter and will review it with Emma at the next meeting.

Purpose for the Project   To bring together all employees into one building. This will improve communication, reduce travel costs, improve productivity, and reduce lease costs. This project will also downsize the data center as part of the move and implement IaaS.

Project Objectives   This project will relocate 1,200 employees from three locations to the Main Street Office Building location. The move will be completed by December 31. All employees will report to work on January 2 at the Main Street Office Building. The data center move to the cloud will be completed by December 31, and all employees will have access to systems needed to perform their jobs on January 2 when they report to work at the new location.

Project Description   Relocate 1,200 employees to one location at the Main Street Office Building. The move is planned over the holiday period so that it's as minimally disruptive as possible. All employees have the period from December 25 to January 1 as paid time off. All employees will pack their personal belongings and take them when they leave for the holiday period. All work-related items will be packed before leaving the evening of December 24.

The IT team will migrate the appropriate systems, services, and applications to the IaaS cloud by December 20 to allow enough time for testing and adjustments that may be needed.

Key Deliverables   Communication to all employees regarding the purpose for the move and instructions regarding packing belongings, location of new office, and timelines. Communication should occur in multiple forms at least five times before the move.

Procure the services of a moving company to move boxes and furniture. Procurement process to start six months prior to the move date.

Survey the Main Street Office Building and work with functional managers to determine seating charts.

Procure new office furniture. Delivery and setup take place between December 26 and December 30.

Procure an IaaS provider and hire consultants to assist the IT team with the migration of servers, databases, and applications.

High-Level Requirements   Communication methods include all-hands meetings at each existing office location to explain the move. Establish a wiki site on the intranet with details as they become available.

The moving company chosen to perform this move will have experience in relocating offices.

All furniture will conform to the chosen color and pattern theme.

Database backups will be performed prior to beginning the migration to the cloud. An inventory of IT equipment, services, and applications will be performed prior to hiring a vendor.

High-Level Milestones

- Communication to employees completed
- Moving company procurement completed
- Seating charts approved and finalized
- New furniture delivered and placed by December 31
- Office 1 move completed
- Office 2 move completed

- Office 3 move completed

- IaaS vendor procurement completed

- IT inventory completed prior to vendor procurement

High-Level Budget

The total budget for this project is $450,000.

High-Level Assumptions

- Employees are supportive of the move.

- Moving companies are available during the move week.

- Employees will have personal belongings packed and removed from premises prior to move.

- Furniture is delivered on time.

- Key IT staff members including the infrastructure architect will be available during the migration.

High-Level Constraints

- December 31 completion date

- $450,000 budget

High-Level Risks

Bad weather during the move week.

IT systems do not perform as expected once migrated to the cloud.

Data is lost.

Name of the Project Manager

You. Your authority level consists of managing the budget, expending funds to perform the work, requesting resources to assist you, and contracting with a moving company for services. You will work with a director in IT to ensure the procurement of the IaaS platform meets the timeline and budget constraints.

Criteria for Project Approval

The project will be considered successful when all three offices are relocated by December 31, the IaaS platform functions as designed, and the project stays within the $450,000 budget.

Summary

Project stakeholders are anyone who has a vested interest in the outcomes of the project. Some project stakeholders you will encounter are the project sponsor, business analyst, IT team members, end users, project manager, subject matter experts, and the PMO, among others.

A project sponsor is an executive in the organization who has the authority to assign budget and resources to the project. Project sponsors serve as the final decision-maker on the project, sign and approve the project charter, and remove obstacles so that the team can perform their work. Project sponsors often act as the project champion as well. They spread enthusiasm for the project and act as a cheerleader regarding its benefits.

The business analyst is responsible for gathering and documenting requirements and assisting in their implementation. IT team members help design and set up the environment to support IT projects. This team may include an architect, developers, and testers/QA technicians. The end users are the people who will use the software or services produced by the project. They may be internal or external to the organization and may also be customers. The project manager is responsible for coordinating and managing the project team, communications, scope, risk, budget, and time. They also manage quality assurance and are responsible for the project artifacts. SMEs have specific knowledge and skills in their line of business. They contribute expertise to the project, work on deliverables, estimate task durations, estimates costs, estimate dependencies, and more. A PMO provides guidelines, templates, and processes for managing the project. Program managers typically work in the PMO and the project managers in their program report to them.

Identifying and analyzing stakeholders is important to the project. Missing a key stakeholder could spell disaster for the project. The project manager should identify the project stakeholders, assess their influence and level of involvement, determine their needs and interests, and record stakeholder information in the stakeholder register. Project managers should also categorize stakeholders in one of several ways, including power/interest grid, power/influence grid, impact/influence grid, stakeholder cube, the Salience model, and prioritization.

Initiating is the second project phase in the project management life cycle, and this is where formal authorization for the project to begin occurs. The preliminary scope statement is written first; it describes the project objectives and the reason for the project. It also describes the relationship between the business need and the product or service requested.

The project charter is the next document produced in the Initiating phase. This document becomes the basis for more detailed project planning later in the project. It should contain the purpose or justification for the project, project goals, project description, high-level requirements, high-level milestones, high-level budget, assumptions, constraints, high-level risks, name of the sponsor, name of the project manager, and criteria for approval. The project charter provides formal approval for the project to begin and authorizes the project manager to apply resources to the project. The project sponsor is the one who publishes, signs, and approves the project charter.

A records management system is used to manage the life cycle of the organization's records. The life cycle of a record includes creation, use, maintenance, and archival or disposal. A record is documents or data used to conduct business. The definition of a record, including classification of the record, retention policies, and more, should be documented in the records management plan.

Access controls are applied to systems to restrict access, functions, and data within the system according to the principle of least privilege. This principle involves assigning the least amount of privilege needed to perform the job to humans and systems alike. The principle of least privilege will help protect the organization from cyberattacks.

The project kickoff meeting should include the sponsor, project team members, and stakeholders. The goal is to make certain stakeholders understand the purpose and objectives of the project and for them to understand their role on the project. Be sure to publish an agenda ahead of time and make time for questions and answers at the end of the meeting.

Exam Essentials

Be able to define project stakeholders.   A stakeholder is anyone who has a vested interest in the project and has something to gain or lose from the project. Stakeholders include the sponsor, project manager, project team members, functional managers, customers, team members, and others with an interest in the project.

Be able to define a project manager.   The project manager manages the team, communication, scope, risk, budget, and time. They also manage quality assurance and are responsible for the project artifacts.

Be able to define a project sponsor.   A project sponsor is an executive in the organization who has the authority to allocate dollars and resources to the project. The sponsor approves funding, the project charter, the project baseline, and high-level requirements. They have final decision-making authority for the project, help with marketing the benefits of the project, remove roadblocks for the team, and participate in business case justification.

Be able to define a business analyst's role on the project.   A business analyst interviews stakeholders to gather and document requirements for the project. They also help implement the requirements into the final product, service, or result of the project.

Be able to define an SME.   The subject matter experts have specific knowledge and skills in their line of business. They contribute expertise to the project, work on deliverables, estimate task durations, estimate costs, estimate dependencies, and more.

Be able to define an end user.   The end users are the people who will use the software or services produced by the project. They may be internal or external to the organization and may also be customers.

Be able to define the project management office.   The PMO provides guidance to project managers and helps present a consistent, reliable approach to managing projects across the organization. PMOs are responsible for maintaining standards, processes, procedures, and templates. The program manager typically works in the PMO and has responsibility for overseeing all of the projects within their program.

Be able to define the IT team.   The IT team consists of the IT architect, developers, and testing/QA specialists. The architect is responsible for designing technology solutions and services for business applications, infrastructure networks storage, cloud, security and more. The developers write programming code, develop applications, and maintain and modify existing applications. The testing/QA specialists ensure that the application functions according to the requirements.

Know how to identify and analyze stakeholders.   The project manager should identify the project stakeholders, assess their influence and level of involvement, determine their needs and interests, and record stakeholder information in the stakeholder register.

Understand the ways to categorize and display stakeholder analysis.   Categorizing and displaying stakeholder analysis can take several forms, including power/interest grid, power/influence grid, impact/influence grid, stakeholder cube, the Salience model, and prioritization.

Understand the purpose for the preliminary scope statement.   The preliminary scope statement describes the objectives of the project and documents the business problem the project is attempting to solve.

Be able to describe a project charter and list the key components.   A project charter provides formal approval for the project to begin and authorizes the project manager to apply resources to the project. The key components are the purpose or justification for the project, project goals and objectives, project description, key deliverables, high-level list of requirements, high-level milestones, high-level budget, high-level assumptions, high-level constraints, high-level list of risks, name of the sponsor, name of the project manager, and criteria for project approval.

Be able to define success criteria for a project.   Success criteria are used to determine whether the deliverables and final outcomes of the project are acceptable and satisfactory to the stakeholders.

Describe the purpose of a records management system.   This is a system that manages the life cycle functionality of a record, starting with creation, use, maintenance, and archival or disposal.

Understand access controls and the principle of least access.   Access controls restrict access to systems, functions, data, and more. Access controls are applied to both humans and computing systems. The principle of least privilege is a matter of assigning the least amount of privilege needed to perform the job.

Understand the purpose of a kickoff meeting. This meeting should include the sponsor, key project team members, and the key stakeholders. The goal is to make certain stakeholders understand the purpose and objectives of the project, and to understand their role in the project. Be sure to publish an agenda ahead of time and make time for questions and answers at the end of the meeting.

Key Terms

Before you take the exam, be certain you are familiar with the following terms:

architect

artifacts

assumptions

business analyst

champion

constraints

customer

deliverables

developers

end users

engineers

milestone

objectives

preliminary scope statement

principle of least privilege

program managers

project baseline

project charter

project description

project management office (PMO)

project team

quality assurance (QA)

record

records management plan

records management system

requirements

sponsor

stakeholder analysis

subject matter experts (SMEs)

success criteria

Review Questions

1. The Initiating phase includes which task?

   A. Assigning work to project team members

   B. Sequencing project activities

   C. Approving a project and authorizing work to begin

   D. Coordinating resources to complete the project work

2. Which person is responsible for authorizing the project to begin and for signing the project charter?

   A. Project sponsor

   B. Executive in the organization who requested the project

   C. Program manager

   D. Project manager

3. You have identified all the key stakeholders on the project. You've listed their names, departments, interests in the project, and level of influence. What have you created? (Choose two.)

   A. A stakeholder contact list

   B. A stakeholder register

   C. An artifact

   D. A business case with a list of key stakeholders

   E. A preliminary scope statement with a list of key stakeholders

4. Zoe is a key resource for the project. She has certifications on the PaaS product you are implementing. She will help determine duration estimates, cost estimates, and perform application development. What type of stakeholder is Zoe?

   A. Tester/QA technician

   B. SME

   C. Business analyst

   D. Architect

5. Zack is a key resource for the project. He is responsible for designing the overall technology infrastructure, network, storage, and security for the cloud application the IT team is developing. What type of stakeholder is Zack?

   A. QA technician

   B. Developer/engineer

   C. End user

   D. Architect

6. Your project's objective is to implement a new financial system. Ravi is a key stakeholder on the project. He, along with others from his team, will provide critical input on the functioning of the system. One of the objectives Ravi would like to see is reducing the amount of clicks it takes to process and invoice. He'd really like to see this process streamlined. What type of stakeholder is Ravi? (Choose two.)

   A. Architect

   B. Developer/engineer

   C. End user

   D. QA technician

   E. SME

7. You are using a document from the Discovery phase to help you write a document produced in the Initiating phase. You have documented the objectives of the project as well as the business problem the project is attempting to resolve, which you know are the primary purposes for this document. Which document are you writing?

   A. Business case

   B. Objectives

   C. Project charter

   D. Preliminary scope statement

8. Which of the following does a PMO provide to the overall project management processes? (Choose three.)

   A. Preliminary scope statement

   B. Business case

   C. Tools

   D. Governance process

   E. Change control

   F. Templates

9. The project sponsor (who is also the project champion in this question) provides which of these functions to the project? (Choose three.)

   A. Preparing the stakeholder matrix

   B. Marketing the project

   C. Removing roadblocks

   D. Preparing the project charter

   E. Defining the business justification

   F. Managing project artifacts

10. Your project team members and key stakeholders are confused about the project you are all working on. What is the most compelling reason for this?

   A. The problem or need generating the project request was not defined well in the preliminary scope statement.

   B. The project sponsor has not signed the project charter document authorizing the project to begin.

   C. The business case is not well documented.

   D. The project team members don't understand their roles and responsibilities.

11. Which of the following are true regarding the project baseline? (Choose four.)

   A. The project baseline is approved by the project manager.

   B. The project baseline includes the approved project scope.

   C. The project baseline includes the approved business justification.

   D. The project baseline includes the approved project quality plan.

   E. The project baseline includes the approved project request.

   F. The project baseline includes the approved project schedule.

   G. The project baseline is approved by the project sponsor.

12. Which of the following is true concerning the project charter?

   A. Describes the project schedule

   B. Contains cost estimates for each task

   C. Authorizes the start of the project work

   D. Lists the responsibilities of the project selection committee

13. Which of the following is performed once the project charter is signed?

   A. You should hold a project kickoff meeting.

   B. You should write the preliminary scope statement.

   C. You should begin the Planning phase.

   D. You should develop the project schedule.

14. This software system manages the life cycle of these items that starts with creation, use, maintenance, and archival or disposal.

   A. Enterprise resource planning system

   B. Customer relationship management system

   C. Records management system

   D. Cloud management system

15. This stakeholder analysis tool is most useful on small projects where it's easier to identify the relationship. It's a quadrant that describes how to maintain relationships, including whether you should meet expectations, maintain good relationships, keep stakeholders updated, or keep them engaged and informed.

   A. Salience model

   B. Prioritization model

   C. Stakeholder cube

   D. Power/interest grid

16. Your project involves implementing a new human resources system. Certain roles with the human resources department will have differing levels of access. The director of human resources can access all human resources–related data while a recruiting manager may only access applicant data. Which of the following are true regarding this question? (Choose two.)

   A. This describes the functions each stakeholder will perform for testing purposes.

   B. This describes an access control system that restricts access to data based on roles.

   C. This describes one of the success criteria for the project.

   D. You should implement the principle of least privilege to guard against cyberattacks.

17. You have just defined the major events for the project that will be used to determine and measure checkpoints throughout the project and determine whether the project is on time. What are they?

   A. Deliverables

   B. Objectives

   C. Milestones

   D. Tasks

18. Identify the items that should *not* be included in a project charter. (Choose two.)

   A. High-level budget

   B. Project objectives

   C. High-level cost–benefit analysis

   D. Equipment and resources

   E. Project description

   F. High-level list of risks

19. Greg is a key technical resource for your project. You've worked with Greg on past projects and have identified him as one of the team members who will work on the project. The charter has been published, and there is great excitement about this project. You've scheduled a meeting to talk to Greg's manager next week about his participation on the project. Which of the following conditions does this describe?

   A. Risk

   B. Assumption

   C. Deliverable

   D. Constraint

20. Which of the following does *not* describe a constraint?

    A. The project team is directed to report to the main headquarters for all project meetings.

    B. The budget is $1.8 million.

    C. The deadline to complete the project is June 27.

    D. The project sponsor will remain the sponsor for the duration of the project.

Chapter

4

Planning the Project

THE COMPTIA PROJECT+ EXAM TOPICS COVERED IN THIS CHAPTER INCLUDE:

✓ **1.0 Project Management Concepts**

- **1.1 Explain the basic characteristics of a project and various methodologies and frameworks used in IT projects**

- **1.2 Compare and contrast Agile vs. Waterfall concepts**

- **1.10 Given a scenario, perform basic activities related to team and resource management**

✓ **2.0 Project Life Cycle Phases**

- **2.2 Given a scenario, perform activities during the project initiation phase**

- **2.3 Given a scenario, perform activities during the project planning phase**

Now that you have an approved project charter, it is time to talk about project planning. I've seen people who want to start working on the project activities immediately after the project is approved. They say something like, "Who has time for planning? We need to get this project started!"

As the project manager, it's your responsibility to write the project management plan and make certain everyone, including team members and key stakeholders, understand it. The project management plan will consist of several important documents, starting with the preliminary scope statement and project charter that we covered in the last chapter. In this chapter, the first Planning phase document we will discuss is the project scope document.

Project scope includes all the components that make up the product or service of the project and what it intends to produce. Scope planning will assist you in understanding what's included in the project boundaries and what is excluded.

You'll need to define and document three scope components to complete scope planning: the scope-management plan, the scope statement, and the work breakdown structure (WBS). The scope management plan documents how the project scope will be defined and verified and how scope will be monitored and controlled throughout the life of the project. The scope statement provides a common understanding of the project by documenting the project objectives and deliverables. And the final component of scope is the work breakdown structure, which breaks the project deliverables down into smaller components from which you can estimate task durations, assign resources, and estimate costs. We will cover work breakdowns in the next chapter.

Next we will discuss several frameworks and methodologies used in IT projects, including waterfall and agile. We will look at the criteria for selecting one method over another and examine solutions design. I'll conclude the chapter with an introduction of the types of human resources on an agile project. Let's get started.

Defining the Planning Phase

Planning is, in my opinion, the most important phase of all. Of course, it takes all phases to achieve a successful project, but if you don't have a well-thought-out and well-documented project plan, it could spell disaster for the project. Planning entails many activities, and you'll see that almost half of this book is dedicated to the Planning phase. Planning involves activities such as creating the scope management plan, the work breakdown structure, the project schedule, the risk plan, the resource plan, the communication plan, and much more.

The *project management plan* is an assortment of documents that describes what the project is, what the project will deliver, and how all the project processes will be managed. You will use this document throughout the Executing phase of the project life cycle to track and measure project performance and as a basis to make future project decisions. It's also used as a communication and information tool for stakeholders, team members, and management. The project management plan also includes baselines such as the scope baseline, schedule baseline, budget baseline, and more. Many of the project documents also have their own individual management plans to help describe how the project document itself will be prepared and maintained, and how processes associated with the document will be administered and verified. We'll start with the scope management plan.

Documenting the Scope Management Plan

The *scope management plan* describes how the project team will define project scope, verify the work of the project, and manage and control scope. The scope management plan should contain the following elements:

- The process you'll use to prepare the scope statement

- A process for creating, maintaining, and approving the work breakdown structure (WBS)

- A definition of how the deliverables will be verified for accuracy and the process used for accepting deliverables

- A description of the process for controlling scope change requests, including the procedure for requesting changes and how to obtain a change request form

One of the most important elements of the scope management plan, the change request process, will help you master that dreaded demon that plagues every project manager at one time or another—*scope creep*. Scope creep involves changing the project or product scope without considering the impacts it will have to the project schedule, budget, and resources. It is the term commonly used to describe the changes and additions that seem to make their way onto the project to the point where you're not managing the same project anymore. Scope creep usually occurs in small increments over time. A small change here, a new little addition there, and the next thing you know the project's overall objectives have changed. I think I can safely say that every project I've ever managed involved change. It is inevitable on most projects. The key to managing the change requests is a well-documented process that includes examining the impacts of change to the project. This process should be documented in the scope management plan.

Everyone involved in the project should understand the process for requesting a change to scope. This will also protect team members from those stakeholders who may come to them with "something they forgot to mention." They can remind stakeholders to submit their change requests according to the process outlined in the scope management plan.

NOTE   You may not encounter a lot of questions on the exam regarding the scope management plan. However, it is an important element in building the scope statement, controlling scope creep, and preparing the work breakdown structure. It's also a component of the *scope baseline*, which consists of the scope management plan, the scope statement, and the work breakdown structure.

Writing the Scope Statement

The *scope statement* includes all the components that make up the product or service of the project and the results the project intends to produce. Although this sounds straightforward, a poorly defined scope statement can lead to missed deadlines, cost overruns, poor morale, and unhappy customers. Good scope planning helps ensure that all the work required to complete the project is defined, agreed on, and clearly documented.

The scope statement builds on and adds detail to the preliminary scope statement and the project charter. However, you may find that much of the work required for scope planning was already completed and documented in those documents. If that's the case, congratulations—you are now ahead of the game.

NOTE   The processes to define the scope elements are *iterative*—that is, you will continue to define and refine the project scope (and other planning elements) going back over them several times until you and the team are satisfied everything has been identified and documented.

The purpose of the scope statement is to document the project objectives, the deliverables, and the work required to produce the deliverables. It is then used to direct the project team's work during the Executing phase and as a basis for future project decisions. The scope statement is an agreement between the project and the project customer that states precisely what the work of the project will produce. Simply put, the scope statement tells everyone concerned with the project exactly what they're going to get when the work is finished. Any major deliverable, feature, or function that is not documented in the scope statement is *not* part of the project.

Typically, the scope statement includes the project objectives, a project description, product scope, success criteria, key deliverables, exclusions from scope, time and cost estimates, project assumptions, and constraints. The scope statement may also include a detailed analysis of the product, an additional cost–benefit analysis, and an examination of alternative solutions. The scope statement can be as detailed as needed, depending on the complexity of the project.

Project Objectives

Objectives describe the overall goal the project hopes to achieve. Objectives should be measurable and verifiable and are often time-bound. For example, you may have a final completion date for the entire project or for some of the project's key objectives. You can copy the objectives you documented in the preliminary scope statement and the project charter. If you've learned new or more detailed information on the objectives since writing these documents, be sure to include it here.

Project and Product Description

The project scope description explains the key characteristics of the product or service you are creating with this project. Again, you could reuse the project description you documented in the project charter and add more details to it in this document.

If the result of your project is a tangible product, you should include the product scope description here as well. The *product scope* describes the features and functions of the product, as well as documents the major characteristics of the product. The *product manager* oversees the existing products and the development of new products for the organization. They are like a project manager in that they meet with stakeholders and customers, determine strategy, create requirements, and oversee development of the products, but their focus is on the product itself, not the project management life cycle.

Success Criteria and Key Performance Indicators

We talked about success criteria, also known as acceptance criteria, in Chapter 3, "Creating the Project Charter." It includes the process and criteria you'll use to determine that the deliverables are complete and satisfactorily meet expectations. Final acceptance criteria are the criteria that describes how you'll determine whether the entire project is complete and meets expectations.

Key performance indicators (KPIs) are metrics that help you determine whether the project is on track and progressing as planned and whether deliverables meet expectations. KPIs can be monitored incrementally to determine performance results and alert you that you must take action to get the project back on track. KPIs should be outlined by the project sponsor and perhaps a few key stakeholders. The KPIs should be documented in the scope statement and used throughout the remainder of the project to measure progress. Financial KPIs are among the easiest to measure, as are time frames and quality metrics. Some examples of KPIs follow:

- Increase profit
- Improve employee retention
- Avoid penalties for regulatory and compliance violations
- Reduce expense

- Improve customer satisfaction
- Decrease the number of call center interactions
- Decrease workers' compensation claims
- Improve vendor partnerships

As stated, KPIs are measurements; this list outlines some KPI ideas but you will need to add a specific metric to make them KPIs—for example, "reduce expenses by 8 percent," or "incur zero penalties for compliance violations by adding physical inspections at the completion of each phase of production."

Key Deliverables

Deliverables, as you recall, are measurable outcomes, measurable results, or specific items that must be produced to consider the project or project phase completed. Deliverables should be specific and verifiable. Key deliverables are those that are critical to the success of the project.

Critical Success Factors

Deliverables and requirements are sometimes referred to as *critical success factors*. Critical success factors are those elements that must be completed accurately and on schedule in order for the project to be considered complete. They are often key deliverables on the project, and if they are not accurate or complete, they will likely cause project failure.

Exclusions from Scope

Exclusions from scope are anything that isn't included as a deliverable or work of the project. It's important to document exclusions from scope so there is no misunderstanding about features or deliverables once the product is complete. For example, your project might involve the implementation of new ERP software for accounting, procurement, human resources, and payroll functions. Exclusions from scope might include budget and inventory functions.

Time and Cost Estimates

Depending on the organization, you may come across scope statement templates that require time and cost estimates. In this section, you'll provide an estimate of the time it will take to complete all the work and the high-level estimates for the cost of the project. These will be *order of magnitude* estimates based on actual duration and cost of similar projects or the expert judgment of someone familiar with the work of the project. Order-of-magnitude estimates are usually wide ranging and do not have to be precise estimates at this stage in the project.

Assumptions

You'll recall from Chapter 3 that an *assumption* is an action, a condition, or an event that is believed to be true. Assumptions can get you into trouble if they are not documented and clearly understood by the stakeholders and project team members. You may think something is obvious, but if it's not written down, chances are other team members or stakeholders will have a different opinion on the matter. Assumptions must be documented and validated.

Exam Spotlight

The purpose of the scope statement is to document the project objectives, the deliverables, and the work required to produce the deliverables.

Constraints

The last section of the scope statement is a list of constraints and influencers. Remember that a *constraint* is anything that restricts or dictates the actions of the project team. Every project faces potential constraints regarding time, budget, scope, or quality. From the start of any project, at least one of these areas is limited. If you are developing a new product with a short time-to-market window, time will be your primary constraint. If you have a fixed budget, money will be the constraint. If both time and money are constrained, quality may suffer.

A predefined budget or a mandated finish date needs to be factored into any discussion on project scope. Scope will be impacted if either time or budget is constrained. As the project progresses and changes to scope are requested, scope may become a constraint that in turn drives changes to time, cost, or quality.

 Make certain you understand the definition of a constraint and its influence and the types of constraints and influences that exist on any project.

Constraints

The following are common constraints found on most projects:

- Budget
- Scope
- Deliverables
- Quality
- Environment
- Resources
- Requirements
- Scheduling

We'll look at each of these next.

Budget

I have never had the experience of working on a project where budget was *not* a constraint. All projects have a limited amount of funding available to perform the work or to purchase the services required to complete the project. The project costs must be monitored and controlled throughout the project so that you stay within budget. Work with your sponsor and key stakeholders to determine the project budget as early as possible in the Planning phase.

Scope

Earlier in the chapter you learned that scope describes the project deliverables and outlines the expectations and acceptance criteria for the deliverables and for a successful project. Scope is a constraint because it dictates the actions of the project team in relation to fulfilling the deliverables. If you perform work other than what's required to fulfill the deliverables outlined in the scope statement (oh no, the dreaded scope creep problem), you have a runaway project on your hands and won't likely have a successful outcome.

 If scope is not fully understood, defined, and documented, you will find that time or budget or both are also impacted.

Deliverables

Deliverables, as we discussed earlier, are measurable outcomes, measurable results, or specific items that must be produced to consider the project completed. Deliverables should be specific and verifiable. Deliverables are constraints because the requirements or measurable results drive (or restrict) the actions of the project team.

Quality

Quality concerns measuring or quantifying performance, deliverables, functionality, specifications, and so on. Quality assurance is defined during the Planning phase and measured and controlled throughout the project. For example, if a quality standard requires deliverables weigh 9 ounces or more, a deliverable weighing 7.5 ounces will not meet quality standards.

Environment

Environment can be a constraint in any number of circumstances. Weather is an environmental factor that can be a constraint, as are the rugged conditions of the Outback or Antarctica. Environment could also pertain to air quality or water quality standards, for example, or emissions regulations. It's important to be familiar with any environmental factors that may restrict or dictate the actions of the team.

Resources

Resources can range from human resources, to materials, to equipment, to funding, and more. Resources can be a constraint when they are scarce, have limited availability, or cannot be delivered on time. Your organization may not have the funding, technology, equipment, or human resources with the skill sets needed to fulfill the deliverables in the time frame required, and therefore, resources become a constraint.

Requirements

Requirements describe the characteristics of the deliverables that must be met in order to satisfy the needs of the project. Requirements might also describe results or outcomes that must be produced in order to satisfy the deliverables as documented in the scope statement.

Scheduling

The project schedule is another constraint that exists on virtually all projects. As with budget, I've never had the privilege of working on a project that didn't have a time constraint. Time can take a couple of forms. It could be a due date set by your executive management. It could also be driven by forces external to the project. For example, the summer Olympic games must be held during the summer months. Perhaps a resource you need for your project is unavailable during the month of April, September, and October. Scheduling then becomes a constraint because you must work within their availability window to complete the deliverable for your project. Scheduling is often a constraint on IT projects as well. Let's say you're implementing a new financial system and your organization undergoes annual audits in July. You won't have resources available for project work during that month and should not schedule the implementation in July. Maintenance windows for IT programs and hardware are another consideration when creating the project schedule. Again, work with your project sponsor and key stakeholders to determine as early as possible in the project what their expectations are regarding deliverable due dates, project completion dates, and other time frames or dates that may be off-limits.

NOTE   You do not have the luxury of working on a project with no constraints. Remember that the most common constraints on any project are scope, budget, and time. You will need to balance and weigh constraints against each other to determine the best way to accomplish the goals of the project while also deciding which constraint is more important or impactful versus which constraint has more flexibility. This requires communication with your sponsor and stakeholders and actively managing expectations.

Influences

Influences are those factors that may impact or change an existing constraint or may bring about a new constraint. The following are common influences:

- Change request
- Scope creep
- Constraint reprioritization
- Interaction between constraints
- Stakeholder/sponsors/management
- Other projects

We'll look at each of these next.

Change Request

A change request can impact existing constraints or bring about a new constraint on the project. For example, if your project is already time constrained and the change request your stakeholders just approved changes to the project due date, the scheduling constraint is impacted.

Scope Creep

We've talked a lot about scope creep. It is imperative that you control changes to scope with an established change management procedure to assure project success.

Constraint Reprioritization

Reprioritizing the constraints may change their impacts or influence on the project. For example, let's say the primary constraint on your project is scheduling because you have a due date that is required by the project sponsor. Let's also say the company is undergoing some financial difficulties and you've just learned that the budget for your project has been reduced. The budget reduction is so significant it now becomes the primary constraint on your project.

Interaction Between Constraints

An example of interaction between constraints may occur when you have changes to scope that in turn impact the schedule and/or budget. Scope can change through the formal change control process or through scope creep. Perhaps your project sponsor has decided you need one more deliverable in order to satisfy the overall objectives of the project. This is approved in a formal change request process. However, scope changes drive schedule changes, budget changes, and changes to product scope. The interaction here is like a domino effect, and all the constraints should be reexamined to assure they still accurately reflect the conditions of the project. This interaction may also cause a reprioritization of the constraints.

Stakeholders, Sponsors, and Management, Oh My

Project sponsors and executive management are notorious for changing project priorities on a moment's notice. Today they want deliverable A, tomorrow they want deliverable Z. It's a constantly changing target! They also sometimes lose interest in the project. Newer projects may gain in importance in the organization (or wane) causing changes to your project that could bring about new constraints or change existing ones. For example, if your project is time constrained and another project comes about that rises in importance, you may lose resources or budget to the new project, which will bring about new constraints on your project. In my experience, the single biggest influence on project constraints is sponsors and executive management changing their priorities.

 **Real World Scenario**

Sample Scope Statement

You have been asked to set up a fund-raising project for your school. Here is a sample of what the scope statement might look like:

Project Objective (from the Project Charter)   Establish a fund-raising golf tournament to raise $20,000.

Project Description   Hold a golf tournament the last week of the school year to raise funds for classroom equipment and resources. Our target goal is $20,000 in donations.

Acceptance Criteria   Golf tournament raises $20,000. Participants enjoy the tournament and would recommend it to their friends next year.

Key Deliverables   The major deliverables are as follows:

- Establish a minimum of two major sponsors willing to contribute $5,000 each.

- Establish multiple minor sponsorships between $500 and $1,000 that will total another $5,000 at a minimum.

- Establish pricing for golf tournament participants that will cover green fees and cart fees, and provide $50 toward the fundraiser.

- Reserve a golf course for the tournament.

- Devise challenges for participants such as longest drive, longest putt, and best scores.

- Procure prizes.

- Develop marketing materials to advertise the event.

- Train volunteers to work at the event.

Exclusions from Scope Alcohol is available at the golf course but is not included in the entrance fees and must be purchased separately.

Time and Cost Estimates The time estimate is one full-time employee (FTE) for a full year to coordinate the event and procure sponsors, prizes, and the golf course agreement. Costs are minimal as sponsors will be providing the funds to purchase prizes.

Assumptions

- Golf courses are available the day of the tournament.

- The number of sponsors and funding needed will be obtained.

- Players will attend the tournament and all available spaces will be filled.

Constraints The date of the tournament is within one week of the last week of school.

Approval of the Scope Statement

Once you have completed the scope statement, your next step is to conduct a review session with your project team to make sure that everyone is in agreement and there are no unresolved issues or missing information.

The next step is to present the scope statement to all the stakeholders, including the project sponsor and the customer. Attach a sign-off and approval sheet to the back of the scope statement with enough signature lines for the sponsor and each of the major stakeholders on the project. Their approval on this document assures their buy-in regarding the scope of the project and should be required before any project work is undertaken.

If you've defined the scope of the project and gained stakeholder approval, and all the major stakeholders and the sponsor have signed the scope statement, you're well on your way to a successful project outcome. Taking the time to create a well-documented scope statement will also help in establishing a solid basis for future change management decisions.

Documenting the Requirements

You may recall from Chapter 3 that requirements describe the characteristics of the deliverables. Requirements might also describe results or outcomes that must be produced to satisfy a contract, specification, standard, or other project document. Requirements quantify and prioritize the wants, needs, and expectations of the project sponsor and stakeholders.

Requirements definition can be part of the scope statement, or it can be an independent document, depending on the size and complexity of the project. In my experience, the scope statement works fine to document the requirements for small projects.

Requirement Categories

Requirements fall into several categories. Having a good grasp of the differences in requirements can help you when writing a requirements document. Your stakeholders won't know the difference and will mix business requirements with functional and nonfunctional requirements when discussing their expectations. On larger projects it helps to categorize the requirements so that when you're constructing the work breakdown structure and later assigning resources, they will already be somewhat organized.

Business Requirements

An organization's *business requirements* are the big-picture results of fulfilling a project and how they satisfy business goals, strategy, and perspective. Business results can be anything from a planned increase in revenue, to a decrease in overall spending, to increased market awareness, and more.

 When gathering requirements, your focus should be on the "what," not on the "how." Stakeholders are passionate about their needs and will likely have a list of ideas on "how" to solve the problem and implement the project. You want to drive them to the "what" and to answer the question, "What problem are we trying to solve?"

When documenting business requirements, sometimes it's helpful to use a process diagram. This shows step-by-step how a process works, where approvals or decisions need to be made, and so on. Process diagrams also come in handy when mapping out business processes. For example, the PMO may have a process diagram that documents how a project idea transforms into a project. It starts with a project idea, goes to the selection committee, and returns to the PMO to either proceed into a full-fledged project or for the idea to be archived or placed in a hold status. Figure 4.1 shows a simple process diagram.

FIGURE 4.1   Sample process diagram

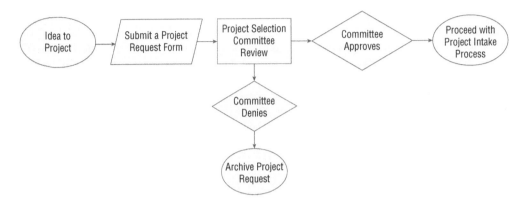

Functional Requirements

Functional requirements are the product characteristics needed for the product to perform. They are typically behavioral in nature or performance-oriented and may also describe elements such as color, quantity, and other specifications. For example, if you're designing a new toaster, a functional requirement might look like this: pushing the red button will begin the toasting process and pushing the green button will pop the toast out of the toaster.

Industry or corporate standards may impact your functional requirements. In our toaster example, perhaps industry standards state that electric cords on kitchen appliances must be 20 inches or shorter in length and must contain a tag describing electrical hazards. This requirement needs to be added to the requirements document. You'll need to research any industry standards that may impact the requirements and document them because they could impact activity duration or cost estimates.

 If you work in a regulated industry, make sure you address the question of whether any specific government or industry-related regulations impact the design or delivery of your product. Regulatory noncompliance is a serious offense, and correcting infractions after the fact can be both time-consuming and costly.

Nonfunctional Requirements

Nonfunctional requirements describe the characteristics of the functional requirements. They are not performance- or behavioral-based. For example, a nonfunctional requirement in our toaster example might state that the green button should be 1.5 inches in diameter and the red button should be 2 inches in diameter.

In my experience, stakeholders are typically more prepared to discuss functional requirements than nonfunctional, so come prepared with a list of questions. If all else fails, asking why and what always works. "Why does the green button stop the toaster and pop the toast?" And, "What would happen if I pushed the green button and the red button at the same time?" If your PMO has a requirements template or checklist, use it in your meetings with the stakeholders.

> *Functional requirements* is a term used in software development. It typically describes a behavior, such as calculations or processes, that should occur once data is entered. In non-software terms, *functional requirements* might describe specifications, quantities, colors, and more. *Nonfunctional requirements* refer to elements that are related to the product but they don't describe the product directly. In the case of a software product, this could be a security requirement or performance criteria.

The Requirements Document

Requirements quantify and prioritize the wants, needs, and expectations of the project sponsor and stakeholders to achieve the project objectives. Requirements typically start out high-level and are further defined, or progressively elaborated, as the project progresses. You must be able to track, measure, test, and trace the requirements of the project. You never want to find yourself at the end of the project and discover you have no way to validate the requirements. If you can't measure or test whether the requirement satisfies the business need of the project, the definition of success is left to the subjective opinions of the stakeholders and team members.

You've worked hard to gather and define requirements and you don't want all that effort going to waste. You'll record everything you've learned in a requirements document or in the scope statement. If your requirements document is a stand-alone document, you should include at least the following elements:

- Business need for the project and why it was undertaken

- Project objectives

- Project deliverables

- Requirements

Once the requirements are documented, you will create a requirements traceability matrix.

Requirements Traceability Matrix

The idea behind the traceability matrix is to document where the requirement originated, document what the requirement will be traced to, link each requirement to a testing strategy, and then follow it through to delivery or completion. Table 4.1 shows a sample traceability matrix with several attributes that identify the requirement.

TABLE 4.1   Requirements traceability matrix

Unique ID	Description of requirement	Source	Priority	Test scenario	Owner	Status and date
001	Requirement one	Project objective	B	User acceptance	HR specialist	Approved 3/15

Each requirement should have its own unique identifier. You could devise a numbering system that defines both the category of the requirement and a unique, ascending number—for example, HR (for human resources) 001—or a simple numbering system, as shown in this example, may suffice. The description should be brief but have enough information to easily identify the requirement. The source column refers to where the requirement originated. Requirements may come from many sources, including project objectives, business needs, product design, the work breakdown structure, and deliverables.

Priority refers to the priority of the requirement. You can use any prioritization process, like a simple numbering system or an alpha system, as the example shows. For example, perhaps an "A" is essential to project success and a "B" is highly desirable. The description and definition of the priority system should be included in the requirements management plan.

The test scenario in this example is where you record how the requirement will be tested (or during which project phase) and the owner of the test item, who will also decide whether the test scenario passes or fails. Status may capture information that refers to whether the requirement was approved; if it was added, deferred, or canceled; and so on.

The traceability matrix may also include the WBS deliverable the requirement is associated with, how it ties to the product design, and/or the product development.

The requirements traceability matrix helps ensure the project meets expectations by linking each requirement to a project objective.

Next, I will introduce project methodologies for IT projects. A good number of questions on the exam will focus on agile methodologies. We'll start with an overview here and I'll incorporate agile topics in all the remaining Planning, Executing, and Closing phases throughout the remainder of the book.

Determining a Project Methodology

Project life cycles are similar to the life cycle that parents experience raising their children to adulthood. Children start out as infants and generate lots of excitement wherever they go. However, not much is known about them at first. So, you study them as they grow, and you assess their needs. Over time, they mature and grow until one day the parents' job is done.

Projects start out just like this and progress along a similar path. Someone comes up with a great idea for a project and actively solicits support for it. The project, after being approved, progresses through several phases to the ending phase, where it is completed and closed out.

All the collective phases the project progresses through from the start of the project until the end are called the *project life cycle*. Project life cycles are similar for all projects regardless of their size or complexity.

The phases that occur within the project life cycle may be sequential or may sometimes overlap each other. Depending on the industry, these phases may be known by different names. Most projects consist of the following life cycle structure:

- Beginning the project
- Planning and organizing the work of the project
- Performing the work of the project
- Closing out the project

This project life cycle looks eerily familiar to the project management phases we've discussed, which consists of the Discovery, Initiating, Planning, Executing, and Closing phases. The project life cycle typically parallels the project management life cycle phases once the project is approved.

Project Life Cycles vs. Project Management Phases

Don't confuse project life cycles with project management phases. Project life cycles describe how the *work* associated with the product of the project will be completed. For example, a construction project might have project life cycle phases such as feasibility study, design, build, inspection, and turnover. The five project management phases (Discovery, Initiating, Planning, Executing, and Closing) organize and describe how the *project* activities will be conducted to meet the project requirements.

Many industries use a *feasibility study* as one of the first phases of the project (this is also another potential phase name). A feasibility study is used to determine whether the project is worth undertaking and whether the project will be profitable to the organization. It's a preliminary assessment of the viability of the project; the viability or perhaps marketability of the product, service, or result of the project; and the project's value to the organization. It might also determine whether the product, service, or result of the project is safe and meets industry or governmental standards and regulations. The completion and approval of the feasibility study triggers the beginning of the Planning phase where requirements are documented and then handed off to the design phase, where blueprints are produced, and so on through the phases. The feasibility study might also show that the project is not worth pursuing and the project is then terminated; therefore, the next phase never begins.

Before we move into development methodologies, I want to introduce a project management life cycle approach called PRINCE2.

Projects in Control (PRINCE2)

PRINCE2 stands for PRojects IN Controlled Environments. This is a project management methodology that divides up projects into small stages that are logically organized. When using this methodology, you will define a project plan early in the project that will be used to manage the project in stages, step by step, and keep it in control throughout the project life cycle. PRINCE2 can be used for any size project in any industry. The "2" was added to the end of the name when the process was updated in 1996. PRINCE2 is a project management process just as the one outlined in the *PMBOK® Guide*, published and defined by the Project Management Institute (PMI®). PRINCE2 is the standard project management methodology used in the United Kingdom. Some sources believe that PRINCE2 is the most widely used project management methodology in the world. I will cover this methodology in more depth in Chapter 9, "Processing Change Requests."

DevOps

DevOps is a framework whereby the development and operations staff members are embedded on one team. It is a combination of the development team, which is responsible for developing and maintaining applications, and the operations team, which is responsible for implementing and maintaining the servers and networks that applications run on. This structure allows the teams to deliver projects faster, provide more reliable systems, and improve collaboration and communication among the team members.

Prior to the concept of DevOps, the development team and operations team were separated organizationally and reported to different managers. In this type of organizational structure, it isn't out of the ordinary for the applications team to forget to involve the operations team in a timely manner. Developers work long hard hours to get the system ready for deployment and then realize they need the assistance of the operations team. The call goes out to the ops team the week before go-live and they are expected to stand up servers, procure networking gear, and have the environment ready for the new application by go-live. This is often impossible on short notice. Integrating these teams helps to eliminate communication issues and improves turnaround times, ensures the solutions being developed fit within the technology environment, ensures the team members are working on the same project or priorities, and enhances collaboration.

When you add digital security operations to the mix, you have a *DevSecOps* team. This team performs the same functions the DevOps team does while incorporating cyber- and digital security operations into the framework. The idea is to provide synergies between teams and functions so that projects are delivered more quickly with more reliability and fidelity.

Development Life Cycle Methodologies

A *development life cycle* consists of the phases of the project associated with producing the product, service, or result of the project. A development life cycle is performed within the project life cycle.

The CompTIA objectives describe several development life cycle methodologies or frameworks used on IT projects. The grandfather of them all is the *software development life cycle (SDLC)*. This methodology has been around for many years and is used to assist in delivering high-quality software. The SDLC consists of several development phases that define the life cycle for creating software applications. A *phase* generally consists of segments of work that allow for easier management, planning, and control of the work and generally produce at least one deliverable by the end of the phase. The work and the deliverables produced during a phase are typically unique to that phase. The work of each phase is usually distinct and not repeated in other phases. Each phase has an emphasis on a different portion of the development activities, and different project management phases are performed during each phase. This phased approach is commonly used in a waterfall methodology. We'll cover that shortly.

There are differing versions of the SDLC phases, but most include at least the following.

Planning   This involves determining scope, what problem are we trying to solve, resources, costs, and more.

Defining   The functional requirements are defined here. This involves determining the "what" the application should do.

Designing   The system design involves determining the specifications of the system and defining the features of the requirements.

Building   This is the actual process of writing the code.

Testing   Testing of the code is performed by the quality assurance team, end users, and others. This ensures the application works as intended and the requirements, features, and functionality perform as designed.

Deploying   After testing is performed and corrections are made to code and retested, the code is deployed to production, where end users can access and use the application.

SDLC methodologies encompass two categories: waterfall and agile. I will discuss them in detail next.

Using the Waterfall Methodology

A *waterfall* approach, also known as a predictive methodology, is a step-by-step methodology whereby each stage of the project work is completed in order. Typically, you don't move from one stage to another until the previous stage is completed, although there are exceptions that we'll get to later in this section. For example, once the project is kicked off, requirements are defined in detail and approved before any programming work begins. In this approach, it is difficult to change requirements or incorporate new ideas as the project progresses. The customer may not see any deliverables or functionality, or understand if business value is being created until the project is close to the end of its life cycle.

The waterfall development life cycle approach defines the scope and deliverable at the beginning of the life cycle. Changes are monitored closely and typically permitted only if they are essential for completing the project. Each development life cycle phase must be completed before moving to the next.

Waterfall or predictive life cycles are an excellent choice for projects where the requirements are well understood, the project is low risk, and the project team is well established and stable.

Using Agile Methodologies

Agile is a method of managing projects in small, incremental portions of work that can be easily assigned, easily managed, and completed within a short period of time. An agile project has continually evolving requirements, a high degree of uncertainty, and high risk. Small increments of work are produced in each iteration that the customer reviews for accuracy and completeness. Prototypes are often used for this review. This methodology provides frequent feedback to the team and allows them to adapt to new requirements and make modifications to the work so that the deliverables align with customer expectations. It also allows the team to perform a continual assessment of the goals, deliverables, and functionality of the product.

You'll want to choose an agile methodology when active participation of your stakeholders is required throughout the project, when you are not certain of all the requirements at the beginning of the project, when the project is high risk, or when you work in a changing environment.

Agile is a highly iterative approach where requirements can be continually defined and refined based on continuous feedback from the product owner. This allows the development team to quickly adapt to changes and accommodate new or modified functionality requests.

Agile has been around for many years in one form or another. In 2001, several software developers converged to formalize the agile approach. They published the *Manifesto for Agile Software Development* (http://agilemanifesto.org) and identified 12 principles that are the focus of any agile approach. These principles include factors such as daily interactions between the business and agile teams, frequent deliverables, and self-motivated teams, with a focus on continuous improvement.

One of the key principles in the *Agile Manifesto* is the focus on the value to the customer. Instead of measuring how efficient a certain process runs or the quality of a deliverable, attention is given to the value the customer perceives. For example, this value may include a tangible deliverable that contains functionality that's critical to the success of the project; business value is thereby created during each period of work. Rather than measuring project success based on the "on time and on budget" approach, success is measured by the progress made in incremental steps and the value that the functionality or deliverables bring to the stakeholders as the project is progressively elaborated.

There are several agile methodologies to choose from. All of them have elements that can be applied to your next project. We'll look at several versions of agile next.

Scrum

Scrum is a form of agile project management. Scrum project teams consist of cross-functional team members from various areas of the organization and are self-organized and self-directed. Scrum emphasizes daily communication and the flexible reassessment of plans, which are carried out in short, iterative phases of work called *sprints*. Sprints are always time-bound and generally consist of two-week time periods, but they can consist of any short period of time defined and agreed on by the team. The goal of the sprint is to produce a deliverable, or a tangible portion of a deliverable, by the end of the sprint. Sprint is a term that is specific to the Scrum methodology. Other agile methodologies use this same time-bound approach and call these short work periods *iterations*.

Scrum is most used in software development projects. Using this approach, a development team can assess results and adjust processes in order to meet new or modified requirements during or after each sprint. Prototypes can be delivered early and tangible progress is made in each sprint. Scrum requirements are documented and managed by the product owner, who is the liaison between the stakeholders and the Scrum team. Scrum teams should only have one product owner. Scrum requirements are known as user stories, and they are kept in a product backlog to be pulled at the beginning of each sprint. I will cover user stories and product backlogs in detail in the section, "Determining Scope on Agile Projects" later in this chapter.

Kanban

Kanban is a lean scheduling agile methodology that was developed by the Toyota Motor Corporation. Kanban is an agile project management methodology that is typically seen in manufacturing projects, but it also makes a presence in the information technology field. With Kanban, the work is balanced against available resources or available capacity for work. It's a pull-based concept where work progresses to the next step only when resources are available. It's also considered an on-demand scheduling methodology because the work is pulled through the system according to demand.

Kanban means "billboard" or "sign." Using Kanban, you construct a board that represents your project. The Kanban board can be physical, like a whiteboard, or you can use software to manage the board. The Kanban board is simple to construct and looks some-what like Figure 4.2 in the beginning of the project.

FIGURE 4.2   Kanban board at the start of the project

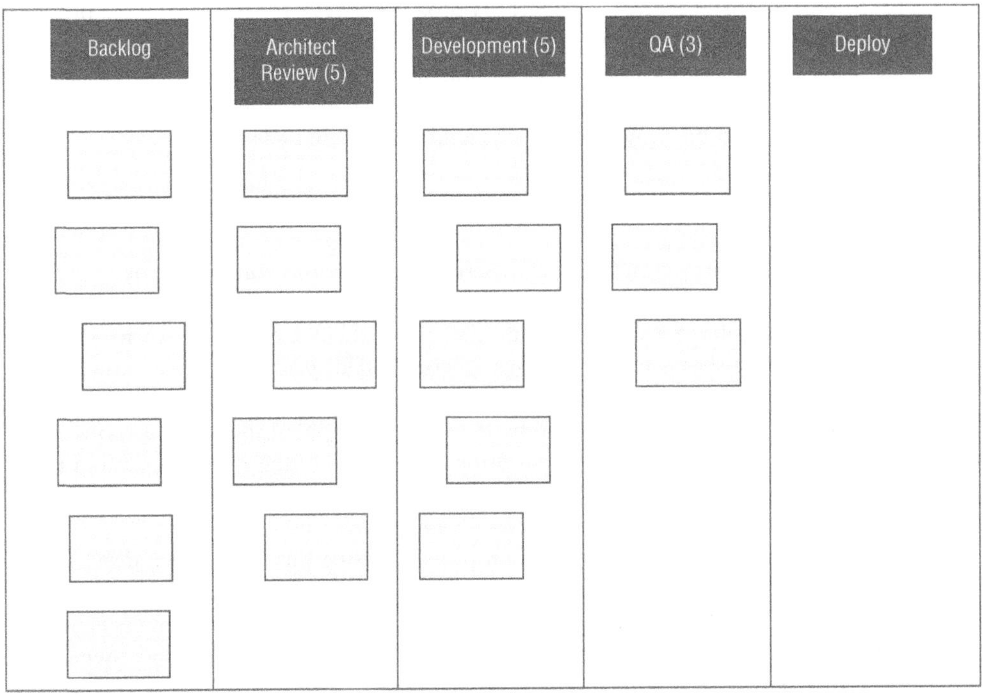

Any number of columns can exist between the Product Backlog and Done columns. It's up to the team to define the stages of work represented by the columns on the board.

Kanban consists of one or more product owners, who are responsible for creating the work list. Each of the tasks are called user stories, tasks, or cards. In Figure 4.2, each of the sticky notes represents a task. Initially the product backlog contains all the notes, but as the project begins and team members start to work on tasks, the notes are moved from the prod-uct backlog to the next column to the right. As a task is completed in a given column, it is moved to the next column to the right, and so on. Once a note has vacated a column, a new note can move into its place. You can use the terms *story*, *task*, or *card* interchangeably. They all mean the same thing: time-bound modularized tasks with discrete deliverables.

In this regard, Kanban is like Scrum. Both are called *pull systems*, meaning that as a task moves from one column or state to the next, a new task is pulled from the previous column or previous state. However, unlike Scrum, which uses sprints that typically consist of two to four weeks' worth of work, Kanban is a continuous system. The work does not start and stop but continues through to completion. There are no sprints in Kanban. The Kanban methodology may involve more than one team working on different functional aspects of the work, although they all work from the same Kanban board in a continuous manner.

Scrumban

This methodology is a hybrid between Scrum and Kanban. The idea is that the work is organized in sprints, as in traditional Scrum, but uses a Kanban board to display the work of the sprint and monitor work in progress. Daily standups are held to review progress and determine whether any obstacles exist that stand in the way of the team. The Kanban board is a good visual backdrop when holding the standups because the team can see the progress of the work and answer the three questions during the standup. The Scrum team roles can be used in this methodology (Scrum master, team members, and product owner, as discussed in the next section).

Lean

Lean is another agile methodology that is concerned with making work processes as efficient as possible while also assuring that the quality of the output is excellent. Lean thinking aims to reduce or eliminate waste. Much of lean thinking is derived from Toyota executives, among them Taiichi Ohno. Although thinking lean is primarily focused on manufacturing, it does not mean that the principles cannot be used in other project management efforts.

Kaizen is a lean methodology. Kaizen means "continuous improvement" in Japanese. The idea behind Kaizen is to continually improve service and quality and reduce waste. Waste is anything the project team is doing that doesn't add value to the process. The foundational belief of Kaizen is that everything can be improved. Kaizen involves every person in the organization—from the CEO to project managers to line workers. They are charged with looking at their job and activities in a new light and finding ways to improve productivity and decrease waste in small steps over time. This isn't about looking for a large, onerous problem (although if you find one, you should deal with it) but about looking for small things that produce inefficiencies or waste in the process. For example, perhaps your PMO requires approvals and signoffs on every document and nearly every task performed on the project. This is likely overkill, and eliminating many of the unnecessary approvals can free up the project managers to work on actual project tasks, thereby delivering project value more quickly. Other examples that come to mind are holding too many meetings that don't add value, implementing tools or processes that aren't effective and that the team avoids using, and requiring too much movement because team members are in different physical locations across the city or the globe. This philosophy could be applied to any number of activities.

Using the Kaizen approach, workers look for places where the seven wastes may appear and then take steps to reduce or eliminate them. The seven wastes are listed here. Reducing or eliminating them by changing your work to make it more efficient is the essence of Kaizen.

Motion   This concerns the movement, or amount of motion, employees go through while performing their work. Examine whether they move too much or too little.

Waiting   Examine whether workers have times where they are simply waiting for the next task and find ways to decrease that wasted time.

Transportation   Moving items or elements of work takes time; put the items needed to complete a task next to the employee.

Storage   Storing materials for tasks or storing completed items for shipment can create waste. Keep materials and supplies organized and easily accessible to employees to reduce waste.

Defects   Defects may be introduced by manufacturing defective parts or by making mistakes in the work. Examine the causes of defects and determine ways to eliminate them.

Processing   This could involve creating too much or too little effort when processing goods or services. Reducing efforts in processing will reduce waste.

Overproduction   This involves making too much of something. This could impact waiting times or storage as well.

Extreme Programming

Extreme Programming (XP) is another agile methodology used in software development. Technology changes rapidly and development teams today do not usually have the luxury of taking years to develop new products. XP involves delivering the software that's needed when the customer needs it. Consider using XP under these conditions:

- When there are dynamically changing user requirements. This typically happens when the customer, or end user, doesn't have a clear idea of what they need.
- When a high amount of risk is associated with the project.
- When you have small development teams of between two and 12 programmers.

XP requires that all project team members work together collaboratively to create the product of the project. They need to work side by side in order to bring about cohesiveness and be able to collaborate instantly. XP also requires automated unit and functional tests. Unit tests are tests on small, whole units of code to determine whether the code is functional. Integration testing involves testing several pieces of the code together to see if they perform as expected. Functional testing is an end-to-end test to ensure the code works throughout the entire process.

XP operates on a set of core values that will help improve software projects:

- Communication
- Simplicity
- Feedback

- Courage

- Respect

XP encourages teams to sit together in a collocated workspace. Programmers share code and make use of *refactoring* techniques whereby they can improve the quality of the code without changing its functionality. Refactoring reduces duplication and eliminates poor code. The idea is to start with a solid, simple design and test the code often, which will help the team increase the speed in which they can program.

XP delivers business value in each iteration and starts with creating *story cards*. Story cards are like user stories and contain requirements, features, and functionality. The story cards are designed in an incremental fashion, much like other agile methodologies. As the project progresses, more information is known and more requirements are developed. The user stories are worked on by pairs of programmers and as a group. There is never a single programmer working alone in this methodology. They perform what's known as *pair programming*. That is, there are always two developers working in pairs at the same computer. It's important that programmers use a consistent style and pattern when writing the code so that all team members can understand what's been done. Having two programmers work on the same code increases the quality of the code because there are two people writing and reviewing the code and one may see something the other does not.

As in other agile methodologies, XP relies heavily on feedback. One important form of feedback comes from *test-driven development*, or a test-first approach. As code is released by the pair programmers, it is tested rigorously. The tests for the new code are combined with existing unit tests, and all the tests are run each time there is a release. Each test is run against the entire program (including the new code) and all the tests, including the new test, must pass with no errors. Code may be released twice a day or more, so this provides a significant amount of feedback for the team.

XP also concerns continuous integration. Everyone on the team has a shared meaning of what the end product looks like. The XP process keeps all the work integrated continuously throughout the project. For example, once testing is completed for a particular piece of code, it is kept up and running correctly throughout the remainder of the iteration (and project) and becomes integrated into new code or functionality as the project progresses.

XP may use both release planning and iteration planning to accomplish work. At the end of each iteration, the team delivers a functioning piece of software to the customer that they can use and/or validate meets the business value. There isn't a set time frame for iterations, but they can vary from daily to quarterly, depending on the project.

Here is a list of the benefits and techniques of the XP methodology:

- Delivers business value in each iteration.

- Based on frequent cycles, delivers software to the customer when they need it.

- Encourages collocation of team members.

- User stories are worked on by pair programmers at the same computer, which improves quality of the code.

- Refactoring reduces duplication and eliminates poor code.

- Test-driven development provides significant feedback to the team because tests for new code are combined with existing unit tests and all the tests are run each time there is a release.
- Tests must pass with no errors in every iteration.
- Keeps all of the work integrated continuously.
- May use both release planning and iteration planning.

Feature-Driven Development

The feature-driven development (FDD) methodology was developed to address large software development projects. It focuses on delivering usable, working software continually in a timely manner. It consists of a five-step approach to develop code rapidly:

- Developing a model
- Creating a features list
- Planning based on features
- Designing based on features
- Building based on features

FDD is a simple, five-step approach that allows teams to develop code rapidly. The first three steps are the Planning phase. First is developing the model on which the team will build the solution and creating the features list that contains all the functionality the end product should include. The features are then broken down into components of work that each team will build during an iteration. The last two steps, design and build, are the development phase and are typically performed in short iterations of two weeks or less. If a feature takes more than two weeks to complete, it will be broken down in the planning step into smaller components that can be completed during the iteration.

FDD is performed using software development best practices. FDD assumes the team has a predefined set of standards for development and that by using these standards, they can move quickly. FDD works well for large projects but not so well for small development projects. This methodology relies on a more top-down approach to decision-making than other methodologies, due to the size of the project.

There are six roles in this methodology: project manager, chief architect, development manager, chief programmer, class owner, and domain expert. Team members may take on one or more of these roles at any one time. Stakeholders in the FDD methodology are called clients.

Dynamic Systems Development Method

The dynamic systems development method (DSDM) was introduced in the mid-1990s as a software development methodology that focuses on the entire project life cycle. It has been revised over the years so that the methodology can be used for any project, not just software development projects. At the onset of the project, DSDM establishes the cost of the project, the quality standards, and the time frame to completion and, as such, is constraint-driven. Scope is prioritized to meet the cost, quality, and time frame constraints. There are eight guiding principles of DSDM:

- Focus on the business need.
- Ensure on-time delivery.
- Collaborate with team members and stakeholders.
- Never compromise on quality.
- Build incrementally.
- Use iterative development techniques.
- Use continual communications that are clear and concise.
- Demonstrate control.

Agile Unified Process

The Agile Unified Process (AUP or AgileUP) methodology is also used in software development projects. It incorporates several other agile processes that help improve productivity. It is an iterative approach that includes feedback during the work cycle (before the end product is delivered).

The benefits of AUP are based on the following philosophies and disciplines:

- Team members who know what they're doing and can work on their own with occasional high-level guidance
- Simplicity in the process and documentation
- Agility by following agile processes and principles
- A focus only on activities that produce high value
- Tool independence, which allows team members to choose the tools they want to use to perform the work
- Tailoring of AUP techniques to fit the organization and team's needs
- Situationally specific, much like tailoring, using AUP when appropriate and efficient

Hybrid

A hybrid methodology is just like the name implies: it's a combination of one or more methodologies to create what works best for your team. This combination could include aspects of waterfall and agile methodologies, or a combination of various agile methodologies. Hybrid does not mean that there is an equal distribution of methodologies. You may work on a project where a waterfall approach is used to document requirements and it accounts for a third of the project time. The remainder of the project will utilize an agile approach, but the combination of approaches means this is technically a hybrid development life cycle. Consider using a hybrid approach when there is uncertainty or complexity, or there are uncertain risks about the project requirements. Then switch to a predictive approach to perform the work of the project. I have used this approach when managing technology projects. The customer may have some idea about the functionality required but can't articulate what the final product should look like. They may express it this way: "I'll know it when I see it." Using an agile approach, we can produce a prototype and continually evolve the requirements as the project progresses.

Hybrid is a great methodology to use to introduce the team and the organization to the principles of agile. You might start the team out on a simple project (one without a lot of risk to the organization), working in iterations and obtaining continual feedback from the customer. As the team learns and becomes increasingly comfortable with this methodology, you can graduate to using agile on more complex projects. A good friend of mine calls the combination of waterfall and agile "Wagile."

We have looked at each of these methodologies independently. However, it is possible, and very popular, to combine the approaches. For example, combining an iteration-based approached with a flow-based approach (such as Scrum and Kanban) as we discussed in the "Scrumban" section earlier, brings the best of both approaches to the team. You can use time-bound iterations to produce work while using the Kanban board to visually see capacity constraints, bottlenecks, and where tasks are in the workflow.

It's also possible to combine Scrum, Kanban, and XP. Scrum utilizes the product backlog and user stories while visually displaying the flow of the work on the Kanban board. Work can be managed using capacity limits in each workflow. The XP principles, such as using test-driven development, working in a continuous integration fashion, and refactoring, all help to improve the team's effectiveness.

Summary of Project Life Cycles

Life cycles, as you'll recall from an earlier section in this chapter, are all the phases a project progresses through from the beginning of the project to the end.

Table 4.2 highlights the differences in the life cycles between an agile approach (highly adaptive) and a waterfall approach (highly predictive), with the hybrid of the two methodologies in the middle of the chart. This hybrid column could read "It depends" for every entry, because the more the organization leans toward waterfall, the more the hybrid approach will behave as waterfall does and will produce similar results. If it's more agile, the approach will be iterative in nature and behave like an agile approach.

TABLE 4.2   Life cycle differences

	Highly predictive (waterfall)	Hybrid	Highly adaptive (agile)
Requirements	Detailed specifications.	High-level planning with iterative refinements.	Progressively elaborated during each iteration.
Risks	A good deal of time is spent at the beginning of the project identifying risks. They are continually identified throughout the project.	Risks are iteratively identified throughout the project.	Risks are identified at the beginning of each iteration.
Costs	A good deal of time is spent at the beginning of the project documenting costs. Once the budget is established, changes must be requested using the change control process.	Costs may be identified at the beginning of the project, with some consideration for changes as the project progresses.	Costs are identified at each of the iterations. A high-level budget may be established at the beginning of the project, but cost and time estimates are determined at the beginning of the iteration.
Stakeholders	Heavily involved in gathering and documenting requirements. Their involvement tapers off as the project progresses.	More involvement than the highly predictive approach and less involvement than the highly adaptive approach.	Continuous involvement and frequent feedback because the stakeholders work beside the project team.
Schedule	Created once for the project, and changes must be approved via the change control process.	May be created once with high-level milestones and further defined as the project progresses.	Each iteration is its own schedule. The work of the iteration is defined at the beginning of each iteration.
Planning	Once the plan is approved, changes that impact scope, time, or budget are controlled and minimized.	A high-level plan is developed at the beginning of the project and further elaborated as the project progresses.	There is progressive elaboration of scope in each iteration based on continuous feedback.

Selecting a Methodology

Selecting a methodology for your project can be a daunting task, especially for teams new to agile. I've found that combining aspects of two or three methodologies is the best approach. This allows the team to tailor the best of the methodologies to the organization and to the project. Combining approaches tends to increase the effectiveness of the team and creates a synergy that will exceed what any individual team member can contribute on their own.

Each project, and each organization, has its own set of unique characteristics that should be examined when choosing a methodology or a combination of them. The CompTIA Project+ exam objectives outline several factors:

Tolerance for Change/Flexibility   The organization's tolerance for change and flexibility should be considered when choosing an agile approach. Agile is highly adaptive and change must be encouraged and embraced. If the organization is not receptive to change, a waterfall methodology may be more appropriate. For example, some organizations are embedded in tradition, methods, and frameworks and may not have the ability to change quickly. Others may be cutting-edge startups or progressive organizations always on the lookout to improve. They are willing to take risks on new methodologies and jump in with both feet. You'll need to examine not only the organization, but the departments within the organization involved on the project to determine their tolerance for change. For those organizations embedded in tradition, your best option is to use the established methodology and incorporate aspects of others you'd like to introduce to the team. Perhaps start with waterfall and create the project plan as you normally do and then incorporate some agile techniques as the work of the project gets underway.

Requirements   Project requirements can help drive the methodology you'll use to run the project. For example, waterfall is an excellent choice for projects where the requirements are well understood and well-defined. Agile is best when you are not certain of all the requirements at the beginning of the project and when you know they will likely change and evolve as the project progresses.

Budget   Budgets can influence your choice of methodology because of the differing ways costs are estimated and calculated on waterfall versus agile projects. On a waterfall project, the budget is derived from the project management plan. The estimates for activities and resources are thoroughly calculated and monitored throughout the project. The total cost of the project is calculated up front. Agile projects estimate costs as they go, at the beginning of each iteration. It is possible to determine a rough order of magnitude estimate with agile, but if requirements are mostly unknown or will change throughout the project, the total costs can be substantially different than the estimates.

Schedules   Schedules can influence your choice of methodology in similar ways that budgets can. Schedules are determined in great detail when using a waterfall methodology with major milestones and deliverables plotted on the schedule. Agile projects don't run on a predetermined schedule. They use iterations, or sprints, that are usually time -boxed periods of time. Tasks, time estimates, cost estimates, and more are determined at the beginning of the iteration. It is possible to come up with a rough order of magnitude estimate for the overall schedule, but just like with budgets, if the requirements are largely unknown or subject to a good deal of change throughout the project, the estimate won't likely be accurate.

Environmental Factors   Environmental factors are closely related to culture, which we'll discuss next. The organization's physical structure or geography is one environmental factor that should be considered. Agile team members sit near each other, often within the same room. This is the most effective way to engage all team members and keep them focused on the iteration. If agile teams are spread out across multiple locations, they aren't as effective as being collocated. You can overcome some of these issues using teleconferencing and other techniques we will discuss in Chapter 6, "Resource Planning and Management."

Waterfall teams are not necessarily collocated and, in my experience, only tend to meet together at a project or status meeting. There are occasions where the team meets together to define requirements or to discuss a particularly difficult issue, but by and large they sit in their own departments at their own desks and come together at the next project status meeting. Consider whether your organization has the space to collocate agile teams and provide the resources such as whiteboards, monitors, and so on to assist the team with the iteration. This can be accomplished virtually as well with videoconferencing resources, chat rooms, virtual whiteboards, and more. This requires the organization have the technology and bandwidth to support the setup.

Risk tolerance is another environmental factor to consider. Agile projects are typically high risk, and the process of agile also contains risk because if it's not conducted well, the team could be in an endless loop of developing and modifying and never get to the end result. Waterfall projects examine all risks and have a clear understanding of the final results before the work begins.

Culture   The organization's culture will influence your decision when choosing methodologies. For example, an agile project requires a culture of learning and continual improvement. Mistakes are tolerated, almost encouraged, but real learning must occur from the mistakes and applied to future behavior. A culture of teamwork and collaboration versus individual contributors is highly valued on agile projects. The team operates as a whole, with both business users and IT developers sitting side by side. No team member is more important than another, and decisions are made by the team. Agile teams are empowered to make decisions and do not need to stop work to escalate to a project manager or key stakeholder. Waterfall projects tend to follow a more traditional approach. Teams typically have an established hierarchy, issues are escalated to the project manager and beyond when needed, mistakes are minimally tolerated, and the team can make recommendations but final decisions belong to the project manager and/ or project sponsor.

Developmental   Developmental standards and considerations apply heavily to choosing among multiple agile methodologies. In this category, be sure to consider elements such as the team's communication skills, knowledge and ability of team members, team members' experience with the agile methodology you're choosing, the size of the project, criticality of the project, business users' collaboration, and so on.

Industry Standards   Industry standards may dictate the type of methodology you'll use for the project. Perhaps you are required to report progress at certain points along the project, or specific quality criteria must be met, or regulations dictate the characteristics of the deliverables, and more. Any number of factors may apply in this category, so be sure to find out what industry standards may impact your project and consider how meeting those requirements will work within the methodology you're using.

Keep in mind that all of the factors discussed in this section apply to choosing waterfall versus agile, as well as choosing among multiple agile methodologies.

Determining Scope on Agile Projects

Agile projects define scope and requirements as the work progresses. The requirements on a Scrum and Kanban project are known as *user stories*. User stories document the functionality or requirement of the application and the person or people who will benefit from this requirement. This isn't usually a named person but rather a role, responsibility, or department. The "who" of the user stories are known as actors. The user story should be written from the perspective of the customer using plain language. It should contain a brief description of the features or functionality that are desired by the actor. It also describes why the requirement is needed by the actor and why it's valuable to them.

User stories should be small, detailed units of work that the team can understand and finish during an iteration. They should contain acceptance criteria so that the team can test or measure whether the deliverable meets the criteria at the end of the iteration.

A *product backlog* contains all the user stories that are needed to complete the project. The user stories will be created throughout the project and added to the backlog as the project progresses. However, you need enough user stories in the product backlog to start the work, so some of them will be created before the work begins.

The product owner (this is the liaison on the agile team who speaks on behalf of the stakeholders) is responsible for maintaining and prioritizing the product backlog. The user stories are prioritized so that the most important are at the top of the backlog list and those with less importance fall beneath these on the list. The product owner will pull user stories from the backlog at the beginning of the iteration and give them to the team. The team estimates the amount of work involved to complete each user story at the beginning of the iteration and breaks them down into tasks that can be accomplished during the iteration. The completed products are released at the end of the iteration for the customer to validate. User stories that were not completed in the previous iteration, or those that require changes, along with new user stories are chosen for the next iteration, and the cycle repeats until the project is completed.

When using a Scrum methodology, the project team will create what's known as the *minimum viable product (MVP)* during each iteration. This involves producing tangible outputs that have enough features and functionality to allow the customer to examine them and provide feedback to the team. These results should be produced quickly, with as little effort as possible. This might take the form of a prototype or mock-up. It's a test of sorts to see what the customer wants and whether the prototype produces positive results and realizes business value. It isn't a full version of the final product, but it does represent the end product. It gives the organization, and the project team, data and information about what the customer likes, what works, and what doesn't. The idea is that the product owner or customer can "see" the deliverable and realize the value it brings to the project in a short time frame. Adjustments can be made quickly if business value is not realized or problems are spotted.

 The minimum viable product is used to validate whether the product has value, if the results meet the needs of the customers, and it allows the team to adapt the product based on feedback as they learn more about the customer and the product.

Agile Team Members

Agile teams are cross-functional teams that consist of members from several departments across the organization. They are self-organized and self-directed and are usually small in number. An agile development team rarely has more than five to nine members, and seven members is the ideal number. One of the greatest benefits of agile teams is active stakeholder involvement in all aspects of the project. Agile is a flexible methodology that is highly interactive. It encourages a great deal of communication among the team. It keeps the stakeholders and project team members engaged and utilizes a facilitated process so that the team can interact daily.

Scrum is one of the most well-known agile processes used on software development projects. Scrum teams are self-directed, self-managed, adaptable, and highly aware of customer needs. Scrum uses the term sprints to describe the iteration. The Scrum team consists of several members: team facilitator, product owner, stakeholders, and cross-functional team members. Here is a brief description of each:

Scrum Master   The Scrum master coordinates the work of the sprint. They also run interference between the team and distractions that might keep them from the work at hand. Scrum masters are facilitators and help educate others in the agile process. They typically do not perform development tasks, but they assist the product owner in maintaining the backlog, prioritizing work, and defining when the work is done. The Scrum master is a facilitator and not a manager. Project team members do not report to the Scrum master.

Product Owner   The *product owner* represents the stakeholders and is the liaison between the stakeholders and the Scrum master. Product owners speak on behalf of the business unit, customer, or the end user of the product and are considered the *voice of the customer*. There should be only one product owner on a Scrum team, but Kanban teams may have more than one product owner. Communicating with the stakeholders is a critical responsibility of product owners. They communicate progress and milestones achieved. They determine project scope and schedule, and they request the funding needed to complete the work of the project. They manage and prioritize the backlog, which contains the user stories the Scrum team will work on in each sprint.

Stakeholders   Stakeholders are people with a vested interest in the project or the outcomes of the project. They interface with the product owner, who informs them of work progress. It's the product owner's responsibility to keep the stakeholders informed.

Team Members   Team members are responsible for completing backlog items. They sign up for tasks associated with user stories that have been chosen for the sprint, based on the priority of the work and their skill sets. They establish estimates for the work and take on enough tasks to fill the sprint. Agile teams are self-directed, self-organized, and self-managed.

Determine a Solutions Design

We'll switch gears in this section and talk about solutions design. This involves determining how to configure the solution, typically a software program, application, or other technology deployment, to meet the needs of the business. A *solutions architect* is the person responsible for this task. They work with the enterprise architect that we talked about in Chapter 3 to ensure the solution fits within the IT enterprise and to ensure it meets the overall objectives of the organization. They also work with the development team to determine a design, develop prototypes, and measure the outcomes to ensure the final product meets the business expectations. The solution architect must understand the business problem the software or technology product is trying to solve. They also need to know how the business performs that function today and how the technology solution will improve the pain points business staff members are experiencing.

The solutions architect assists the business analyst in requirements gathering, recommends technology frameworks for the final solution, examines and evaluates risk, and determines how the ongoing support for this system will be incorporated into the organization. Ultimately, the solutions architect is responsible for finding the technical solution that will best solve the business problem and then implementing it. They work closely with the business users and must be able to speak with them in common language. (No tech jargon allowed—they can use all the tech jargon they like when working with the development team to design and develop the solution.) Finally, the solutions architect also must work closely with the project manager. They will act as the liaison between the business, project manager, and the development team to ensure requirements and other information are translated accurately and produced in a timely manner. Keep in mind that the solution may encompass several aspects of IT that we've discussed previously, such as cloud development, multitiered architecture, networking, storage, databases, DevOps, project management fundamentals, and more. The solutions architect must be well versed in all aspects of IT.

 Real World Scenario

Main Street Office Move

After the kickoff meeting, you're ready to write the scope statement. Your scope statement contains the following elements:

Project Objectives   To bring together all employees into one building. This move will improve communication, reduce travel costs, improve productivity, and reduce lease costs. This project will relocate 1,200 employees from three locations to the Main Street Office Building location. The move will be completed by December 31. All employees will report to work on January 2 at the Main Street Office Building. The data center move to the cloud will be completed by December 31 and all employees will have access to systems needed to perform their jobs on January 2 when they report to work at the new location.

Acceptance Criteria   The move will be made on time and on budget, with minimal disruption to employees. Employees will return to work on January 2, and their computers and phones will be available for use, the printers will be online, all office spaces will be completed (including pictures hung on the walls), and office kitchens will be fully stocked with beverages and snacks. All fleet cars will be moved to the new garage located in the new building and will be available for checkout on January 2. The designated systems, services, and applications will be moved to the IaaS provider and will be fully tested and functional by December 31.

Major Deliverables   The deliverables include the following:

- Communication to all employees regarding the purpose for the move and instructions regarding packing belongings, location of the new office, and timelines. Communication should occur in multiple forms at least five times before the move.

- Procure the services of a moving company to move boxes and furniture. The procurement process to start nine months prior to the move date.

- Procure general contracting services and perform building remodeling on the three floors occupied by Kate's organization.

- Survey the Main Street Office Building and work with functional managers to determine seating charts.

- Procure new office furniture. Delivery and setup between December 15 and December 31.

- Procure and install cubicle furnishings.

- Work with an interior designer to maximize space and provide aesthetically pleasing workspace and common areas.

- Install employee desktops, peripherals, and telephones.

- Install three networked printers on each floor.

- Relocate fleet cars to the new garage.

- Perform system assessments and migration plans for the systems, services, and applications being moved to the cloud.

Exclusions from Scope   This project does not include moving the satellite office located 90 miles south of the three main campuses.

Time and Cost Estimates   The high-level budget for this project is $450,000.

The high-level timeline for this project is 12 months. Kickoff occurred December 27. The move will occur 12 months from that date.

Assumptions   You have the following assumptions:

- Employees are supportive of the move.

- Moving companies are available during the move week.

- Employees will have personal belongings packed and removed from the premises prior to the move.

- Furniture is delivered on time.

- All sites will provide reasonable access for installers and movers.

- The IaaS provider will assign a project manager from their organization to work with the IT team.

Constraints   December 31 completion date.

$450,000 budget.

You discovered new deliverables and a stakeholder who was missed during the Initiating phase. You also changed one of the deliverables (procure moving company) to begin nine months prior to the move rather than six. The information technology (IT) team is integral to the success of this project as all employee workstations and phones must be set up and functioning before returning on January 2. IT will also manage the transition of the data center to the cloud as well as retiring the current data center. Additional deliverables and assumptions have been added to the scope statement.

Methodology Selection   The project team will use a hybrid approach to accomplish the project objectives. The move will be managed using a waterfall approach, and the initial assessments and Planning phases for the data center migration will also be waterfall. After planning is complete for the cloud deployment, the IT team will use an agile approach to migrate programs and shut down equipment on premises.

Summary

This was another action-packed chapter with lots of information for the exam. We kicked it off with scope planning, which starts with the scope management plan. The scope management plan documents the process you'll use to prepare the scope statement and WBS, a definition of how the deliverables will be verified, and a description of the process for controlling scope change requests.

The scope statement is the basis for many of the planning processes and future change decisions. It is also the basis for setting the boundaries of the project with the customer and stakeholders. A scope statement includes the product description, key deliverables, success and acceptance criteria, key performance indicators, exclusions, time and cost estimates, assumptions, and constraints. Work that is not listed in the scope statement is not included in the project.

Requirements describe the characteristics of the deliverables. They might also describe functionality that a deliverable must have or specific conditions a deliverable must meet to satisfy the objective of the project. They are typically conditions that must be met or criteria that the product or service of the project must possess to satisfy the objectives of the project. Requirements quantify and prioritize the wants, needs, and expectations of the project sponsor and stakeholders. They are documented in the scope statement or in a stand-alone requirements document. Requirements categories include business, functional, and non-functional. The requirements traceability matrix is a document that helps ensure the project meets expectations by linking each requirement to a project objective.

A project life cycle consists of the phases of the project from the start to the end. Most project life cycles include a beginning, Planning phase, performing phase, and Closing phase. These are not the same as the project management phases. Project management phases are preformed within the project life cycle.

PRINCE2 is a project management methodology that can be used for any size project in any industry. It manages the project in stages, step by step, to keep the project in control. DevOps is a framework whereby the development team and the operations team are embedded on one team. This facilitates collaboration, improved communications, and faster, more reliable delivery of systems.

A development life cycle consists of phases associated with producing the product or as a result of the project. SDLC is a common software development life cycle. This is performed within the project life cycle. SDLC includes waterfall and agile methodologies. Waterfall is a step-by-step approach whereby each stage of the work is completed in order. Agile is a method of managing projects in small, incremental portions of work that can be easily assigned, easily managed, and completed within a short period of time.

Agile consists of several methodologies, including Scrum, Kanban, Scrumban, lean, Extreme Programming, feature-driven development, dynamic systems development method, Agile Unified Process, hybrid, and more. Scrum is likely the most used agile methodology on development projects. Scrum teams work from user stories that are chosen at the beginning of a sprint and broken down into work tasks by the team. Scrum is a pull-based system. Kanban is also a pull-based concept where work progresses to the next step when resources are available. Kanban is not time-boxed like Scrum. XP involves delivering software that's needed when the customer needs it. Hybrid is any combination of methodologies.

Criteria for selecting a methodology include tolerance for change, requirements, budgets, schedules, environment factors, culture, developmental factors, and industry standards.

Agile projects, particularly Scrum and Kanban methodologies, use user stories to document requirements. The product owner writes the user stories and pulls them from the backlog (where user stories are kept until needed) at the beginning of the sprint. The team then breaks these down into manageable tasks and produces a minimally viable product (MVP) by the end of the sprint. An MVP is a prototype or mock-up of the final deliverable. It contains only enough features to determine if the product will meet the objectives.

Agile team members are cross-functional teams that are self-organized and self-directed. Scrum teams consist of a Scrum master, product owner, stakeholders, and team members who are often collocated to improve collaboration and communication.

Solutions design is the responsibility of a solutions architect. They work closely with the enterprise architect, the business users, and the project manager to find a technical solution that will best solve the business problem at hand, and then implement it.

Exam Essentials

Understand the purpose of the scope statement.   The scope statement is the basis of the agreement between the project team and the customer concerning what comprises the work of the project. It defines the deliverables and success criteria that will meet those objectives.

Be able to list the components of a scope statement.   A scope statement includes a project description, acceptance criteria, key deliverables, exclusions from scope, assumptions, and constraints. It could also contain a high-level time and cost estimate to complete the project.

Be able to define requirements.   Requirements describe the characteristics of the deliverables, or functionality that a deliverable must have, or specific conditions a deliverable must meet to satisfy the objective of the project.

Be able to define project constraints and assumptions.   Project constraints limit the options of the project team and restrict their actions. Sometimes constraints dictate actions. Time, budget, and scope are the most common constraints. Assumptions are conditions that are presumed to be true or real. They are both documented in the assumption log.

Be able to describe the PRINCE2 methodology.   PRINCE2 is a project management methodology that can be used for any size project in any industry. It manages the project in stages, step by step, to keep the project in control.

Understand the concept of the DevOps and DevSecOps framework.   DevOps combines the development team and operations team into one team to improve collaboration, communication, and deliver products more efficiently. DevSecOps adds security responsibilities to the team to deliver projects with fidelity.

Be able to describe SDLC.   The software development life cycle (SDLC) consists of phases such as planning, defining, designing, building, testing, and deploying. Waterfall and agile are types of SDLC methodologies.

Be able to name three types of development life cycles.   They are waterfall, agile, and hybrid.

Understand the hybrid development life cycle.   Hybrid is a combination of aspects of waterfall and agile, or a combination of multiple agile methodologies.

Be able to describe the agile project management methodology.   A method of managing projects in small, incremental portions of work that can be easily assigned, easily managed, and completed within a short period of time. Agile involves continuous stakeholder involvement and feedback.

Be able to describe the difference between Scrum and Kanban.   Scrum and Kanban are both agile methodologies. Scrum teams complete work in short, time-bound periods called sprints. Kanban is a continuous system. The work does not start and stop but continues through to completion. Kanban is also known as an on-demand scheduling system. Both Scrum and Kanban are known as pull systems.

Be able to name the key roles on a Scrum team. The key roles are the product owner (also known as the voice of the customer), the Scrum team members, and the Scrum master.

Be able to describe a minimum viable product. The minimum viable product involves breaking down tasks into tangible components that have enough features and functionality to allow the customer to examine value and provide feedback to the team. They are often prototypes or mock-ups.

Be able to describe the product backlog. The product backlog is a list of all the user stories that are needed to complete the project.

Be able to name several agile methodologies. Examples are Extreme Programming, Scrumban, feature-driven development, dynamic systems development method, and Agile Unified Process.

Understand the role of the solutions architect in solutions design. Solutions design is determining the best technical solution for the business problem at hand. The solutions architect is the person determining the solution and works closely with the enterprise architect, the business team, and the project manager to implement the solution.

Key Terms

agile

business requirements

critical success factors

DevOps

DevSecOps

Extreme Programming (XP)

functional requirements

iterative

Kaizen

Kanban

key performance indicators (KPIs)

lean

minimum viable product (MVP)

nonfunctional requirements

product backlog

product manager

product owner

product scope

project management plan

pull system

refactoring

scope baseline

scope creep

scope management plan

scope statement

software development life cycle (SDLC)

solutions architect

sprint

order of magnitude

pair programming

phase

PRINCE2

test-driven development

user stories

voice of the customer

waterfall

Review Questions

1. Which of the following is not a key component of scope planning?

   A. Work breakdown structure (WBS)

   B. Scope statement

   C. Project charter

   D. Scope management plan

2. The scope statement provides which of the following?

   A. A basis for a common understanding of the project and for making future decisions regarding the project

   B. A detailed list of all resources required for project completion

   C. A schedule of all the key project activities

   D. A process for managing change control

3. Which of the following are components of a scope statement? (Choose three.)

   A. General project approach

   B. Project description

   C. Assumptions and constraints

   D. Exclusions

   E. Stakeholder list

   F. High-level milestones

   G. Change request process

4. Which of the following describes influencers?

   A. Influencers can impact, change, or create a new constraint.

   B. Scope creep is an example of an influencer.

   C. Change request is an influencer.

   D. Interaction between constraints is an example of an influencer.

   E. All of the above.

   F. A, B, D.

5. Which of the following involves changing the project or product scope without considering the impacts it will have to the project schedule, budget, and scope statement?

   A. Change request

   B. Scope creep

   C. Stakeholder/management directive

   D. Quality deficiency

6. There are three primary constraints on most projects. Your customer, or project sponsor, will stipulate which of the three is the most important to them. Which three are the typical constraints found on the majority of projects? (Choose three.)

    A. Budget

    B. Team members

    C. Scope

    D. Quality

    E. Time

    F. Sponsors and stakeholders

    G. Scope management plan

7. Your sprint is nearing completion. The product owner reminds you they will not accept the deliverable unless it measures 3 centimeters exactly. If the measurements are off, the next sprint will be delayed, and the entire project could be at risk. This is an example of which of the following?

    A. Acceptance criteria

    B. Change request

    C. Stability of scope

    D. Product scope description

8. Agile project life cycle methodologies are characterized by which of the following? (Choose three.)

    A. Dividing tasks into small deliverables that can be completed in a short time frame.

    B. Using a step-by-step process where one task is completed followed by another.

    C. This methodology is used primarily in the software development industry but can be applied across other industry areas.

    D. This methodology allows the project team to quickly adapt to new requirements and receive continuous feedback.

9. Which of the following agile methodologies describes the seven wastes?

    A. Scrum

    B. Six Sigma

    C. Kaizen

    D. Kanban

10. Which of the following agile methodologies are a type of pull system? (Choose two.)

    A. Kaizen

    B. AUP

    C. Lean

    D. XP

    E. Scrum

    F. Kanban

11. Which agile methodology strongly encourages teams to sit in collocated workspaces and programmers make use of refactoring techniques?

    A. FDD

    B. XP

    C. Scrum

    D. Kanban

12. Which of the following are characteristics of a waterfall methodology? (Choose three.)

    A. The results of the work of the project are often not delivered until the end of the project.

    B. This methodology requires continuous feedback from your stakeholders throughout the project.

    C. Changes to the project require a review of project plans and documenting the changes in the project plan.

    D. Predictive methodologies might use a phased approach where deliverables are produced at the end of each phase.

    E. The project team reviews the work of the project with the stakeholders in an iterative fashion so that they can incorporate modifications to functionality in the next phase.

13. Which of the following are true regarding the *Agile Manifesto*? (Choose two.)

    A. It is concerned with the quality of the deliverable.

    B. Success is measured in incremental steps.

    C. The focus is on the value to the customer.

    D. It measures how efficient the process was performed.

    E. It is concerned with business process improvements.

14. Your project team has a solid idea of the requirements for the project up front. Some specific elements of the deliverables are known at this point. Not all deliverables have been completely defined yet. The team would like to start with the known requirements and specific deliverables and then change their approach later in the development phase to incrementally deliver results. What development life cycle does this describe?

    A. Incremental

    B. Predictive

    C. Hybrid

    D. Agile

15. You are using an agile project management methodology to deliver your project. During each iteration, you and the team members are breaking down tasks into tangible components that have enough features and functionality to allow the customer to examine value and provide feedback to the team. Which of the following are true regarding this question when using a Scrum methodology? (Choose two.)

    A. The product owner will determine whether the requirements have been achieved.

    B. The project team will manage and prioritize the product backlog and choose the user stories for the upcoming sprint that can be broken down to the minimum viable product.

    C. The Scrum master will assist the team in breaking down the user stories and assign each team member tasks for the upcoming iteration.

    D. You are creating the minimum viable product.

16. Which of the following are true regarding assisting the team in subdividing tasks into the minimum viable product?

   A. Each iteration will produce enough features to examine whether the product is viable.

   B. Each iteration will provide an opportunity for feedback on future iterations.

   C. The minimum viable product allows the customer to see or experience the results and business value that was created.

   D. All the options are correct.

17. You are working on a project where the requirements and scope are well-defined, but you know there will be changes when performing the work of the project. Your stakeholders will need to provide continuous feedback during the development stages of this project. Which of the following are true when determining the deliverables for the project? (Choose three.)

   A. You should use a waterfall approach to manage this project. You will document a project scope statement because it describes how the team will define and develop the work breakdown structure.

   B. You should use a hybrid approach for this project. Because the requirements and deliverables are well-defined, you may choose to document a project scope statement that further elaborates the deliverables of the project and serves as a basis for future project decisions.

   C. You should document the project scope statement so there is agreement between the project management team and the project customer and everyone knows what the work of the project will produce.

   D. You may choose to document the project scope statement because it assesses the reliability of the project scope and describes the process for verifying and accepting completed deliverables.

   E. You should use a hybrid approach for this project because the stakeholders would like to provide continuous feedback on the deliverables once the work of the project starts. User stories will be used to fulfill the deliverables of the project and will be pulled to the backlog.

18. You are a project manager for a plumbing supply company and are heading up a project that will replace the current inventory system. You have interviewed stakeholders and gathered their project requirements. Which of the following is true regarding this question?

   A. The requirements traceability matrix ties requirements to project objectives, business needs, WBS deliverables, product design, and test strategies and traces them through to project completion.

   B. Requirements documentation consists of formal, complex documents that include elements such as the business need of the project, functional requirements, nonfunctional requirements, impacts to others inside and outside the organization, and requirements assumptions and constraints.

   C. The requirements documentation details the work required to create the deliverables of the project, including deliverables description, product acceptance criteria, exclusions from requirements, and requirements assumptions and constraints.

   D. The requirements document lists the requirements and describes how they will be analyzed, documented, and managed throughout the project.

19. This person assists the business analyst in requirements gathering and serves as a translator of sorts between the business and development team. They are responsible for ensuring the technical solution will solve the business problem. What role does this question describe?

    A. Enterprise architect

    B. Scrum master

    C. Solutions architect

    D. Project manager

20. Which framework combines teams from different areas in IT to deliver projects faster, provide more reliable systems, and improve collaboration and communication among team members?

    A. XP

    B. DevOps

    C. PRINCE2

    D. FDD

Chapter

5

Creating the Project Schedule

THE COMPTIA PROJECT+ EXAM TOPICS COVERED IN THIS CHAPTER INCLUDE:

✓ **1.0 Project Management Concepts**

- 1.6 Given a scenario, apply schedule development and management activities and techniques

✓ **2.0 Project Life Cycle Phases**

- 2.3 Given a scenario, perform activities during the project planning phase

✓ **3.0 Tools and Documentation**

- 3.1 Given a scenario, use the appropriate tools throughout the project life cycle

- 3.3 Given a scenario, analyze quality and performance charts to inform project decisions

This chapter is all about defining units of work and creating a project schedule (for waterfall projects) and sprint planning (for agile projects). We will cover work breakdown structures, defining tasks, sequencing tasks, and establishing dependencies. Next, we'll look at the documents that comprise the project management plan, including several baselines. We will examine how to create a project schedule, establishing milestones, determining the critical path, and baselining the schedule. From there we will move on to examine how sprint planning works, including prioritizing the backlog, breaking down backlog items, estimating tasks for the sprint, creating burndown and burnup charts, and more. Here we go.

Creating the Work Breakdown Structure

The work breakdown structure is part of scope planning. You'll recall we started our discussion on scope planning in Chapter 4, "Planning the Project." In that chapter, we created the scope management plan, which defines the process for preparing the scope statement and the work breakdown structure, and we also discussed the scope statement and what it entails. Now we'll look at the final element of scope planning, which is the *work breakdown structure (WBS)*. The WBS is a deliverables-oriented hierarchy that defines all the work of the project. Each level of the WBS is a further breakdown of the level above it. *Decomposition* is the process of breaking down the high-level deliverables (and each successive level of the WBS) into smaller, more manageable work units. Once the work is broken down to the lowest level, you can establish time estimates, resource assignments, and cost estimates.

A WBS is one of the fundamental building blocks of project planning. It will be used as a reference to numerous other planning processes. It's also the basis for estimating activity duration, assigning resources to activities, estimating work effort, and creating a budget. Because the WBS is typically displayed as a graphical representation, it can be a great way of visually communicating the project scope. It contains more details of the deliverables than the scope statement does and helps further clarify the magnitude of the project deliverables.

The WBS puts boundaries around the project work because any work not included in the WBS is considered outside the scope of the project.

Decomposing the Major Deliverables

The quality of your WBS depends on having the right team members involved in its development. You won't want a large team of people to assist in this process, but it's helpful if you can involve some of your more experienced team members. Work with the business unit managers to get representation from each business area that has a major deliverable for the project.

A WBS is typically created using either a tree structure diagram or an outline form. The tree structure can be created using software, using a whiteboard, or using easel paper with sticky notes for each level and each component of the WBS. This allows the components to be moved around as you work through the process and get everything in proper order.

A typical WBS starts with the project itself at the topmost level. The next level consists of the major deliverables, project phases, or subprojects that support the main project. From there, each deliverable is decomposed into smaller and smaller units of work. The lowest level of any WBS is called the *work package level*. This is the level where resources, time, and cost estimates are determined. Work packages are assigned to team members or organizational units to complete the activities associated with this work.

Make sure that all the team members have reviewed the project charter, scope statement, and requirements document and have a clear understanding of all the deliverables. Have copies of these documents available as a reference. The team may go through several iterations of constructing the WBS before it's considered complete.

Figure 5.1 is an abbreviated example of a WBS for a conference event project.

FIGURE 5.1 Sample WBS

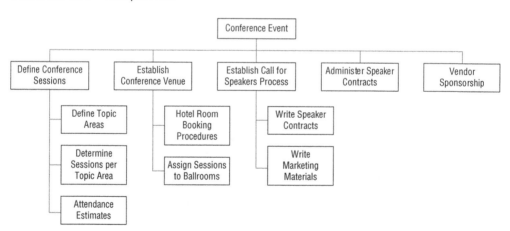

The second method for depicting a WBS is the outline form. Regardless of how you depict the WBS, each level in the WBS should have a unique identifier. This identifier is typically a number, and it's used to sum and track the costs, schedule, and resources associated with the WBS elements. These numbers are usually associated with the corporation's chart of accounts, which is used to track costs by category. Collectively, these numeric identifiers are known as the *code of accounts*. If you took the example from Figure 5.1 and converted it to outline form using the code of accounts, it would look like this:

Conference Event Project

1. Define conference sessions.

      1.1   Define topic areas.

      1.2   Determine number of sessions per topic.

      1.3   Determine approximate attendance at each session.

2. Establish conference venue.

      2.1   Research hotel booking procedures.

      2.2   Assign sessions to ballrooms.

3. Establish a call-for-speakers process.

      3.1   Write speaker contracts.

      3.2   Write marketing materials.

4. Administer speaker contracts.

5. Contact and sign up vendors for sponsorships.

> The project description, project scope, deliverables, and work breakdown structure will be progressively elaborated throughout the Planning phase. As more information becomes available and as you decompose deliverables, you may discover elements of scope or the deliverables that need additional detail or clarification.

Guidelines for Creating a WBS

Getting started creating a WBS can sometimes seem overwhelming. Once you start breaking down your deliverables into smaller units of work, it's tempting to immediately put these work units in logical order and start assigning them to team members. You'll need to keep reminding the group that the purpose of the WBS is to make certain each deliverable is identified (usually as a level 2 element) and that each subdeliverable is decomposed from there. This isn't the process where activities are put into logical order or where predecessor or successor work is determined. That will occur when the project schedule is developed. For now, focus on the deliverables and their decomposition.

Although there is no one right way to complete a WBS, there are some tips you can use to help be more successful. Here are some helpful guidelines to review with the project team before diving into a WBS session:

Recruit knowledgeable resources.   Do not try to complete the WBS yourself in the interest of saving time. If you are not an expert on the deliverables, you will miss key elements. You also want the team members to assist in this process so that they understand the work of the project and can see the level of effort needed to bring about a successful conclusion. Involving knowledgeable team members in the creation of a WBS is far more effective at communicating what the project is about than handing someone a completed WBS.

Each item in a lower level is a component of the level above.   Completing all the items at the lower levels of a WBS leads to the completion of the higher-level components. As a checkpoint, you should review the items at the lower level and ask the team whether completion of those items will result in completion of the components of the next higher level. If the answer to this question is no, then you have not identified all the lower-level tasks.

Define the work package level.   Make sure you work the WBS to a level where the team feels comfortable that resources can be assigned and held accountable for completing the work and estimates can be determined. This is the primary goal of constructing the WBS. Sequencing, assigning resources, and estimating are all separate activities that you will perform after the WBS is complete.

Do not create a to-do list.   You should not decompose work components into individual activities. Otherwise, you will spend your entire project management experience managing individual tasks for the work packages. The person who is assigned to the work package level is the one responsible for determining and managing all the activities that make up the work package.

Use the appropriate number of levels.   Each major deliverable may have a different level of decomposition. It is not uncommon for one portion of the WBS to have three levels and another to have five levels. You should be concerned about getting to a manageable work package, not about balancing the WBS. If you try to force an even number of levels across all deliverables, you will end up with some deliverables that are not broken down in adequate detail and others that end up listing every minor activity to complete a simple task.

Benefits of the WBS

The WBS is often listed as one of the most important components of a successful project. As you will see in later chapters, the WBS is an input reference for many of the documents that comprise the project management plan.

The WBS is an excellent tool for team building and team communication. A graphic representation of the major project deliverables and the underlying subcomponents allows team members to see the big picture and understand how their part in the project fits in. The direct link between a given work package and a major project deliverable can also help clarify the impact on individual team members. Additionally, as new resources are added to the project, the WBS can help bring these new team members quickly up to speed.

If your organization typically undertakes projects that are similar in size, scope, and complexity, consider using your existing WBS as a template for future projects. It's a great starting point for the new project and can help kick off the brainstorming session with the project team.

A detailed WBS will not only prevent critical work from being overlooked, but it will also help control change. If the project team has a clear picture of the project objectives and the map to reach these objectives, they are less likely to go down a path unrelated to the project scope. I don't mean to imply that a WBS will prevent change; there are almost always changes during the project life cycle. But a WBS will clarify that a request is a change and not part of the original project scope. The WBS is also useful when discussing staffing requirements or budgets.

The WBS is an excellent tool for communicating with customers and stakeholders. People don't always comprehend the magnitude of a project until they see the diagram of the project deliverables and the subcomponents required to reach the objectives of the project. Seeing the work of the project displayed on a WBS will help you convey to the project team and the stakeholders the need for communicating at all levels of the project, coordinating work efforts, and adhering to the project scope.

WBS Dictionary

There's one more component of the WBS, called the *WBS dictionary*. This is where the WBS levels and work component descriptions are documented. These are some of the elements you should list in the WBS dictionary:

- Code of accounts identifier
- Description of the work of the component
- Organization responsible for completing the component
- Resources
- Cost estimates
- Criteria for acceptance

All the WBS components should be listed in the dictionary. This serves as a reference for you and the team regarding the WBS and should be easily accessible to all project team members.

Scope Baseline

Now that you have an approved scope statement, a WBS, and a WBS dictionary, you have what's known as the *scope baseline*. This baseline will be used throughout the remainder of documents. The scope baseline will also be used as a basis to determine the outcomes of change requests. Speaking of project management documents, before we jump into creating a schedule, let's look at what comprises the project management plan.

Documenting the Project Management Plan

The *project management plan* defines how the project is executed, how you'll measure performance, and how it's closed. It is progressively elaborated over the life of the project. All of the documents and plans you'll be using for this project make up the project management plan. For example, so far, we have created the scope management plan, scope statement, WBS, and WBS dictionary. These are all part of the project management plan. All of the new plans you'll create going forward, including the schedule, cost management plan, quality management plan, risk plans, the change management plan, and more, will be included as well. The project management plan also includes project baselines, such as these:

- Scope baseline
- Schedule baseline
- Cost baseline

We've already talked about the scope baseline, and we'll cover the schedule baseline later in this chapter, and the cost baseline in Chapter 7, "Defining the Project Budget and Risk Plans." Together, the scope, schedule, and cost baselines make up what's called the *performance measurement baseline*.

 Understand that the purpose of the project management plan is to define how the project is executed, how performance is measured, and how the project is closed. It is made up of project management plans, documents, and project baselines.

The project management plan should also document or discuss the following components:

- Processes you'll use to perform each phase of the project, how the processes have been tailored to the project, and the interactions and dependencies among the processes
- The life cycle methodology you'll use for the project
- The development approach you'll use, such as waterfall, agile, or hybrid
- When management reviews should be established (for example, at certain times during the project or at completion of milestones) so that the stakeholders can review project progress and ensure it's meeting the objectives and/or take action if it is not on track as planned
- Change management plan describing methods for monitoring and controlling change
- Methods for determining and maintaining the validity of performance baselines, especially scope, schedule, and cost

The project management plan has been progressively elaborated to include all the details as you progress through the Planning phases. However, once the project management plan is complete, you'll seek approval from the sponsor and key stakeholders. Once you have approval and sign-offs, the project management plan is *baselined*. No changes can be made from this point forward without going through the change control process. If changes to the project are approved, the project management plan should be updated to reflect those changes.

The project management plan is used for a waterfall or hybrid methodology. It's your roadmap for the project, and every future decision, work effort, change request, and corrective action will be weighed against this plan. Creating the plan is a collaborative effort between the project manager, project team, and key stakeholders. Collaborating and then documenting the project management plan help fulfill these objectives:

- Manage customer expectations and direct the work of the project to achieve the project objectives by documenting them and ensuring that the project management plan is available to all project participants.

- Optimize alignment between stakeholder needs, expectations, and project objectives by making certain key stakeholders contribute to the plan and by encouraging them to sign off on the plan, thereby gaining their commitment to the project's success.

- Survey all necessary stakeholders to reach consensus on the objectives of the project, the project management plan, and its contents by including them in the development of the planning documents.

When using an adaptive methodology to manage the project, you will define the work as the project progresses. You won't have a detailed roadmap to rely on as you have in a predictive approach. You will have other tools such as the project backlog, user stories, task definition, burndown charts, and more. We'll look at these in more depth later in this chapter.

Schedule Planning

After the WBS is completed, the next planning document you'll develop is the project schedule. As with the WBS, there isn't one right way to create the schedule. Here I've outlined the steps typically followed in creating a project schedule. On small projects you'll usually find all these steps performed in one sitting, whereas larger projects may require separate sessions for each step to complete the schedule, and you may also need to perform some planning steps more than once as you gather information from stakeholders and team members. Here is the list of steps I typically follow when constructing a project schedule.

1. Determine tasks.
2. Sequence tasks.
3. Allocate resources.
4. Determine task durations including start and end dates.
5. Determine milestones.
6. Construct the schedule.

7. Determine the critical path.

8. Set the baseline and obtain approval.

 For the purposes of this exam, the terms *task* and *activity* are interchangeable.

At first glance, it would seem that putting together a schedule is fairly basic. All you need to do is enter the work packages from the WBS into a project-scheduling software program, and you have the schedule. However, a sound project schedule takes a lot of planning. All the tasks must be identified, they must be sequenced in the order they can be completed, they need an estimated time frame and effort for completion, resource assignments must be derived, and finally all this information must be organized logically to come up with the overall project schedule.

The schedule documents the planned start and finish dates of each of the tasks included in the project, and the total project duration is calculated once the schedule is complete. Once it is finalized, checking the schedule becomes part of the project manager's weekly, if not daily, routine until the project is completed. Progress is reported against the schedule, and status updates regarding activities are provided to the stakeholders on a regular basis.

If you don't take the time up front to create an accurate schedule, you'll be spending a lot of time during the project making changes to the schedule and explaining why deliverables are not being completed as anticipated.

You'll want several subject matter experts to assist you with identifying and estimating tasks and creating the schedule, and it's a good idea to let everyone know up front that it could take more than one session to finalize the schedule.

Defining Tasks

The foundation for developing a project schedule is defining the list of tasks required to complete the project deliverables. This is an iterative process that involves further decomposing the WBS work packages into individual tasks. On small projects, it's a natural progression to break down the work packages into tasks as you're decomposing the WBS, because you have all the right people in the room and you've got the momentum going. However, remember that tasks are not recorded on the WBS but they are listed on the project schedule.

 Keep tasks at a high enough level that they can be managed effectively without breaking them down so far that you're finding yourself managing each team member's to-do list.

It is helpful to have the team members who are assigned to the work package levels involved in task definition. Their expertise can help you not only with defining tasks but also with assigning resources and determining estimates for the tasks. A good rule of thumb I use for most projects is to define tasks at a level that will take 40 to 80 hours to complete. If you have a critical task that's shorter in duration than this, or a very small project, you may want to make an exception.

You'll want to list each activity you've defined on an *activity list* or *task list*. This list should include every activity needed to complete the work of the project, along with an identifier or code so that you can track each task independently. It's also good practice to list the WBS code this activity is associated with, along with a short description of the work.

Once you have all your tasks defined, you're ready to start putting them into the sequence in which they will be worked.

Task Sequencing

Sequencing is the process of identifying dependency relationships between project activities and sequencing them in proper order. First you need to identify the type of dependency, and then you need to determine the specific relationship between the activities.

Dependencies are relationships between activities. For example, one activity may not be able to start until another has finished, or perhaps one activity is dependent on another activity starting before it can finish. Let's look at several types of dependencies next.

Types of Dependencies

Dependencies will influence the way tasks are scheduled. For example, a mandatory dependency, as its name implies, must be scheduled in successive order. Let's look at the four categories of dependencies:

- Mandatory dependencies
- Discretionary dependencies
- External dependencies
- Internal dependencies

A *mandatory dependency* is directly related to the type of work being performed. For example, a utility crew can't lay the cable for a new housing area until a trench has been dug. The nature of the work, needing a trench before laying the cable, dictates the order in which activities are performed. On the schedule, this means the "digging the trench" task must be scheduled before the "laying the cable" task. Mandatory dependencies are also known as *hard logic*. The project team determines mandatory, or hard logic, dependencies.

A *discretionary dependency* is defined by the project team and is usually process-or procedure-driven and/or may include best-practice techniques. An example is a process that requires approvals and sign-off on planning documents before proceeding with the work of the project. Discretionary dependencies are also known as *soft logic*.

An *external dependency* is a relationship between a project task and some factor outside the project that drives the scheduling of that task. For example, installation of a new server depends on when the vendor can deliver the equipment. The project team has little or no control over the scheduling of this type of dependency.

An *internal dependency* is a relationship between tasks within an individual project or within the organization. For example, developing programming code is dependent on the database administrators performing their tasks first. This would be an internal, mandatory dependency. The project team has control over these tasks.

It is important to know the type of dependency you're dealing with because you will need to know which tasks have flexibility, or which do not, when creating the schedule. This distinction becomes important later when you're looking at ways to shorten the schedule and complete a project in less time.

Logical Relationships

Now that you know the task dependency type, you'll need to answer several other questions: How does the dependency of the task impact the start and finish of other activities associated with this task? Does one activity have to start first? Can you start the second activity before the first activity is finished? All these variables impact what your overall project schedule looks like and involves establishing the logical relationship between the tasks so you can sequence them properly. Before covering the logical relationships, I'll present a few key terms related to understanding task dependencies.

A *predecessor* activity is one that comes before another activity. A *successor* activity is one that comes after the activity in question.

Four possible *logical relationships* can exist between the predecessor activity and the successor activity. Understanding these relationships will help you determine if you can schedule the activities in parallel or if one activity must wait until the predecessor task is completed. The four logical relationships are as follows:

Finish-to-Start (FS)   In a finish-to-start relationship, the successor activity cannot begin until the predecessor activity has completed. This is the most frequently used logical relationship and is the default setting for most project-scheduling software packages.

Start-to-Finish (SF)   In a start-to-finish relationship, the predecessor activity must start before the successor activity can finish. This relationship is seldom used.

Finish-to-Finish (FF)   A finish-to-finish relationship is where the predecessor activity must finish before the successor activity finishes.

Start-to-Start (SS)   In a start-to-start relationship, the predecessor activity must start before the successor activity can start.

Once the activity dependency relationships have been identified, your next step is creating a network diagram.

Creating a Network Diagram

One technique used by project managers to sequence activities is a network diagram. Understanding activity relationships is fundamental to using this technique. A *network diagram* depicts the project activities and the interrelationships among these activities. It is a great tool to develop with the project team. Use a whiteboard and label one sticky note with one activity. This will make it easy to see the workflow, and you can move the sticky notes around to make changes.

The most commonly used network diagramming method is the *precedence diagramming method (PDM)*. PDM uses boxes to represent the project milestones and arrows that represent activities. They also show the dependencies between the tasks. You'll see an example of a PDM diagram known as a PERT chart in Figure 5.2 in the "Program Evaluation and Review Technique" section later in this chapter.

Now that the activities are sequenced based on their logical dependencies, you're ready to assign resources to the activities and estimate how long it will take to complete each activity.

Assigning Resources

Resources on a project schedule typically refer to human resources and/or consulting or contracting resources who will work on the tasks. As I mentioned earlier, it's a good idea to have the work package–level owners present while constructing the schedule, because they are typically the supervisors of the teams who will work on the tasks. They should know at a glance which person on their team to assign to the tasks. They are also typically expert enough in their areas to determine estimates and start and end dates for tasks. When there are multiple tasks within a work package, it's best to have the resources who are assigned to those tasks determine duration estimates.

Another helpful tool you can use when assigning resources is a resource calendar. The *resource calendar* describes the time frames in which resources are available. It defines a particular resource or groups of resources and may also include their skills, abilities, and quantity, as well as availability. Perhaps your project calls for a marketing resource and the person assigned to the marketing activities is on an extended vacation in October. The resource calendar would show this person's vacation schedule. Resource calendars also examine the quantity, capability, and availability of equipment and material resources that have a potential to impact the project schedule. For example, suppose your project calls for a hydraulic drill and your organization owns only one. The resource calendar will tell you whether it's scheduled for another job at the same time it's needed for your project.

Determining Task Durations

Determining task durations is the next step in constructing the project schedule using a waterfall methodology. Duration estimating can be as easy as an expert giving you an educated estimate based on their experience, or it can be a complex process involving techniques and calculations to develop estimates—albeit most of these estimates are still based on expert opinions.

Before explaining some of the techniques you can use to complete your task duration estimates, let's make sure you have a common understanding of activity duration.

Defining Duration

When you are estimating duration, you need to make sure that you are looking at the total elapsed time to complete the activity. For example, let's say you have a task that is estimated to take five days to complete based on an eight-hour workday. You have one full-time resource assigned to this task, but they have only four hours a day to work on it. That means the actual duration estimate for this task is 10 days.

You also need to be aware of the difference between workdays and calendar days. If your workweek is Monday through Friday and you have a four-day task starting on Thursday, the duration for that task will be six calendar days because no work will be done on Saturday and Sunday.

 Make certain that everyone who is providing estimates is in agreement up front as to whether they will be provided in workdays or calendar days. Most project management software packages allow you to establish a calendar that accounts for nonwork days and will exclude these days when computing duration.

Now that you have a common understanding of duration, I'll discuss the various techniques used to create duration estimates.

Estimating Techniques

You can use several techniques to determine task duration estimates. These methods can be used when estimating tasks in a waterfall or agile methodology. When working in sprints, the team may use any of these techniques at the beginning of the sprint to estimate task durations. We'll talk more about agile estimation and scheduling techniques later in this chapter. Let's look at some of the most common estimating methods:

Analogous Estimating   *Analogous estimating*, also known as *top-down estimating*, is a technique that uses actual durations from similar tasks on a previous project. It is most frequently used at the early stages of project planning, when you have limited information about the project. Although analogous estimating can provide a good approximation of task duration, it is typically the least accurate means of obtaining an estimate. No two projects are the same, and there is the risk that the project used to obtain the analogous estimates is not as similar to the current project as it appears.

Results from analogous estimating are more accurate if the person doing the estimating is familiar with both projects and is able to understand the differences that could impact the activity durations on the new project.

Expert Judgment   *Expert judgment* is a technique where the people most familiar with the work determine the estimate. Ideally, the project team member who will perform the task should provide the estimate. If all the team members haven't been identified yet, recruit people with expertise for the tasks you need estimated. Ask for people who have completed a similar task on a previous project to assist with the estimates for this project.

Remember that people with more experience will likely provide a shorter estimate for an activity than someone who doesn't have as much experience. You should validate the estimate or ask other experts in the department to validate it for you.

Parametric Estimating   *Parametric estimating* is a quantitatively based estimating method that multiplies the quantity of work by the rate. To apply quantitatively based durations, you must know the productivity rate of the resource performing the task or have a company or industry standard that can be applied to the task in question. The duration is obtained by multiplying the unit of work produced by the productivity rate. For example, the IT team received 10 laptops to image for new employees. It takes one IT technician 90 minutes to perform this task. Therefore, it will take 900 minutes, or 15 hours, for one IT technician to image all 10 laptops. If you had two IT technicians perform this task, it could be completed in 7.5 hours.

Bottom-Up Estimating   *Bottom-up estimating* is performed by obtaining individual estimates for each project activity and then adding them all to arrive at a total estimate for the work package. Bottom-up estimating is a good technique to use when you aren't confident about the type or quantity of resources you'll need for the project. This is an accurate means of estimating provided the estimates at the schedule activity level are accurate. However, it takes a considerable amount of time to perform bottom-up estimating because every activity must be assessed and estimated accurately to be included in the bottom-up calculation. The smaller and more detailed the activity, the greater the accuracy and cost of this technique.

Now that you know their durations and dependencies, you can establish start and end dates for each task and construct the project schedule. We'll look at that next.

🌐 Real World Scenario

The Bathroom Remodel Project

You have been assigned to manage the bathroom remodel project for your building. All restrooms will undergo a remodel, including the two large restrooms in the basement that also have lockers and showers.

Team members from the facilities department will be working on this project along with a contractor who was hired to perform the plumbing work. Some of the major deliverables include removing all the old fixtures and stalls, removing the existing tile, reconfiguring the space to add additional wheelchair-accessible stalls in each restroom, removing the old lockers, and installing all new fixtures, stalls, counters, sinks, showers, and lockers.

You work with the team members from the facilities department to break down the tasks from each work package level. They inform you of predecessor activities, such as running electric lines for overhead lighting before setting countertops or mirrors. Because they have been involved in other projects of a similar nature, they use expert judgment to provide you with duration estimates for their tasks and provide a rough order of magnitude estimate for the plumbing work. You all agree that the work should be estimated in workday increments.

Once all the work of the project is recorded on the schedule, you assign resources and calculate the duration of all the critical path tasks, and you find that the project will take 120 days to complete.

Developing the Project Schedule

Creating the schedule involves all the work you've done so far, including defining the tasks, sequencing the tasks, and determining duration estimates. You will now plug this information into the schedule and establish a start date and a finish date for each of the project activities. Let's walk through an example. Your project involves painting a house. One of the tasks is scraping the old paint off the walls. Another task is applying the new paint to the walls, and another task is painting the trim. You really shouldn't apply the new paint until the scraping is finished. That means the scraping task is a predecessor to the painting task. And the painting can't start until the scraping is finished (an FS relationship). You know from the experts providing estimates for these tasks that the scraping task will take two days and painting five days. If scraping starts on Wednesday, June 1, scraping should end on Thursday, June 2. All day June 1 and all day June 2 are spent on scraping. That means painting can start on Friday, June 3. The painters work on Saturday but not Sunday. If this is a five-day task, painting will finish on Wednesday, June 8. The total duration for these two tasks is eight days (including the Sunday the painters don't work).

It may take several iterations to get the schedule finalized. Once it's approved, it serves as the schedule baseline for the project. Once you begin the work of the project, you'll use this baseline to track actual progress against what was planned.

Before creating the schedule, let's revisit milestones and how they interact with the project schedule.

Milestones

Milestones are typically major accomplishments of the project and mark the completion of major deliverables or some other key event in the project. For example, approval and sign-off on project deliverables might be considered milestones. Other examples might be the completion of a prototype, functional testing, or contract approval. A milestone is typically denoted on a project schedule as an event that is achieved once all the deliverables associated with that milestone are completed and it has a duration of 0.

Milestone charts are one method to display your schedule information. A milestone chart tracks the scheduled dates and actual completion dates for the major milestones. Table 5.1 shows an example of a milestone chart. As the project manager, you should pay close attention to milestone dates because they are also a communication trigger. Stakeholders need to be informed when major deliverables are completed or when a project has successfully moved to a new phase. If these dates are not met, you need to communicate the current status, the plans to bring the project back on track, and the new milestone date.

TABLE 5.1   A sample milestone chart

Milestone	Scheduled start date	Actual start date	Scheduled completion date	Actual completion date
Sign-off on scope statement	12/18	12/18	12/18	12/18
Sign-off on contract	2/02	2/02	2/02	2/02
Acceptance of deliverable 1	3/05	3/05	5/31	6/07
Acceptance of deliverable 2	3/15	4/01	6/30	7/15
Testing completed	7/01	7/16	7/31	8/16
Project acceptance and sign-off	8/10	8/20	8/10	8/20

Program Evaluation and Review Technique

The *Program Evaluation and Review Technique (PERT)* is a method that the U.S. Navy developed in the 1950s. The Navy was working on one of the most complex engineering projects in history at the time—the Polaris Missile Program—and needed a way to manage the project and forecast the project schedule with a high degree of reliability. PERT was developed to do just that.

Before you can construct a PERT chart, you need to estimate the duration of the tasks or milestones that will be depicted on the chart. PERT uses three-point estimates known as the *weighted average* to calculate estimates for task duration. Weighted average consists of three estimates: the optimistic, the pessimistic, and the most likely estimates. You'll want to involve the team members who will be working on the tasks, or others who are experts in the tasks, to give you these estimates. It's as simple as asking: "If everything goes right, when is the soonest this task could be completed?" (optimistic estimate); "If things don't go so well, what would be the longest amount of time it would take to complete this task?" (pessimistic estimate); and "What is the most likely amount of time it will take to complete this task?"

The formula to calculate the weighted average is as follows:

optimistic + pessimistic + (4 × most likely)/6

Let's use an example to calculate the weighted average for one of the tasks on the PERT chart shown in Figure 5.2. The optimistic estimate is 6 days, the pessimistic estimate is 14 days, and the most likely estimate is 10 days. Let's plug this into the formula:

6 + 14 + (4 × 10)/6 = 10 days

A PERT chart is a type of precedence network diagram. The nodes might represent milestones or tasks and the arrows represent the sequence of tasks. You can add other information on the nodes such as start and end dates, and task duration. It is also acceptable to put task durations on the arrows. Figure 5.2 shows a simple PERT chart.

FIGURE 5.2   PERT chart

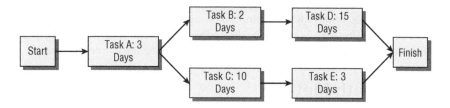

Keep in mind that most project managers use some combination of estimating techniques to determine task durations.

Gantt Charts

One of the most common ways to display project schedules is using a *Gantt chart*. Gantt charts display much of the same information a PERT chart shows. Gantt charts are displayed as bar charts that span the entire project timeline. It's possible to visually show the entire project on one page using this method. Gantt charts might show milestones, deliverables, and all the tasks of the project, including their durations, start and end dates, and the resources assigned to each task. I know project managers who have constructed Gantt charts for small projects using only a spreadsheet. Figure 5.3 shows a sample Gantt chart including resource names and task durations.

FIGURE 5.3   Gantt chart

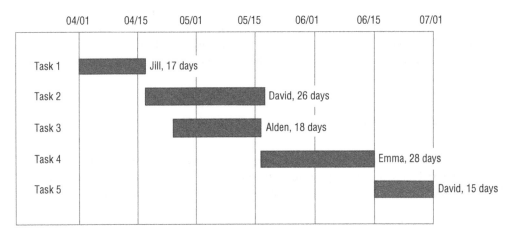

PERT charts are typically used for large, complex projects whereas Gantt charts are more often used for medium and small projects. As you saw in Figure 5.2, PERT charts use nodes to represent tasks or milestones and arrows that show the dependencies between the tasks. PERT charts focus on dependencies. However, there is no way to visually see all the tasks across the project timeline.

Gantt charts show all the tasks over the entire project timeline, but it's difficult to display dependencies between the tasks. Gantt charts focus on the time needed to work on the tasks. Each chart has its place, and it's not uncommon to create both a PERT chart and a Gantt chart for the project. This way, you can see dependencies and examine the critical path on the PERT chart and use the Gantt chart to see all the activities across the timeline.

The Critical Path Method

One of the most widely used techniques in schedule development is the *critical path method (CPM)*. CPM determines the amount of *float time* for each activity on the schedule by calculating the earliest start date, earliest finish date, latest start date, and latest finish date for each task. Float is the amount of time you can delay the earliest start of an activity without delaying the ending of the project. Tasks with the same early and late start dates and the same early and late finish dates have zero float and are considered critical path tasks. If a critical path task does not finish as scheduled, the project end date will be affected.

> For the exam, remember that tasks with zero float are critical path tasks. It is possible to calculate float time manually, but the formulas are beyond the scope of this book and the exam. Float time calculations are easily performed in project-scheduling software.

The *critical path* is the longest full path on the project. If you refer to Figure 5.2, you'll see that the longest path for this project has a duration of 20 days. This is calculated by adding the durations for the A-B-D path (Task A, Task B, and Task D). Simply add up the task durations for that path.

Table 5.2 shows the start and end dates and durations for the project tasks in table form. When calculating the start and end dates, the first day counts as day 1. Task A starts on 10/6, and it's worked on all day on the 6th, 7th, and 8th because it has a duration of three days. The next task can start on the 9th. In this example, there are no holidays or vacation days.

TABLE 5.2 Finding a critical path

Task	Start date	End date	Predecessor	Duration in days
A	10/6	10/8	None	3
B	10/9	10/10	A	2
C	10/9	10/18	A	10
D	10/11	10/25	B	15
E	10/19	10/21	C	3

Again refer to Figure 5.2 and Table 5.2. What happens to the critical path if you eliminate Task E? Nothing changes, because the longest path (or the activities with the longest durations that are in the same path or that have the same predecessors) is still A-B-D with 20 days. Path A-C-E has a duration of 16 days. If you eliminated Task B, the critical path changes to 18 days, which is along the new path A-D.

For the exam, make certain you understand that the critical path is the longest full path on the project. The simplest calculation you can use for the exam is to add up the duration of each activity for each path on the project and determine which one is the longest. It might be helpful to draw a network diagram on scrap paper so that you can more easily see which tasks are dependent on each other and add up the durations of each path.

In addition to calculating the overall time to complete the project and identifying tasks on the critical path, CPM provides other useful information. You will be able to determine which tasks can start late or which can take more time than planned without impacting the project end date. During project execution, the project manager can use this information to focus attention on the tasks that have the most impact on the overall project completion date.

So far, we've talked about creating the schedule using precise estimates and dates. It's often good practice to add what's known as *contingency reserves* (or *buffers*) to milestone dates in the schedule. This means adding a cushion of extra time to give the team some breathing room if things don't go as planned. This is especially useful when the team is working on new tasks, when they are inexperienced, or when the project is high risk. The idea is to add a buffer of additional time to the milestone completion dates. You will have to analyze project risks, team capabilities, and other factors that may impact the schedule to determine how much additional time to add. Your project management office may also have recommendations on the amount of time to add, based on past projects of a similar nature. Some project managers use a certain percentage, such as an additional 10 percent, and add this as the buffer. Be aware that this could backfire on you. If you consistently add too much, or too little, buffer time to your projects, your stakeholders will get wise and begin to "adjust" the project schedules you present to them according to their past experience with your projects. They will come to expect the project to be completed sooner (or later) than the schedule says, so try to be as accurate as you can in your buffer estimates.

When you complete the schedule and calculate the critical path, you may learn that the duration of the project is unacceptable to the project stakeholders. If you find yourself in that situation, you can use duration compression techniques, discussed next, to help shorten the schedule.

Duration Compression

What happens if your calculation of the total project duration is longer than your target project completion date?

This is where *duration compression* scheduling techniques come into play. These techniques can be used during planning to shorten the planned duration of the project or during project execution to help resolve schedule slippage. The two duration compression techniques are crashing and fast tracking.

Crashing

Crashing is a technique that looks at cost and schedule trade-offs. Crashing is typically implemented by adding more resources to the critical path tasks in order to complete the project more quickly. Crashing can also be accomplished by requiring mandatory overtime for those team members working on critical path tasks or by speeding up delivery times from team members, vendors, and so on.

> One common misconception about adding resources is that if you double the resources, you can cut the duration in half. In other words, if two people can finish the work in four weeks, then four people must be able to finish in two weeks. This isn't always the case. Typically, the original resources assigned to the task are less productive when you add new resources because they're busy helping the new resources come up to speed on the work. Or you may have so many resources working on the project that they are in each other's way.

Crashing can produce the desired results if used wisely, but you should be aware that crashing the schedule may increase risks and will impact your budget. Be certain you've examined these impacts to the project when using this technique.

Fast Tracking

Fast tracking is performing multiple tasks in parallel that were previously scheduled to start sequentially.

Let's go back to our painting example. Scraping and painting cannot start at the same time. However, we have two painting tasks. One is painting the walls; the other is painting the trim. The schedule currently shows the trim starting when the paint finishes (an FS relationship). We could fast-track these activities and have the trim start at the same time as the walls. Logistically, the crews will have to start from different points in the building so that they aren't in each other's way, but the tasks can be started in parallel.

There is a great deal of risk in fast tracking. If you decide to compress your project schedule using this method, be sure you get input from the team members as to what could go wrong. Document all the risks and present them to your sponsor and other key stakeholders. Don't make the mistake of trying to do the project faster without communicating any of the potential risks or impacts. You need to make sure that everyone understands the potential consequences and agrees to the schedule change.

Resource Loading

Now that you have a schedule of activities and have determined the critical path, it's time to plug in resources for those activities and adjust the schedule or resources according to any resource constraints you discover. The CPM and PERT methods do not consider resource availability, so assigning resources to the activities is the next step in creating the schedule.

Usually, you'll find that your initial schedule has periods of time with more activities than you have resources to work on them. You will also find that it isn't always possible to assign 100 percent of your team members' time to tasks. Sometimes your schedule will show a team member who is overallocated, meaning that individual is assigned to more work than they can physically perform in the given time period. Other times, they might not be assigned enough work to keep them busy during the time period. This problem is easy to fix. You can assign underallocated resources to multiple tasks to keep the resource busy. Adjusting the schedule for overallocated resources is a harder problem to fix. We will look at three techniques that optimize resources to prevent overallocation where possible: resource leveling, resource smoothing, and reverse resource allocation scheduling. You should use these techniques with CPM-based schedules.

Resource Leveling

Resource leveling is used when resources are overallocated, when they are only available at certain times, or when they are assigned to more than one activity at a time. In a nutshell, resource leveling attempts to balance out the resource assignments to get tasks completed without overloading the individual. You accomplish this by adjusting the start and finish dates of schedule activities based on the availability of resources. This typically means allocating resources to critical path tasks first, which often changes the critical path and, in turn, the overall project end date.

The project manager can accomplish resource leveling in a couple of other ways as well. You might delay the start of a task to match the availability of a key team member, or you might adjust the resource assignments so that more tasks are given to team members who are underallocated. Generally speaking, resource leveling of overallocated team members extends the project end date. If you're under a date constraint, you'll have to rework the schedule after assigning resources to keep the project on track with the committed completion date. You can accomplish this with resource smoothing, which we'll look at next.

Resource Smoothing

Resource smoothing accommodates resource availability by modifying activities within their float times without changing the critical path or project end date. That means you'll also use this technique when you need to meet specific schedule dates and are concerned about resource availability.

There are several ways you can accomplish this. You can adjust the resource assignments so that more tasks are given to team members who are underallocated. You could also require the resources to work mandatory overtime—that one always goes over well! Perhaps you can split some tasks so that the team member with the pertinent knowledge or skill performs the critical part of the task and the noncritical part of the task is given to a less skilled team member. Other methods might include moving key resources from noncritical tasks and assigning them to critical path tasks or adjusting assignments. Reallocating those team members with slack time to critical path tasks to keep them on schedule is another option. Don't forget—fast tracking is another way to keep the project on schedule.

Reverse Resource Allocation Scheduling

Reverse resource allocation scheduling is a technique used when key resources—like a thermodynamic expert, for example—are required at a specific point in the project and they are the only resource, or resources, available to perform these activities. This technique requires the resources to be scheduled in reverse order (that is, from the end date of the project rather than the beginning) in order to assign this key resource at the correct time.

Resource leveling can cause the original critical path to change and can delay the project's completion date. Resource smoothing modifies activities within their floats without changing the critical path or project end date. It's used when changes to the critical path cannot or should not be made. Reverse resource allocation scheduling is used when specific resources are needed at certain times.

Project Scheduling Software

Project management software is a tool that can save you a lot of time when creating your schedule. You can enter tasks, durations, and/or start and end dates; assign resources; and generate a graphical representation of the project. It will automatically calculate task durations, determine the critical path, and help you balance resources. It provides you with the ability to display a number of different views for the project, which can be a great communication tool, and you can tailor the views for your audience. For example, executives typically don't want to see every line in a project schedule. They are interested in milestone views or in seeing the major deliverables and their due dates. The software will also allow you to save the original baseline schedule for historical reference as well as provide version control for future revisions to the schedule. Let's look at that next.

Setting the Baseline and Obtaining Approval

The *schedule baseline* is the final, approved version of the project schedule that includes the start and finish dates and resource assignments. It's important that you obtain sign-off on the project schedule from your stakeholders and the managers who are supplying resources to the project. This ensures they have read the schedule, understand the dates, and understand the resource commitments. Ideally, it will also keep them from reneging on commitments they've made and promises of resources at specific times on the project. Be certain to publish the baselined schedule in the project repository so that stakeholders have access to it.

The schedule baseline will be used throughout the project to monitor progress. The schedule baseline is the original schedule with the original estimates, start and finish dates, resources, and costs that can be used to assess results throughout the project. In an ideal world, the schedule baseline will remain the same throughout the project. In the real world, this doesn't happen often. Changes occur all the time on projects, particularly to the schedule, and this calls for either revising the project schedule, or re-baselining the schedule.

Let's say the change control board approves a change that adds scope to the project. This will likely impact the end date of the project and you'll need to re-baseline the schedule to include the new dates for the added scope. The re-baselined schedule should be approved by the project sponsor and key stakeholders. However, you should preserve the original baseline for comparison purposes and lessons learned. Most scheduling software programs offer the option to save the original baseline. Once it's saved, plug in the new dates for the tasks that have changed and save a new version of the schedule baseline. This re-baselined version replaces the original baseline and is now the version you'll use throughout the remainder of the project to monitor progress.

Remember that if the end date is moving, you are impacting a critical path task.

Changes to the schedule that do not impact the project end date can be managed using a schedule revision. Revisions are typically used when there are changes to noncritical path tasks. In this instance, changes occur to some tasks but not to the overall schedule. Changes to scope or cost usually trigger a need for a schedule revision or a new baseline.

Changes, as we've discussed previously, must be managed using the change control process, which you'll learn about in Chapter 9, "Processing Change Requests." Any changes to the schedule end date will require modifying the schedule baseline and obtaining approvals of the re-baselined schedule.

Quality Gates

Quality gates in the project schedule are similar to milestones. They don't produce something per se; they are used to determine quality checks at strategic points in the project and ensure that the work is accurate and meets quality standards. In the painting example, you may have a quality gate that occurs after the scraping is finished but before the painting task begins. Painting should not begin until the quality gate is verified. In this case, the quality gate is to assure the work has been performed correctly and completely.

Your organization or PMO may have processes, checklists, or templates for use during quality gates. The activities associated with quality gates are not usually unique to the project; rather, they pertain to the product or service and can be used repeatedly on multiple projects.

Establishing Governance Gates

Governance gates are used as approval points in the project. On large projects, they can also be used as additional approval checkpoints or go/no-go decision points during the project.

The CompTIA objectives list three governance gates: client sign-off, management approval, and legislative approval. You learned about sponsor and stakeholder sign-offs earlier. You'll also want your customer to sign off on the project schedule (and the project plan when completed) as well. Remember that sign-offs help assure adherence to the schedule, agreement to the dates, and agreement to resource commitments. Legislative approvals, in my experience, actually occur prior to starting the project. However, I can imagine that a really large, complex public sector project, such as building a space station, may require periodic legislative approval and oversight at strategic points in the project.

Scheduling Techniques Using Agile Methodologies

Agile methodologies perform work in short, frequent cycles. Each cycle produces a minimum viable product (MVP) that the stakeholders review. They provide immediate feedback to the team in order to modify or adjust the requirements to produce business value.

User stories are the requirements of the project (somewhat akin to a work package) that are kept in the backlog and then decomposed into activities that are prioritized and worked on during each iteration. You'll recall from Chapter 4 that the product owner is responsible for maintaining and prioritizing the product backlog. The user stories are prioritized so that the most important are at the top of the list (and are usually well-defined) and that user stories with less importance fall beneath these on the list.

Before we go into detail on this concept, let's also look at another agile artifact called an *epic* that relates to the project requirements and backlog. Epics are large units of work such as a business requirement or features that are not usually well-defined. Epics may also be large user stories, but they cannot be easily broken down into tasks or estimated in this form, and they can't be completed in one iteration. Epics are placeholders that contain big ideas or concepts that are not fully defined. They are similar to the second level of a work breakdown structure and need to be decomposed into units of work, or user stories. Multiple user stories can result from one epic. When visually displayed on a burndown chart (like the one in Figure 5.4 later in this chapter), epics can help the team see the big picture view of the project and how all of the requirements and user stories fit together.

 NOTE   Think of an epic like a movie trailer. There's enough information in the trailer to give you an idea of what the movie is about, but the details are left out and won't be known until you start watching the movie.

Estimating Techniques Using Agile

Estimating techniques in agile begin with breaking down epics into user stories, and then user stories into individual tasks. Breaking down user stories happens at the beginning of the iteration, or sprint as it's known in the Scrum methodology. An iteration or sprint is a short, time-bound period of work (usually two to four weeks in length) where the tasks are worked on and the MVP is produced. The sprint kicks off with a *sprint planning meeting*. During the meeting, the product owner identifies the user stories that should be worked on during the upcoming sprint, pulls them from the product backlog, and places them into the sprint backlog. Team members then choose which user stories to work on during the sprint and break them down into activities or tasks. They also estimate the time it will take to complete the activities and determine how much of the work can be accomplished during the sprint. Because the agile team is self-directed, they have the ability to use the tools and techniques that work best for them to break down tasks and determine estimates. They are the experts in the work and therefore have the freedom to choose their tasks and the tools and techniques they will use to perform the tasks.

The Scrum master works with the team members to examine all the user stories and estimate how many iterations will be required to complete all of the user stories (in other words, all the work of the project). This estimate can be expressed in hours or team days. Team days are the total cumulative hours all the team members make up together. For example, if you have six team members working full time on the project, one team day consists of 48 hours (8 hours a day × 6 team members). The team may use any or all of the estimating techniques discussed in this chapter to estimate the task durations. Expert judgment is used frequently to estimate agile tasks because agile teams are small, and the resources providing the estimates are also performing the work of the project. After estimating the tasks and their approximate durations, the Scrum master will roll this up into a total number of iterations needed to complete the project. Remember that iterations are typically two to four weeks in length, and agile is flexible. There will be changes and new requirements introduced as the project progresses, so the number of iterations may change.

Burndown Chart

Let's say our project estimate shows that 20 sprints are needed to complete the work. The Scrum master may use what's called a *burndown chart* to track this work. A burndown chart shows the remaining time and work effort for the iteration, and it can also be used to display remaining work for small projects. It displays the number of days in the iteration on the horizontal axis and the hours of effort for tasks on the vertical axis. At the end of each day, team members update their estimates for the remaining amount of work, which then updates the burndown chart. As the project progresses and iterations are completed, the amount of work will decrease. Team members and stakeholders can visually see the amount of work remaining in the iteration or the project. Figure 5.4 shows a sample burndown chart for a small project.

In Figure 5.4, the sprint shows 10 working days on the x-axis and 80 hours of time on the y-axis. This assumes an 8-hour day and a 5-day workweek. Burndown charts are unique to the teams that create them. They are only as accurate as the estimates the team submitted for the tasks. It takes about four to eight sprints or iterations before the team develops a steady cadence and becomes more accurate with estimates.

FIGURE 5.4   Burndown chart

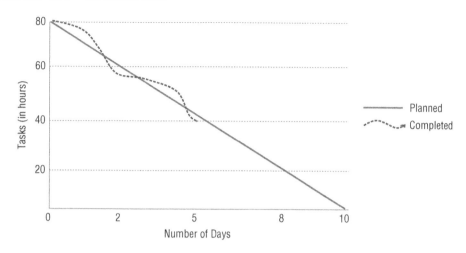

   Burndown charts are a moment-in-time display of the remaining work of the iteration. Burndown charts go to zero over time and they do not show changes to scope.

Story Points and Velocity

Another way to estimate task durations using agile techniques is by identifying story points. *Story points* are defined by the project team members themselves. They are a unit of measure agreed on by the team and are used to estimate the amount of work to complete a user story. Typically, the story point is a comparative approach based on complexity of the tasks as they relate to one another, and on team members' past experience working on similar tasks. However, story points can be anything the team agrees on as a measurement. You could use a chart similar to Figure 5.4 to show story points and the amount of work remaining on the project. Story points in this case could be plotted on the y-axis in Figure 5.4 instead of task hours.

Another estimating concept you should know for the exam is *velocity*. Velocity is generally used in Scrum to determine how long it will take to complete the backlog. Velocity reflects the speed at which the team is working. You can use velocity to estimate the duration of the iteration or the duration of the project. For example, let's say the team has worked on a similar project in the past. They know that their average velocity on that project was 20 story points per iteration. If your project has 100 total story points, it will take 5 iterations to complete the project (100 story points ÷ 20 story points per iteration). If your iterations are 2 weeks in duration, the total duration of the project will be 10 weeks (2 week iteration × 5 total iterations = 10 weeks). Velocity estimates will improve as iterations are completed and the team improves their estimates. You can use this same concept with user stories instead of velocity. For example, let's say your team can complete one user story in two days. If you have 50 user stories total, it will take 100 days to complete all the user stories (50 user stories × 2 days each = 100 days).

Kanban Board

You'll recall from Chapter 4 that Kanban pulls work from the backlog according to the team's capacity to perform the work. This is known as *on-demand scheduling* or *pull-based scheduling*. Kanban uses a scheduling technique whereby work is pulled on demand, as capacity is available. Kanban is a visual process where the work is displayed on a board known as a *Kanban board*. The board has columns that represent stages of work, and cards that represent units of work that are moved from stage to stage as the work progresses. These stages are not time-bound; they are capacity-bound. You can have any number of columns on a Kanban board, but fewer is better. The idea is that you can visually see the stages of work and where bottlenecks in the process are occurring so that you can solve them and ultimately improve the process.

Let's look at the Kanban board again in more detail. Figure 5.5 is the same board you saw in Chapter 4.

FIGURE 5.5   Kanban board at the start of the project

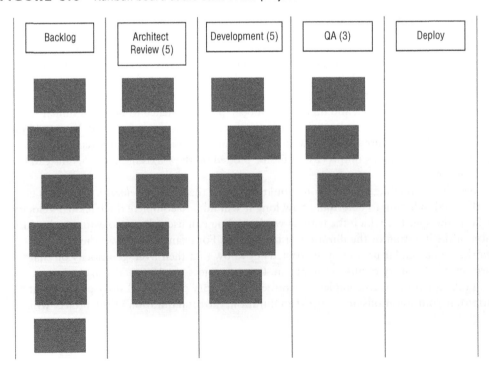

Your team has one software architect, five software developers, and one quality assurance (QA) reviewer. All of the cards start in the Backlog column and wait for team members to pull them to the next stage. The architect pulls cards from the backlog as they have capacity, but their work capacity is limited to five cards. The developers are also limited to five cards at a time. The QA reviewer has the capacity to review and test only three cards at a time. The maximum number of cards are represented in the column headings in Figure 5.5. In this example, you can see that the quality assurance area is the bottleneck because the QA reviewer can't pull work at the same rate their teammates can produce and complete their cards. The QA reviewer must wait for a card to be pulled into the Deploy stage before they are able to pull the next card from development into QA.

In Kanban, the topmost card in any column is the most important. Team members are always aware which card to work on next. As the card is pulled from one column to the next, team members might add notes to the card and the card owner will change hands. This is the case in Figure 5.5. The developers pull cards from the architect review column and become the new owner of the task. When all the cards have moved to the deploy stage, the project is finished.

Kanban starts with the current state and works incrementally toward the future state. It provides a way to visualize the work of the project in stages. Kanban encourages all team members to act as leaders. It is capacity-based and limits the amount of work in each stage. Feedback is built into the process at every stage, and the team works collaboratively toward continuous improvement.

Scrum Board

In the Scrum methodology, the project team keeps track of work using a *Scrum board* or *task board*. Visually, this board looks almost identical to the Kanban board. The difference between a Scrum board and a Kanban board is that the Scrum board only shows the work of the sprint, and it is only used by that one team working on that sprint. Kanban boards are used by all the teams working on the project. A Scrum board is time-bound, not capacity-bound. User stories are added to the first column of the Scrum board, the tasks are broken down and added to the second column, and the remaining columns show the stages of work during the sprint. Scrum boards can be divided into categories such as to-do, in progress, review, and done, or other categories that work for the team. This enables all team members and the product owner to see the progress of the sprint at a glance and ensures that important tasks are not forgotten. Table 5.3 shows what a sample Scrum board might look like. Work that isn't completed in a sprint becomes the first priority in the next sprint, unless the product owner says otherwise.

TABLE 5.3   Scrum board

User stories	To-do	In progress	In testing	Done
User story 1			Task 1 (user story 1)	
		Task 2 (user story 1)		
	Task 3 (user story 1)			
User story 2	Task 1 (user story 2)			

The Scrum master may choose to use either the Scrum board or a burndown chart to show the progress of the sprint. You can construct a burndown chart for a sprint showing the time on the x-axis (10 workdays for a 2-week sprint, for example) and task hours or story points on the y-axis.

Both Kanban and Scrum allow the project team to deliver value incrementally because work is produced in each stage or each sprint and the product owner can provide real-time feedback on the work results. These agile methodologies allow for changes, as well as additions to scope. Keep in mind that many software programs are available that help you manage and prioritize the backlog items, Kanban boards, and Scrum boards in a more automated fashion. Some teams like the sticky notes on a whiteboard that's hung in the work area because they can see the progress of the work at any time, without having to log in to a program.

Agile Release Planning

Agile release planning is a method you can use to accommodate large projects using an agile development methodology. Agile release planning involves defining releases, which are usually a significant feature or portion of functionality that will exist in the final product. You can think of release planning somewhat like project phases, which are used in a predictive methodology. Release planning starts at a high level with a product vision that drives the roadmap for the project (think of this as the project scope description), as well as the release plans. Based on this product vision, the team estimates how many releases it will take to complete the final product, service, or result of the project. The product owner will define user stories at the beginning of the project, but they need to define only enough user stories for the first release. User stories may also be created and added at the beginning of each release. The team will assess the user stories at the beginning of each release and determine how many iterations it will take to complete the release.

Let's say we are implementing an enterprise resource planning system with three modules. The releases might look like this:

Release 1 = Accounting

Release 2 = Human Resources

Release 3 = Procurement

Release 1 contains four iterations. Iteration 1 within Release 1 contains two user stories, each with their own tasks. Each release has its own release plan with the number of iterations required for that release and the user stories within each iteration. A visual example of Release 1 might look like Figure 5.6.

FIGURE 5.6   Example product vision release plan and iteration plan

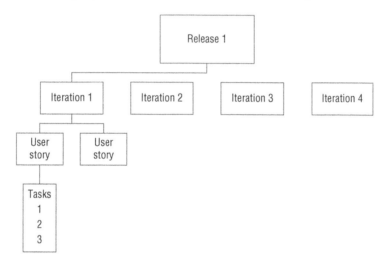

 **Real World Scenario**

Main Street Office Move: Scheduling

One of the deliverables noted in the scope statement is "Survey the Main Street Office Building and work with functional managers to determine seating charts." Working with two key functional managers on the project, you define the following tasks:

- Obtain floor plans for the Main Street Office Building.

- Perform a walk-through of the Main Street Office Building.

- Interview functional managers.

- Obtain the current organizational chart from each functional manager.

- Provide draft seating charts to functional managers.

- Determine office placements and sizes.

- Determine cubicle placements.

- Determine printer placement.

- Determine breakroom areas.

- Provide final seating charts to functional managers.

The next step involves sequencing these tasks in the correct order and determining start and finish dates. You determined the following dependencies:

Task number	Task	Dependency
1	Obtain floor plans.	NA
2	Building walk-through.	NA
3	Interview functional managers.	Task 1
4	Obtain current org charts.	Task 3
5	Office and conference room placements and sizing.	Tasks 1–3
6	Determine cubicle placements.	Tasks 1–3 and "Interior Designer" deliverable
7	Determine office placements.	Tasks 1–3
8	Determine printer locations.	Tasks 1–2
9	Determine breakroom areas.	Tasks 1, 2 and "Interior Designer" deliverable
10	Draft seating charts to managers.	Tasks 1–9
11	Functional managers review draft seating charts.	Task 10
12	Final seating chart approved.	Task 11

You need to determine some rough order-of-magnitude estimates for these tasks to determine start and end dates. For example, based on the recommendation from the functional managers that the final seating chart be approved before the cube build-outs begin, you know that Task 12 must finish before you place the order for the cubicle furnishings.

When breaking down the tasks for the "Procure and install cubicle furnishings" deliverable and determining start and finish dates, you realize you are working with a constraint that requires all cubicles and office furniture be delivered and installed by December 31. When you met with the IT director shortly after the scope statement was written, you discovered two weeks is needed to place computer equipment, monitors, and telephones on each desk. The cubicle buildouts and furniture delivery are predecessors to the computer equipment setup deliverable, so you need to determine when the cubicle furnishing order should be placed.

You've obtained an estimate from a vendor that it takes roughly two days to install 250 cubicles. Based on assumptions you've made in your conversations with Emma and the two functional managers who helped develop the task list, you think there will be a minimum of 1,000 cubicles. To allow IT two weeks to install the computer equipment, you determine delivery of the cubicle materials must occur by December 6. Cubicle buildouts can begin December 7 and must finish by December 15 (taking into account weekend days).

In summary, your cubicle furnishing order will take six weeks to fill according to your vendor contacts. If the materials must be delivered no later than December 6, that means Task 12 from the "Survey the Main Street Office Building" deliverable has to finish by October 25. You can work backward from October 25 to determine the start and end dates for each task in this deliverable.

You continue breaking down each deliverable into a list of tasks, sequence them in the proper order, determine start and end dates, and assign resources to the tasks to come up with the final schedule.

The IT team will use agile release planning for the data center activities. There are several releases, including transfer Active Directory domain, transfer email services, and migrate databases. The small amount of equipment needed to be retained and moved to the new premises will be managed in the office move portion of the project.

Once the schedule is approved by the management team, it becomes the base-line schedule for the project, and all changes to the schedule must follow the change management process.

Summary

The work breakdown structure is created by taking the major deliverables from the scope statement and decomposing them into smaller, more manageable components. The breakdown continues through multiple levels until the components can be estimated and have resources assigned to them. The lowest level of decomposition is the work package level. The WBS includes all the work required to complete the project. Any deliverable or work not listed on the WBS is excluded from the project. The WBS is a critical component of project planning. A WBS is the basis for time estimates, cost estimates, and resource assignments.

The WBS dictionary should list every deliverable and each of their components contained in the WBS. It should include a description of the component, code of account identifiers, responsible party, estimates, criteria for acceptance, and any other information that helps clarify the deliverables and work components.

Many steps are involved in schedule planning. Task definition takes the work packages from your WBS and breaks them down into individual tasks that can be estimated and assigned to team members. Sequencing looks at dependencies between tasks. These dependencies can be mandatory, discretionary, internal, or external. A dependent task is either a successor or a predecessor of a linked task.

There are four types of logical relationships: finish-to-start, start-to-start, start-to-finish, and finish-to-finish. Duration estimating is obtained using analogous (also called top-down) estimating, parametric estimating, and expert judgment.

The critical path method (CPM) creates a schedule by determining float time. Float is the difference between the early and late start dates and the early and late finish dates. The critical path is the longest full path on the project.

Duration compression is the technique used to shorten a project schedule to meet a mandated completion date. Crashing shortens task duration by adding more resources to the project. Fast tracking is where two tasks are started in parallel that were previously scheduled to start sequentially.

A project schedule may be displayed as a milestone chart. Milestones mark major project events such as the completion of a key deliverable or project phase. Gantt charts are a common method to display schedule data as well. The completed, approved project schedule becomes the baseline for tracking and reporting project progress.

Resource leveling is used when resources are overallocated and may create changes to the critical path and project end date. Resource smoothing modifies activities within their floats without changing the critical path or project end date.

When using an agile approach, the user stories are defined at the beginning of the project and kept in the backlog. Activity estimates can be performed using the techniques outlined in the chapter to determine the number of sprints or iterations the project will take. The Scrum team determines velocity by defining story points. The number of total story points is divided by the team's average velocity per iteration to determine the number of iterations needed to complete the work of the project. Agile methodologies use Kanban boards, Scrum boards, and burndown charts to display the work of the project.

Exam Essentials

Know how to define and create a work breakdown structure.   The WBS is a deliverable-oriented hierarchy that describes the work required to complete the project. The WBS is a multilevel diagram that starts with the project, includes the major deliverables, and decomposes the major deliverables into smaller units of work to the point where time and cost estimates can be provided and resources assigned.

Understand the levels in a WBS.   The highest level of the WBS is the project name. The major deliverables, project phases, or subprojects make up the next level. The number of levels in a WBS will vary by project; however, the lowest level of the WBS is a work package.

Describe a WBS dictionary.   The WBS dictionary describes each of the deliverables and their components and includes a code of accounts identifier, estimates, resources, criteria for acceptance, and any other information that helps clarify the deliverables.

Know the difference between analogous estimating and bottom-up estimating.   Analogous estimating is a top-down technique that uses expert judgment and historical information. Bottom-up estimating performs estimates for each work item and rolls them up to a total.

Describe the task sequencing process.   Sequencing is the process of identifying dependency relationships between the project activities and scheduling activities in the proper order.

Name the two major relationships between dependent tasks.   A predecessor is a task that exists on a path with another task and occurs before the task in question. A successor is a task that exists on a common path with another task and occurs after the task in question.

Name the four types of logical relationships.   The four types of logical relationships are finish-to-start, start-to-start, start-to-finish, and finish-to-finish.

Know and understand the three most commonly used techniques to estimate activity duration.   Expert judgment relies on the knowledge of someone familiar with the tasks. Analogous or top-down estimating bases the estimate on similar activities from a previous project. Parametric estimates are quantitatively-based estimates that typically calculate the rate times the quantity.

Be able to calculate the critical path.   The critical path includes the activities with durations that add up to the longest path of the project schedule network diagram. This path controls the finish date of the project. Any delay to a critical path task will delay the completion date of the project.

Be able to define a critical path task.   A critical path task is a project activity with zero or negative float.

Define the purpose of CPM.   CPM calculates the longest full path in the project. This path controls the finish date of the project. Any delay to a critical path task will delay the completion date of the project.

Explain a network diagram.   A network diagram is used to depict project activities and the interrelationships and dependencies among these activities.

Name three common ways project schedules are displayed.   Project schedules are typically displayed as milestone charts, PERT network diagrams, or Gantt charts; a Gantt chart is a type of bar chart.

Be able to describe the difference between resource leveling and resource smoothing. Resource leveling can change the critical path and project end date. Resource smoothing does not change the critical path or project end date.

Be familiar with the duration compression techniques.   The duration compression techniques are crashing and fast tracking.

Understand the estimating techniques for an agile project.   Expert judgment is used most frequently on agile projects, but other techniques such as parametric estimating or bottom-up estimating will also work.

Understand how to determine activity durations for an agile project.   Activity durations can be calculated using the number of iterations needed to complete the work, using the number of story points needed to complete the work, or using average velocity to determine how many story points can be completed in each iteration.

Be able to describe a Kanban board and a Scrum board and the difference between them.   Kanban boards and Scrum boards are visual displays of the work of the project. Kanban uses cards or tasks, and Scrum uses tasks. Tasks are added to the first column, usually the backlog or user story column, and then broken down into tasks and pulled into the remaining columns as the work finishes. Kanban boards and their work are capacity-bound. The work is progressive and continuous. There isn't a start and stop date. Scrum boards are time-bound and display the work of the sprint.

Key Terms

Before you take the exam, be certain you are familiar with the following terms:

activity list	parametric estimating
analogous estimating	performance measurement baseline
bottom-up estimating	
buffers	precedence diagramming method (PDM)
burndown chart	predecessor
code of accounts	Program Evaluation and Review Technique (PERT)
contingency reserves	project management plan
crashing	pull-based scheduling
critical path	quality gates
critical path method (CPM)	resource calendar
decomposition	resource leveling
dependencies	resource smoothing
discretionary dependency	reverse resource allocation

duration compression

epics

expert judgment

external dependency

fast tracking

float time

Gantt chart

governance gates

hard logic

internal dependency

Kanban board

logical relationships

mandatory dependency

network diagram

on-demand scheduling

schedule baseline

scope baseline

Scrum board

sequencing

soft logic

sprint planning meeting

story points

successor

task board

task list

top-down estimating

velocity

work breakdown structure (WBS)

work breakdown structure (WBS) dictionary

work package level

Review Questions

1. Which of the following is a characteristic of a WBS?

   A. A cost center structure for the project that describes the work of the project and the costs per work component to complete the deliverable

   B. A deliverables-oriented chart of the work of the project, with assignments showing the project teams responsible for the work components

   C. A deliverables-oriented structure that describes the detailed tasks required to complete the deliverables

   D. A deliverables-oriented structure that defines the work of the project

2. A WBS is created using a technique called decomposition. What is decomposition?

   A. Matching resources with deliverables

   B. Breaking down the project deliverables into smaller, more manageable components

   C. Estimating the cost of each individual deliverable

   D. Creating a detailed to-do list for each work package

3. What is the lowest level of the WBS?

   A. Work package

   B. Level 5

   C. Milestone

   D. Activities

4. Which of the following is not a benefit of a WBS?

   A. A WBS is an excellent tool for team building.

   B. A WBS helps prevents critical work from being overlooked.

   C. A WBS can become a template for future projects.

   D. A WBS can be used to describe how the deliverables will be validated.

5. All of the following are true regarding code of accounts identifiers except for which one?

   A. They are unique numbers for each component on the WBS.

   B. They are documented in the WBS dictionary.

   C. They are tied to the organization's chart of accounts.

   D. They are assigned to the resources who are associated with the work package level.

6. Your team has already created a WBS for the ABC product launch project. You are kicking off phase II of this project, which is the product Development phase. Which of the following is an example of what might appear in the second level of your project's WBS?

   A. ABC Product Launch Project

   B. Project deliverables

    C. Project phases

    D. Activities

7. Which of the following is not true for the critical path?

    A. It has zero float.

    B. It's the shortest activity sequence in the network.

    C. You can determine which tasks can start late without impacting the project end date.

    D. It controls the project finish date.

8. You are a project manager for a major movie studio. You need to schedule a shoot in Vail, Colorado during ski season. This is an example of which of the following?

    A. External dependency

    B. Finish-to-start relationship

    C. Mandatory dependency

    D. Discretionary dependency

9. What is analogous estimating also referred to as?

    A. Bottom-up estimating

    B. Expert judgment

    C. Parametric estimating

    D. Top-down estimating

10. You are working on your network diagram. Activity A is a predecessor to Activity B. Activity B cannot begin until Activity A is completed. What is this telling you?

    A. There is a mandatory dependency between Activity A and Activity B.

    B. There is a finish-to-start dependency relationship between Activity A and Activity B.

    C. Activity A and Activity B are both on the critical path.

    D. Activity B is a successor to multiple tasks.

11. What are the crashing and fast-track techniques used for?

    A. Duration compression

    B. Activity sequencing

    C. Precedence diagramming

    D. Task definition

12. Which of the following is true for float?

    A. It's calculated by adding the durations of all tasks and dividing by the number of tasks.

    B. It's time that you add to the project schedule to provide a buffer or contingency.

    C. It's the amount of time an activity can be delayed without affecting the project completion date.

    D. It is calculated only on the longest path of the project schedule.

13. Activity B on your project schedule starts on Monday, October 3, and ends on Wednesday, October 12. You calculate duration in workdays, and the team does not work on Saturdays or Sundays. How many days is the total duration of this task in workdays?

A. 9 days

B. 10 days

C. 8 days

D. 7 days

14. You have been hired as a contract project manager for Grapevine Vineyards. You have been told to use an agile methodology to develop this project. Grapevine wants you to design an Internet wine club for its customers. You'll need to develop a programming routine for customers to register with Grapevine before being allowed to order wine so that legal age can be established. You will also develop a module to allow customers to pick wine selections for the month based on their preferences. Lastly, you also need to develop a module to determine inventory on hand, which will interface with the monthly wine selection code. Which of the following techniques is the most beneficial for completing the work of this project?

A. Using agile release planning, because this is a large project that can be broken into releases and user stories can be created for each release

B. Using a Kanban board, because this is a large project that can be broken into releases that can be easily managed in small increments of time

C. Using a Scrum board, because this is a large project that can be broken into releases that can be easily managed as resources are available

D. Using epics, because this is a large project that can be broken into releases and user stories can be created for each release

15. Your task requires 4 miles of paving, and it will take 30 hours to complete one mile. On a past project similar to this one, it took 150 hours to complete. Which of the following is true regarding this estimate?

A. The total estimate for this task is 120 hours, which was derived using expert judgment.

B. The total estimate for this task is 120 hours, which was derived using parametric estimating.

C. The total estimate for this task is 150 hours, which was derived using analogous estimating.

D. The total estimate for this task is 150 hours, which was derived using expert judgment.

16. All of the following are true regarding milestone charts except for which one?

A. Milestone charts list the major deliverables or phases of a project.

B. Milestone charts show the scheduled completion dates.

C. Milestone charts show the actual completion dates.

D. Milestone charts are commonly displayed in bar chart format.

17. Your Scrum team's velocity rate is 24 story points per iteration. There are 165 total story points. Which of the following statements are true regarding this question? (Choose two.)

  A. Velocity is used to estimate the capacity of the Scrum team.

  B. This information can be tracked on a burndown chart.

  C. The project needs 7 iterations to complete all of the work of the project.

  D. A Kanban board can display this information.

18. Which of the following describes the difference between a Kanban board and a Scrum board?

  A. A Scrum board is capacity-based.

  B. A Kanban board is known as on-demand scheduling.

  C. A Scrum board is developed using rolling wave planning.

  D. A Kanban board is capacity-based.

19. Which of the following options describes iterative scheduling? (Choose two.)

  A. User stories are pulled from the product backlog as the team has the capacity to work on them.

  B. User stories are decomposed into tasks and managed on a task board. Tasks cannot proceed from one work column to another on the board until the team has the capacity to work on them.

  C. User stories are pulled from the product backlog and placed on the sprint backlog for the team to work on in the upcoming sprint.

  D. User stories that are in the sprint backlog will be decomposed into tasks and team members will choose the tasks they want to work on during the sprint.

20. Your project entails developing an app that will unlock your front door to allow deliveries from your favorite online services. The app will unlock the front door, detect and record how long the door was open, detect that a package or box was deposited on a delivery mat that is just inside the door, and then relock the door 60 seconds after the mat senses a package was placed there. At the beginning of the sprint, the product owner will pull the user stories that should be worked on during the upcoming sprint and team members will break them down into tasks and estimate their durations. Which of the following are true regarding this question?

  A. The product owner will develop the project timeline based on the estimates the team members give for each sprint.

  B. This question describes the sprint planning meeting that is held at the beginning of each sprint.

  C. The Scrum master will provide the team with the tools and techniques that will work best to break down tasks and determine estimates.

  D. This question describes agile release planning because it's a large project that can be broken down into releases and then user stories can be created for each release.

Chapter

6

Resource Planning and Management

THE COMPTIA PROJECT+ EXAM TOPICS COVERED IN THIS CHAPTER INCLUDE:

✓ **1.0 Project Management Concepts**

- ▪ **1.2 Compare and contract Agile vs. Waterfall concepts**

- ▪ **1.10 Given a scenario, perform basic activities related to team and resource management**

- ▪ **1.11 Explain important project procurement and vendor selection concepts**

✓ **2.0 Project Life Cycle Phases**

- ▪ **2.2 Given a scenario, perform activities during the project initiation phase**

- ▪ **2.3 Given a scenario, perform activities during the project planning phase**

- ▪ **2.4 Given a scenario, perform activities during the project execution phase**

✓ **3.0 Tools and Documentation**

- ▪ **3.1 Given a scenario, use the appropriate tools throughout the project life cycle**

- ▪ **3.3 Given a scenario, analyze quality and performance charts to inform project decisions**

We'll kick off this chapter with a discussion about the organizational structures in which people work. Project work is performed by people. Successful project outcomes involve developing the project team, managing the work according to the project plan, and managing conflict.

You'll have relationships with a number of individuals and groups during the life of the project. All of your people management skills will come into play as you negotiate with the sponsor, team members, vendors, functional managers, clients, users, and other internal organizations.

If you talk to veteran project managers about what makes their projects successful, most will list the project team. Understanding how to build this temporary group into a team, making sure appropriate training is provided, managing conflict, and implementing a meaningful rewards and recognition plan are all challenges you'll face in developing a cohesive team.

You'll often find that you need to engage contract resources to help with project activities. And you'll likely need supplies or equipment for the project or to perform project activities. This will require contracting with vendors. We'll cover procurement and vendor selection in this chapter. Let's dive in.

Understanding Organizational Structures

The structure of your organization has an impact on many aspects of project management, including the authority of the project manager and the process to assign resources.

Project managers are often frustrated by what appear to be roadblocks in moving the project forward, but in many cases, the root issue is the organizational structure itself and how it operates. The following sections will cover the different types of organizational structures and how they influence the way projects are conducted.

The Functional Organization

The classic organizational structure is the *functional organization*, as shown in Figure 6.1. In this structure, the staff is organized along departmental lines, such as IT, marketing, sales, network, human resources, public relations, customer support, and legal. Each department is managed independently with a limited span of control. This organizational type is hierarchical, with each staff member reporting to one supervisor, who in turn reports to one supervisor, and so on up the chain. Figure 6.1 shows a typical functional organization.

FIGURE 6.1   The functional organization

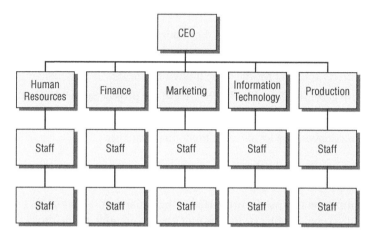

A functional organization often goes about the work of the project in a siloed fashion. That is, the project deliverables are worked on independently in different departments. This can cause frustration among project managers because they are the ones held accountable for the results of the project, but they have no means of holding team members from other departments accountable for completing project deliverables.

A project manager in a functional organization should develop strong working relationships with the functional managers. Functional managers are responsible for assigning work to the employees who report to them. They are also responsible for rating the performance of the employees and determining their raises or bonuses. This, as you can imagine, sets up a strong loyalty between the employee and the functional manager as opposed to the employee and the project manager. However, that doesn't mean project managers can't be successful in this type of organization. Building a relationship with the functional managers and maintaining open communications is the key to successful projects in this type of structure. It also helps a great deal if you can contribute to the employee's performance ratings by rating their work on the project.

Project managers have little formal authority in a functional organizational structure, but it doesn't mean their projects are destined for failure. Communication skills, negotiation skills, and strong interpersonal skills will help assure your success in working within this type of environment.

The functional organization is the most common organizational structure and has endured for centuries. The advantages of a functional organization include the following:

- Growth potential and a career path for employees
- The opportunity for those with unique skills to flourish
- A clear chain of command (each staff member has one supervisor—the functional manager)

The typical disadvantages of a functional organization include the following:

- Project managers have limited to no authority.
- Multiple projects compete for the same limited resources.
- Resources are generally committed part-time to the project rather than full-time.
- Issue resolution follows the department chain of command.
- Project team members are loyal to the functional manager.

The Matrix Organization

The *matrix organization* is typically organized along departmental lines, like a functional organization, but resources assigned to a project are accountable to the project manager for all work associated with the project. The project manager is often a peer of the functional staff managers. The team members working on the project often have two or more supervisors—their functional manager and the project manager (or managers) they are reporting to. Figure 6.2 shows a balanced matrix organization.

FIGURE 6.2   The balanced matrix organization

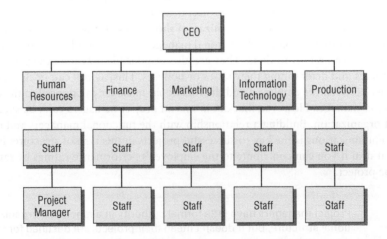

Project managers working in a matrix organization need to be clear with both the project team members and their respective functional managers about assignments and results regarding the following:

- Those outcomes for which the team member is accountable to the project manager

- Those outcomes for which the team member is accountable to the functional manager

The team member should be accountable to only one person for any given outcome so as to avoid confusion and conflicting direction.

Another trouble area in a matrix organization is availability of resources. If you have a resource assigned 50 percent of the time to your project, it's critical that the functional manager, or other project managers working with this resource, be aware of the time commitment this resource has allocated to your project. If time-constraint issues like this are not addressed, project managers may well discover they have fewer human resources for the project than first anticipated. Addressing resource commitments at the beginning of the project, both during pre-project setup and again during the Planning phase, will help prevent problems down the road.

 In a typical matrix organization, functional managers assign employees to the project, while project managers assign tasks associated with the project to the employee.

The following are the typical characteristics of a matrix organization:

- Project manager authority ranges from weak to strong.

- There is a mix of full-time and part-time project resources.

- Resources are assigned to the project within their respective functional areas by a functional manager.

- Project managers and functional managers share authority levels.

- There is better interdepartmental communication.

Matrix Organizations Times Three

There are three types of matrix organizations:

Strong Matrix The strong matrix organization emphasizes project work over functional duties. The project manager has the majority of power in this type of organization.

Weak Matrix The weak matrix organization emphasizes functional work over project work and operates more like a functional hierarchy. The functional managers have the majority of power in this type of organization.

Balanced Matrix A balanced matrix organization shares equal emphasis between projects and functional work. Both the project manager and the functional manager share power in this type of structure.

Matrix organizations allow project managers to focus on the work of the project. The project team members, once assigned to a project, are free to focus on the project objectives with minimal distractions from the functional department.

It is important that you understand what type of matrix organization you're working in because the organizational type dictates the level of authority you'll have. But don't be fooled into thinking you will have your way more easily in a strong matrix environment. It is still essential that you keep the lines of communication open with functional managers and inform them of status, employee performance, future needs, project progress, and so on.

The Projectized Organization

The *projectized organizational* structure is shown in Figure 6.3. This organizational structure is far less common than the functional or matrix structure. In this environment, the focus of the organization is projects rather than functional work units.

FIGURE 6.3   The projectized organization

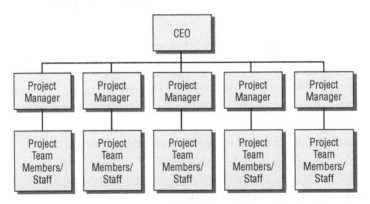

Project managers have the majority of power in this type of structure. They are responsible for making decisions regarding the project and for acquiring and assigning resources from inside or outside the organization. Support staff, such as human resources, administrative support, and accounting, often report to the project manager in a projectized environment.

One of the advantages of this type of organization is that team members are *collocated*, meaning they work together at the same physical location. Other advantages of this structure are as follows:

- The project manager has full authority to manage the project and resources.
- Full-time resources are assigned to the project and report to the project manager.
- Loyalty is established with the project manager.

- Other ad hoc resources may report to the project manager.
- There is dedicated project support staff.

One of the biggest drawbacks of a projectized organization is reassigning project team members once the project ends. There may not always be a new project waiting for these resources. Again, it's essential that communication occurs among project managers across the organization so that the complex timing of increasing or decreasing resources is managed as efficiently as possible.

Now that you have a good understanding of organizational structures, let's move on to determining the types of resources you'll need for the project.

Determining Resource Needs

All projects require resources to complete the tasks and deliver a successful project. Usually when someone talks about resources, it's assumed they are talking about human resources. While I would argue they are one of the most critical resources needed for the project, there are many other types that may be needed for the project as well. According to the CompTIA objectives, there are human, physical, capital, internal, external, and shared versus dedicated resources on a project. Let's look at each of these:

Human Resources   All projects require human resources. Even if you are relying on robotic technology, automated processes, artificial intelligence, and more, there are still humans behind each of these technologies. Human resources are unique, diverse, and complicated. We will spend a good portion of this chapter discussing managing human resources and resolving conflict.

Physical Resources   Most projects will likely require *physical resources* to perform the work of the project. This might take the form of equipment, materials, supplies, and more. IT projects often require computers, servers, software programs, and so on.

Capital Resources   *Capital resources* are physical resources used to create the product of the project or that are used by the organization to perform the project. The definition of capital resources can vary by industry or company. For example, in my organization, any asset valued at $5,000 or more is considered a capital resource. Typically, capital resources have a high value and are in resources with long life expectancies. Again, the definition of "long" can vary. For example, let's say your project requires the purchase of a new server to host the case management software application you are purchasing. Both the server and software in this case would be considered capital assets. They both should last at least three years and maybe up to five years. Let's say you also purchase cell phones and tablets for the project team working on the project. They are likely not considered capital resources because they are not high-dollar items and are only expected to last a couple of years at best. Make certain to check with your organization on the definition of *capital* so that you can account for these resources appropriately in the project budget.

Internal vs. External Resources   Internal resources are those the company owns or employs. They may be human, physical, or capital resources. External resources are those you will acquire, lease, or contract from outside the organization. Project staff, whether internal or external, may also come from remote locations. *Remote resources* located in other parts of the company, who are geographically dispersed, or who are external to the organization, sometimes feel disconnected from the project team. When possible, you should collocate the resources so they all work together in the same location.

Here is a word of caution when working with functional managers in the case of internal resources, especially human resources. They may jump at the opportunity to assign resources to your project and begin giving you names before you've even stated what skills are needed. I've learned from experience that overeager offers to provide team members to my project sometimes means the resources are *low-quality resources*. This doesn't mean they're bad resources, but it generally means they don't have the skill sets needed and require a lot of training or, worse, they may have abrasive personalities or a history of conflicts with other team members. If you must accept an employee like this on the team, I recommend meeting with them as soon as possible and setting clear expectations so that there are no misunderstandings on how team members are expected to interact with one another. When negotiating for external resources with contracting companies, be certain to specify the skills and experience levels needed and explain organizational culture issues with the contracting agency so that you get the resources needed. Some contracting agencies will present resources to you during the procurement process, declaring their expertise only to switch them with a lower-quality resource once the contract is signed. Also, beware of low-quality physical resources that won't hold up to the wear and tear needed to complete the task.

Shared vs. Dedicated Resources   *Dedicated resources* are found in projectized organizational structures and are the ideal scenario for a project manager because you have full authority and control of the resource time and the tasks they work on. You don't have to coordinate schedules with another manager or fear having the resource pulled off the project because of an "emergency" in the functional area. You may also have resources assigned to the project for the duration of its life cycle in a functional organization. I have worked on projects where expert resources were assigned, or dedicated to the project, due to the criticality of the project. They were temporarily backfilled with contract resources to perform their daily duties until the project was complete.

In a functional or matrix organization, you'll find you often have to share resources. A *shared resource* works for both the functional manager and the project manager. Typically, the team member will remain loyal to the person writing their performance appraisals and reviews. And in my experience, shared resources are often torn between their functional work and project work and find themselves defaulting to functional work because the business has to continue operating and they fear their work might pile up while they are busy working on project tasks. Project managers working with shared resources should negotiate with the functional managers to make certain the shared resource has the appropriate amount of time available to work on the project. They should also negotiate the ability to have some say in the team member's performance ratings. This will help you reinforce that the project work is important and needs to be addressed and prioritized by the team member.

Resource Overallocation

Resources are sometimes scarce. At the time of this writing, there are more jobs in the United States than there are people applying for them. Additionally, organizations are poaching employees and enticing them with higher pay, better benefits, and opportunities for remote work. The organization that has lost employees now finds themselves with vacancies that remain unfilled for quite some time. This in turn can lead to *resource overallocation* for existing employees. Due to vacancies and lack of qualified applicants, the existing employees pick up the work of those who left. This means if you need a person with a specific skill for your project, you may have to wait in line because that person is working on multiple projects as well as operational activities; they are overallocated, which can lead to burnout, and they may end up leaving the organization for better working conditions. It's a vicious cycle, but I digress.

Resource shortages are not always the cause of resource overallocation. It could be that you've scheduled the resource to complete more tasks than the time available. Overallocated resources will show up on a project schedule as 100 percent (or more) allocated. In reality, resources never have 100 percent of their time available for any task because they also have administrative functions they need to perform, such as filling out timecards, attending staff meetings, and answering emails.

 Generally speaking, when your organization has only one person or one physical resource who can perform a task, you will be dealing with overallocation issues.

I'm sorry to say there isn't an easy answer for overallocated resources. This might mean you'll have to work with the senior management team to determine project priorities. If the one and only resource needed for two competing projects can't work on both projects, management will have to decide which one has priority.

The opposite of overallocating team members is having *benched resources*. Benched resources are those who have typically finished a project and are not yet assigned to a new project or who have a time gap between the finish and start of the new project. Benched resources are costly to the organization because, well, they're being paid to sit around and wait for the next assignment. This scenario typically occurs in a projectized organization.

Interproject Work

When you're determining resource needs, you'll need to take *interproject dependencies* and *interproject resource contention* into consideration.

Interproject dependencies occur when you need the completed deliverables from one project to work on the current project. For example, perhaps your organization is constructing a new highway lane on an existing highway in your city. However, there are other projects in this program that must be completed before you can finish the highway lane construction. One of those projects is performing the environmental studies on the ground where the new lane is planned. Another might be digging a trench to lay fiber-optic cable along the highway. Both of these projects must be completed before you can begin your project. Thus, you have an interproject dependency.

It's important to meet with the project managers from the other projects and understand their schedules and risks. You should also discuss the possibility of removing dependencies wherever possible. Make certain that you are receiving up-to-date status reports on the other projects so that you can track the key dependencies and keep your project on schedule or take corrective action where necessary.

Interproject resource contention is similar in nature to the overallocation problem discussed previously. Your resource may be scheduled for similar tasks on other projects. You'll need to work in coordination with the project managers on those other projects to schedule the resource so that they are available to both of you when needed.

Resource Life Cycle

Resources, particularly physical resources, won't last forever. They have a life cycle that consists of several stages: acquisition, maintenance, hardware decommissioning, end-of-life software, and successor planning. We'll look at each of these next.

Acquisition   Acquiring resources usually starts with a needs assessment. Much like a project charter or scope statement that's prepared for a project, a needs assessment examines requirements, functionality, life span, cost, and other factors, and the justification for the resource. This may be as simple as obtaining a few quotes from vendors, or it may involve a written acquisition and justification process. Check with the organization to determine how resources are procured. Typically, resources obtained from an operating budget follow a different process than capital resources. In my experience, acquiring capital resources is a more rigorous process, with lots of reviews and approvals. Once the resource is acquired, it is implemented and begins its purposeful life cycle.

Maintenance   Maintenance involves the ongoing care and feeding of the resource. This may include elements such as patching and updating in the case of software or updating firmware on hardware, while other resources may require physical maintenance such as oiling or painting, and so on. Maintenance duties will depend on the resource type. Resources that require regular maintenance will not last their expected life span without it. Maintenance routines should be documented. There should also be a maintenance log where routine maintenance activities are recorded. This should at a minimum include the date, the maintenance activity, and who performed the activity.

Hardware Decommissioning   In the IT world, hardware such as servers and workstations need to be decommissioned at the end of their life cycle. In some cases, the hardware may still be usable and could be donated to a charitable organization or school. The decommissioning process ensures that no data remains on the hardware before disposal or donation, and these processes should be documented.

Data on the old hardware may need to be preserved and transferred to the new hardware. Or data may need to be archived or destroyed. In either case, before disposing of the old hardware, you'll need to ensure the data that resides on it has been destroyed. In Chapter 2, "Understanding IT Fundamentals," we talked about personal information, sensitive data, protected health information (PHI), and sensitive personally identifiable information (SPII) data, all of which may reside on the old equipment. In addition, sensitive company data or trade secrets may reside on this hardware. The decommissioning process should outline steps required to destroy the data on the hard drives. This may include using special software that will wipe the drive clean of its data and overwrite the empty spaces so that the data cannot be retrieved. It may include degaussing techniques, which is using a magnet to erase the data and ensure it's unrecoverable. Or it may include physically destroying the hard drive by shredding it, crushing it, and so on. Do not ever throw away, donate, or otherwise dispose of old equipment without first destroying the data residing on the drives.

End-of-Life Software   Software is a resource that also has a useful life. It may physically reside on a server or workstation or other device, or it may be accessed via the cloud. Software that physically resides on devices needs to be decommissioned just like hardware as described earlier. You'll need to determine if the data in the software needs to be retained, transferred to the new software system, archived, or destroyed. Keep in mind that the software may also include hard-coded information that is sensitive to the company. If it's determined the data should be destroyed, you can use the same process described in the hardware decommissioning section. When decommissioning data from the cloud, you'll need to follow the processes outlined by your provider. Make certain when contracting with cloud providers that the contract ensures complete and total destruction of your organization's data when the contract is terminated.

Be certain to meet with key stakeholders before destroying any data. The stakeholders are the owners of the data and are responsible for determining its usefulness. It may need to be retained for legal purposes, regulatory reporting purposes, and so on. They should approve data destruction in writing. I strongly recommend having a sign-off document that specifies the type of data, data ranges if known, and other pertinent information and that requires the business owner to sign off approving the destruction.

Successor Planning   Long before the hardware, software, or other resource reaches end of life, decisions should be made about their successors. Some of the questions you can start asking are: Should the resource be replaced with a newer version? Or can the resource move to the cloud or be retired altogether? Purchasing replacement resources may require a long lead time. If you're replacing a resource with a cloud version, you've just taken on a project and will need at least a year or more to implement. It's important to begin thinking about what comes next for your hardware and software resources before they reach end of life so that you have adequate time to prepare and acquire new resources. If you are caught unawares, you may incur hefty fees from your software vendor to continue maintenance and support for end-of-life systems.

Personnel Management

Managing a project team differs from managing a functional work group. Project teams are temporary, and getting everyone to work together on a common goal can be challenging, especially if your team members are specialists in a given discipline and don't have a broad business background. As the project manager, you must mold this group into an effective team that can work together to deliver the project on time, on budget, and within scope, all while producing quality results. This is not always an easy undertaking, especially if you factor in a combination of full- and part-time team members, technical and nontechnical team members, internal and external resources, and in some cases a team dispersed over a large geographic area.

Team Composition

Teams are made up of people and, as such, are diverse, complex, and unique, and have varying needs. No two teams are alike. Team composition is as diverse and unique as the individuals that make it up. We have discussed some of the topics associated with team composition in previous chapters, but I'd like to highlight some key references here as it ties together with other resource topics in this chapter. Agile teams are self-managed and self-directed and should consist of between five and 11 members. Waterfall teams are not limited to size and are typically very large. Waterfall teams are made up of members from all over the organization. Product owners in agile methodologies represent the stakeholders and are responsible for managing and prioritizing the backlog and creating and choosing user stories for the upcoming iteration. Each team member, no matter the development methodology you're using, has a role and a set of responsibilities on the team. It's also important to gain commitment from team members and product owners to work with the project throughout its life cycle and to encourage continuity throughout the project.

Selecting Team Members

Acquiring team members with the right skills and demeanor is important to the success of your project. On all but the smallest of projects, you'll find you have a diverse set of team members working on the project at various times during its life cycle. Some team members will join the project team and then leave when their work is done; others will be involved from the beginning to the end of the project. These team members are known as *core team members*. They are core to the project because of their expertise and knowledge of the business process, the technology associated with the project, and/or the skills needed to perform the work of the project, and their expertise is required throughout the project. Core team members are critical to the success of the project.

Those team members who come in for an assignment or two and then go back to their departments are known as *functional/extended team members*. They may have skills or expertise needed for a specific task, but not for the entire project life cycle. Functional/extended team members may also include business unit stakeholders, advisers, or subject matter experts who can answer questions, review requirements, verify deliverables, and so on. They will be called upon when needed throughout the project but are not committed full time.

You may often find that you don't have control over the selection of team members. Functional managers may assign team members to the project according to their availability. Other times, you'll know the team members you want on the project and can request them. When you're not familiar with the resource or their skill set, spend some time with the functional manager discussing the skills and abilities you need for the tasks. Interview the resource being recommended and ask specific skill-related questions and how they might go about approaching the tasks you'll be assigning to them. If you are doubtful about their skills and abilities, meet with the functional manager, share your concerns, and ask them if someone else is available.

You should consider performing a *gap analysis* when selecting team members. A gap analysis determines the difference between where you are now and where you want to be in the future. In the case of resources, it's a comparison of the resources you have to the resources you need. This can include an assessment of skills as well. This technique may be used to compare performance capability, financial assessments, resource assignments, goal planning, and much more. In the case of resource planning, you'll need to start by understanding the skills needed to perform the work of the project and if those skills reside within the organization. Perhaps you need a programmer, a server administrator, a database administrator, and key business personnel. You'll need to know if the organization has those resources and, if not, begin the process to procure them from an external source, either contract or as employees.

Once you know the skills needed and the resources available for the project, you can perform a skills assessment. You can do this by interviewing potential team members about their past experience on projects similar to this one, asking them to fill out a questionnaire with skills-related questions, talking with their managers, and so on. Next, learn how many team members with certain skills will be needed to do the work and determine how those team members will be utilized on the project. You may need core team members as well as extended team members. You should work with a few key team members and functional managers to help perform this analysis and determine what skills are needed and in what quantity.

Gap analysis is a useful technique when determining the features and functionality needed for the product of the project. You can perform gap analysis before or during the requirements gathering process. Ask the stakeholders questions such as: What features are available today in the program you currently use? What features are a must-have to consider the implementation a success? What functionality or specifications should the system possess to ensure your business processes follow best practices?

Another consideration when selecting resources is determining the criticality of the resource. For example, if you need a thermodynamic expert for the project and that expert becomes unavailable, you can't replace this resource with someone who does not have this skill. You'll need to understand the criticality that each resource has to the project and perhaps devise a contingency plan if that resource becomes unavailable. You can document resources and their criticality in the roles and responsibility document, which we'll look at next.

Roles and Responsibilities

A roles and responsibilities document lists each group or individual team member on the project along with their skills, criticality, and responsibilities. Roles and responsibilities of project team members are more than just the assigned tasks. There are standards and methodologies to be adhered to, documentation to be completed, and time-reporting responsibilities, to name a few. It's a good idea to develop a template to document roles and responsibilities beyond just the task assignment. The more clarity around who is responsible for what, the better. We discussed the various roles and responsibilities of team members in Chapter 2 if you need a refresher on specific project roles. You could use that information as a starting point for the roles and responsibilities document.

Be clear and precise in defining the key areas of accountability for each team member in the roles and responsibilities document. Roles and responsibilities may change over the course of the project, so be sure to update this document as needed.

Organization Charts and Position Descriptions

Once your team members have been selected, it's a good idea to create a *project organization chart*. We've all seen an organization chart. It usually documents your name, your position, your boss, your boss's boss, your boss's boss's boss, and so on. It's hierarchical in nature, similar to a WBS. In the case of a project organization chart, you can present the information in a couple of different ways, including the traditional org chart, with the project manager and project team member names, as shown in Figure 6.4.

FIGURE 6.4   Project organization chart

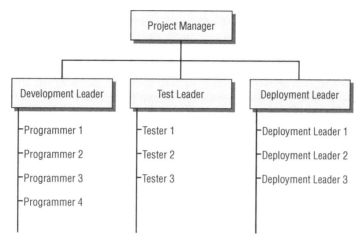

You may also present the work of the project in an *organization breakdown structure (OBS)*. This form of organization chart shows the departments, work units, or teams within an organization (rather than individuals) and their respective work packages.

A *resource breakdown structure (RBS)* is another type of hierarchical chart that breaks down the work of the project according to the types of resources needed. For example, you might have painters, carpenters, and electricians as resource types on the RBS.

Matrix-Based Charts

A *responsibility assignment matrix (RAM)* is a matrix-based chart that maps your WBS elements to the required resources. Table 6.1 shows a sample portion of a RAM for an IT development project. It lists the WBS identifier, the type of resource required, and the number of resources needed for each skill set.

TABLE 6.1   Sample project responsibility assignment matrix

WBS identifier	Programmer	Tester	Marketing	Tech writer	Server
10-1-1-1				1	
10-1-1-2	2				
10-1-1-3		3			1
10-1-1-4	4				
10-1-1-5			1		

Another type of responsibility assignment chart I like to use is called a RACI chart. These are used to show the types of resources and the responsibility they each have on the project. A RACI is usually depicted as a chart with resource names (or the individual names of team members) listed in each column and work elements such as milestones or work packages listed as the row. Indicators in the intersections show where the resources are needed.

Table 6.2 shows a *RACI chart* for a conference event project team. In this example, the RACI chart shows the level of accountability each of the participants has on the project. The letters in the acronym RACI are the designations shown in the chart.

R = Responsible for performing the work

A = Accountable, the one who ensures the deliverable or work package is completed and approves or signs off on the work

C = Consulted; someone who has input to the work or decisions

I = Informed; someone who must be informed of the decisions or results

TABLE 6.2   Sample RACI chart

	Olga	Rae	Charlie	Lolita
Hotel conference rooms	R*	A	C	C/I
Food and snack service	C/I	C	I	R/A
Speaker contracts	C	I	R	A

* R = Responsible, A = Accountable, C = Consult, I = Inform

In this example, Olga is responsible for booking and assigning the hotel conference rooms, but Rae is accountable and is the one who must make sure this task is completed and approved. Charlie is responsible for securing speakers, but Lolita is accountable for making sure this task is completed. Charlie also needs to be consulted regarding hotel conference rooms so that speakers are assigned to a room large enough to hold the projected number of attendees. Lolita is responsible and accountable for the food and snack service and needs to be consulted and informed about the hotel conference room task.

The responsibility, consulting, and informing elements may have multiple team members assigned on the RACI. There should only be one person designated as accountable.

This is a great tool because it shows at a glance not only where a resource is working but what the resource's responsibility level is on the project.

Building and Managing a Cohesive Team

Every team progresses through a series of development stages. It's important to understand these stages because team member behaviors will change as you progress through them, and the stage they're in affects their interactions with each other.

Bruce Tuckman developed a model that describes how teams develop and mature over time. According to Tuckman, all teams progress through the following five stages of development:

Forming   *Forming* is the beginning stage of team formation, when all the members are brought together, introduced, and told the objectives of the project. This is where team members learn why they're working together. During this stage, team members tend to be formal and reserved and take on an "all-business" approach.

Storming   *Storming* is where the action begins. They're working through who is going to have the most influence and they're jockeying for status.

Norming   *Norming* is where things begin to calm down. Team members know one another fairly well by now. They're comfortable with their positions in the team, and they begin to deal with project problems instead of people problems. Decisions are made jointly at this stage, and team members exhibit mutual respect and familiarity with one another.

Performing   Ahh, perfection. Well, almost, anyway. *Performing* is the stage where great teams end up. This is where the team is productive and effective. The level of trust among team members is high, and great things are achieved. This is the mature development stage. Not all teams make it to performing; many churn between storming and norming. It is a real joy to work with a team that has made it to the performing stage.

Adjourning   As the name implies, *adjourning* refers to breaking up the team after the work is completed and returning the team members to their functional managers and teams.

Different teams progress through the stages of development at different rates. When new team members are brought onto the team, the development stages start all over again. It doesn't matter where the team is in the first four phases of the development process—a new member will start the cycle all over again.

Progressing through these stages can be enhanced with the use of team-building activities. *Team building* is a set of activities or exercises designed to get a diverse group of people to work together in an efficient and effective manner. It helps them to form social bonds and identify common interests, and it can help clarify the roles and responsibilities of each team member. Organized team-building activities are most effective when a team is in the forming and storming stages, especially if they don't know each other well. Search the web or ask your human resources department for team-building activities that will help your new staff get to know each other better. In my experience, once the team moves into the norming stage and beyond, there may not be as much of a need for organized team activities; however, informal activities are a great benefit in this stage, especially if the team arranges them, such as lunches, pizza nights, sports outings, or drinks after work.

You may also find team-building activities helpful if your team is experiencing personality clashes or if there are changes to the team makeup where old members have rolled off and new members have rolled on. Organizational changes are another good reason to employ team-building activities.

Trust Building

Building trust with and among your team members is in my experience the most important thing a project manager can do to ensure a top-performing team. Trust, as the old saying goes, is earned, not given.

> To build and maintain the trust of your project team members, you need to demonstrate competence, respect, honesty, integrity, and openness. You must also demonstrate that you are willing to act on performance problems.

Trust building occurs over time, not overnight. In my experience, trust building includes doing what you say you'll do, supporting your team, showing concern for your team, holding the good of the organization above your own, and being humble. Not many folks want to work for or with someone whose primary concern is themselves.

Teams that trust one another and their project manager are more comfortable stating their opinions and objecting to ideas that don't make sense. This may sound contrary, but teams who are able to speak their minds are much more likely to be successful. They have buy-in to ideas and tasks because they had some say in the matter.

If the project manager is not open to this type of feedback or thinks they have all the answers and don't require input from the team, they aren't likely to experience their teams moving to the performing stage.

Take the time to get to know your team members. Ask them questions about their outside interests and show genuine concern when they have issues or conflicts. This can go a long way in establishing a trusting relationship.

Monitoring Team Performance

Managing team member performance can be a complex undertaking. A successful project manager understands that most people work at their best when they're allowed to do the work they were assigned without someone preapproving every action they take. As long as the end result is accomplished according to plan and there is no impact on scope, schedule, budget, or quality, team members should be given freedom and choices as to how to complete their tasks.

Although you shouldn't micromanage team members, they do need feedback on how they're doing. Most team members perform well in some areas and need improvement in others. Even if your organization does not require project managers to conduct formal written appraisals, you should take the time to provide feedback to the team members. It's easy to get caught up in managing the project issues, but don't get so deep into the issues that you neglect your team members. The following are important areas of focus as you prepare to discuss performance with your team members:

- Specifying performance expectations
- Identifying inadequate performance behaviors
- Rewarding superior performance
- Reprimanding inadequate performance
- Providing specific consequences for choices made

Performance Feedback

The first meeting you should have with any new team member, and at the beginning of every project, is the expectations-setting meeting. This is where you discuss the following: their role on the project, due dates, performance expectations, team interactions, industry standards and regulations that must be followed, and your expectations of their work quality. You'll want them to know the best way to contact you and that you are available for any questions they may have.

Performance feedback should be given in a timely fashion. It is of little value to attempt corrective action on something that happened several weeks or months ago. The team member may not even remember the specifics of the performance in question. It is best to deal with negative situations as soon as they occur. Be objective about your observations and ask the team member to explain the issue from their perspective. The best case is that you and the team member come to an understanding on what occurred and how the behavior should be corrected. The not-so-best case is you'll have to remove this team member.

You must work with your human resources department if the team member refuses to correct their behavior or if they don't have the ability to perform their tasks. If your team member came from a functional area, you'll need to write up the issues and provide this information to the functional manager.

It isn't easy to have to remove or replace personnel from a project. But if all other actions fail and the team member refuses to improve, you must take steps to prevent a serious decline in morale. Taking this action also builds trust in you as a leader. Your team will see that you're willing take the actions needed in a compassionate manner to deal with team issues.

Rewarding Superior Performance

Recognition and rewards are important elements of both individual and team motivation. They are formal ways of recognizing and promoting desirable behavior and are most effective when carried out by the project manager or management team. Project teams work hard and often overcome numerous challenges to deliver a project. If your company has a functional organizational structure, the project work may not receive the appropriate recognition from the functional managers. That means it's up to you to recognize the job your team is doing and to implement a recognition and reward system.

When you think of rewards, you generally think of monetary rewards. And that's great if you're lucky enough to have money for a reward system, either as a direct budget line or as part of a managerial reserve. But there are options besides money that you can use as a reward—for example, time off, movie tickets, sporting or cultural events, team dinners, trophies, and so on. I've worked in organizations where an ordinary object was designated the "trophy" for outstanding performance. Individual team members were responsible for recognizing each other by presenting the trophy to the team member who went above and beyond.

Another no-cost idea is a letter of recognition sent to an employee's manager, with copies to the appropriate organizational executives and the project sponsor. This can be a powerful means of communicating your appreciation for outstanding performance.

Not all project managers have the resources to reward team members either individually or collectively, but that does not mean superior performance should go unrecognized. One of the easiest things you can do is simply tell people that you are aware of their accomplishments and that you appreciate their efforts. A simple thank-you works wonders. A handwritten note of appreciation only takes a few minutes and is something the employee can keep in their file.

Make certain that rewards are proportional to the achievement and are distributed equitably among team members. Playing favorites or recognizing the same team member with awards multiple times can kill morale rather than improve it.

Also, be sensitive to your team members and their cultural backgrounds. Some people love to be praised in public, and others may actually be shamed by this action rather than feeling appreciated.

You should develop and document the criteria for rewards, especially monetary awards. Work with your human resources department to understand the guidelines for reward systems in your organization. The key is to establish a program to acknowledge the efforts of your project team members, whether it involves money, prizes, letters of commendation, or a simple thank-you. Whatever form your rewards and recognition program takes, you must make sure that it is applied consistently to all project team members and that the reward is appropriate for the level of effort expended or the results that were achieved. Inconsistent application of rewards is often construed as favoritism.

Rewards for superior performance can be given publicly, but a discussion of inadequate performance should always be done privately. Berating a team member in front of others is inappropriate and will likely make the person angry and defensive. It may also negatively impact the morale of the team members who witnessed the berating.

Developing your team and improving overall performance can also be accomplished through training. I'll discuss this next.

Training

Training involves determining your team members' skills and abilities, assessing the project needs, and providing the training necessary for the team members to perform their activities. In some industries or organizations, one of the perks associated with being assigned to a new project is the opportunity to expand a skill set or get training on new products or processes. Training needs may come to light when you perform the skill gap analysis as well.

One of the most common types of training provided to project teams is project management training. Project management training may include a session developed by the project manager, formal training provided by an outside company, or training from an internal PMO on the standard methodologies, tools, and templates all project members are expected to use.

Conflict management is an important aspect of team building, communication, and team cohesiveness. We'll look at this topic next.

 **Real World Scenario**

Project Management 101

One of the more successful experiences I've had with project management training involved a project team in an organization that was just starting to implement project management disciplines. Based on the chaos surrounding earlier attempts at running projects, it was clear that the team members needed a common understanding of what project management was all about.

We contracted with a professional project management training company to teach a beginning class in project management concepts. All project team members were required to attend this session. All of the exercises associated with the class were based on the actual project the team members were assigned to. Not only did the team members gain knowledge of the project management discipline, but they were able to contribute to the project itself while in class.

Although this took some time and money, it was well worth the effort. All the team members used common definitions of terms, and it was much easier to talk about the meeting requirements, the project baseline, scope creep, and other fundamental project management concepts. The success of this project resulted in the organization setting goals for project management training for the entire department.

Conflict Management

One thing is certain: if you have people working on your project, you'll likely experience conflict at least once, if not many times, during the course of the project. *Conflict* is the incompatibility of desires, needs, or goals between two parties or individuals. This can lead to one party resisting or blocking the other party from attaining their goals.

Conflict may arise on a project for any of several reasons. As I've discussed in several places throughout the book, resources in most organizations are in high demand. Competition for resources can cause conflicts among the project managers, functional managers, and even project team members who may not be happy with less stellar selections as teammates.

Work styles can sometimes cause conflict. For example, we've all worked with team members whose desks were so buried in papers and books and other items that you couldn't see the desktop. And of course, we've seen the opposite as well—those team members without a speck of paper on the desk, only the telephone and a computer monitor. Some team members are early birds and show up for work before the sun is up but are tired and cranky by 4 p.m., whereas others do their best work in the afternoon and early evening hours. There are hundreds of ways that work styles can vary and cause conflicts on the team. You should be aware of the preferences of your team members and accommodate reasonable solutions whenever possible.

Constraints are another area that can cause conflict on a project. Change requests, scope creep, and stakeholders are just a few examples of constraints that may drive incompatible goals.

Another common cause of conflict is communication issues. Perhaps team members don't understand the goals of the project, or maybe they lack solid interpersonal skills and are not adept at communicating their needs or issues. Sometimes team members don't communicate well with each other and deadlines are missed or tasks don't meet quality standards. Communication is such an important issue in project management I've dedicated almost an entire chapter to the topic. I'll talk more about communication in Chapter 8, "Communicating the Plan."

There are several techniques you can use to address and ideally resolve conflict among team members. We'll look at them next.

Managing Conflict

One of the most important concepts I can share with you that I've learned during my career managing hundreds of projects and personnel is that conflict will not go away on its own. You can't wish it away and hope for the best. Unfortunately, ignoring conflict will not make it go away either. I tried that tactic once or twice early in my career and it was a resounding failure. You need to address conflict head on before it grows and gets out of hand.

NOTE   This is such an important concept that I'm going to say it again. As soon as you are alerted that conflict is lurking among the team, even if you simply suspect there is conflict (listen to your gut on this), deal with it immediately. Conflict is like a cancer and will grow and fester out of control without intervention.

The CompTIA exam objectives list several ways to detect and resolve conflict. Let's look at each technique next.

Smoothing   *Smoothing* is a temporary way to resolve conflict. In this technique, the areas of agreement are emphasized over the areas of difference, so the real issue stays buried. This technique does not lead to a permanent solution. Smoothing can also occur when someone attempts to make the conflict appear less important than it really is. Smoothing is an example of a lose-lose conflict-resolution technique because neither side wins.

Forcing   *Forcing* is just as it sounds. One person forces a solution on the other parties. Although this is a permanent solution, it isn't necessarily the best solution. People will go along with it because, well, they're forced to go along with it. It doesn't mean they agree with the solution. This isn't the best technique to use when you're trying to build a team. This is an example of a win-lose conflict-resolution technique. The forcing party wins, and the losers are forced to go along with the decision.

Compromising   *Compromising* is achieved when each of the parties involved in the conflict gives up something to reach a solution. Everyone involved decides what they'll give on and what they won't give on, and eventually through all the give-and-take, a solution is reached. Neither side wins or loses in this situation. As a result, neither side really buys in to the decision that was reached. If, however, both parties make firm commitments to the resolution, then the solution can become a permanent one.

Collaborating   *Collaborating* is the best way to resolve conflict. This involves working together with other team members to derive a solution. You can use brainstorming techniques or interviews, or go on a fact-finding mission. The idea is to work together in a cordial manner with other team members to find the right solution to the problem. Once the brainstorming sessions are complete and the facts are uncovered, the team presents the solutions to the parties involved, and the decision will be clear. Thus, the solution becomes a permanent one, and the conflict expires. This is the conflict-resolution approach project managers use most often and is an example of a win-win technique.

Avoiding   *Avoiding*, sometimes known as withdrawal, never results in resolution. This occurs when one of the parties gets up and leaves and refuses to discuss the conflict. It is probably the worst of all the techniques because nothing gets resolved. This is an example of a lose-lose conflict-resolution technique.

These conflict management styles can help you understand the behaviors you're observing and help you reach resolution. Two additional situations that require special treatment are dealing with team member disputes and handling disgruntled team members, which I'll discuss next.

Team Member Disputes

Given the diverse backgrounds and varying areas of expertise among project team members, it should come as no surprise that team members will have disagreements. Sometimes people simply need to have a conversation and work through the issues, but other times disputes require the intervention of the project manager.

You may be tempted to make a snap judgment based on what you see at any given point in time, but this may only exacerbate the situation. You need to get the facts and understand what is behind the dispute. Interview each of the team members involved to get as much information as you can. If it's a minor dispute, you might consider hosting a meeting, with you as the moderator, and ask each person to explain their issues and offer potential solutions. You could turn this into a brainstorming session in order to engage everyone and place the burden of finding a solution on them.

Sometimes, the dispute is very deep or potentially involves threats or other workplace issues. Always get your human resources department involved in these issues as soon as you are made aware of the problem. Most organizations have strict policies and guidelines in place regarding disputes of this nature. They may recommend mediation, training, disciplinary action, or replacing one of the team members. Don't attempt to resolve these types of issues on your own. If you do, you may find yourself entangled in legal issues, especially if you acted outside of the company policy.

It's always a good idea to check with your human resources department before jumping into the middle of dispute resolution. You want to make certain you are following company policies and don't end up as part of the problem yourself, rather than as part of the solution.

Disgruntled Team Members

Few situations can poison team morale more quickly than a disgruntled team member. This can happen at any time during the project and can involve anyone on the team.

The behavior of a discontented team member can take a variety of forms. They may become argumentative in meetings or continually make snide comments putting down the project. Even worse, this unhappy person may spend time "cube hopping" in order to share these negative feelings about the project with other team members. When otherwise-satisfied team members constantly hear statements that the project is worthless, is doomed to fail, or is on the cutting block, overall team productivity will be impacted.

As the project manager, you need to spend some private time with this employee to determine the cause of the dissatisfaction. It may be that the unhappy team member doesn't fully understand the project scope or how their contribution will lead to the project success. Or, it could be this person never wanted this assignment in the first place and feels forced onto a project they don't believe in.

It is best to start by listening. Stick to the facts and ask the person to clarify the negative comments. If the team member is repeating incorrect information, set the record straight. If they are frustrated about some aspect of the project and feel no one is listening, find out what the issue is and explain that going around bad-mouthing the project is not the way issues get resolved. If the person truly does not want to be part of the project team or does not want to do their assigned tasks, work quickly with the functional manager or your sponsor to get this person replaced.

It's your responsibility as the project manager to hold your team members accountable. Once you've given them an opportunity to state their case and have made a few positive changes to address their concerns, make it clear you expect their negative behavior to stop. If they don't, you'll need to get your HR experts involved and begin disciplinary action.

Ideally, conflict resolution should not dominate your time with the team. In my experience, this is typically a one- or two-time issue on most projects, depending on the length and complexity of the project. Most likely, you'll be more involved with building and managing a cohesive team and using an effective rewards and recognition system to motivate the team. We'll look at rewards and recognition systems next.

Now that you have the team established and assembled, and have assigned team members to tasks, it's time to have the project kickoff meeting.

Project Kickoff Part Two

A project kickoff meeting is generally held after the project charter is signed, as we discussed in Chapter 3, "Creating the Project Charter." However, in some cases you may not have all the project team members assigned at that time. If that's the case, it's a good idea to wait and hold the kickoff meeting after the majority of the team members are assigned. Another tactic is to hold a project kickoff after signing the project charter and another meeting once all the team members are assigned. Remember that the timing of the kickoff isn't as important as actually holding the meeting.

As a refresher, the key agenda items for this meeting should include the following: welcome, introductions, project sponsor and key stakeholder introductions, project overview, stakeholder expectations, roles and responsibilities, and time for questions and answers. Please refer to Chapter 3 for the details of the kickoff meeting.

 **Real World Scenario**

Kickoff for Remote Team Members

For a project kickoff to work effectively, it needs to include all team members. But what do you do if part of your team is located in a different city or state?

Remote team members often feel left out, especially if the majority of the team, including the project manager, sponsor, and client, is located at corporate headquarters where all of the action is.

Getting approval to bring in remote team members is a battle worth fighting, because it's so important in making everyone feel like part of the team. When making your case with the project sponsor, make sure you explain the importance of this meeting and the benefits it will have to the project. Your sponsor will be much more receptive to the idea if they know what will be covered and can see that this exercise is far more than people getting together for a free lunch.

But with more companies tightening their belts and looking closely at travel-related expenses, bringing in remote team members may not be possible. Perhaps if you can't get the budget to bring in all the team members, maybe you can do the next best thing: fly the sponsor, the project manager, and a key stakeholder or two to the place where the other team members reside and hold a separate kickoff for them. Last but not least, there are tele-conferencing, videoconferencing, and web-based meeting options that you can use to at least virtually bring everyone together during the kickoff meeting.

Procurement Planning

Procurement planning is the process of identifying the goods and services required for your project that will be purchased from outside the organization.

One of the first techniques you should use when thinking about the procurement planning process is whether you should make or buy the goods and services needed for the project. *Make-or-buy analysis* determines whether it's more cost-effective to produce the needed resources in-house or to procure them from outside the organization. CompTIA lists four scenarios you can use for this analysis: build, buy, lease, or subscription/pay-as-you-go ser-vice. For example, you can use make-or-buy analysis to determine if it's more cost-effective to buy equipment or to lease it, or whether to use a pay-as-you-go subscription service like in the cloud, or build the application in-house, and so on.

You should include both direct costs and indirect costs when performing make-or-buy analysis. Direct costs are those that are directly attributed to the project, such as costs needed to produce the resource. Indirect costs are those costs associated with overhead, management, and ongoing maintenance costs. Other considerations to take into account in make-or-buy analysis are capacity, skill sets, availability, and company trade secrets.

Most organizations have a procurement department that manages all aspects of procuring goods and services. If that's the case in your organization, you'll want to make certain you understand the forms and processes you're required to follow, or you may end up with some significant schedule delays. Most procurement departments are highly process-driven, and if you miss something along the way, the procurement folks may or may not choose to show mercy and lend a hand in getting the forms through the workflow. The procurement pro-cess is complex and large contracts or difficult purchases often require a review by the legal department, so be sure to build enough lead time to account for these processes.

Do not underestimate the power your procurement department possesses. I have been involved on projects that were delayed for months because the procurement process was not started in time or I missed one of the myriads of forms they require to complete the transaction. Make certain you know and understand your procurement department's rules and processes so that you don't bring about unnecessary time delays on your project.

As the project manager, you're the buyer of goods and services for your project, so I'll cover the procurement process from the buyer's perspective. The organization selling the goods or services is referred to as a vendor, a seller, a supplier, a consultant, or a contractor.

The typical areas where you may need to procure goods or services are discussed next:

Equipment   For some projects, the equipment needs may be easy to determine. If you are developing a new application that requires new hardware, you'll need to obtain the hardware from outside your company. If you're working on a project that requires equipment your organization routinely has available, you'll want to reserve the equipment for the tasks and time frames needed for the project.

Staff Augmentation   Staff augmentation may come about for several reasons. Perhaps your gap analysis shows a lack of expertise or skills needed for certain tasks. Or there may be other critical projects that have reserved the same resources you need for your project. Projects with a time constraint may also require more resources than are currently available. Contract resources can help fill this gap.

Staff augmentation may range from contracting with a vendor to run the entire project to contracting for specific resources to perform certain tasks. In my experience, staff augmentation is often needed for large, complex projects.

Other Goods and Services   Goods and services that your organization typically does not produce or keep on hand are good candidates for procurement. You may also find that some of the project deliverables are best met by procuring them from outside the organization.

Procurement planning starts with the decision to procure goods or services outside the organization. Once that decision has been made, you need to determine what type of procurement vehicle is best for the purchase you need to make. A simple purchase order may suffice, or you may need a contract.

Statement of Work

If you're working with vendors to perform some or all of the work of the project, it's critical that they know exactly what you are asking them to do. The *statement of work (SOW)* details the goods or services you want to procure. In many respects it's similar to the project scope statement, except that it focuses on the work being procured. It contains the project description, major deliverables, success criteria, assumptions, and constraints. The project scope statement is a good starting point for documenting the SOW.

The project manager should be involved in the process of creating the SOW to ensure accuracy of the project requirements. Vendors use the SOW to determine whether they can produce the deliverables and to determine their interest in bidding on your project work. The SOW must be very clear and precise. Anything in the SOW that is ambiguous could lead to a less-than-satisfactory deliverable.

Many organizations have templates for creating a SOW. This ensures that all required items are covered, and it provides consistent information to vendors. Once the SOW is complete, you're ready to ask for vendors to bid on the work.

Vendor Solicitation

Solicitation is the process of obtaining responses from vendors to complete the project work as documented in the SOW. Typically, a procurement document is prepared to notify prospective sellers of upcoming work. You can prepare the solicitation notice in several ways. The most common are as follows:

Request for Information (RFI)   A *request for information (RFI)* is used when you have to gather more information about the goods or services you need to procure. This process will give you a sense for the number of providers or contractors who can provide the goods or services, and you will get an idea of cost. An RFI or request for quote (RFQ) is used when the costs are unknown to you and you need an estimate for the goods or services.

Request for Proposal (RFP)   A *request for proposal (RFP)* is submitted when you are ready to procure and begin the work. This process includes creating the SOW and publishing it in the RFP, receiving bids from vendors and suppliers, evaluating the responses, and making a selection. After selection, you will engage in negotiations for the best price, service, warranty periods, and more. The vendor proposals should include costs, high-level timelines, background information such as financials, their experience on previous projects of a similar nature, and more. This is usually a complex request, and you'll want to be as detailed as possible about expectations and outcomes. In many cases, an RFI precedes an RFP so that you can gather more information about vendor solutions and incorporate into the RFP requirements you might not have thought about at the RFI stage.

Request for Quote (RFQ)   A *request for quote (RFQ)* is often used when you know what you want to buy, typically a commodity of some sort like a fleet of trucks or piece of equipment that is readily available in the marketplace. The RFQ is used to compare estimates among various vendors who can supply your needs with ready-made goods and services. RFQs can require background information about the vendors.

Request for Bid (RFB)   A *request for bid (RFB)* is used when the items or services you are procuring are readily available in the marketplace. This is a sealed bid process, unlike an RFQ, and is solely based on price. This process doesn't include an evaluation of the company providing the goods and services, and because it's based on price alone, the organization can't practice favoritism among vendors.

I've found that RFIs and RFQs are used interchangeably in organizations I've worked in, but be certain to check your procurement department and understand which document to use according to their process. Regardless of what these documents are called, they should include your SOW or a detailed description of the goods or services needed, information regarding how responses are to be formatted and delivered, and a date by which responses must be submitted. Potential vendors may also be required to make a formal presentation as part of the bidding process.

When using an RFP, most procurement processes allow for a meeting between you and the prospective vendors prior to their completing the RFP; this is called a *bidder conference*. This meeting usually occurs right after the RFP is published, and all prospective vendors are invited to the meeting so that they can ask questions and clarify issues they may have identified with the RFP. The bidder conference helps assure that vendors prepare responses that address the project requirements.

At the time the procurement documents are distributed (or earlier), you need to develop the criteria the selection committee will use to evaluate the bids, quotes, or proposals you receive.

Vendor Selection Criteria

Most organizations have a procurement department that will assist you with vendor solicitation and selection. They will advise you regarding the information you need to provide and will usually assign a member of their team to manage the vendor selection process and the contract for your project. Some organizations have approved vendor lists made up of prequalified vendors that have already met the basic criteria the company requires to do business with them, as we discussed in Chapter 1, "Introducing the Project." If that's the case, your solicitation and selection process will be easier because you'll be working with preapproved vendors that have already crossed several of the procurement hurdles required to proceed.

If you're responsible for vendor selection, you'll need to develop criteria to use when evaluating vendor bids or proposals. It helps to decide up front with the sponsor and other key stakeholders who will be involved in the review and selection of vendor proposals. This group should develop the selection criteria as a team and reach agreement ahead of time regarding the weighting of the criteria. These are some of the criteria you should consider when evaluating bids and proposals:

- The vendor's understanding of the needs and requirements of the project
- Cost
- Warranty period
- Technical ability of the vendor to perform the work of the project
- References
- Vendor's experience on projects of similar size and scope
- Vendor's project management approach

- Financial stability of the vendor's company
- Intellectual property rights and proprietary rights

You can use several techniques to evaluate the proposals that we'll talk about next. One of the most common methods is using a weighted scoring model or system. The idea is that each of the criteria you're using to evaluate the vendor is assigned a weight. Each vendor is then given a score for each of the evaluation elements, and the weight is multiplied by the score to give an overall score. Table 6.3 shows a sample weighted scoring model using some of the evaluation criteria shown earlier. The scores are assigned a value of 1 to 5, with 5 being the highest score a vendor can earn. You multiply the weight by the score for each element and then sum the totals to come up with an overall score for each vendor. You would almost always choose the vendor with the highest score using this selection method.

TABLE 6.3 Weighted scoring model

Criteria	Weight	Vendor A score	Vendor A total	Vendor B score	Vendor B total
Understand requirements	5	2	**10**	4	**20**
Cost	3	3	**9**	4	**12**
Experience	4	1	**4**	2	**8**
Financial stability	3	4	**12**	3	**9**
Final weighted score			**35**		**49**

In this example, vendor B has the highest score and is the vendor you should choose.

Other vendor evaluation techniques as listed in the CompTIA objectives include the following:

Best Value vs. Lowest Cost Value may include any number of elements, including quality, conditions, features, warranty, and more. Cost is what you pay. Be aware that lowest cost does not mean best value—they are two different things. Government contracts often use a "lowest cost" approach and are often burned in the process because the value or quality of the goods are not on par with their expectations. Then they cancel the current contract and go out for bid for the next vendor and end up paying for the project twice.

Cost-Benefit Analysis We discussed this technique in Chapter 1. When choosing among vendors cost–benefit analysis compares the cost to produce the product or service to the benefits the organization stands to gain by choosing a particular vendor.

Market Research   This involves a bit of detective work on your part. Jump on your favorite search engine and find out what you can about the vendor you are considering. Examine their reputation, social media standing, financial standing (if a public company), experience with projects such as yours, product viability, and more.

Competitive Analysis   This analysis involves comparing the bids you receive to each other. Compare elements such as costs, resource experience and skills, warranty periods, features/functionality, and more.

Qualifications   Qualifications may include years of experience performing similar projects, the skills and abilities of resources committed to the project, experience in your industry, and more.

Prequalified Vendors/Sellers   We covered this in Chapter 1. The organization may have a list of prequalified vendors who have already been researched, qualifications verified, and references checked.

Demonstration   This may occur before the RFP is written and/or during the bidders conference. In my experience, when purchasing IT software or subscription services, it's helpful to have a few potential vendors demonstrate their products to the IT team and the business users so that we can get an idea of how their product performs, business processes, and so on.

Technical Approach   This evaluation technique is used to determine how the vendor will go about implementing the project, software, hardware, or items you are procuring. Compare the technical approach of the various vendors to determine which one will work best for the organization.

Physical and Financial Capacity   It's a good idea to review the financial stability of the vendor you are considering hiring. If their financial capacity and stability is on shaky ground, they could go out of business or be acquired by another business before your contract ends. This could leave you stranded, especially in the case of proprietary technology because there aren't other vendors who can pick up the work. They should also have the financial capacity to continue to deliver goods and services to you while awaiting payments on invoices. Additionally, you'll want to ensure they have the physical capacity to fulfill your needs. For example, if the vendor plans to hire the resources needed for the project after you sign the contract, beware. The resources may not be available or not easily attained, or the supplies or parts needed for physical goods may be on backorder or otherwise unavailable. As of this writing, for example, computer chip shortages are affecting everything from ink cartridge replacements to new car production.

References   Last but not least is a reference check. As most cybersecurity professionals everywhere will tell you, "Trust but verify." Require vendors to provide you with references for past projects they've worked on similar to yours so that you can verify they do have the qualifications, they met expectations on previous jobs, and there weren't any issues that couldn't be resolved. Don't skip this step. Better safe than sorry.

Sole-Source Documentation

Sometimes you'll have a procurement situation where you can use only one vendor to fulfill your needs. For example, suppose you have a computer system that is unique to your line of business. You've used that software for several years and are ready for an upgrade. You don't want to go through the headache of installing a new system—you simply want to update the one you already have. This situation calls for a sole-source procurement because there's only one vendor that can meet your requirements.

Types of Contracts

A *contract* is a legal, mutually binding document that describes the goods or services that will be provided, the costs of the goods or services, and any penalties for noncompliance. Let's take a look at several contract types here:

Fixed-Price Contract A *fixed-price contract* states a fixed fee or price for the goods or services provided. This type of contract works best when the product is very well-defined and the statement of work is clear and concise. Using a fixed-price contract for a product or service that is not well-defined or that has never been done before is risky for both the buyer and the seller. This type of contract is the riskiest for the seller. If problems arise during the course of the project and it takes longer to complete a task than anticipated or the goods they were to supply can't be obtained in a timely manner, the seller bears the burden of paying the additional wages needed to complete the task or paying the penalty for not delivering the goods on time.

Cost-Reimbursable Contract A *cost-reimbursable contract* reimburses the seller for all the allowable costs associated with producing the goods or services outlined in the contract. This type of contract is riskiest for the buyer because the total costs are unknown until the project is completed. The advantage in this type of contract is that the buyer can easily change scope. A cost-plus contract is like a cost-reimbursable contract and contains provisions for additional fees or incentives above the reimbursable cost amounts. The contract should outline the criteria for the additional fees or incentives. There are four types of cost plus contracts:

Cost Plus Fixed Fee The *cost plus fixed fee contract (CPFF)* adds a fixed fee that is paid upon completion of the contract.

Cost Plus Incentive Fee A *cost plus incentive fee contract (CPIF)* includes an incentive for meeting or exceeding performance criteria described in the contract.

Cost Plus Percentage Fee   A *cost plus percentage of cost (CPPC)* includes a fee that's calculated as a percentage of the reimbursable costs.

Cost Plus Award Fee   A *cost plus award fee (CPAF)* is an award fee paid at the end of the contract at the discretion of the buyer. This is the riskiest of all cost-reimbursable contracts for the seller.

Time and Materials Contract   A *time and materials(T&M) contract* is a cross between fixed-price and cost-reimbursable contracts. The buyer and the seller agree on a unit rate, such as the hourly rate for a programmer, but the total cost is unknown and will depend on the amount of time spent to produce the product or service. This type of contract is often used for staff augmentation, where contract workers are brought on to perform specific tasks on the project. Time and materials contracts are typically written with a not-to-exceed clause outlining the maximum amount of money that will be paid. Once that amount is reached, the contract is ended, or an amendment is written to revise the statement of work or the not-to-exceed amount.

Unit Price Contract   A *unit price contract* is priced according to the units of work that make up the project or materials needed to complete the work, or both. Rather than price the project as a whole, each unit of work has a price, and the contractor is paid when that unit of work is delivered.

Master Service Agreement   Agile projects may use what's known as a *master service agreement (MSA) contract*. Agile projects involve frequent deliveries produced during an iteration, and you may not know much about future iterations at the beginning of the project. An MSA may outline service rates and warranties in one section while allowing elements such as scope, budget, and timeline to be added as needed. For example, scope details for each iteration or release might be included in the MSA as an appendix, allowing scope to be fluid and flexible. If your organization is new to agile, your procurement department may need to develop contracts that are agile-based so that you can quickly move through procurement processes as iterations or releases are completed.

Most contracts, and most particularly the master service agreement, may use purchase orders or terms of reference to execute work. A *purchaser order (PO)* is typically written by a buyer and describes the specifications and quantities of the goods or services being purchased and the price. Once the PO is accepted by the seller, it is a legally binding document. The *terms of reference (TOR)* document describe the work requirements for the project, or in the case of agile projects, for each iteration. The TOR should contain a scope of work, the timeline for the work, the resources that will be assigned, and any other regulations or requirements needed. In either case, the contract itself must have a high-level description of the types of resources or services that may be needed. The specifics, quantities, timelines, and more can be detailed as needed in the PO or the TOR.

Vendor-Related Documents

Organizations may use a variety of documents to manage relationships in addition to the contracts mentioned earlier. Let's take a brief look at each.

Nondisclosure Agreement   *Nondisclosure agreements (NDA)* are used when organizations engage the services of an outside entity and want to assure that sensitive company or trade secret information is not shared outside the organization. An NDA assures that what's discussed, discovered, or developed is kept between the parties and isn't shared with anyone else.

Cease-and-Desist Letter   A *cease-and-desist letter* informs the other party to stop (cease) doing the activity they are doing and not do it again (desist). A cease-and-desist letter might be sent to someone who is violating copyright laws.

Letter of Intent   A *letter of intent* outlines the intent or actions of both parties before entering into a contract or other mutually binding agreement. It's a negotiable document and can be thought of as an agreement to agree on the terms and conditions.

Memorandum of Understanding (MOU)   A *memorandum of understanding (MOU)* is an agreement that may outline specific performance criteria or other actions between two or more parties. An MOU is used when a legal agreement can't be created between the parties. For example, two or more government agencies may have an MOU that describes the actions, services, or performance criteria between them. Government agencies cannot hold one another accountable legally as you could with a vendor who is not performing per the terms of a contract. Nonperformance by either party under a contract is enforceable in court. An MOU is not legally enforceable.

Service Level Agreement (SLA)   A *service level agreement (SLA)* defines service level performance expectations among two or more parties. For example, the information technology department may have SLAs in place that outline how quickly they will respond to a critical service desk ticket.

Maintenance Agreement   A *maintenance agreement* outlines the actions and duties the vendor will take to keep the products you purchased running efficiently. For example, software maintenance agreements may include upgrades, patches, security fixes, and so on as part of the maintenance agreement. A vehicle may have maintenance agreements that perform regular service checks, oil changes, and replacements for certain parts. Maintenance agreements may also contain warranties, which is explained next.

Warranty   A *warranty* is usually associated with equipment, materials, software, or supplies. It is a guarantee that the product will meet expectations and perform as stated. A warranty is typically in effect for a specified period of time and expires once the time period is reached.

Real World Scenario

Main Street Office Move: Building the Team

You've worked with the functional managers to select team members for your project. You've created a project organization chart and also developed a RACI matrix. A sample portion of the RACI is shown here. Juliette heads up the communication department. Leah is the manager of the procurement department, Jason is the manager of information technology, Joe is the fleet manager, and Emma is the executive sponsor.

Deliverable/ stakeholder	Juliette: Communication	Leah: Procurement	Jason: IT	Joe: Fleet	Emma: Sponsor
Communication	R	C	C	C	A/C
Moving company	I	A/R	C	I	C/I
Seating charts	A/R	I	C		C/I
Technical installs	I	I	A/R		C/I
Fleet cars	I	C	I	A/R	I

Since all the team members are new to the project and some have not worked together before, you decide to hold some team-building activities. Your human resources department assists you with some exercises that help to break the ice and allow team members to get to know one another. They progress through the forming stage of development quickly and stall a bit during the storming stage. This isn't unusual, and the team continues becoming more cohesive as the project continues.

A conflict arises between two of the team members concerning the choices of furniture and fixtures for the new office space. As soon as you realize the tension is building between these team members, you speak with each of them and use the confronting (problem-solving) conflict-resolution technique to reach agreement between them.

You issued an RFP to procure a moving company service to perform the office move. Your selection criteria were as follows: references from recent past moves of similar size, delivery dates, and cost. The contract was signed with the moving company after a round of negotiations with them to agree on delivery dates and times. The moving company responded to the RFP stating they could meet the dates and then wanted to change them during the contract negotiation. You and your procurement officer stuck to the terms of the

SOW and the RFP and told them they had to meet the delivery dates stated in the procurement documents or you would find a different moving company.

You held some demonstrations with three leading vendors in the IaaS space. After the demos, you worked with IT to write an RFP for the cloud procurement, including consultant resources to help with implementation.

Summary

Organizational structures impact how projects are managed and staffed. The primary structures are functional, matrix, and projectized. The traditional departmental hierarchy in a functional organization provides the project manager with the least authority. The other end of the spectrum is the projectized organization, where resources are organized around projects; in these types of organizations, the project manager has the greatest level of authority to take action and make decisions regarding the project. The matrix organization is a middle ground between the functional organization and the project-based organization.

All projects require resources. Resources include the human type and physical resources such as material and equipment.

Capital resources are used to create the product of the project or are used by the organization to perform the project. Shared resources work for more than one manager. They may report to both a functional manager and a project manager. If you're working with a shared resource, be certain you have some input into each team member's performance appraisal. Dedicated resources are dedicated to the project. Low-quality resources may not have the skills needed to complete the tasks assigned. In the case of low-quality physical resources, look elsewhere.

Resource allocation identifies the type of resources, skills sets, and time frames needed. Resource shortages occur when there aren't enough resources available with the skills needed to perform the task. Resource overallocation occurs when one resource (or set of resources) is scheduled to work on too many tasks at the same time. These tasks may be on the same project or a combination of tasks from different projects and their normal operational work. Benched resources are those who have rolled off one project and are waiting for the next project to begin. These are costly resources to the organization, so work in coordination with other project and functional managers to assign these resources as soon as possible. A gap analysis determines the difference between the resources you have and the resources you need or the skills the existing resources have versus the skills needed.

Interproject dependencies occur when you need the completed deliverables from one project in order to start work on the next project. Interproject resources contention occurs when resources are scheduled for similar tasks on competing projects and may be unavailable for your project when needed.

Project organization charts help you see the project resources at a glance. Examples include a project organization chart, an organization breakdown structure, a resource breakdown structure, and a RACI. A project organization chart is a hierarchical chart that shows the sponsor, project manager, and team members. An organization breakdown structure chart shows the hierarchy of the reporting structure of all employees within an organization. A resource breakdown structure shows the work packages and the types of resources needed. A RACI chart shows the roles and responsibilities of team members (or it can depict teams or business units.) RACI stands for responsible, accountable, consulted, and informed.

Physical resources have a life cycle of their own, including acquisition, maintenance, hardware decommissioning, end-of-life software, and successor planning.

All teams progress through five stages of development: forming, storming, norming, performing, and adjourning. Core team members are those who are committed to the project for its life cycle because of their expertise, knowledge of the business, and/or skills. Functional/extended team members may have skills or expertise needed for a specific task or are stakeholders or subject matter experts who can answer questions, verify requirements, and so on.

Team-building activities help diverse groups of people work together in an efficient and effective manner. Trust building is an important activity. It takes time to build trust with team members and requires that the project manager demonstrate competence, respect, honesty, integrity, and openness.

Provide feedback to your team members in a timely manner and deal with negative situations as soon as they occur. Removing personnel from the project should be done in coordination with the human resources department.

Rewards and recognition are important motivators for individuals and teams. Be certain the reward is in keeping with the achievement. Also make sure that reward criteria and processes are written down.

Conflict will occur on nearly all projects. The common techniques for conflict resolution include smoothing, forcing, compromising, collaborating, and avoiding. Collaborating is the technique project managers should use.

The procurement processes are used when you are purchasing goods or services for the project outside of the organization. You might use an RFI, RFQ, RFP, RFB, MSA, PO, or TOR to procure your goods and services. Sometimes, you may also use resources from other parts of the organization that require formal agreements regarding their use such as an MOU. An NDA ensures your discussions with the vendor will remain private.

Fixed-price contracts state a fixed fee for the goods or services provided. Cost-reimbursable contracts reimburse the seller for all the allowable costs. Cost-reimbursable contracts may include CPFF, CPIF, CPPC, and CPAF. Time and materials contracts charge a unit rate for goods and services, but the total cost is unknown until all the work or goods are provided. Unit price contracts charge by using units of work such as a major deliverable or milestone, rather than charging for the entire project. Master service agreements are often used on agile projects where you don't know all of the deliverables or work up front.

Exam Essentials

Name the three types of organizational structures. The three types of organizational structures are functional, matrix, and projectized structures. Matrix organizations may be structured as a strong matrix, weak matrix, or balanced matrix organization.

Understand the definition of resources. Resources can be human resources or physical resources. They are used to complete the work of the project. Resources include human, physical, capital, shared resources, dedicated resources, low-quality resources, internal resources, external resources, benched resources, and remote resources.

Define resource allocation. Resource allocation is identifying resource availability and skills sets and assigning them to project tasks.

Define resource overallocation and resource shortage. Resource overallocation occurs when resources are assigned too many tasks within a given time frame. Resource shortage occurs when there are not enough resources with the required skills or abilities to complete the tasks.

Define interproject dependencies and interproject resource contention. Interproject dependencies occur when one project must complete its deliverables before another project can begin. Interproject resource contention occurs when resources are assigned to more than one project, resulting in timing and availability conflict.

Describe a RACI chart and define the acronym. This is a matrix-based chart that shows the resource role and responsibility level for the work product. RACI stands for responsible, accountable, consulted, and informed.

Name the five stages of team development. They are forming, storming, norming, performing, and adjourning.

Describe team building and trust building. Team building consists of activities that help diverse groups of people work together in an efficient and effective manner. Trust building involves building trust with the project manager and among team members. This takes time and is accomplished by being true to your word and having the team's best interests at heart.

Name the conflict-resolution techniques and the technique that is best for project managers. The techniques are smoothing, forcing, compromising, collaborating, and avoiding. Project managers should use the collaborating technique.

State the purpose of a project kickoff meeting. The project kickoff meeting is a way to formally introduce all project team members, to review the goals and the deliverables for the project, to discuss roles and responsibilities, and to review stakeholder expectations.

Be able to name the types of contracts. The contract types include fixed-price, cost-reimbursable, and time and materials.

Be able to name the types of vendor-centric documents.   The types of vendor documents include nondisclosure agreements, cease-and-desist letters, letters of intent, statements of work, memoranda of understanding, service level agreements, purchase orders, maintenance agreements, and warranties.

Be able to name the type of contract that's best for an agile project.   A master service agreement (MSA) is the best type of contract to use for an agile project. Agile projects involve frequent, small deliveries, and an MSA allows you to add work to the contract via an appendix without having to rewrite the contract.

Key Terms

Before you take the exam, make certain you are familiar with the following terms:

adjourning	memorandum of understanding (MOU)
avoiding	nondisclosure agreements (NDA)
benched resources	norming
bidder conference	organization breakdown structure (OBS)
capital resources	performing
cease-and-desist letter	physical resources
collaborating	procurement planning
collocate	project organization chart
compromise	projectized organizational structure
conflict	purchaser order (PO)
contract	RACI chart
core team members	remote resources
cost plus award fee (CPAF)	request for bid (RFB)
cost plus fixed fee (CPFF)	request for information (RFI)
cost plus incentive fee (CPIF)	request for proposal (RFP)
cost plus percentage of cost (CPPC)	request for quote (RFQ)
cost-reimbursable contract	resource breakdown structure (RBS)
dedicated resources	resource overallocation
fixed-price contract	responsibility assignment matrix (RAM)

forcing

forming

functional organization

functional/extended team members

gap analysis

interproject dependencies

interproject resource contention

letter of intent

low-quality resources

maintenance agreement

make-or-buy analysis

master service agreement (MSA) contract

matrix organization

service level agreement (SLA)

shared resource

smoothing

solicitation

statement of work (SOW)

storming

team building

terms of reference (TOR)

time and materials (T&M) contract

trust building

unit price contract

warranty

Review Questions

1. Your project is underway, and your team members are working well together, anticipating the needs of the project, and they all understand their roles in the project. A new team member has been introduced and started working with the team this week. Which stage of team development does this situation represent?

    A. Forming

    B. Storming

    C. Performing

    D. Norming

    E. Adjourning

2. Which type of contract assigns a unit rate for work or goods, but the total cost is unknown?

    A. Time and materials

    B. Fixed price

    C. Cost plus incentive fee

    D. Cost reimbursable

3. A team member has come to your office to complain that a fellow team member is never available for meetings before noon and seems to ignore their requests to follow proper processes. Which of the following does this describe? (Choose two.)

    A. This describes an interproject resource contention.

    B. This describes a low-quality resource.

    C. This describes a conflict.

    D. This describes a situation where the negotiating conflict technique should be used.

    E. This describes varying work styles.

4. All of the following are stages of team development except for which one?

    A. Adjourning

    B. Collaborating

    C. Performing

    D. Storming

5. What is one disadvantage of a projectized organization?

    A. The organization doesn't work on anything that isn't project-related.

    B. Costs are high because specialized skills are required to complete projects in this type of structure.

    C. The functional managers have control over which team members are assigned to projects.

    D. Once the project is completed, the project team members may not have other projects to work on.

6. Your project is undergoing some difficulties. You've determined that the primary problem is vendor performance. A key stakeholder insists the problem is not the vendor; the problem is the project team. However, the key stakeholder spends most of the meeting emphasizing the areas of agreement. Which conflict-resolution technique does this describe?

   A. Avoiding

   B. Forcing

   C. Confronting

   D. Smoothing

7. Which vendor selection method weighs various criteria from the RFP, scores each vendor on each of the criteria, and determines an overall score for each vendor?

   A. Weighted scoring model

   B. Screening system

   C. Seller rating system

   D. Independent estimates

8. Which type of contract is the riskiest for the buyer?

   A. Time and materials

   B. Fixed price

   C. Fixed price plus incentive

   D. Cost reimbursable

9. Your system engineer has started making negative comments during your weekly team meeting. He has had a heated argument with the marketing manager, and you have heard from various team members that he has become difficult to work with. What is the best course of action for you to take?

   A. You should write a memo to the system engineer's functional manager and request a replacement as soon as possible.

   B. The system engineer is critical to the project, so you should give him some slack and wait to see whether the behavior stops.

   C. You should confront the system engineer openly at the next team meeting. Let him know that his behavior is unacceptable and that he will be replaced if there is not an immediate change.

   D. You should schedule an individual meeting with the system engineer to determine whether he has issues with the project that need to be resolved. Get his perspective on how the project is progressing and how he feels about his role.

10. Which of the following is true regarding a RACI chart? (Choose three.)

    A. A RACI chart shows roles and responsibilities of team members or business units and how they intersect with project tasks.

    B. RACI stands for responsible, approved, consulted, and informed.

    C. A RACI is a matrix-based chart.

    D. A RACI is a type of organization breakdown structure.

    E. RACI stands for responsible, accountable, consulted, and informed.

11. All of the following are true regarding rewards and recognition except for which one?

A. You should have a written procedure describing the criteria for rewarding team members.

B. Rewards and recognition are a form of motivation.

C. Rewards and recognition should be applied consistently to all project team members.

D. Rewards and recognition almost always involve money.

12. You are working on a construction project. Your organization owns one crane, and the crane is needed for two tasks on your project at the same time. This is known as which of the following?

A. Resource shortage

B. Resource allocation

C. Interproject dependencies

D. Shared resource

13. You are working in a matrix organization. Choose two responses that describe this type of structure.

A. Project resources are members of another business unit and may or may not be able to help you full-time.

B. Matrix organizations can be structured as strong, weak, or balanced.

C. Project managers have the majority of power in this type of structure.

D. This organizational structure is similar to a functional organization.

E. Employees are assigned project tasks by their project manager in this type of structure.

14. The project sponsor will approve the final deliverables of the project. On a RACI chart, how would this be designated?

A. R

B. I

C. A

D. C

15. Your team is working well together. They understand their roles on the project, perform the work with the best effort possible, and really enjoy working with one another. A new team member will be introduced next week who is well respected by the current team. Which of the following is true regarding this situation? (Choose two.)

A. The team is currently in the performing stage of team development.

B. Once the new team member is introduced, the team will revert to the forming stage of team development.

C. The team is currently in the performing stage of team development and will stay in performing because they know the new team member.

D. Once the new team member is introduced, the team will revert to the norming stage of team development.

E. The team is currently in the performing stage of team development and will revert to the storming stage of team development because they know the new team member.

16. You are working on resource assignments and need to determine the types and criticality of the resources needed for the project, along with the skill sets of the existing project team members. If you don't have the skills on staff, you'll need to contract with an external vendor to procure the resources needed. You are examining resources that will need to be engaged for the entire project. What does this question describe? (Choose three.)

   A. These are extended resources.

   B. You are performing a gap analysis.

   C. These are core resources.

   D. The size of this team should be between 5 and 11 team members.

   E. You can procure resources much faster by using a prequalified vendor.

17. All the following are elements of the project kickoff meeting except for which one?

   A. Introductions

   B. Overview of goals and objectives

   C. High-level budget overview

   D. Roles and responsibilities overview

   E. WBS overview

   F. Stakeholder expectations

18. Which conflict-resolution technique is known as win-lose?

   A. Smoothing

   B. Avoiding

   C. Confronting

   D. Forcing

19. Resources who are awaiting new assignments between projects are costly to an organization and typically reside in a projectized organizational structure. Which of the following does this describe?

   A. Overallocated resources

   B. Benched resources

   C. In-house resources

   D. Remote resources

20. One way you are presenting the work of the project is by listing the departments responsible for the work along the work packages they're assigned to. What type of chart is this?

   A. RBS

   B. Project organization chart

   C. OBS

   D. Organization chart

Chapter

7

Defining the Project Budget and Risk Plans

THE COMPTIA PROJECT+ EXAM TOPICS COVERED IN THIS CHAPTER INCLUDE:

✓ **1.0 Project Management Concepts**

- 1.4 Given a scenario, perform risk management activities

- 1.6 Given a scenario, apply schedule development and management activities and techniques

✓ **2.0 Project Life Cycle Phases**

- 2.1 Explain the value of artifacts in the discovery/concept preparation phase for a project

- 2.3 Given a scenario, perform activities during the project planning phase

✓ **3.0 Tools and Documentation**

- 3.1 Given a scenario, use the appropriate tools throughout the project life cycle

✓ **4.0 Basic of IT and Governance**

- 4.2 Explain the relevant information security concepts impacting project management concepts

This chapter will cover several topics, including security, budgeting, and risk activities and strategies for your project.

Security involves physical, operational, digital, and data security, and we'll look at how these should be addressed on the project. Security also includes creating and abiding by corporate policies and restrictions. You'll learn the various considerations and requirements for each type of security.

To many project managers, the most important components of a project plan are the scope statement, schedule, and budget. As you probably recall, these also happen to constitute the classic definition of the triple constraints. We've already covered the scope statement and the schedule. We will cover the budget and cost principles in this chapter as well.

Next, we will examine risks and how they may impact your projects, mitigation techniques, and how to monitor and report on risks. Let's get going—there's a lot of ground to cover.

Understanding Information Security Concepts

The CompTIA exam objectives cover several aspects of security, including corporate IT policies. In today's technology-driven world, security in all of its forms must take high priority. Whether you are building applications in-house, subscribing to cloud services, employing vendors to assist with development or services, decommissioning hardware, hiring full-time employees, or other similar tasks, all should follow security protocols. We'll look at several areas of security, including physical, operational, digital, data, and corporate IT policies. Let's start with the policies that drive security for physical and digital assets.

Corporate IT Security Policies

A *security policy* is a document (or documents) that outlines the minimum standards required to secure the organization's technology-related systems, assets, and data. It also outlines the rules and procedures for accessing the organization's systems and data. Most policies include a purpose, scope, definitions section, and an appendix where readers can find other policies and procedures related to it. Some policies may also include a roles and responsibilities section describing what actions need to be taken by whom to ensure adherence to the policy. The purpose section states what the policy is protecting and why.

The scope section defines the people impacted by the policy, such as employees and contractors, and a description of the systems the policy is covering. Most importantly, this section will outline the rules and procedures regarding accessing the organization's systems and data. The definitions section provides clarification on terms found in the policy.

At a minimum, the policy should outline what systems, assets, employees, and contractors are subject to the policy; a description of the types of devices, assets, and human resources that are covered by the policy; the rules and procedures to access systems and information; and where additional information can be found. In my experience, policies typically describe the *what* we are going to accomplish. A procedure document outlines the *how*. It is perfectly acceptable to create a policy that outlines both the *what* and the *how* and not create a separate procedure document. This process will vary by organization, so be certain to understand how your organization goes about creating these documents and what they should include.

IT security policies may cover many aspects of IT. Here are some examples:

- Acceptable use policy
- Protection for electronic confidential and sensitive information
- Network and system configuration
- Cybersecurity incident response
- Acquisition and disposal of technology assets

Let's walk through a typical acceptable use policy as an example. The purpose of the policy is to instruct the reader on how to use the organization's technology resources. This may also describe activities such as maintenance, inventory, and disposal of equipment and data. The scope section outlines who the policy impacts, typically employees and contractors. It also includes a description of the types of resources the users may use or come in contact with during their daily duties. Some examples are computers, laptops, phones, mobile devices, externally hosted services, electronic information, networks, and repositories. The rules and procedures description may include elements such as "do not use corporate resources to conduct personal business," "limit usage of the Internet to brief checks of the weather or news headlines," "access to sites that involve violence or pornographic materials are prohibited." The definitions section may include further descriptions of equipment, data, services, and more. Roles and responsibilities will outline who performs the inventory and disposal and the employee's role in allowing access for these activities.

Branding restrictions are a type of security for those who create products, intellectual property, or unique services. Branding typically involves a trademark, copyright, registered trademark, or patent. For example, you might reach for a Kleenex® when you sneeze. Kleenex® is a registered brand name and cannot be cited without using the registered trademark symbol. If instead you reach for a tissue when you sneeze, this term is not trademarked because it's used generically to describe a product. A trademark is generally used to identify a company, brand names, logos, and such. It is identified with this symbol: ™. A registered trademark is one that identifies the intellectual property of the company just like a trademark, and it has been registered with the U.S. Patent and Trademark Office. It is designated with this symbol: ®. A copyright is used for intellectual property such as books, music, recordings, and so on. It is designated with this symbol: ©. Intellectual property that is awaiting acceptance by the Patent and Trademark Office may be designated as "patent pending."

It's important to research and understand the policies that may impact your project. If you are implementing a patient health management system, for example, you'll need to know how sensitive data should be protected, how to establish access rights to this data, how to classify the data, and more.

Categorizing Security Policies

Now that you have an understanding of how a policy is constructed and what it contains, let's look at categories of policies by asset type:

Physical Security   Physical security involves securing physical assets such as mobile devices, removable media devices, access to facilities, and more.

Mobile devices, whether issued by the organization or a personal device used to access corporate data and systems, should require a passcode to activate the device. If the device is lost or stolen, it would make it difficult for a casual user to access the organization's data because they couldn't log in to the phone.

Removable media may include SD cards, USB drives, external hard drives, and more. These devices should use encryption protocols, outlined in the policy, to restrict access to the device. If the device is lost or stolen and it's encrypted, it will make it very difficult for a casual user to plug the device into their own laptop and access the data.

Facilities, including buildings, data centers, storage facilities, and research laboratories, among others, should be secured if they contain, for example, sensitive information, trade secrets, protected governmental information, or experimental equipment for research activities. A data center, for example, may not necessarily contain trade secrets, but employees who are not trained in IT procedures could wreak havoc if they accidentally turned off equipment or otherwise disturbed the equipment. Therefore, access should be limited to those with the proper skills and knowledge to manage this area.

Facilities may also require access control so that only people with a reason to enter can get into the facility, to protect employees, to protect controlled environments such as food production, and more.

There are a host of ways to secure facilities, such as badge systems, biometric readers, and guards stationed at entrances who scan people and packages entering the building.

Facility access control policies should be reviewed on a periodic basis, no less than annually. The access control systems should be updated whenever employees are terminated, when new employees are hired, or when employees change roles in the organization. The policy should outline the procedures for these activities. It is critical to describe the procedures for terminated employees, including who to contact to revoke access upon termination. Employees with high levels of access or security clearances should not be able to access the facilities once terminated.

Operational Security   Operational security includes policies for performing background checks and security clearances. The policy in this case should define the types of roles and responsibilities that require either a background check or a security clearance. Background checks usually entail verifying potential employees or contract employees' financial status, criminal history, sex offender registry status, Social Security number, driving history, and more. Background checks are important elements in the hiring process for many organizations. Most organizations I've worked for required background checks for all employees, regardless of their role in the organization. Some organizations may require them for certain positions such as those with access to corporate bank accounts or research and development procedures. For example, if you are hiring bus drivers who transport school-age children back and forth to school, a background check will show if the potential employee has a previous history of driving while impaired or is listed on a sex-offender registry. I think we can all agree we wouldn't want this person driving our children to school.

Security clearances are generally required for government organizations or contractors who work with the government. These clearances will vary depending on whether the government entity is national, military, regional, or local. For example, security clearances for the U.S. Department of State include three levels: confidential, secret, and top secret. The level of security defines the types or classifications of information the employee (or contractor) has access to. The process to obtain a security clearance is quite extensive and generally includes a background check, interviews with past and current employers, interviews with people who know the potential employee well, questionnaires, fingerprint check, interviews with the potential employee, and more.

Digital Security   Digital security policies are related to access and permissions to digital assets. This may include systems, data, communication equipment, and more. Access to digital information and systems is typically role-based. Here's an example. Payroll employees have access to some human resources (HR) records that pertain to employee pay, benefits, time-off requests, and similar information. But payroll employees have no need to see a performance appraisal or information related to an employee investigation. The HR recruiter has access to potential employees' home address, phone number, current or former employers, references, and more. They do not have access to existing employees' information. The HR director has access to all information related to all employees. Each of these roles has a different purpose in the organization, and as such, their access and permissions to systems and data should be limited to their functional area.

Remote access provides a way for users who are not physically located at the organization's site to access information. Remote access follows the same protocol for digital access and permissions to systems and data and may have additional security levels to ensure the person logging into the system is who they say they are. *Multifactor authentication (MFA)* is a process whereby the user must use two or more methods to verify their identity during the sign-in process. The first step typically involves entering a username and password. The second step could include receiving a passcode on a registered mobile device or email account, a biometric scan, geographic or network location detection, answering security-related questions, or other methods as outlined in the policy. MFA helps protect access to information and verifies the person's identity. For example, perhaps you have a high-ranking executive in your organization who is attending a conference that is open to the public. Let's say the conference publishes its attendees on their website. A bad actor (someone with malicious intent) could easily find your executive's name and sign up for the conference. Once on-site, the bad actor performs a bit of cyber-hacking using Bluetooth or Wi-Fi techniques and obtains the username and password the executive uses to access systems and data back at headquarters. However, even with username and password at hand, the bad actor will be shut out of these systems if MFA is implemented. MFA can be hacked, but it is very difficult and requires a level of skill most bad actors don't possess.

Data Security   Data security policies typically define access by roles and responsibilities and/or by *data classification*. Data classification is a way to describe data according to its sensitivity, type, and value to the organization. We talked about data confidentiality in Chapter 2, "Understanding IT Fundamentals," and in that discussion you'll recall that we talked about two types of data classifications: personally identifiable information (PII) and personal health information (PHI). Both PII and PHI are considered sensitive data. Data that is valuable to the organization might include trade secrets, financial information, client lists, and more. Other classifications might include intellectual property, national security information, public information, internal information, confidential information, classified data, restricted use, and many more. The policy should include the location of the data, or a reference in the appendix to where the data is located, as well as the security requirements needed to secure the data based on its classification. The policy should also describe the rules and processes for managing, handling, and archiving or disposing of data.

 It is the project manager's responsibility to confirm and adhere to the types of data, data classifications, and handling procedures outlined in the organization's policies and incorporate these procedures into the project.

Another classification that is widely used is called *need-to-know basis*. Need-to-know is just as it sounds: information should only be shared with those who have a need-to-know to perform a task or fulfill their job function. Need-to-know involves relaying the least amount of information needed for the activity, and nothing more. Need-to-know can apply to system access, data, information, and so on.

Estimating Costs

Estimating the costs to complete the work of the project, determine the project budget, and estimate the total cost of the project is one of the primary roles of a project manager. Budgets are monitored closely by executives, and you'll need to provide status on the budget in your project status reports. Estimating costs is an iterative process that culminates in the cost baseline. The cost baseline and schedule baseline are two areas where you want to be as accurate as possible when presenting estimates.

Stakeholders have a way of declaring both cost and schedule estimates as final. Make certain they are aware that these are estimates and that more information will be known about total cost as the project progresses. Estimates become final once you determine the cost baseline.

Cost-Estimating Techniques

You can use several techniques to determine cost estimates. We will revisit four techniques in this chapter from the perspective of cost estimating, including analogous (also known as *top-down*), parametric, bottom-up, and three-point estimates. I'll also provide some tips to help you work through the estimating process. Remember that these estimating techniques can be used for estimating activity durations for the schedule like we discussed in Chapter 5, "Creating the Project Schedule," as well as costs.

Estimating methods have varying degrees of accuracy, and each method can produce different results, so it is important to communicate which method you are using when you provide cost estimates. Let's look at each of these estimating methods in more detail and discuss how they work.

Analogous Estimating (Top-Down Estimating)

I talked about analogous estimating when discussing schedule planning in Chapter 5. For cost-estimating purposes, an analogous estimate approximates the cost of the project at a high level by using a similar past project as a basis for the estimate. (You may also hear this technique referred to as *top-down estimating* or an *order-of-magnitude* estimate.) This type of estimate is typically done as part of the business case development or during the early stages of scope planning when there isn't a lot of detail on the project. Analogous estimating uses historical data from past projects along with expert judgment to create a big-picture estimate. Remember that expert judgment relies on people who have experience working on projects of similar size and complexity or who have expertise in a certain area. An analogous estimate may be done for the project as a whole or for selected phases or deliverables. It is not typically used to estimate individual work packages.

Analogous estimates are the least accurate of all the estimating techniques but also the least costly. Analogous estimates rely on expert judgment.

Analogous estimating will likely be the best technique to use at the early stage of the project because you'll have very little detail to go on. The key here is to make sure that everyone involved understands how imprecise this estimate is.

Parametric Estimating

You'll recall that this technique uses a mathematical model to compute costs, and it most often uses the quantity of work multiplied by the rate. Commercial parametric modeling packages are available for complex projects or those performed within specialized industries.

Parametric estimating is dependent on the accuracy of the data used to create the model. If your organization uses parametric modeling, spend some time learning about the specific models that are available and whether this technique is appropriate for your project.

Bottom-Up Estimating

The most precise cost-estimating technique is called the *bottom-up estimate*, which assigns a cost estimate to each work package on the project. The WBS and the project resource requirements are critical inputs for a bottom-up estimate. The idea is that you start at the work package level of the WBS and calculate the cost of each activity assigned to that work package. The sum of all the work package estimates provides the estimate of the total project cost.

 Bottom-up estimates are the most accurate of all the estimating techniques, but they're also the most time-consuming to perform.

When I discussed schedule planning in Chapter 5, I talked about calculating duration estimates for each task to determine the length of time your project will take. When you are calculating cost estimates, you need to base the estimate on *work effort*, which is the total time it will take for a person to complete the task if they do nothing else from the time they start until the task is complete. For example, assume a task to perform technical writing has an activity duration estimate of four days. When you perform cost planning, you need to know the actual number of hours spent performing the task. So, let's say the technical writer is allocating 5 hours a day to the project over the course of 4 days. The work effort estimate is 5 hours a day multiplied by 4 days, which equals 20 hours.

 The duration estimates that you complete in schedule planning help you define how long the project will take to complete. The work effort estimates that you obtain in cost planning are used to define how much the project will cost.

The final piece of data you need for a bottom-up estimate is the rate for each resource. Rates for labor and leased equipment are typically calculated on an hourly or daily rate, while the purchase of materials or equipment will generally have a fixed price.

Deciding the correct rate to use for cost estimates can be tricky. For materials or equipment, the current cost of a similar item is probably as accurate as you can get. The largest cost for many projects is the human resource or labor cost. The actual rate that someone will be paid to perform work, even within the same job title, can fluctuate based on education and experience level. If you're procuring contract resources, you'll get a rate sheet that describes the rates for a given job title and the resource's travel rates if they're coming from out of town.

Table 7.1 shows the work effort and rate assigned for each of the resources in a sample project.

TABLE 7.1   Sample project resource rates

Task	Resource	Work effort	Rate
4.1.1	Tech writer	20 hours	$30/hr
4.1.2	Programmer	100 hours	$150/hr
4.1.3	Server	Fixed rate	$100,000
4.1.4	Testers	60 hours	$80/hr
4.1.5	Programmer	200 hours	$150/hr
4.1.6	Marketing	30 hours	$60/hr

Now that you have the resource requirements, the work effort estimates, and the rate for each task, you can complete the cost estimate by adding a Total Cost column to the table. The cost of each task is calculated by multiplying the work effort for each resource by the rate for that resource. This will give you the total project cost estimate. Table 7.2 shows a completed cost estimate for the tasks in the sample project.

TABLE 7.2   Sample project cost estimate

Task	Resource	Work effort	Rate	Total cost
4.1.1	Tech writer	20 hours	$30/hr	$600
4.1.2	Programmer	100 hours	$150/hr	$15,000
4.1.3	Server	Fixed rate	$100,000	$100,000

TABLE 7.2   Sample project cost estimate *(continued)*

Task	Resource	Work effort	Rate	Total cost
4.1.4	Testers	60 hours	$80/hr	$4,800
4.1.5	Programmer	200 hours	$150/hr	$30,000
4.1.6	Marketing	30 hours	$60/hr	$1,800
Total				**$152,200**

Three-Point Estimates

Three-point estimates are an average of the most likely estimate, the optimistic estimate, and the pessimistic estimate. We looked at this in Chapter 5 in the context of constructing a PERT chart. Three-point estimates are also useful for cost estimates.

You should ask team members and/or ask subject matter experts who are familiar with the type of purchase or consulting work to give you estimates. They should base these estimates on their past experience with similar work or their best guess based on their knowledge.

The most likely estimate assumes that costs will come in as expected. You'll recall if you are using this to estimate activity durations, this estimate assumes work proceeds according to plan, that there won't be any obstacles, and that the team member is confident they have the skills to complete the task.

The optimistic estimate is an estimate that is better than expected. For example, you may have estimated internally that the consulting work you are requesting will be $225 per hour. The optimistic estimate might be $212 per hour, which is better than what you expected. If you are using this estimate for activity duration, this estimate is the fastest time frame in which your resources can complete the activity. This might assume that other tasks the resource is working on are completed early or no longer need to be worked on during the same time frame as the current task. It could also mean that the work is easier than anticipated, so the task could complete early.

The pessimistic estimate assumes the goods or services will cost more than expected. If you are using this for activity duration, it assumes the work will take longer than anticipated to complete or that obstacles will crop up along the way that will delay completing the work.

Calculating the three-point estimate is straightforward, as you saw in Chapter 5. It's an average of the sum of the estimates. We'll walk through another example here. Let's say your most likely estimate for contracting work is $120 per hour. The optimistic estimate is $110 per hour, and the pessimistic estimate is $150 per hour. The three-point estimate is calculated this way:

$$(\$120 + \$110 + \$150) / 3 = \$126.67 \text{ per hour}$$

The three-point estimate for this work is $126.67 per hour. This estimate is only as good as the estimates given for the three points in the calculation. This estimate can swing between accurate and poor based on the quality of the estimates provided by the subject matter experts.

All the estimating techniques discussed in this section can also be used to determine task durations on the project schedule.

You may use some or all of these methods at various stages of project planning, or you may use one type of estimating for certain types of purchases or costs and another method for the rest.

Estimating Tips

Cost estimating can be complex, and cost estimates often turn into the official cost of the project before you have the proper level of detail. You will probably never have all the information that you'd like when calculating cost estimates, but that's the nature of project management. Here are some thoughts to keep in mind as you work through the estimating process:

Brainstorm with your project team.   Work with your team and other subject matter experts to make certain you've accounted for cost estimates that may not be so obvious. For example, do any of your project team members require special training in order to perform their duties on the project? Are there travel costs involved for team members or consultants? Getting the team together to talk about other possible costs is a good way to catch these items.

Communicate the type of estimate you are providing.   Make certain your stakeholders are aware of the types of estimates you're using and the level of accuracy they provide. If you're preparing an analogous cost estimate based on a similar project, be up front regarding the possibility of this estimate deviating from the actual cost of the project.

In addition to emphasizing the potential inaccuracies of an analogous estimate, provide stakeholders with a timeline for a definitive estimate. A project sponsor is more willing to accept that your current estimate may be lower than the actual cost of the project if they understand why the current estimate is vague and what is being done to provide a more accurate estimate.

Make use of any available templates.   Many companies have cost-estimating templates or worksheets that you can use to make this job easier. They will also help you in identifying hidden costs you may not have thought of and may list the rates from the vendor agreements the organization has entered into.

Templates may also be a good source of rate estimates for internal resources. The salary of the people on your project will vary based on both their job title and specific experience. Your organization may require you use to a loaded rate, which is typically a percentage of the employee's salary to cover benefits such as medical, disability, or pension plans. Individual corporate policies will determine whether loaded rates should be used for project cost estimates.

Get estimates from the people doing the work.   A bottom-up estimate is the most accurate because effort estimates are provided for each activity and then rolled up into an overall estimate for the deliverable or the project. The person performing the activities should be the one to develop the estimate. If your project includes tasks new to your team or uses an untested methodology, you may need to look outside for assistance with work effort estimates. You could consult published industry standards or hire a consultant to assist with the estimating process.

Document any assumptions you have made.   Be certain to document any assumptions you've made when performing cost estimates. For example, you may need to note that you are assuming the rate sheet you're using to determine contractor costs will still be valid once the work of the project begins.

The cost estimates will be used to create the project budget, which you'll learn about next.

Creating the Project Budget

When you have the cost estimates completed, it's time to prepare the budget. *Budgeting* is the process of aggregating all the cost estimates and establishing a cost baseline for the project. The *cost baseline* is the total expected cost for the project. Once approved, it's used throughout the remainder of the project to measure the overall cost performance.

The project budget is used to track the actual expenses incurred against the estimates. You'll look at tracking and reporting expenses more closely in the "Expenditure Tracking and Reporting" section later in this chapter.

Before learning about the mechanics of the budget itself, you should make sure you have an understanding of the processes within your organization regarding budgets, authority levels, how expenses are approved, and more. Here are a few questions you can use to help get you started:

- Are all project expenses submitted to the project manager for approval?
- What spending authority or approval levels does the project manager have regarding project expenses?
- Does the project manager approve timesheets for project team members?
- Are there categories of cost or threshold dollar amounts that require approval from the project sponsor or customer?
- What portions of the budget are capital expenses and which are operational expenses?

Getting the answers to these questions before spending the money will eliminate problems and confusion later in the project.

Tracking project expenses as they're incurred is not always the responsibility of the project manager. Once the cost estimates have been provided and the project budget is established, the actual tracking of expenses may be performed by the accounting or finance department. Some organizations use their program management office (PMO) to oversee project budgets, approve expenses, track all the project budgets, and so on. Make certain you know who is responsible for what actions regarding the budget.

No matter who actually tracks the budget expenditures, as the project manager you're the person accountable for how the money is spent and for completing the work of the project within budget. You'll want to monitor the budget reports regularly so that you can identify any overruns and take corrective action to get the budget back on track.

 Set up a routine meeting with all the budget analysts from the various departments providing project funding so that everyone is aware of the status of the project budget at any point in the project.

Now let's look at how to create the project budget.

Creating the Project Budget

Project budgets are usually broken down by specific cost categories that are defined by the accounting department. A few examples of common cost categories include salary, hardware, software, travel, training, and materials and supplies. Project budgets may also incorporate both *capital expenses (CapEx)* and *operational expenses (OpEx)*. Capital expenses typically apply to assets that are expected to provide benefit to the organization for an extended time into the future. Some examples of capital expenses include equipment purchases, large software purchases, entitlements or licensing costs for large software subscriptions that extend over several years, building purchases, and vehicle purchases. Capital funds are usually a separate account in the organization's code of accounts and are managed differently than operating expenses. All budget items that require capital expenses must come from the capital expense account.

Operational expenses include all expenses needed to run the day-to-day activities of the business such as administrative costs, training, travel, supplies, materials, salaries, rent, and leases. Be certain to obtain a copy of your organization's cost categories so that you understand how each of your resources should be tracked and classified.

 Check with your PMO or accounting department to see whether there are standard budget templates that you can use for the project.

Project budgets are as varied as projects themselves. Although the format for budgets may be similar from project to project, the expenses, budget amounts, and categories you use will change for each project.

Budgets can be created in a spreadsheet format or in a budgeting software program and may be divided into monthly or quarterly increments or more depending on the size and length of the project. If you don't have a template available to start your budget, contact your accounting department to get the chart of accounts information needed to construct the budget. The chart of accounts lists the account number and description for each category of expense you'll use on the budget. You may remember that we used the chart of accounts codes earlier in the book for the work package level of the WBS as well.

To begin creating the budget, list categories such as salaries, contract expenses, materials, travel, training, and others, and record the cost estimates you derived for each. Add a column for actual expenditures to date. You'll use this information during the Monitoring and Controlling phase of the project to determine the financial health of the project. Table 7.3 shows a high-level sample budget.

TABLE 7.3   Sample project budget

Account code	Category	Estimated costs
1001	Contract labor	$50,000
1003	Materials	$2,500
1005	Hardware	$22,700
1010	Training	$7,000
Total Budget		**$82,200**

You may want to include two additional types of expenses in the project budget: contingency reserves and management reserves. Make certain you check with your organization regarding the policies that dictate the allocation of these funds and the approvals needed to spend them.

> **Contingency Reserve**   A *contingency reserve,* also known as a buffer, is a certain amount of money set aside to cover costs resulting from possible adverse events or unexpected issues on the project. These costs may come about for many reasons, including scope creep, risks, change requests, variances in estimates, cost overruns, and so on. There is no set rule for defining the amount you should put in a contingency fund, but most organizations that use this allocation often set the contingency fund amount as a percentage of the total project cost.
>
> Be aware that stakeholders may misunderstand the meaning of a contingency reserve and see it as a source of funding for project enhancements or additional functionality they didn't plan into the project. Make sure they understand the purpose of this fund

is to cover possible adverse or unexpected events. With the exception of very small projects, it seems there are always expenses that come up later during the project that weren't planned for up front. The contingency fund is designed to cover these types of expenses. Contingency reserves are included in the budget and the cost baseline.

Management Reserve   A *management reserve* is an amount set aside by upper management to cover future situations that can't be predicted. As with the contingency reserve, the amount of a management reserve is typically based on a percentage of the total project cost.

What makes the management reserve different from the contingency reserve is the spending authority and the fact that it covers unforeseen costs. The project manager controls how the contingency funds are used. The management fund is usually controlled by upper management, and the project manager can't spend money out of this fund without approval from upper management. Management reserves are not included as part of the project budget or cost baseline.

The terms *contingency reserve* and *management reserve* may be considered interchangeable in some organizations.

The project budget is used to create the cost baseline, which is a tool used during project execution and during the Monitoring and Controlling phase to monitor project expenditures.

Cost Baseline

The key members of the project team should review the draft budget. It may be appropriate to have a representative from the accounting department or the PMO review the draft as well. The project team needs to understand the critical link between the schedule and the budget. Any questions about budget categories or how the dollars are spread across the project timeline should be addressed at this time.

Once the budget review with the project team is complete, it is time to get the project sponsor's approval and then create a cost baseline. The cost baseline is the total approved expected cost for the project. This should be approved before any work begins. All future expenditures and variances will be measured against this baseline.

Cost baselines can be displayed graphically, with time increments on one axis and dollars expended on the other axis, as shown in Figure 7.1. The costs shown on this graph are cumulative costs, meaning that what you spent this period is added to what was spent last period and then charted. Many variations of this graph exist showing dollars budgeted against dollars expended to date. Cost budgets can be displayed using this type of graph as well, by plotting the sum of the estimated costs excepted per period.

FIGURE 7.1   Cost baseline

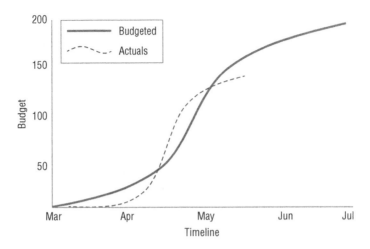

 Cost baselines are displayed as S curves. The reason for this is that project spending starts out slowly, then gradually increases over the project's life until it reaches a peak, and then tapers off again as the project wraps up. Large projects are difficult to graph in this manner because the timescale isn't wide enough to accurately show fluctuations in spending.

The cost baseline is used throughout the remainder of the project to track the actual cost of the project against the estimated or planned costs. It is also used to predict future costs based on what's been spent to date and to calculate the projected cost of the remaining work.

The project manager should communicate the cost baseline to the project stakeholders. Some stakeholders may want a copy of the total project budget, whereas others may be interested in the budget only for specific phases of the project. You should note each stakeholder's needs regarding budget information in the communication plan.

Expenditure Tracking and Reporting

Now that the budget is established and the cost baseline is approved, you will need to track the project expenditures and report the state of the budget to your stakeholders and sponsor. It's common to include budget updates as an agenda item during your project update meetings.

Expenditure tracking includes measuring the project spending to date, determining the burn rate (or how fast you're going through the money), and tracking expenditures to the cost baseline so that stakeholders can see what was planned versus what was actually spent on the project. *Expenditure reporting* is the mechanism you'll use to report on the current state of the project budget.

Project management software is useful in tracking project spending. You can run reports that show spending to date versus what was planned, and you can also use software to look at the impact of adding new tasks or resources using what-if scenarios.

You can also use your handy spreadsheet program for expenditure tracking and reporting. Table 7.4 is a sample of a budget report showing the estimated costs (what was planned) versus the actual costs to date and the variance, or difference between the two.

TABLE 7.4   Sample project budget report

Account code	Category	Estimated costs	Actual cost at reporting date	Variance
1001	Contract labor	$50,000	$48,500	$1,500
1003	Materials	$2,500	$2,500	$0
1005	Hardware	$22,700	$24,500	$(1,800)
1010	Training	$7,000	$5,000	$2,000
Total Variance This Period		$82,200	$80,500	**$1,700**

Budget Burndown Chart

Another way to report on budget expenditures is using a budget burndown chart. We talked about burndown charts in Chapter 5 when reporting on agile projects. You'll recall that the agile burndown chart shows the remaining time and work effort for the iteration. A budget burndown chart shows the burn rate for the budget over the scheduled timeline, as shown in the example in Figure 7.2.

Burn rate is the rate at which you are spending funds over time. You can see that the total budget in Figure 7.2 is $200,000. The entire project is expected to take five months; therefore, your expected burn rate is $40,000 per month. It is calculated this way: total budget / time period.

The current reporting date is in May. As of May, there is approximately $75,000 of funds remaining. Actual burn rate is calculated this way: expenses to date / time periods at measurement date. In this case, we must first determine expenses to date. We had $200,000 to start and have $75,000 remaining, so that means we've spent $125,000 as of the reporting date. That is calculated this way: $200,000 − $75,000 = $125,0000.

FIGURE 7.2   Budget burndown chart

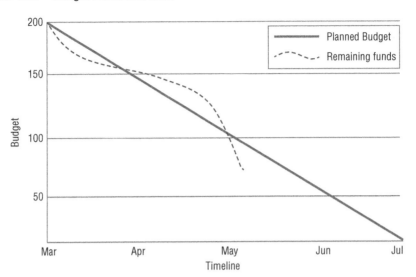

In our example, expenses to date are $125,000 / 3 months = $41,667. You are slightly over the projected burn rate of $40,000 per month, so you'd want to keep an eye on the budget to keep things in check and on track so as not to exceed the project budget.

You can use a budget burndown chart for agile projects as well. In this case, the timeline on the x-axis would show iterations instead of dates.

Earned Value Management

One of your duties as a project manager is to control and monitor the costs of the project. There are several techniques you can use to do this. *Earned value measurement (EVM)* is a performance measurement technique that compares what your project has produced to what you've spent by monitoring the planned value, earned value, and actual costs expended to produce the work of the project. When variances that result in changes to the cost baseline are discovered, those changes should be managed using the project change control system. If the budget needs updating and/or funding has been added to the project, you'll need approval and sign-off from the sponsor for the new cost baseline.

The primary functions of EVM analysis techniques are to determine and document the cause of the variance, to determine the impact of the variance, and to determine whether a corrective action should be implemented as a result.

EVM looks at schedule, cost, and scope project measurements together and compares them to the actual work completed to date. These measures allow you to forecast where the project is headed. You may be ahead of schedule, behind schedule, spending money too fast, and so on. EVM is usually performed on the work packages or other WBS components.

To perform the EVM calculations, you need to first gather these three measurements: planned value, actual cost, and earned value.

Planned Value The *planned value (PV)* is the cost of work that has been authorized and budgeted for a specific schedule activity or WBS component (such as a work package) during a given time period or phase.

Actual Cost *Actual cost (AC)* is the actual cost of completing the work component in a given time period. Actual costs might include direct and indirect costs but must correspond to what was budgeted for the activity. For example, if the budgeted amount did not include indirect costs, do not include them here.

Earned Value *Earned value (EV)* is the value of the work completed to date as it compares to the budgeted amount (PV) for that period. EV is typically expressed as a percentage of the work completed compared to the budget. For example, if our budgeted amount is $1,000 and you have completed 30 percent of the work so far, your EV is $300. EV cannot exceed the total project budget, but it may exceed the PV for a work component or period of performance if the team is ahead of schedule because they completed work planned for a future period during the measurement period.

The concepts of PV, AC, and EV are really easy to mix up. In their simplest forms, here's what each means:

PV The approved budget assigned to the work to be completed during a given time period

AC Money that's actually been expended during a given time period for completed work

EV The value of the work completed to date compared to the budget

Cost Variance

Cost variance (CV) tells you whether your costs are higher than budgeted (with a resulting negative number) or lower than budgeted (with a resulting positive number). It measures the actual performance to date against what's been spent.

The formula for CV is as follows:

$$CV = EV - AC$$

Suppose that as of December 1 (the measurement date), the performance measurements are as follows:

$$PV = 75,000$$

$$AC = 71,000$$

$$EV = 70,000$$

Now let's calculate the CV using these numbers:

$$70,000 - 71,000 = -1,000$$

The result is a negative number, which means that costs were higher than what was planned for the work that was completed as of December 1. These costs are usually not recoverable. If the result was a positive number, it would mean you spent less than what you planned for the work that was completed as of December 1.

Schedule Variance

Schedule variance, another popular EVM variance, compares an activity's actual progress to date to the estimated progress and is represented in terms of cost. It tells you whether the schedule is ahead of or behind what was planned for this period. This formula is most helpful when you've used the critical path methodology to build the project schedule. The schedule variance (SV) is calculated as follows:

$$SV = EV - PV$$

Plug in the numbers:

$$70,000 - 75,000 = -5,000$$

The resulting schedule variance is negative, which means you are behind schedule or behind where you planned to be as of December 1.

Together, the CV and SV are known as efficiency indicators for the project and can be used to compare the performance of all the projects in a portfolio.

Performance Indexes

Cost and schedule performance indexes are primarily used to calculate performance efficiencies, and they're often used to help predict future project performance.

The *cost performance index (CPI)* measures the value of the work completed at the measurement date against the actual cost. It is the most critical of all the EVM measurements because it tells you the cost efficiency for the work completed to date or at the completion of the project. If CPI is greater than 1, you are spending less than anticipated at the measurement date. If CPI is less than 1, you are spending more than anticipated for the work completed at the measurement date.

The cost performance index (CPI) is calculated this way:

$$CPI = EV / AC$$

Plug in the numbers to see where you stand:

$$70,000 / 71,000 = .99$$

Since the result is less than 1, it means cost performance is worse than expected.

The *schedule performance index (SPI)* measures the progress to date against the progress that was planned. This formula should be used in conjunction with an analysis of the critical path activities to determine whether the project will finish ahead of or behind schedule. If SPI is greater than 1, your performance is better than expected, and you're ahead of schedule. If SPI is less than 1, you're behind schedule at the measurement date.

The schedule performance index (SPI) is calculated this way:

$$SPI = EV / PV$$

Again, let's see where you stand with this example:

$$70,000 / 75,000 = .93$$

Schedule performance is not what you expected as of December 1.

Keep in mind that all of these formulas start with EV. Remember that the variances use subtraction and the performance indexes use division. Cost performance uses actual costs, and schedule performance uses planned value. Here's a recap of the formulas:

CV

EV − AC

CPI

EV / AC

SV

EV − PV

SPI

EV / PV

Burn Rate

Burn rate is the rate you are spending money over time. For example, if you had a $12,000 budget and you're spending $2,000 a month, you'll run out of money in six months. That's great if you are running a five- or six-month project. It's not so great if you're running a 12-month project. Unfortunately, spending is rarely spread out evenly over the course of the project, so calculating burn rate isn't quite as simple as I've just explained. Burn rate on a project is typically calculated using the cost performance index (CPI) calculation.

Another method of determining burn rate uses the *estimate to complete (ETC)* formula. This is the cost estimate for the remaining project work. It is typically provided by the team members actually working on the project activities. Using the previous example, the project budget is $12,000, you've spent $8,000 to date, and the ETC is $6,000. Your spending is outpacing the project work, and you will likely run out of money unless corrections are made.

 For the exam, remember that the cost processes include cost estimating, creating the project budget, and controlling costs.

Expenditure Reporting

Expenditure reporting can take many different forms. As shown earlier in Table 7.4, a simple spreadsheet showing planned versus actual costs to date and their variance should suffice for most small projects. Project management software gives you many options for tracking and reporting on the budget. Pie charts, bar charts, and budgets broken down by work components are other ways to report on and display project spending. You can also use much more advanced EVM measurements to report on project expenditures.

Take the time to define estimates, create an overall budget based on the estimates, and then track what you're spending against what you planned and report this status to the stakeholders. Be certain to alert your sponsor at the earliest signs of trouble with the budget. You may be able to take action to get the budget back on track, but don't assume this can or will happen. The sponsor isn't likely going to be happy with negative budget news, but the sooner you make them aware, the sooner they can assist in solving the issue. Spending overruns are often outside the project manager's control, but you'll need documentation and budget reports when you talk with the sponsor.

Risk Planning

Risk is something that we deal with in our everyday lives. Some people seek out jobs or leisure activities that are considered high risk. They may get a thrill or a feeling of great accomplishment from taking on the challenge of skydiving or mountain climbing or from working on high-voltage electrical lines as part of the line crew.

A *risk* is a potential future event that can have either negative or positive impacts on the project. However, if you mention the word *risk* in association with a project, the majority of people will immediately think of something negative. In my experience, most of the time when a risk event occurs, it has negative consequences. But risks are not always negative. There is the potential for positive consequences as a result of a risk occurrence.

Risk planning deals with how you manage the areas of uncertainty in your project. There are three major components to risk planning: identifying the potential risks to your project, analyzing the potential impact of each risk, and developing an appropriate response for those risks with the greatest probability and impact. Let's take a look at each of these next.

Risk Identification

All projects have risks. *Risk identification* is the process of determining and documenting the potential risks that could occur on your project.

You can view risks both by looking at the project as a whole and by analyzing individual components of the project such as resources, schedule, costs, tasks, and so on. Risks can include such items as the level of funding committed to the project, the overall experience level of the core project team, the use of project management practices, or the strategic significance of the project. Risks may also be associated with particular phases of the project or with certain key tasks.

You should include stakeholders, core team members, and any other subject matter experts who may have experience or knowledge of this project in your risk identification and analysis process. You can use several techniques to help define the initial risk list, including brainstorming, interviews, and facilitated workshops.

One way to get a jump start on a brainstorming session is to review a list of common potential risks:

- Budgets or funding
- Schedules
- Scope
- Requirements changes
- Contracts
- Hardware
- Political concerns
- Management risks
- Legal risks
- Technical issues

In my experience, brainstorming meetings are a great way to identify risks. You can conduct the brainstorming meeting in a couple of ways. Provide everyone with a marker and a sticky-note pad and ask them to write one risk per sticky note as they review the risk types and the questions. Then post the risks to a whiteboard and begin to categorize them.

You can also invite someone to attend the meeting and take notes as ideas are shared. No matter which method you use to identify the risks, at the conclusion of the meeting you should have a completed *risk register*. This is a list of risks that includes an identification number, risk name, risk description, risk owner, and response plan (or where the response plan can be located). The risk owner is the person responsible for monitoring the project to determine whether the potential for this risk event is high and for implementing the *risk response plan* should it occur.

One type of risk you should be aware of for the exam is called *force majeure*. These risks are catastrophic in nature and are outside of the control of the organization. Force majeure risks might include war, employees going on strike, pandemics, cyber ransom attacks, asteroids hitting the earth, and so on. These risks almost always have negative consequences to the project and the organization and cannot be addressed with a risk response plan. From an IT perspective, force majeure risks are most often addressed using disaster recovery plans or cybersecurity incident response plans, not risk response plans.

What Could Possibly Go Wrong?

Another brainstorming technique you can use to identify risks is to hand out sticky notes and ask the risk team to answer one question: what could go wrong?

By letting people freely think and blurt out all the possibilities that occur to them, you may get some input that proves to be valuable in the risk identification process.

Strengths, Weaknesses, Opportunities, and Threats (SWOT)

Another technique you can use to identify risks is called *SWOT analysis*. This involves analyzing the project from each of these perspectives: strengths, weaknesses, opportunities, and threats. It also requires examining other elements such as the project management processes, resources, the organization, and so on. SWOT analysis is sometimes known as internal-external analysis.

Strengths and weaknesses are generally related to issues that are internal to the organization. Strengths examine what your organization does well and what your customers, or the stakeholders, view as your strengths. Weaknesses are areas the organization could improve upon. Typically, negative risks are associated with the organization's weaknesses, and positive risks are associated with its strengths.

Opportunities and threats are usually external to the organization. For example, the weather, political climates in other countries where you may be performing parts of the project, the financial markets, and so on, are external to the project and could present either opportunities or threats. SWOT analysis can be used in combination with brainstorming techniques to help discover and document potential risks.

Once you have identified all the possible risks to the project, you need to analyze the risks to determine the potential for the risk event to occur and the impact it will have on the project if it does occur.

Risk Analysis

The purpose of *risk analysis* is to identify those risks that have the greatest possibility of occurring and the greatest impact to the project if they do occur. You will create a risk response plan for those risks with high probability and impact after completing the analysis process.

It's important to understand your stakeholders' risk tolerance levels. This may be partially based on the type of industry you work in, corporate culture, departmental culture, or individual preferences of stakeholders. For example, research and development industries tend to have a high-risk tolerance, whereas the banking industry leans toward a very low risk tolerance. Make certain you understand the risk tolerances of your stakeholders before assigning probability and impacts to the risk events.

Risk analysis involves several techniques, including impact analysis, qualitative analysis, quantitative analysis, and situational or scenario-based analysis. We will look at each next.

Impact Analysis

Impact analysis is a way to prioritize and quantify risks so they are easy to understand and highlights at a glance those risks that will need a risk response plan should they occur. One of the easiest ways to do this is by creating a *probability and impact matrix*.

Probability is the likelihood that a risk event will occur. For example, if you a flip a coin, there's a 0.5 probability the coin will come up heads. Probability is expressed as a number between 0.0 and 1.0, with 1.0 being an absolute certainty the risk event will occur.

The quickest way to determine probability is by using expert judgment. This typically comes from knowledgeable project team members, stakeholders, or subject matter experts who have experience on similar projects. Ask them to rate the probability of occurrence of each risk on the list. You could also review historical data from past projects that are similar to the current project to rate the probability of risk occurrence.

Impact is the consequence (or opportunity) the risk poses to the project if it occurs. Some risks have impacts that are very low and won't impact the overall success of the project if they were to occur, while others could have impacts that cause a delay in the project completion or a significant budget overrun. Again, rely on the expert knowledge and judgment of the team members and on historical data to rate the severity of each risk. You can use a simple high-medium-low score to rate impact.

Next, you'll convert the high-medium-low scores to a range of numbers determined by the team or the PMO. The impact numbers can be stated in terms of impact to the organization using a scale such as 1 to 10, or costs. You'll plug the scores into the probability and impact matrix. For this example, a high impact has a score of 10, a medium impact has a score of 5, and a low impact has a score of 1.

Next, you'll construct a probability and impact matrix to calculate a final risk score for each of the risks on your list. The final score is determined by multiplying the probability by the impact. Table 7.5 shows a basic probability and impact matrix.

TABLE 7.5   Probability and impact matrix

Risk	Probability	Impact	Risk score
Risk A	0.9	10	9
Risk B	0.3	5	1.5
Risk C	0.8	1	0.8
Risk D	0.5	5	2.5

The higher the risk score, the more likely the risk will occur and have a significant impact on the project. The organization, or the PMO, may have predetermined risk score ranges that indicate if a response plan is needed. In Table 7.5, any risk score 2.0 or higher needs a response plan. Risk A has a high probability of occurring and has a significant impact. This risk needs a response plan. Risk B has a low probability of occurring and a medium impact. Its total risk score is low, and it does not need a risk response plan. Risk C has a high probability of occurring but a low impact if it does occur and does not need a risk response plan. Risk D should have a response plan.

Make certain you understand the risk tolerances of your stakeholders before assigning probability and impacts to the risk events. If your stakeholders are primarily risk-averse but the project team is assigning probability and impact scores that are allowing for a higher tolerance toward risks, when a risk event occurs your stakeholders may react in a way you didn't expect. For example, if they perceive a certain risk as high and the team rated it as medium and then the risk event comes about, you may have stakeholders recommending canceling the project because of their unwillingness to deal with the risk event. Stakeholder reactions may bring about unintended consequences on the project, so be certain you're in tune with their comfort level regarding risk.

Qualitative Analysis

Qualitative analysis is the process of determining the probability and impact of the risks and ranking them in order of priority to determine which ones need response plans. Qualitative analysis considers risk threshold levels, especially as they relate to the project constraints (scope, time, cost, and quality) and the time frames of the potential risk events. This analysis involves prioritizing risks according to their probability of occurring and their impact. Qualitative analysis is fast, relatively easy to perform, and cost effective. The probability and impact analysis we discussed previously is a type of qualitative analysis.

Risk analysis should be performed throughout the project. If you're using an agile approach, you'll perform this process at the beginning of each iteration.

Here are some further elements you should consider when defining probability and impact and prioritizing the lists of risk:

Urgency   Determining how quickly a response needs to be implemented

Proximity   Determining how quickly the risk will impact one or more of the project objectives

Dormancy   The period of time between the risk occurrence and discovery of the risk

Manageability   How well the risk owner manages the risk event

Controllability   The ability of the risk owner to control the impact of the risk

Detectability   The ability to detect a risk trigger and understand a risk event is about to occur

Interconnectivity   The relationship between the individual risks and how one risk may raise or lower the probability and/or impact of another should it occur

Strategic Impact   The impact to the organization's strategic goals if the risk event occurs

Propinquity   The stakeholder's perception of the risk significance

Let's walk through an example of how you would use some of these risk parameters to prioritize risk. Perhaps you are implementing a new, on-premises ERP system. Your Internet newsfeed pops up with a message about supply chain issues due to weather events and political unrest (this describes detectability). You are reliant on hardware components coming from the location noted in the newsfeed to arrive before you can proceed with the project. The delay of this equipment will delay the software implementation and configuration and cause delays to the project timeline (this describes interconnectivity). Both factors in this example would lead to prioritizing this risk as a high risk with high impact.

Quantitative Analysis

Quantitative analysis quantifies the aggregate risk exposure for the project by assigning numeric probabilities to risks and their impacts on project objectives. This quantitative approach is accomplished using techniques such as Monte Carlo simulation, which we will get to shortly.

Quantitative analysis helps determine the probability of achieving the project objectives, identifying the risks that should be closely monitored, and more. Quantitative analysis, like qualitative analysis, examines risk and its potential impact on the project objectives. You might choose to use both of these processes to assess all the project risks or only one or two of them, depending on the complexity of the project. If you do choose to use both, you will perform qualitative analysis before determining quantitative analysis.

Simulation techniques are often used for schedule risk analysis and cost risk analysis. For example, simulations allow you to translate the potential risks at specific points in the project into their impacts so that you can determine how the project objectives are affected. Simulation techniques are "what if" scenarios that analyze the project outcomes using various inputs, such as cost estimates or activity durations, to determine a probability distribution for the variable chosen. We might examine some of the following, for example: "What if a risk occurs that increases costs and we exceed our total budget? What if a risk event impacts the schedule? What if the supply chain is disrupted and we don't receive our hardware on schedule?"

Cost variables typically use either a work breakdown structure or a cost breakdown structure as the input variable. Schedule variables always use the schedule network diagram and duration estimates as the input variable. If you used simulation techniques to determine project cost and use the cost of the project elements as the input variable, a probability distribution for the total cost of the project would be produced after running the simulation numerous times. Simulation techniques examine the identified risks and their potential impacts on the project objectives from the perspective of the whole project.

Monte Carlo analysis is a type of simulation technique you should know for the exam. Monte Carlo analysis typically uses cost or schedule variables that are input into the model and then replicated several times to estimate potential outcomes for each of the variables used. Every time the analysis is performed, the values for the variable are changed using a probability distribution for each variable. This way, you can determine the likely outcome of potential risks, cost risks or changes, schedule risk or changes, and other what-if scenarios. You can then create risk response plans for the risks that are most likely to occur, and/or for the worst-case scenario for each risk, or input variable, used in the analysis. Monte Carlo analysis can also be used to perform cost and schedule analysis.

Situational/Scenario Analysis

Situational/scenario analysis looks at risk from the perspective of various situations or scenarios that may occur as the project progresses. The idea is to think about what could occur and identify potential risks or outcomes from those situations and prepare for them. You'll want to be reasonable in your assumptions about the scenarios. For example, an asteroid could hit the earth, but the probability of this happening and disrupting your project is almost zero, so it's not a risk you'll need to analyze. Situation/scenario analysis should consider internal factors to the organization as well as external factors that may bring about a risk. You'll also want to consider several scenarios while thinking through the different directions the project could take and the risks that could occur. Make certain to examine internal influences such as organizational change, a new project sponsor, or new management. The CompTIA objectives list several situation/scenario-based risks you should know for the exam:

- New projects
- New management
- Regulatory environment changes
- Digital transformation
- Infrastructure end of life
- Merger and acquisition
- Reorganization
- Cybersecurity events

Most of these risk scenarios are self-explanatory and each has the potential to significantly impact your project. I have experienced most of these scenarios during my career. One of my all-time favorites is a change in management that brings about new projects. This almost always means the number one priority project you're working on now will take a backseat to the new project proposed by new management and all the hard work the team has accomplished to date is trashed. But I digress. Be sure to examine the potential for each of these scenarios on your next project.

The last step in the risk process is to create an appropriate course of action for those risks with the highest scores.

Preparing Risk Responses

Risk is, after all, uncertainty. The more you know about risks and their impacts beforehand, the better equipped you will be to handle a risk event when it occurs. The processes that involve risk concern balance. You want to find that point where you and the stakeholders are comfortable with the risk based on the benefits you can potentially gain. In a nutshell, you're balancing the action of taking a risk against avoiding the consequences or impacts of a risk event or enjoying the benefits it may bring.

Risk response planning is the process of reviewing the risk analysis and determining what, if any, action should be taken to reduce negative impacts and take advantage of opportunities because of a risk event occurring.

Your organization may have a predetermined formula for identifying risks that require a response plan. For example, they may require that all risks with a total risk score greater than 0.6 have a response plan.

You'll use several strategies when determining both negative risks and opportunities and formulating your response plans. The strategies to deal with negative risks include the following:

- *Avoid*: Avoiding the risk altogether or eliminating the cause of the risk event
- *Transfer*: Moving the liability for the risk to a third party by purchasing insurance, performance bonds, and so on
- *Mitigate*: Reducing the impact or the probability of the risk
- *Accept*: Choosing to accept the consequences of the risk

 Real World Scenario

The Road Trip

You decide to take a road trip. However, you've had some rather unfortunate driving incidents lately. You've received two speeding tickets and were involved in a minor fender bender all within the last six months. You don't want to take a chance on another ticket, because your insurance rates are already astronomical. So, you hire a driver to go with you. The driver will do all the driving while you sit back and enjoy the scenery. You consider yourself very clever because you've transferred the risk of receiving a speeding ticket to the driver.

Your driver checks the road conditions and traffic reports before you leave. The driver discovers that the highway you planned to take is clogged with congestion because of an accident. You both decide to avoid the risk by taking an alternate route that will go around the accident and put you on the highway a few miles down the road, avoiding the congestion and the accident altogether.

A few days into the road trip, you find yourself on a mountain pass in the middle of a beautiful sunny day. All of a sudden, a rock tumbles down the side of the hill and lands squarely on the road in front of your car. The rock is so big you can't go around it. You and your driver accept this risk occurrence and perform a U-turn and go back to the town you just passed a few miles ago and wait for the road crew to clear the pass.

The strategies associated with positive risks or opportunities include the following:

- *Exploit*: Looking for opportunities to take advantage of positive impacts
- *Share*: Assigning the risk to a third party who is best able to bring about the opportunity
- *Enhance*: Monitoring the probability or impact of the risk event to assure benefits are realized
- *Accept*: Choosing to accept the consequences of the risk

As you perform risk analysis, assign owners, and determine whether response plans are needed, you should record this information in the *risk register*. Table 7.6 shows a sample risk register.

TABLE 7.6   Risk register

Risk #	Risk description	Probability	Impact	Risk score	Response plan	Risk owner	Location
1	Bad weather	1.0	1.0	1.0	Y	Peterson	H Drive
2	Vendor delays	0.3	0.5	0.15	N	Hernandez	H Drive
3	Budget overrun	0.8	0.1	0.08	Y	Whatley	H Drive
4	Technical issues	0.5	0.5	0.25	N	White	IT Dept

Risk triggers are a sign or a precursor signaling that a risk event is about to occur. For example, clouds rolling in midday of a planned outdoor event is a trigger that rain is at hand, and you'll need to activate the response plan.

The *risk owner* is responsible for monitoring the risks assigned to them and watching for risk triggers. It's the risk owner's responsibility to alert the project manager that risks are about to occur, and to review and enact the response plan if necessary. The risk owner is also responsible for monitoring the response plan and its effectiveness until the risk is resolved. The project manager may in turn need to escalate to the project sponsor and inform them of the risk event, the response plan, and the progress of the response plan. These *points of escalation* should be documented in the risk response plan. Points of escalation describe who should be alerted once a risk event occurs. The risk ranking can be used to designate escalation. For example, all risks rated as high, or perhaps all risks with a probability and impact rating of 0.7 and greater need to be escalated to the project sponsor. Medium risks might be escalated to a key stakeholder and so on. The project manager is usually the first point of escalation.

We've spent a good deal of time discussing known risks—that is, risk you've identified ahead of time that have the potential to cause issues (or reap rewards) on the project. But unknown risks can appear on the project as well. Unknown risks, by their nature, are not known until they occur. Many of the strategies we discussed in this section can be activated when unknown risks occur. Force majeure risks are often unknown risks. One of the best strategies to deal with unknown risk is putting aside contingency reserves and/or management reserves specifically to address this issue.

Risk Monitoring

Use the risk register to communicate the project risks and action plans to the stakeholders. Include a risk update in your project status meetings and periodically set up a risk review meeting to go through each risk on the risk register and determine whether they have occurred or are likely to occur. Risk typically diminishes over time, so risk rankings should change to reflect the current state of the project. New risks can come to light as you proceed with the work of the project, and you'll want to add them to the risk register and perform a risk analysis to determine if a response plan is needed. Risk identification and risk monitoring should be performed throughout the entire project life cycle.

 Risk events have a higher probability of occurring and causing more impact early in the project, whereas probability and impact decrease as you approach closing out the project.

If you're working on a large project or one with an extended time frame, it's good practice to reevaluate risks periodically. This involves starting again at the risk identification process and working through the probability and impact exercise and writing response plans for newly identified risks and updating responses for existing risks.

 **Real World Scenario**

Main Street Office Move

Emma is anxiously awaiting the estimated cost for the project. Now that the schedule is complete and you have resources assigned, you begin the process of estimating the costs of the tasks, including contract resources, supplies, and materials. The work packages are a great place to start. The IaaS platform contract is coming from the capital budget and is not included as part of the project budget. Your estimates are as follows:

Description	Work effort/quantity	Rate/ each	Estimated cost	Budget category	Comments
Communicate move purpose (marketing materials)	2,400 brochures	$1.50	$3,600	OpEx	Estimate provided by Juliette in marketing
Moving company services	18 loads	$3,200	$57,600	OpEx	Estimate based on calls and quotes from several moving companies

Furniture and fixtures	Desks, chairs, tables, artwork		$100,000	OpEx	Estimate based on current pricing with the organization's vendor
Interior design	70 hours	$180/hr	$12,600	OpEx	Estimate provided by Alden in facilities
Relocate fleet cars	16 hours	$75/hr	$1,200	OpEx	Estimate provided by Joe, fleet manager
Network printers in the new building	3	$25,000	$75,000	CapEx	Estimate provided by Jason, IT director
Implementation and configuration of IaaS platform	Fixed rate contract	$225,000	$225,000	OpEx	Estimate provided by Jason, IT director
Equipment move for data center items needed at new location	24 hours	$125/hr	$3,000	OpEx	Estimate provided by Jason, IT director
TOTAL Estimated Cost			**$478,000**		

Early in the project, Emma informed you that the budget was fixed at $450,000. The project estimates are coming in over that amount—not by much, but you know that this budget is a constraint and can't go over.

You also haven't accounted for contingency reserves in case there are unexpected costs. You will meet again with Leah in procurement and Jason in IT to see whether they can negotiate lower implementation costs once the RFP process is complete. You set up a meeting with Alden, the facilities manager, to go over the cost estimates for the interior design services and the furniture and fixtures to see if costs can be trimmed from this area as well. Perhaps you can choose less expensive furniture and artwork for the offices.

Once you get new estimates, you'll revise the budget and then present it to Emma and stakeholders. Once Emma approves and signs off on the budget, this becomes the official cost baseline for the project. You will monitor burn rate and expenditures, and report expenditures and the state of the budget to the stakeholders throughout the remainder of the project.

The IT department is working on refreshing several of their IT security policies to address the new digital platform the organization will be using once the IaaS implementation is complete. They are looking at updating the operational security, data security, and digital security policies. Since the new building will also have a small data center on-site, they decide a refresh to the physical security policy is in order as well. This will also outline the MFA procedures for remote access to the IaaS platform.

You set up a meeting with the key stakeholders to determine the list of risks. Then you perform risk analysis by determining their probability and impact, and determine which risks need response plans. You assign risk owners to each risk and record this information in the risk register. Your sample risk register is shown here:

Risk #	Description	Probability	Impact	Risk score	Response plan	Risk owner
1	Delay in IaaS implementation	.10	90	9	Y	Jason, IT manager
2	Moving company availability on moving days	.25	90	22.5	Y	Leah, procurement manager
3	Bad weather during move	.25	10	2.5	N	Project manager
4	Furniture order delayed	.10	50	5	Y	Alden, facilities manager

All risks with a risk score of 5 or greater will need a response plan. The risk owner will monitor the risk triggers, and the points of escalation are the project manager and then the project sponsor.

Summary

Security policies are important for securing the organization's equipment, data, digital assets and more. Security policies may cover several types of assets, including physical, operational, digital, and more. Operational policies include background checks and security clearances.

Digital policies should incorporate multifactor authentication techniques that use at least two forms of identification to verify identity during sign-in. Data classification is used to classify data based on sensitivity, type, and value to the organization. Security policies can be applied based on the classification.

Cost estimating is performed after the schedule is created and the resources for the project have been determined. You can use several techniques to create project estimates. Analogous or top-down estimates use expert judgment and historical data to provide a high-level estimate for the entire project, a phase of the project, or a deliverable. Parametric estimating uses a mathematical model to create the estimates and, in its simplest form, multiplies the duration of the project task by the resource rate to determine an estimate. The bottom-up method creates the project estimate by adding up the individual estimates from each work package. Three-point estimates are the average of the most likely, optimistic, and pessimistic estimates.

Cost estimates are used to make up the project budget. The project budget is established by using the organization's chart of accounts and then documenting work effort, duration, equipment and material costs, and any other costs that may be incurred during the course of the project. The cost baseline is the total approved expected cost for the project and is used for forecasting and tracking expenditures throughout the project.

Risk planning involves identifying potential risk events that could occur during the project. Risk analysis techniques include impact analysis, qualitative analysis, quantitative analysis, and situational/scenario analysis. Impact analysis concerns determining the probability of a risk occurrence and determining its impact to the project. Probability is always expressed as a number between 0.0 and 1.0. Qualitative analysis also uses probability and impact ranking. Quantitative analysis uses simulation techniques such as Monte Carlo analysis to estimate potential outcomes of multiple risk variables to the project. Situational/scenario analysis involves looking at factors internal to the organization as well as external such as regulatory impacts or cyber threats. Risk response plans should be developed for those risks that have a high probability of occurrence, a significant impact to the project if they occur, or an overall risk score that is high.

It's important to communicate the risks and response plans to the stakeholders throughout the remainder of the project. If you're working on a project with a long timeline, periodically perform the risk processes again to determine whether your risks are still valid and to identify new risks.

Exam Essentials

Describe a security policy.   A security policy defines the minimum standards required to secure the organization's assets and outlines the rules and procedures for accessing them.

Be able to name three types of devices covered in a physical security policy.   Three types of devices covered in a physical security policy include mobile devices, removable media, and facilities.

Be able to name two types of operational policies.   Operational policies include background checks and security clearances.

Describe MFA.   Multifactor authentication is a process that requires two or more methods of verifying identity during the sign-in process.

Describe data classification.   Data classification is a way to classify data based on its sensitivity, type, and value to the organization.

Be able to define need-to-know basis.   Need-to-know concerns relaying the least amount of information needed with only those who have a need-to-know.

Know the difference between analogous, parametric, and bottom-up estimating techniques.   Analogous, or top-down, estimates use expert judgment and historical data to provide a high-level estimate for the entire project, a phase of the project, or a deliverable. Parametric estimates use a mathematical model to create the estimates. The bottom-up method starts at the lowest level of the WBS and calculates the cost of each item within the work packages to obtain a total cost for the project or deliverable.

Name the two discretionary funding allocations a project may receive.   The two types of discretionary funding are a contingency reserve and a management reserve. Contingency reserves are monies set aside to cover the cost of possible adverse events and are used at the discretion of the project manager. Management reserves are set aside by upper management and are used to cover future situations that can't be predicted during project planning.

Explain the purpose of a cost baseline.   The cost baseline is the total approved, expected cost for the project. It's used throughout the project life cycle to monitor the performance of the project budget throughout the project.

Explain the risk identification process.   Risk identification is the process of identifying and documenting the potential risk events that may occur on the project.

Explain the purpose of risk analysis.   Risk analysis evaluates the severity of the impact to the project and the probability that the risk will actually occur.

Be able to name the four risk analysis techniques.   Impact analysis, qualitative analysis, quantitative analysis, and situational/scenario analysis.

Explain Monte Carlo analysis.   Monte Carlo analysis is a simulation technique that uses multiple inputs, usually related to cost and schedule, to estimate potential outcomes for each of the inputs used in the model. This is a "what if"-based analysis that is performed multiple times to determine potential outcomes.

Be able to name at least four situational/scenario-based risks.   They are new projects, new management, regulatory environment changes, digital transformation, infrastructure end-of-life, merger and acquisition, reorganization, and cybersecurity events.

Name the negative risk response strategies. The negative risk response strategies are avoid, transfer, mitigate, and accept.

Name the positive risk response strategies. The positive risk response strategies are exploit, share, enhance, and accept.

Explain the purpose of risk response planning. Risk response planning is the process of reviewing the list of potential risks impacting the project to determine what, if any, action should be taken and then documenting it in a response plan.

Key Terms

Before you take the exam, be certain you are familiar with the following terms:

accept	need-to-know basis
actual cost (AC)	operational expenses (OpEx)
avoid	order-of-magnitude
bottom-up estimate	planned value (PV)
branding restrictions	points of escalation
budgeting	probability
burn rate	probability and impact matrix
capital expenses (CapEx)	qualitative analysis
contingency reserve,	quantitative analysis
cost baseline	risk
cost performance index (CPI)	risk analysis
cost variance (CV)	risk identification
data classification	risk owner
earned value (EV)	risk planning
earned value measurement (EVM)	risk register
enhance	risk response plan
estimate to complete (ETC)	risk triggers
expenditure reporting	schedule performance index (SPI)
expenditure tracking	schedule variance
exploit	security policy
force majeure	share

impact

management reserve

mitigate

Monte Carlo analysis

multi-factor authentication (MFA)

SWOT analysis

three-point estimates

top-down estimating

transfer

work effort

Review Questions

1. You are creating a document that describes the access rights to the financial system in your organization. It defines access by roles and responsibilities and describes the approval process for obtaining access. One of the rules stated in the document dictates that remote access to systems requires MFA. Which of the following are true regarding this question? (Choose two.)

    A. This question describes an operational security policy.

    B. This question describes a digital security policy.

    C. This question describes a process of verifying identity by requiring two or more forms of identification at sign-in.

    D. This question describes a form of data classification.

    E. This question describes a data security policy.

2. Your organization is involved in research and development of botanical cleaning products. Your recent product has just received approval to display the ® (registered) symbol. All potential employees must undergo a background check before being hired and again yearly on the anniversary of their hire date. One of the laboratories contains top-secret research and only certain employees have access to this lab. One of the employees on the project team has just been promoted and will be leaving the team to join their new functional area. This team member previously had access to the top-secret lab, but their new role no longer requires this access. Which of the following is not true regarding this question?

    A. The operational security policy outlines the process for background checks for employees.

    B. Access to the top-secret lab is outlined in the physical security policy.

    C. The new product has not been registered at the U.S. Patent and Trademark office.

    D. The physical security policy should outline the process for revoking access to the top-secret lab as soon as the employee is transferred to their new role.

3. A stranger comes to your door posing as a census taker. They look official in their bright orange vest and have some type of tag or badge hanging from the vest, but you can't read what it says. They begin to ask questions that become rather personal, including your household income on an annual basis, your birthdate, your health status, and more. You become suspicious of this person and stop to think through what to do next. Which of the following are true regarding this question?

    A. Due to your suspicion of this individual, you are classifying your answers as PII and refuse to answer.

    B. Due to your suspicion of this individual, you are classifying your answers as PHI and refuse to answer.

    C. Due to your suspicion of this individual, you ask to see their badge before you decide to answer.

    D. Due to your suspicion of this individual, you are classifying your answers as need-to-know basis and refuse to answer.

    E. All of the answers are true.

    F. Options A, B, and D are true.

4. You are asked to prepare an estimate for a project that involves planting new trees in the parking lot. The trees cost $800 each, and the labor to install them is $75 per hour. You are planting 10 new trees, and each tree takes one hour of labor to plant, stake, and water. What is the estimated cost of the labor for this project, and which technique are you using to determine this estimate? (Choose two.)

    A. $8,000

    B. Three-point estimate

    C. Bottom-up method

    D. $750

    E. Analogous method

    F. Parametric method

    G. $8,750

5. The total time it will take for one person to complete a task from beginning to end without taking into account holidays, time off, or other project work is known as this.

    A. Duration estimate

    B. Work effort estimate

    C. Bottom-up estimate

    D. Parametric estimate

6. A discretionary fund used by the project manager to cover the cost of possible adverse events during the project is known as which of the following?

    A. Management reserve

    B. Chart of accounts

    C. Contingency fund

    D. Cost baseline

7. You are developing a bottom-up cost estimate for the first phase of your project. Which of the following is the most important input to complete this task?

    A. Historic data from a similar project

    B. Chart of accounts

    C. The WBS

    D. The scope statement

8. What is considered the most accurate estimate?

    A. Analogous estimate

    B. Bottom-up estimate

    C. Estimates based on expert judgment

    D. Parametric estimate

9. You are asked to present and explain your project cost baseline. All of the following are true except which one?

   A. The baseline will be used to track actual spending against the cost estimates.

   B. The baseline can be used to predict future project costs.

   C. The baseline is calculated and approved by the project manager.

   D. The baseline is the total expected cost for the project.

10. Your project task is complex, and you decide to use a three-point estimating technique. Which of the following options determine the three-point estimate? (Choose three.)

    A. Quantity estimate

    B. Work package level estimate

    C. Materials estimate

    D. Pessimistic estimate

    E. Resource estimate

    F. Rate estimate

    G. Optimistic estimate

    H. Most likely estimate

11. Which of the following is used in a burn rate calculation?

    A. CV

    B. Determining spending rates over time

    C. CPI

    D. AC - PV

12. Your project has a potential for a future risk event. The sponsor has told you that the organization cannot sustain the consequences of this risk. You recommend purchasing insurance so that if the risk event occurs, the organization can recoup their expenditures for the impacts of the risk. What risk strategy is this known as?

    A. Avoid

    B. Mitigate

    C. Accept

    D. Transfer

13. Which technique can be used to help identify risks?

    A. SWOT

    B. CPI

    C. EVM

    D. CV

14. The risk register typically contains several pieces of information. Which of the following would you expect to see on a risk register? (Choose three.)

   A. Risk owner

   B. Description of risk

   C. Risk score

   D. Cost estimate for response plan

   E. Resource costs to track risks

   F. Cost estimate of the consequences of the risk

15. You have identified a risk on your project, and the team decides they won't create a response plan; if the risk happens, they'll deal with consequences when they occur. This is an example of which risk strategy?

   A. Exploit

   B. Avoid

   C. Mitigate

   D. Accept

16. The difference between planned expenditures and actual expenditures is known as which of the following?

   A. Planned value

   B. Variance

   C. Expenditure reporting

   D. Burn rate

17. The clouds are rolling in over the horizon and the wind is picking up. Your outdoor event is about to get rained out. What is this an example of?

   A. Risk trigger

   B. Risk analysis

   C. Risk probability

   D. Risk response

18. All of the following are strategies for dealing with negative risks, except for which one?

   A. Accept

   B. Transfer

   C. Share

   D. Mitigate

19. Cost baselines when displayed graphically over time represent which of the following?

   A. S curve

   B. C curve

   C. Evenly distributed expenditures

   D. Erratic expenditures

20. You are determining the risk score for each of the risks in your risk register. You need which of the following to determine this score? (Choose two.)

   A. Risk tolerance levels of the stakeholders

   B. Risk owners

   C. Probability the risk will occur

   D. Contingency reserves

   E. Risk trigger scores

   F. Impact if the risk occurs

Chapter

8

Communicating
the Plan

**THE COMPTIA PROJECT+ EXAM TOPICS
COVERED IN THIS CHAPTER INCLUDE:**

✓ **1.0 Project Management Concepts**

- ▪ **1.2 Compare and contrast Agile vs. Waterfall
  concepts**

- ▪ **1.8 Compare and contrast communication management
  concepts**

- ▪ **1.9 Given a scenario, apply effective meeting management
  techniques**

✓ **2.0 Project Life Cycle Phases**

- ▪ **2.3 Given a scenario, perform activities during the project
  planning phase**

- ▪ **2.4 Given a scenario, perform activities during the project
  execution phase**

✓ **3.0 Tools and Documentation**

- ▪ **3.1 Given a scenario, use the appropriate tools throughout the
  project life cycle**

- ▪ **3.2 Compare and contrast various project management
  productivity tools**

- ▪ **3.3 Given a scenario, analyze quality and performance charts
  to inform project decisions**

Communications is a critical success factor for your project. In this chapter, we'll look at communication methods, factors that influence communication, triggers that bring about communication, how agile teams communicate, communication tools, meeting types, and meeting tools. We'll discuss managing stakeholder expectations and the types of communication requirements for stakeholders, and how to hold effective meetings.

So, let's get started with the most important aspect of any project: communications.

Communications Planning

Good communication is the key to project success. Granted, you need a solid plan that includes the scope statement, schedule, and budget. But if you aren't able to communicate the plan or keep stakeholder expectations in line with the project goals, you could end up with an unsuccessful project on your hands in spite of having a great plan.

Good communication involves far more than just setting up distribution lists and talking with your stakeholders at the watercooler. You need a plan to determine what gets communicated to whom and when. Communications planning is the process of identifying what people or groups need to receive information regarding your project, what information each group needs, and how the information will be distributed. As the project manager, you should use communication systems and methods that satisfy the diverse communication needs of the project's stakeholders.

The need for good communication starts from the day the project charter is issued and you are formally named project manager (perhaps even earlier if you've been filling the project manager role informally). As you've already seen, the project charter is the first of many project artifacts that needs to be reviewed with your stakeholders. The scope statement, project schedule, budget, and final project management plan are all documents that should be discussed, reviewed, and approved by your stakeholders. But the communication can't stop with reviews and approvals. They'll want to know the status of the schedule and budget, and it will be your job to inform them of potential risk events, changes, and issues that may impact the project. To do that, you need a plan.

We'll start by reviewing some of the general principles of exchanging information.

How Much Time?

According to PMI®, project managers should spend as much as 90 percent of their time communicating.

Exchanging Information

The act of communicating is part of your daily life. Every aspect of your job as a project manager involves communicating with others. Communication is the process of exchanging information, which involves these three elements:

Sender   The *sender* is the person responsible for putting the information together in a clear and concise manner and communicating it to the receiver. The information should be complete and presented in a way that the receiver will be able to correctly understand it. Make your messages relevant to the receiver. Junk mail is annoying, and information that doesn't pertain to the receiver is nothing more than that.

Message   The *message* is the information that is being sent and received. Messages can take many forms, including written, verbal, nonverbal, formal, informal, internal, external, horizontal, and vertical. Horizontal communications are messages sent and received between peers. Vertical communications are messages sent and received between subordinates and executive management.

The message should be appropriate and relevant to the receiver. Information that isn't needed or isn't pertinent to the intended audience is considered noise and will likely be discarded before it's read or heard.

Receiver   The *receiver* is the person for whom the message is intended. They are responsible for understanding the information correctly, asking for clarification if they don't understand, and making sure they've received all the information.

Keep in mind that receivers filter the information they receive through their knowledge of the subject, culture influences, language, emotions, attitudes, and geographic locations. The sender should take these filters into consideration when sending messages so that the receiver will clearly understand the message that was sent.

The sender-message-receiver model, also known as the *basic communication model*, is how all communication exchange occurs, no matter what format it takes. The sender encodes the information (typically in written or verbal format) and transmits it, via a message, to the receiver.

Transmitting is the way the information gets from the sender to the receiver. Spoken words, written documentation, memos, email, instant messages, texts, and voicemail are all transmitting methods.

Decoding is what the receiver does with the information when they get it. They convert it into an understandable format. Usually, this means they read the memo, listen to the voicemail, read the document, and so on. Both the sender and the receiver have responsibility in this process. The sender must make sure the message is clear and understandable and in a format that the receiver can use. The receiver must make certain they understand what was communicated and ask for clarification where needed.

Project communication always involves more than one person. Communication network models are a way to explain the relationship between the number of people engaged in communicating and the actual number of interactions taking place between participants. For example, if you have five people in a meeting exchanging ideas, there are actually 10 lines of communication among all the participants. In Figure 8.1, a network model shows the *lines of communication* among the members.

FIGURE 8.1   Network communication model

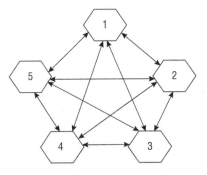

The nodes are the participants, and the lines show the connection between them all. The formula for calculating the lines of communication looks like this:

$$\left[\text{Number of participants} \times (\text{Number of participants} - 1)\right] \div 2$$

Here's the calculation in mathematical terms:

$$n(n-1) \div 2$$

Figure 8.1 shows five participants, so let's plug that into the formula to determine the lines of communication:

$$5(5-1) \div 2 = 10$$

Effective vs. Efficient Communication

Keep in mind there is a difference between effective and efficient communication. *Effective* communication concerns providing the right information in the right format for the intended audience at the right time. *Efficient* communication refers to providing the appropriate level and amount of information at the right time—that is, only the information that's needed at the time.

Listening

In the sender-message-receiver model, there's one critical communication skill that we all need to possess as a receiver, and that is the art of listening. Listening isn't the part where you plan what you're going to say because someone else is speaking. It's the part where you actively engage with the sender and ask clarifying questions to make sure you're understanding the message correctly.

You can use several techniques to improve your listening skills. Many books are devoted to this topic, so I'll highlight some of the most common techniques here:

- Appearing interested in what the speaker is saying will make the speaker feel at ease and will benefit you as well. By acting interested, you become interested and thereby retain more of the information being presented.

- Making eye contact with the speaker is another effective listening tool. This lets the speaker know you are paying attention to what they're saying and are interested.

- Put your speaker at ease by letting them know beforehand that you're interested in what they're going to talk about and that you're looking forward to hearing what they have to say. While they're speaking, nod your head, smile, or make comments when and if appropriate to let the speaker know you understand the message. If you don't understand something and are in the proper setting, ask clarifying questions.

- Another great trick that works well in many situations is to recap what the speaker said in your own words. Start with something like this, "Let me make sure I understand you correctly, you're saying. . . ," and ask the speaker to confirm that you did understand them correctly.

- Interrupting others while they are talking is impolite. Interrupting is a way of telling the speaker that you aren't really listening and that you're more interested in telling them what you have to say than listening to them. Interrupting gets the other person off track, they might forget their point, and it might even make them angry. However, there is a time and a place where an occasional interruption is needed. For example, if you're in a project status meeting and someone wants to take the meeting off course, sometimes the only way to get the meeting back on track is to interrupt them. You can do this politely. Start first by saying the person's name to get their attention. Then let them know that you'd be happy to talk with them about their topic outside of the meeting or add it to the agenda for the next status meeting if it's something everyone needs to hear.

Methods of Communicating

In ancient times, there were a couple of ways of communicating. The primary method was verbal. You talked to your neighbors and others in your community to get the latest news. You also made sure you talked to those traveling through from other towns so you could hear the news from other parts of the world. Written communication was also prevalent in many cultures, but the documents were not easily accessible to all until the invention of the printing press.

Today's technology has brought us dozens of communication methods. We'll touch on a few of them after we first look at the various forms of communication.

Assessing the Forms of Communication

There are several forms of communication. We'll start by comparing synchronous and asynchronous communications. *Synchronous communication* happens in real time such as a face-to-face meeting, phone calls, instant messaging, or watercooler chats. This type of communication offers immediate responses so that issues can be resolved quickly, decisions can be made in the moment, and each party understands the intent and expected outcomes. Face-to-face communication also allows the parties involved to read each other's body language to help interpret the message. Synchronous communication also builds human connections and rapport and reduces the chances of miscommunication or misinterpretation. For example, email (an asynchronous form of communication) does not communicate emotion. I have sometimes misinterpreted the emotion behind an email message only to find I was wrong once I spoke with the person face-to-face.

Expecting an immediate response can sometimes be challenging, especially if you are engaged in a conversation about project details you don't have at your disposal. In this scenario, it is acceptable to say, "I'll find out and get back to you." Another potential negative of synchronous communication is interruptions. You might be deep into plotting the project schedule and plugging in dates and names only to be interrupted by an instant message or someone at your desk wanting to chat. This breaks your concentration, and you'll need to spend some time after the chat to refocus on the task at hand.

Asynchronous communication does not require an immediate response. The response will come sometime after the communication is sent. Asynchronous messages include email, text messages, voicemail messages, and more. Asynchronous communication is useful when you're working with geographically dispersed teams who are in different time zones. Rather than getting up at 2:00 a.m. local time to catch someone live across the world, you can fire off an email or voicemail and wait for a response. Asynchronous communication also helps you have dedicated work time to concentrate on project issues. You can block time on your calendar for the project, and then get to the emails and voicemails after the project work is completed.

The disadvantage to this method is that you can't read team members' emotional reactions to the communication and there is always a chance they will misinterpret the message. Asynchronous communication doesn't work well for urgent issues, which generally require an immediate response.

> There is a time and place for both synchronous and asynchronous messaging. Make certain to examine the situation at hand and then decide whether an immediate face-to-face meeting or phone call is needed versus an email.

Written and Verbal Communication

Two additional forms of communication include verbal and written formats. Verbal communication is synchronous and written communication is asynchronous. Verbal communication is easier and less complicated than written, and it's usually faster. The risk with verbal communication is that there's no record of what was said other than everyone's memories.

Written communications are good for detailed instructions or complex messages that people may need to review. The risk with written communication is that stakeholders are inundated with emails, memos, documents, and other information, and your project information could get lost in the sea of information overload.

Deciding whether your information should be verbal or written is an important decision. Most formal project information, such as the scope statement, budget, and project plan, should be written. You will conduct meetings to discuss the contents of these documents, which means the verbal format will be used as well. It's always good practice to think about what you're communicating beforehand and how it will be communicated. Planning your communications before you speak or write is even more critical if your message is sensitive or controversial. Things will go much easier if you send the right message to begin with, rather than apologizing or retracting it later.

Communication Methods and Tools

There are dozens of ways of communicating today. Let's look at each of the methods found in the CompTIA objectives.

Meetings   Meetings are prevalent during projects. You will have meetings to determine requirements, approve plans, discuss risks, report on project status, and more. Meetings can use both verbal and written forms of communication. For example, you could be sharing the project scope statement with the meeting attendees or have printed copies of the budget or schedule to review, or you might provide written status updates and discuss the updates at the meeting. We will look at meetings in more depth later in this chapter.

Email   Email is a written form of communication. It's useful when conveying succinct, easily understood information quickly to many people. Be careful with email because it's easy for the receiver to misunderstand your tone or intention. Email is great for meeting invites, sharing meeting agendas and minutes, and providing a quick update. If you have complex information to convey, it's best to put this into a written report and present the report in person or via a videoconference. It's a good idea to send the report ahead of the meeting so that everyone has a chance to review it. But the discussion of the contents should occur at a meeting, not in email. And one last tip: please ask yourself twice if everyone needs to know your response before hitting Reply All. Most of the time only the sender needs the reply, not everyone on the distribution list.

Fax   Fax machines used to be stand-alone devices that scanned each page of the document and sent it over the telephone lines to the recipients. Faxes are fading into a communication method of the past. Today, you can scan documents into your computer and attach them to emails (although this is the least preferred method among your server administration team), upload the documents to a shared drive, your organization's intranet, and more.

If you do need to send a fax, you can do so over the Internet or over a phone line. A document that is signed and then faxed (or scanned and sent) to a bank, government agency, or a vendor is considered a legally binding document. Signed contract amendments and change orders might be faxed to a vendor, and these are legally binding as well. Since you have the capability to send multiple-page documents, faxing is appropriate for either simple messages or complex messages.

Instant Messaging   Instant messaging allows you to communicate with another person via a chat message over the Internet. There are many software programs that provide this capability. You can use instant messaging on a computer, tablet, or a phone, provided the software program you're using has that capability. It's a great mechanism to convey a quick, short message. Instant messaging isn't appropriate for meetings or complex information or for communicating with multiple people at the same time.

Video and Voice Conferencing   Videoconferencing is a communication technique that uses the Internet to visually display reports, presentations, and/or people's faces. It also provides audio capabilities so you can both see and hear the other people in the conference. Videoconferencing is a multiway communication where two or more people participate in the conference. Participants can reside anywhere in the world and use their Internet connection and software to connect to the meeting. Cameras and microphones are needed for videoconferencing if you intend to visually see and hear the participants.

Voice conferencing uses telecommunications technology that allows two or more people to participate in a meeting. Voice conferencing can sometimes be awkward if there are too many people in the meeting because it's easy to accidentally interrupt or talk while someone else is talking. Like videoconferencing, voice conferencing allows participants to join the meeting from anywhere in the world as long as they have access to a phone line.

Face-to-Face Meetings   Face-to-face meetings are where two or more participants are physically present in the same room. These types of meeting are best when delivering complicated material, or when you have to discuss negative results or confront a team member to discuss improper behavior or results.

Face-to-Face Always Works

If you are ever unsure what method of communication to use, default to face-to-face. You always have the advantage in face-to-face meetings of not only hearing the other person's words, but also reading their body language. If they tense up or look away from you when you're speaking, there is likely something they don't understand or they may not like the message. Conversely, if they are making eye contact, nodding and asking questions, you can be fairly sure they are understanding the message.

Short Message Service (SMS)   A short message service (SMS) is a text message sent over a cell phone network. This method should be used for quick, short, easy-to-convey messages and is typically used to communicate with one person, not a group of people. Text messaging isn't appropriate for relaying complex information.

Distribution of Printed Media   There are times when you may provide printed materials as a form of communication. I generally like to print the project charter, the project scope statement, the project schedule, the budget, meeting agendas, status reports, and the risk register. The project charter and scope statement should each be reviewed a few times: once in draft form, another when they are believed to be final, and one more time at the approval and sign-off stage. The project schedule, budget, risk register, and meeting agendas are nice to have in printed form at your status meetings. Electronic copies should be distributed a few days prior to the meeting so that participants have the opportunity to review them beforehand. I find two to three days before the meeting is the ideal time to send these types of documents. If you send them out a week ahead or more, they will likely be forgotten and won't be read. Do keep in mind that if you're sending a link to a contract document or one that's dozens of pages or more in length, it is better to send it a week or more in advance because a couple of days isn't enough time to read all the material. Use your judgment on the timing of the distribution based on the complexity of the information.

Documents such as the project status report, meeting minutes, and action items may have a regular distribution schedule. For example, if you hold project status meetings every week, the schedule may call for the distribution of minutes the following day. Distribution schedules should be discussed with your stakeholders.

Social Media   Social media is a way to create and share communication to and from your customer base or project team members in an electronic format. It enables interaction, content sharing, and the ability for anyone connected with the project to provide input.

Scheduled vs. Impromptu Meetings   Scheduled meetings are put on the calendar in advance of the meeting. Typically invites are sent via email with an agenda, the date, time, and location of the meetings. Impromptu meetings typically occur in the moment and are not scheduled ahead of time. This happens on my projects quite often. I will causally ask a team member a question that grows into asking another person or two to join in the discussion, and the next thing you know, we are having an impromptu meeting. Sometimes, these can be a gold mine of inspiration and a good brainstorming opportunity. You wouldn't want all of your meetings to be impromptu, but on those rare occasions when they happen naturally, don't be surprised if you find answers to problems and solve some issues that had previously eluded you and the team.

The Communication Plan

The communication plan details what information will be distributed to whom, in what format, and its frequency. It can be very simple, or it can be detailed, and you can easily construct a template using a spreadsheet or table format.

You can document an overall communications plan by doing the following:

- Defining who needs information on your project
- Defining the types of information each person or group needs
- Identifying the communications format and method of distribution
- Assigning accountability for delivering the communication
- Determining when the communications will occur and how often

Table 8.1 shows a sample communications plan.

TABLE 8.1   Example of a communications plan

Stakeholder name	Communication type	Format of communication	Distribution method	Responsible person	Frequency
Sponsor	Project status reports, monthly executive status meeting	Written and verbal	Email notification, project repository, face-to-face	Project manager	Weekly status meetings, monthly executive meetings
Sponsor	Schedule, budget, and/or risk updates	Written and verbal	Email notification, special meetings, reports stored in project repository, face-to-face	Project manager	Immediate notice of schedule or budget updates and risk events with scores of medium or high

Stakeholder name	Communication type	Format of communication	Distribution method	Responsible person	Frequency
Stakeholder A	Project status reports, schedule updates, risks, changes	Written and verbal	Email notification, project repository, project meetings	Project manager	Weekly, immediate notification of schedule changes
Stakeholder B	Project status reports	Written and verbal	Email notification, project repository, project meetings	Project manager	Weekly
All stakeholders	Project schedule updates, changes, risks	Written and verbal	Email notification, project repository	Scheduler	Weekly

You may also choose to include information in this plan on how to gather and store information, how to obtain information between communications, and how to update the communications plan.

The communications plan should be reviewed with your sponsor. If your project requires communication to executive team members, the sponsor can help you by identifying what information those groups need and how and when communication should take place.

Although you can use the template from this example to create an overall communications plan for all stakeholder groups, there are some additional considerations when it comes to communicating with your project team that we'll cover next.

Communicating with Project Team Members

One of your most important jobs as a project manager is communicating with your project team members. It is your responsibility to make sure all the team members understand the project goals and objectives and how their contribution fits into the big picture. Unfortunately, this is an area that is frequently overlooked in communications planning.

Your interactions with your project team will involve both formal and informal communications. *Formal communications* include project kickoff meetings, team status meetings, written status reports, team-building sessions, or other planned sessions that you hold with the team. *Informal communications* include phone calls and emails to and from your team members, conversations in the hallway, and impromptu meetings.

The challenge that project managers face is matching their communication style with that of each team member. Getting input from your team members will help you better communicate with them. If you are scheduling a kickoff meeting or other team-building session, ask for suggestions on agenda items or areas that require team discussion. Team members may have suggestions for the structure and frequency of the team meetings or for the format for status reporting, based on their previous project experience. The project manager may not be able to accommodate all suggestions, but taking the time to consider input and reviewing the final format will go a long way toward building a cohesive team.

How Much Is Too Much?

I once participated on a project where the project manager created distribution lists for both email and paper documents and sent everything she received that even remotely involved the project to everyone on both lists. She thought she was doing an excellent job of communicating with the team, but the team was going crazy. We were buried with data, and much of it was not relevant to our role on the project. Most of the team members were so overwhelmed with information they stopped reading everything. That, of course, led to the team missing information they actually needed. The project manager did not understand why there was so much confusion among the team members. A more thoughtful approach to distributing the right information at the right time to the right audience could have reduced or eliminated this issue.

Everyone has a communications method they are most comfortable with. Some of your team members may prefer email; others prefer phone calls or face-to-face meetings. Some may prefer to drop in on you and share a piece of information they have or get an update from you. For these informal one-on-one types of communications, try to accommodate what is most comfortable for each team member whenever possible.

You'll want to establish team touchpoints at regular intervals. These typically take the form of team meetings but could include individual one-on-one meetings with team members. Team meetings should cover topics such as the work performed last week, tasks expected to be completed this week, and tasks anticipated to be worked on next week. You should discuss any issues or obstacles standing in the way of the team performing their work, risk triggers they may have noticed, issues or concerns with stakeholders, and more.

Communicating on an Agile Team

Agile teams have an inherent need to communicate on a continuous basis. The amount of change and uncertainty on an agile-based project requires quick and frequent communications so that all team members know and understand the new or emerging details. The agile team holds a series of meetings during the course of the project. We looked at the sprint planning meeting in an earlier chapter. As you'll recall, this is a meeting at the beginning of the sprint where items are chosen from the product backlog and placed in the sprint backlog to be worked on during the upcoming iteration. There are three other meetings in an agile methodology that we'll look at next:

Daily Standups   Agile teams require frequent interactions and team checkpoints. Scrum teams use what's called a daily standup meeting for these checkpoints. *Daily standup* meetings are used to review the work of the sprint and make any changes or adjustments necessary to ensure the work can be completed. It's also an opportunity to discuss any obstacles standing in the way of the team doing their work. Any changes that are needed might be made in the current iteration or documented for inclusion in the next one.

The daily standups should be held at the same time and same place every day and should be timeboxed, usually no more than 15 minutes. These meetings are run by the team. It's a good idea to hold the standup meeting in front of the Scrum board or burndown chart so that the tasks are easily referenced. Team members must come prepared to discuss the answers to three questions at each standup meeting:

1.   What did I accomplish yesterday?

2.   What will I work on today?

3.   Do I have any roadblocks or issues preventing me from doing my work?

Standups are an important element in the agile process. They keep the team informed and alert them to any obstacles blocking the way of completing tasks. The daily standups should focus on the team members.

Daily standups occur for Kanban-based projects as well. These meetings focus on the workflow and capacity to produce work, not the team members. In this standup meeting, the team will review the Kanban board. Let's say the workflow columns on the task board are Plan, Design, Build, Test, and Deploy. Starting with the last column and working toward the left (from Deploy to Plan in our example), the team will answer the following questions:

- What is needed to advance this task?

- Are tasks being worked on that are not on the board?

- What is needed in order for us to finish as a team?

- Are any obstacles or bottlenecks blocking the workflow?

Daily standups are not status meetings for the product owner or the stakeholders, nor are they problem-solving meetings. They are working meetings for the team members and the product owner to determine what work was accomplished and what will be worked on today. Problems may be identified during the meeting but should not be solved during the meeting. Address problem resolution in a separate meeting right after the standup.

Iteration Review   At the end of the sprint, agile teams hold regular stakeholder meetings known as *reviews*. Such a meeting includes team members, the Scrum master, the product owner, customers, stakeholders, and management. This is not a decision-making meeting. The purpose is to review the work that was accomplished or completed during the iteration and gives the team a chance to show off their accomplishments. This may include a demonstration of functionality or a demonstration of the design work completed during the iteration. This meeting demonstrates the progressive completion and improvement of the deliverable during the iteration. Stakeholders will likely provide feedback during this meeting that the team can use to improve the deliverable in the next iteration.

If backlog items were not completed during the current sprint, you'll want to discuss this at the next planning meeting. The product owner will use information from this meeting to inform project stakeholders of the overall progress.

Backlog Refinement   Refinement meetings are used on agile projects. *Backlog refinement* typically occurs midway to a few days before the end of the current sprint. It's a meeting conducted between the product owner and the team to help them learn about upcoming stories for the next iteration, understand the context of the user stories, and identify how the user stories relate to one another and the project as a whole. The idea is for the product owner to explain their ideas to the team so that challenges or problems with the user stories can be discussed. This gives the team the opportunity to determine alternatives, refine the user stories, and break them down into small enough units of work that the team can continue to produce features and results during an iteration or as cards are worked on the task board.

Retrospective   At the end of the iteration, another meeting is held called a *retrospective*. This meeting occurs after the review meeting and includes the agile team members, Scrum master, and product owner. A retrospective examines the following:

- Overall progress of the work
- Changes that are needed to schedule or scope
- Ideas for improvement for the next iteration
- What worked well during this iteration
- A review of lessons learned to determine how the next iteration, and future iterations, can be improved

You've now seen the full circle of agile meetings. I've outlined them here, start to finish, for easy reference.

1. The initial product backlog is defined by the product owner.

2. Sprint planning meetings are held to determine which user stories to work on in the upcoming iteration. User stories are pulled into the backlog or onto the work columns on the task board if you're using Kanban.

3. Daily standups are conducted by a team member.

4. Backlog refinement is conducted midway through the iteration for upcoming user stories to help the team understand the context of the user stories and how they relate to one another.

5. Review meetings are held for the customer to examine the features and provide feedback.

6. Retrospectives are held at the end of an iteration or unit of work, midway through the project, and/or at the end of the project to examine the process, determine what worked well (or not), and make improvements.

The real benefit of agile is that teams can identify and diagnose issues early and often. The continuous feedback from the customer, along with regular retrospectives, helps them to correct the issues, improve the process, and quickly produce a minimally viable product.

Factors That Influence Communications

It's important to keep the lines of communication open with team members so that you're attuned to issues or conflicts that may be brewing. In an ideal world, this is easy to accomplish if your teams are small in number and all the team members have office space right outside your door. You'd know each of them by name and have the opportunity for informal chats to help you all get to know one another better. If that is not possible, go the extra mile in building relationships with and among your team members so that they feel comfortable relating issues and information to you and others on the team.

In today's global world, it's more likely you have team members in various geographical locations. That means several things for you as the project manager. First, you'll have to be aware of time-zone issues when scheduling meetings so that some team members are not required to be up in the middle of the night. Due dates may have to be adjusted in some cases to account for the various time zones. Communication preferences and language barriers also come into play. If you have team members who speak different languages, you'll have to determine the best method for communication. In my experience, it's worked well to use two or three forms of communication, especially for critical information, so that there's less chance for misunderstanding.

Cultural differences can have an impact on teams whether they are collocated or dispersed. If you are used to working in the United States, for example, you know that the culture tends to value accomplishments and individualism. U.S. citizens tend to be informal and call one another by their first names, even if they've just met. In some European countries, people tend to be more formal, using surnames instead of first names in a business setting, even when they know one another well. Their communication style is also more formal than in the United States, and although they tend to value individualism, they also value history, hierarchy, and loyalty. In many Asian cultures, people consider themselves part of a group, not an individual, and they value hard work and success. You should take the time to research the cultural background of your team members and be aware of the customs and practices that will help them succeed and help you in making them feel like part of the team.

> Regardless of cultural backgrounds, people still have individual preferences about the way they communicate, receive feedback, provide updates, and interact with the team. Personal preferences are as varied as your team members, so make every effort to understand them. This will ensure you and the team are making the most of your communications.

Technology barriers can have impacts that are unexpected. For example, in some countries, it's not an uncommon occurrence for the electricity to go out for hours at a time or for Internet connections to drop for no reason. These issues can have significant impacts on the project if you're in the midst of a deliverable or troubleshooting a problem. Team members may also have different levels of proficiency with software programs and other technology you're using on the project. Make certain that training is available where needed or include questions in the interview process about proficiency with the technology used on the project. It wouldn't be a bad idea to add some buffer time to the schedule to account for unforeseen issues with technology.

Remember that the organizational structure itself may also have an impact on the way you manage teams and the way they interact with one another. Intraorganizational differences that exist within your own team can influence the methods you use to communicate. If you have a small team and they are collocated, informal and impromptu meetings may work well.

Interorganizational differences will also influence your communication methods. For example, functional organizations that are hierarchical in nature can have impacts on the team because there are other managers involved in their career and performance evaluation. They also usually direct the work assignments of their team members. This type of interorganizational difference likely calls for formal communications with written reports that are produced on a regular distribution schedule.

Use your best judgment when determining the method and content of your communication, and tailor it to your audience. Be certain to take into account everything that could influence the message such as cultural, language, time zone, or technological factors. Criticality of the message and timeliness of the information are other factors to consider in your communication methods.

The Geographically Dispersed Team

Jim is a senior systems analyst and project manager for a large aerospace contracting firm. He manages aerospace engineers, some of whom live in California, others in Europe and South America, still others in Colorado, and so forth. They design, build, assemble, and deploy rockets. Jim is an expert at managing geographically dispersed teams. Here are some of his tips:

- You have to understand the project thoroughly. All team members have to be clear about what it is you're building. There can be no question about vision.

- When working on large projects, you must break the project into manageable chunks and group similar phases or work efforts together. This assures communication is targeted to the right team members at the right time.

- In the case of geographically dispersed teams, you simply don't have the funding to fly everyone around the country so they can get together to work on the project. Jim and his teams rely heavily on videoconferencing, using instant messaging and voice conferencing to bring people together to discuss drawings, design characteristics, and other components of the project.

- You don't need to be afraid of geographic boundaries when assembling people with the skills you need. A little thinking outside the box might lead to a well-formed, albeit dispersed, team. That being said, you, the project manager, are the one who determines what will and will not work as communications methods for a given team.

The power of the Internet has greatly impacted the speed with which team members can communicate and bring their projects to fruition.

Communication Triggers

There are several factors that may bring about the need to update stakeholders or otherwise communicate new information to them. These *communication triggers* are common on all projects and are mostly self-explanatory, so I'll spend just a moment or two briefly touching on each.

Audits   Your organization may conduct audits of projects periodically to determine if they are receiving adequate value for the money spent and/or to determine if proper processes and procedures are followed. Audits may be conducted from parties inside or outside the organization. This is one of many reasons to have your project plan documented and to save important project artifacts to the project repository.

Project Planning   Communications occurs throughout the project planning process and beyond. As I've discussed throughout the book, anytime you're in the planning stage, whether developing the scope statement, schedule, budget, or something else, you should be actively communicating with your stakeholder and team members.

Project Change   Whenever there is a scope, budget, or schedule change to the project, it needs to be discussed and communicated with the stakeholders. We will talk about change processes in depth in Chapter 9, "Processing Change Requests."

Risk Register Updates   Risks are more likely to occur and have bigger consequences earlier in the project. As risks occur, or new risks are identified, the stakeholders should be informed of the actions taken and the outcomes of the response plans.

Milestones   Milestones can be a communication trigger because it's good news when they are achieved on time and within budget, but not so good news when they are not. Both cases are cause for an update to the stakeholders.

Schedule Changes   Schedules have a way of becoming etched in the minds of project sponsors and key stakeholders and they will continuously remind you of the project end date. They will want to know if the schedule slips for any reason, and it's generally delightful news to share that you have completed deliverables or milestones ahead of schedule.

Task Initiation/Completion   This communication trigger is typically at the team level, rather than the stakeholder level. Project team members appreciate hearing "great job" when tasks are completed on time. Starting new tasks is another opportunity for the project team to communicate with the project manager.

Stakeholder Changes   Stakeholders will sometimes request changes to the project. Executive stakeholders are notorious for thinking they don't have to follow process. They also might think because of their status in the organization, any change they request should be granted. If you find yourself in this situation, enlist the help of your project sponsor or other key stakeholders to explain the importance of communicating changes with all the stakeholders and weighing the pros and cons of the change requests.

Phase Gate Reviews   *Phase gate reviews* occur at predetermined points in the project and are conducted to review project progress to date. These could be defined by the PMO, or the gate reviews can be designated by the project manager and agreed upon by the stakeholders. Phase gate reviews may occur at the end of each project phase (Initiating, Planning, or Executing), or once certain milestones or deliverables are achieved. Gate reviews may also be used as go/no-go decision points. At the end of the gate review, a decision is made to either continue or kill the project.

Business Continuity Response   The business continuity response plan outlines how the business can continue providing its services or products to their customers in case of a disaster. It describes how business will continue operating, including where people should report if they can no longer work at their regular location, an emergency contact list, and how to recover from the disaster and resume operations. Obviously, this is a case where communications should be frequent, effective, and efficient.

Incident Response   Incident response is similar to business continuity response, only on a smaller, individualized basis. For example, a flood might impact a portion of your warehouse. That would require an incident response to deal with that occurrence. Business can still be conducted, but the flooded parts of the warehouse must be addressed along with any damaged goods. A flood that impacts your day-to-day operations and prevents you from conducting business as usual and/or requires you to conduct business operations from another location is an example of a business continuity response.

In my humble opinion, if your organization has had a disaster and is enacting their business continuity response plan, it's extremely likely your project will be suspended until business operations are restored. The same can be true for an incident. Depending on the incident type and impact, you might find the project sponsor putting the project on hold until the incident is resolved and business returns to normal.

Resource Changes Another communication trigger for your project is resource changes, especially if key resources are impacted. Whenever a new project manager takes over the project, there should be a meeting to announce the change. Perhaps you have resources with specialized skills who have taken employment elsewhere or who are experiencing personal circumstances that require an extended absence. This should also be communicated to the stakeholders as soon as you can. Resource changes can have many impacts, including schedule delays, budget increases, and the introduction of new risks to the project.

 A change to any of the triple constraints (schedule, budget, or scope) is a communication trigger.

If a communication trigger occurs, you'll need to inform the appropriate stakeholders or project team members and perhaps set up a meeting to discuss the implications. Not all communication triggers require notification to every stakeholder. You'll want to determine the target audience, based on the type of information or trigger that's transpired.

 Make certain to target your audience and determine the rationale for notifying stakeholders when a communication trigger occurs so that you are providing the right information to the right stakeholders.

You might consider capturing your triggers in a spreadsheet or similar program so that you know who to notify if a communication trigger occurs, when to notify them, and what method to use. Table 8.2 shows a sample communications trigger plan.

TABLE 8.2   Example of a communication trigger plan

Trigger	Stakeholder	Reason	Method	Timing of notification
Project planning complete	All	Obtain sign-off	Sign-off meeting	At completion of Planning phase
Project change	Sponsor and affected stakeholders	Obtain approval/ deferral of change	Project change management meeting	Regularly scheduled change meeting

TABLE 8.2   Example of a communication trigger plan *(continued)*

Trigger	Stakeholder	Reason	Method	Timing of notification
Risk register updates	Stakeholder A, Stakeholder B, Stakeholder C, Stakeholder D	Update of risk events occurring, response plans put into action, or notification of new risks	Special risk meeting, project meeting	Immediate and at regularly scheduled project meeting
Resource changes	Sponsor, impacted stakeholders	Informing stakeholders of impacts, delays, or risks from resource changes	Special meetings, project meetings	Immediate and at regularly scheduled project meeting

Holding Effective Meetings

We have all sat through meetings where we asked ourselves, "What was that about?," or worse, "There's an hour I can never get back." Please, don't put your stakeholders through this torture. There are ways you can hold effective meetings, and we'll examine some of those techniques in this section. Keep in mind that this is only scratching the surface. There are books devoted to holding effective meetings, and I encourage you to check them out.

Let's start with a look at the various types of meetings, and then we'll dive into preparing for those meetings and putting good communication tools to work for us.

Meeting Types

Meetings can take many forms. According to the CompTIA objectives, they are categorized as one of three types: informative, collaborative, or decisive. For example, the project status meeting is probably the most well-known of all project meetings and it is an informative meeting. As you can guess, informative meetings are those where information is shared with others. Collaborative meetings occur when teams come together to brainstorm or work through solutions to risks or issues. Decisive meetings occur when a decision is needed such as changing the timeline or modifying the budget. The CompTIA objectives outline several meeting types, and we'll take a look at each in this section.

Project Status Meeting

The project status meeting is intended to inform stakeholders of project progress. This typically includes reviewing the following:

- Schedule status
- Budget status

- Risk review
- Issue review
- Changes approved in the current reporting period
- Time completion and cost forecasts
- Action items
- Notes/comments/announcements

Project status meetings should occur on a regular schedule, no less than once per month. Be sure to publish an agenda prior to the meeting. A project status meeting is an informative meeting type.

 Status meetings may include separate meetings with stakeholders, project team members, and the customer. Take care that you don't over-burden yourself with meetings that aren't necessary or meetings that could be combined with other meetings. Having more than three or four status meetings per month is unwieldy.

Kickoff Meetings

We talked about project kickoff meetings in Chapter 6, "Resource Planning and Management." These meetings are intended to discuss the project goals, introduce the team members and stakeholders, introduce the project manager, and set expectations for meeting the project timelines and budgets. You may also discuss team member roles and responsibilities at this meeting. Kickoff meetings are informative meetings.

Workshops

Workshops are a collaborative meeting where attendees are asked to participate in exercises, brainstorming sessions, and so on for creating new processes, problem solving, identifying risk, and much more.

Focus Groups

Focus groups are often used for market research purposes to understand the attendees' responses and reactions to the topic at hand. Attendees are carefully chosen ahead of time to participate in the focus group. There are numerous factors the researchers will use to choose these attendees, which are based on the subject matter they are researching. Focus groups are a type of collaborative meeting.

Joint Application Development

Joint application development (JAD) meetings are often used on agile development projects. The meeting focuses on developing the requirements for the system or application. Business users and application developers meet together to focus on the business need or the problem they are trying to solve, and to create a deep understanding of the requirements among all team members. JAD sessions help improve quality and ensure the solution will solve the problem. JAD sessions are a type of collaborative meeting.

Brainstorming

We've talked about brainstorming in previous chapters. This is a meeting where the participants are asked to generate ideas or solutions related to the topic. The facilitator will typically address one topic at a time and ask participants to provide succinct responses, usually one word or one sentence. These ideas or responses should be generated quickly, without a lot of deep thinking. The facilitator will group the responses into common themes and then move onto the next question. Brainstorming meetings can be held in person or virtually; they are a collaborative meeting type.

Demonstrations/Presentations

Demonstrations and presentations are informative meetings where the audience can view a demonstration of how a product works, examine a prototype, or participate in how-to topics.

Standups

We talked about standups earlier in this chapter. They are used on agile projects and are typically performed daily. Standups are an informative meeting type.

Backlog Refinement

We discussed refinement meetings earlier in this chapter. They are used on agile projects and are a decisive type of meeting.

Task Setting

Task setting meetings can occur in many ways. If you are working in a waterfall methodology, tasks are usually assigned by the supervisor of the team performing the work. Or, perhaps the tasks are assigned during a team meeting. On agile projects, this occurs in the sprint planning meeting. You'll recall that the sprint planning meeting occurs at the beginning of the sprint and is when team members pick the items they'll work on during the upcoming sprint. Task setting or sprint planning meetings are a decisive type of meeting.

Steering Committee

The project sponsor, key project stakeholders, and the project manager typically make up the project steering committee. The steering committee is an oversight committee that ensures the project stays on track and helps resolve major issues. It is also an escalation point for the project team. When there are risks, decisions, budget items, or changes that may have a major impact on the project, they should be escalated to the steering committee for decision. This is also an escalation point for the project team when they cannot come to a consensus on a decision or action. The criteria for escalation should be outlined in the communications plan. The steering committee meeting is a decisive meeting type.

Recap of Meeting Types

According to the CompTIA objectives, there are three meeting types: collaborative, informative, and decisive. I've recapped all the meetings in this section into their meeting types:

Collaborative

- Workshops

- Focus groups

- JAD

- Brainstorming

Informative

- Demonstrations/presentations

- Standups

- Project status

Decisive

- Refinement/backlog refinement

- Task setting/sprint planning meeting

- Project steering committee

Preparing for Meetings

Meetings can encompass several communication techniques we've already discussed such as synchronous and asynchronous, written and verbal formats, and more. There are several requirements outlined in the CompTIA objectives that relate to preparing for and conducting meetings. Let's look at each of them next.

> **Creating Agendas**   Agendas outline the purpose for the meeting, the topics that will be covered, who will be presenting the topic, and a time frame for each. They contain the date, time, and location of the meeting and/or a link to the videoconference if the meeting is virtual. I like to add time at the end of every agenda for questions and answers or roundtable discussions. This gives the opportunity for attendees to bring up items that should be on the next meeting agenda, ask questions, and inform others of information

they know that may impact the project. Agendas should be created and published a few days prior to the meeting to give participants the opportunity to review them and come prepared with information and questions.

At a minimum, you'll want to report on the following items:

- Overall project status
- Schedule updates, including changes
- Milestone achievements
- Budget status
- Change requests this period
- Major issues that could impede progress of the project
- Action items

Agenda items should be timeboxed to keep the conversation moving and keep the meeting on track. I've found that topics without start and stop times can get out of hand quickly. The first one or two topics take up the entire meeting and you don't have time to discuss the remaining items. It's amazing how something as simple as timeboxing your agenda items can keep the meeting on track.

Meeting Roles   Meetings should be orderly, and roles help define who does what during a meeting. The facilitator is the person holding the meeting and making certain that items on the agenda are addressed and are staying within their allotted time frames. The project manager is the facilitator in a project status meeting.

A scribe is the person who takes meeting minutes. They will capture discussion items, action items, decision items, and more, which will be published in the meeting minutes.

Attendees are those who attend the meeting and are known as your target audience. They may have items to present during the meeting, or they may simply participate in discussions. Attendees should adhere to the agenda and refrain from introducing topics that are not listed.

Timeboxing   Meetings should be timeboxed—that is, the meeting should have a designated start and stop time. The agenda topics should also be timeboxed to keep the meeting orderly and ensure that you'll finish by the end time. The length of the meeting will depend on the purpose of the meeting, the topics discussed, the attendees, and more. Keep the meetings to the shortest time possible to address the agenda items. Participants will fill up the allotted time no matter how little or how much time you set aside. Set agenda items to a reasonable length of time to allow for discussion and then get to a decision.

Action Items   *Action items* are tasks that come about, usually at a project status meeting, that require follow up or resolution. They are typically about the project, but don't have a direct impact on the work of the project. For example, a stakeholder may ask how much money was spent on the previous work order with the project vendor. This action item is recorded on the action item log, and its results are reported at the next status meeting. Action items can take many forms, such as requests for additional information, to prepare a briefing on a specific topic, to contact someone in the procurement department about an upcoming bid, and so on.

> **NOTE** Action items are not a mechanism to create change requests for the work of the project. Changes must follow the change control process.

Action item logs include the following elements:

- Identification number
- Date the action was recorded
- Action item description
- Action item owner
- Progress or resolution to the action item
- Closed date

Action items should be assigned to the person or team responsible for completing the item, and they should be recorded in the meeting minutes. Project status meetings should devote a portion of time to update the team on the status of action items.

Meeting Minutes Meeting minutes contain several elements, including a list of attendees, discussion items, action items, decision items, questions, and more. Meeting minutes should be published within a day or two of the meeting.

Follow-Ups Follow-ups occur for items that were not completed or couldn't be discussed or decided at the original meeting. These can be conducted as follow-up meetings, or the project manager or action item owner may meet with those who can provide the additional information. The project manager will report the findings at the next project meeting.

Communication Platforms

Communication platforms provide a way for the project team to connect in real time with one another. Some examples include instant messaging, videoconferencing, screen sharing, file sharing, and more. The platform provides the technology on which the team can communicate. Examples include Microsoft Teams, Zoom, OneDrive, and Google Drive, among others. Many people today work remotely or have hybrid schedules. Communication platforms provide a convenient and easy way to meet with teammates and access project documents.

Collaboration Tools

Collaboration tools typically reside on the communications platform. The CompTIA exam objectives list several types of collaboration tools, which we'll look at next:

Multi-Authoring and Editing Software These tools allow multiple people to create and edit documents or presentations in real time, and they have many useful applications—for example, creating requirements lists, conducting brainstorming sessions, reviewing project status reports, creating and reviewing project presentations, and much more. There is no limit to the types of documents and presentations you can create and edit with your project team using this software.

File-Sharing Platforms I gave a few examples of file-sharing platforms earlier when we discussed communication platforms. File sharing allows team members and stakeholders to access project documents from one central repository. Some other examples of file sharing include your organization's intranet site, SharePoint, and DropBox.

> When I wrote the very first edition of this book and others on project management, I had an entire section devoted to creating a project note-book for containing your project documents. You guessed it, an old-fashioned 3-ring binder with paper. Gasp. We've come a long way since then. I'm grateful for file-sharing platforms. No more hunting down the notebook or wondering who has the latest version of the project schedule.

Workflow and E-Signature Platforms These platforms automate document workflows and allow users to sign documents using electronic signatures. In the old days, I would clip a distribution list to the top of the document, and after I signed, it would be routed via interoffice mail to the next person on the list. Workflow platforms take care of this automatically, and because the documents are routed electronically, they don't get lost or buried in a pile of other papers on someone's desk. Electronic signatures are created with a digital identification that is associated with the person signing and is legally binding.

Whiteboard Whiteboards hung on the wall are one way to collaborate with the team, but whiteboards, like many other tools, have also gone digital these days. Many communication platforms have whiteboard tools built in, allowing team members to jot down ideas, draw sketches, erase, and so on with other team members in real time. Physical whiteboards are great tools for brainstorming sessions.

Wiki Knowledge Base A *wiki knowledge base* is a collaboration tool that contains project documents and information that allows for all project team members (or those who have access to the site) to create, add, and update content. Wiki knowledge bases are usually found on the organization's intranet site. You can create a wiki site for the project and upload all project documents to the site so that team members and stakeholders can access information and those with permissions can add, edit, and update information. For example, posting the risk register to the wiki allows all the risk owners to update the register in real time.

Be cautious when using some of these collaboration tools, especially with your baseline documents (scope, cost, and schedule). You'll want to control access to documents like these so that changes can only be made by authorized users.

Meeting Tools

Meeting tools help you conduct effective meetings and provide ways to interact with the audience. CompTIA outlines several meeting tools we'll look at next.

Real-Time Surveys and Polling   Polling is a way to obtain instant feedback from the audience. Real-time surveys and polling are conducted using an app on a cellular device or an Internet-connected laptop. The facilitator should instruct the audience beforehand on where to obtain the app, and it's a good idea for them to ask a practice question or two at the beginning of the meeting to help participants understand how it all works. Once the meeting is underway, the facilitator asks a question about the topic at hand and the participants can type in responses or choose from a list of options depending on how the app is configured. Results are tallied and displayed on a projection screen so that the facilitator and the audience can see the results.

Calendaring Tools   Calendaring tools are used to coordinate meeting times with attendees' schedules. The meeting scheduler can see free and busy times on attendees' calendars and schedule the meeting when everyone is available.

Print Media   Good old-fashioned paper is still the preferred method for reporting project information for many executives. Make certain that your print media is clear and legible, and bring enough copies for all attendees if you are meeting in person. You should distribute the print media at least two or three days prior to the meeting, if possible, especially if you are making decisions at the meeting or discussing alternative solutions to an issue. It's also a good idea to send electronic forms of the materials before the meeting.

Conferencing Platforms   Conferencing platforms work much the same way as collaboration tools. These platforms provide a way to host conferences, live streams, and webinars to multiple attendees at the same time.

Project Management Scheduling Tools   These aren't necessarily meeting tools, but they are a way to facilitate the information you will discuss at your meetings. Project management scheduling tools may be cloud-based or on-premises solutions. This software will assist in creating the project schedule by automatically determining and plotting completion dates for tasks and deliverables, and balancing resource availability. They include multiple ways to display project schedules including PERT, Gantt charts, milestone charts, and so on.

Version Control Tools   Version control tools provide a way to keep track of changes to your project documents. When distributing information or uploading to your project repository, you'll want to ensure everyone is referencing the same version of the document. Changes to the project budget or schedule will be of great interest to key stakeholders, so you'll want to make certain they are referencing the most recent version.

Time-Tracking Tools   Time-tracking tools are used to keep track of the amount of time team members are spending on tasks. You can use this information to update the project schedule and perform schedule variance calculations and forecasts like we talked about in Chapter 7, "Defining the Project Budget and Risk Plans." Enterprise resource planning systems often have time-tracking tools built in. There are also stand-alone systems that include timeclocks or other timekeeping mechanisms to track time by means of swiping a badge or entering a code. The software can calculate complex time-keeping rules for overtime pay, shift differential pay, holiday pay, and so on.

Reporting Project Information

Project status can be reported in a variety of ways, such as status reports, dashboards, and charts. This information may be presented in writing, in person, in a videoconference, or any other number of ways. Status reports are informational meetings, and it's important to target the information to your audience. Let's look at how to do this along with some of the common ways to report status.

Project Status Reports

Status reports are usually intended for a diverse audience. They describe the status of the project at the reporting date and compare current progress against the project management plan. Status reports may cover a range of topics but should always include updates on milestone accomplishments and/or deliverables, project schedule, budget, risks, issues, and changes. It may also include information about the work that was completed during the time period, work that is planned for the next time period, action items, and so on. Status reports may contain several pages of content, or they might be a brief, one-page report. Your PMO may have project status templates that you can use, or ask your stakeholders what information is most important to them on a status report and create your reports to reflect this. Also ask them if they prefer brief reports versus lots of detail about each topic. Be certain to note information about the status report in the communication plan, such as the frequency of the report, how it's distributed, who it's distributed to, and where to find it on the project site.

Project Dashboard

Dashboards visually depict the progress of the project. They are easy to read and are usually updated with real-time information, so they are always up-to-date. A dashboard typically displays the most important elements of the project such as cost, time, and deliverables. The information is usually succinct and abbreviated. The most common way to display this data is using graphs or charts, numbers, and/or status-level indicators such as Red-Yellow-Green. Red means the project element being reported is in trouble (perhaps over budget, behind schedule, and so on), yellow means it's moving toward trouble, and green means everything is going according to plan.

The dashboard is the most effective reporting tool to use for your executive team. They have neither the time nor interest in reading a lengthy report on project status. If something on the dashboard piques their interest, they will contact you for more information on that topic.

Charts

Charts are another great way to display project information, especially for agile-based projects. We discussed the burndown chart in Chapter 5, "Creating the Project Schedule." You'll recall that a burndown chart shows the work remaining for the iteration. At the end of each day, team members update the burndown chart with progress on work completed and revise estimates for the remaining work items, which updates the burndown chart.

The burndown chart should be kept in a prominent place where all stakeholders and team members can visually see the amount of work remaining in the iteration. This allows the team to see at a glance if issues are cropping up so that they can address them before they get out of hand. If there is a variance between the actual work and ideal work remaining, you'll see a trend line emerging that forecasts the likely variance at the end of the iteration. If a large variance exists, you'll want to take action to get the remaining work completed on time or reprioritize it into a later iteration.

The accuracy of the burndown chart relies on the accuracy of the estimates the team provides for the units of work. Keep in mind that it only shows the work of the iteration and does not show the entire backlog. It is a good indicator of trends, but a burndown chart can't tell you if you are working on the right things; only the team can determine that. Figure 8.2 shows the burndown chart you saw in Chapter 5 as a refresher.

FIGURE 8.2 Burndown chart

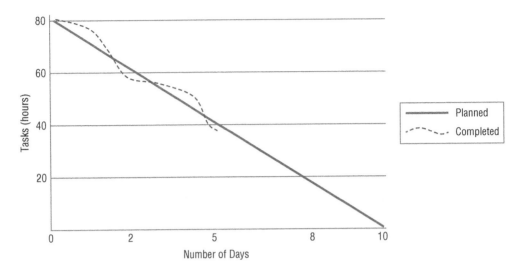

Burnup charts are like burndown charts only they show the work that has been completed for the iteration along with all the work of the project. They can be used for the work of the iteration but are typically used for the entire project. The y-axis shows units of work such as user stories, work hours, or workdays, or other work units the team deems appropriate. The x-axis shows the amount of time in days, weeks, or iterations. A burnup chart can also show changes in scope. If you look at Figure 8.3, you'll see that the original plan for this project was to complete 90 user stories in 8 iterations. The planned number of user stories are shown above the planned line on the graph. Up until iteration 4, the team had fallen behind their estimates. For example, by iteration 3 they had only completed 25 user stories rather than the estimated 40. By iteration 4, the planned number of iterations seemed to be on track with the completed work.

At iteration 4, ten more user stories were added to the scope (as you can see at the top of the chart). This means the team will not likely finish in 8 iterations unless they can manage to complete more user stories per iteration than planned. Looking at the planned user story completions, they will complete 90 user stories in 8 iterations and will need one more iteration to complete 100 user stories. It takes an agile team between 4 and 8 iterations to reach a steady cadence whereby their estimates improve.

Here's the difference between burnup and burndown charts: burndown charts show the remaining work for the iteration and go to zero, whereas burnup charts start at zero and show the work completed for the iteration along with all the remaining work for the project.

FIGURE 8.3   Burnup chart

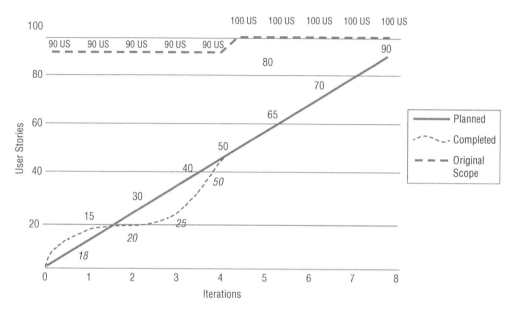

Other types of charts that you can use to display project progress are Kanban boards, Scrum boards, and task boards. We covered these in Chapter 5 if you need a refresher.

Establishing Communication Channels

We've talked about communication channels throughout this chapter, but I'd like to highlight a few points in this section. As we've discussed there are many ways to communicate. It's important that you, as the project manager, find out your stakeholders' preferences for project information. You'll want to establish communication channels that are meaningful and most effective for your stakeholders. They may desire to see written status reports as well as a dashboard, for example. They may prefer to hold in-person meetings rather than videoconferences. No matter the preference, it's up to you to establish the communication channels that work best for the stakeholders and the team and document them in the communication plan.

Maintaining Communication Records

Creating communication is one part of the equation; maintaining those records is the other. It isn't unusual for stakeholders to forget decisions that were made several weeks or months ago on the project. If you are properly storing and maintaining project records, it's easy to retrieve the status meetings minutes or other notes that documented the decision and refresh everyone's memory. Most project documents should be stored in the project repository, be it an intranet site, an electronic document and records management software (EDRMS) system, or an online document site such as OneDrive or Google.

Maintaining communication records, according to the CompTIA objectives, incorporates three elements: security, integrity, and archiving. Let's look at each.

Document Security

We've talked a good deal about security throughout this book, and security shouldn't be overlooked when it comes to project documents. It's easy enough to think a status report should be shared with everyone, but think twice about this if the report contains sensitive information. Your project might be dealing with personally identifiable information or trade secrets. Keep in mind that project documents may have references to some of these items such as requirements documents, scope documents, risk registers, project status reports, and so on. If the documents do contain sensitive information, they should be protected according to the security policies your organization has in place. You should also scrutinize who has access to project documents that may contain sensitive or need-to-know information. You should record access permissions for project documents in the communication plan and be certain to keep it updated. Don't overlook security when it comes to project documents. If a team member accidentally shares a project document with sensitive information, it could result in reputational damage, fines, penalties, and more.

Document Integrity

Document integrity concerns ensuring the document accurately reflects what the author created and intended. This means that others have not added, deleted, or otherwise altered the information. It also means that the document is valid and useful for imparting information. Version control procedures help ensure that only those with proper access can edit information, and it provides an audit trail so that you can see who created, modified, or deleted the document. Your organization may have policies regarding creating, storing, and archiving documents, so make sure your documents adhere to these standards to ensure integrity.

Archiving

There comes a time when project information is no longer needed on a day-to-day basis. Once the project is closed, the project documents become inactive and static. However, you'll want the ability to reference them in the future. Remember that artifacts and documents from past projects are a great starting point when initiating new projects. Risks, costs, estimates, timelines, and more from past projects can be used as a reference to start creating the project management plan for the new project. You'll want to ensure that key project documents are archived so that they can be accessed for this purpose. You won't save all project documents—only those that are finalized and approved. For example, you'll want to archive the approved scope statement, schedule baseline, cost baseline, scope baseline, and contract documents. Once they are archived, they are static documents, meaning they will not change.

In addition, there could be regulations, compliance issues, or legal reasons for retaining project documents. Be certain to review your organization's document retention policy for guidance on archiving procedures.

Archiving is not the same as backup procedures. Backing up your documents on a regular basis is good business practice and enables you to restore files if they are accidentally deleted. The backup will restore the files to their previous state. For example, perhaps you are in the middle of drafting the project schedule but the next time you look for the file to continue your work, it has disappeared. Hopefully, your IT department performs regular backups, and after a quick phone call to the service desk, your file can be restored and you're back to work. Archived documents are retained in long-term storage and are only referenced when needed.

There are many systems available for archiving documents. Most EDRMS systems include a process for this function. Archiving documents helps IT free up storage space, increase processing times, and reduce costs. Archived documents are accessed infrequently, and moving these documents to secondary storage devices frees up primary storage for active documents. Archive files may exist on the cloud, on hardware on-premises, on tape, and more.

Controlling Communications

Communication with stakeholders, team members, vendors, and others occur throughout the project life cycle from Discovery/Conception to Closing. It's your responsibility, as the project manager, to ensure you are monitoring communication throughout the project and that stakeholders are receiving what they need when they need it. The most effective way you can control communication is to create, update, maintain, and follow a communication plan. As we talked about earlier in this chapter, the communication plan should describe the type of communication, format, frequency, distribution methods, who will receive the information, and the person responsible for communicating and distributing the information. Having a plan for communication ensures that stakeholders receive the information they need to make decisions, perform tasks, and be informed of project status in a timely and consistent manner.

Controlling communications also involves updating the communication plan periodically throughout the project. Sometimes stakeholders will leave the project and others will join. This will require an update to the plan to reflect the new stakeholder, their preferences for communication, and so on. Any number of factors can initiate the need to update the communication plan. For example, risk events with adverse impacts, changes to the project schedule or budget, or changes in scope might drive the stakeholders to request more frequent updates on project status. Whether or not changes occur, it's a good idea to periodically review the plan and keep it up-to-date.

The last element of controlling communications we will discuss is escalating communication issues. For example, the project manager is responsible for escalating issues that are beyond their decision-making authority to the project sponsor. Team members should have an established escalation path so they know when to alert the project manager on issues.

You could include a section in the communication plan to describe escalation paths. This section could also define the types of information that need to be escalated and to which stakeholders.

Escalating communications can also occur on a personal level. For example, let's say you receive an email from a team member that you respond to, and they jump right back with what appears to be an inappropriate or cutting response. In this sense, the email, and the emotions behind it, are escalating, and as the project manager, you should take a moment to think about your next steps. Is another email response appropriate, or would it be better to walk over to the team member's desk and address this face to face? I would vote for the face-to-face approach at this stage. Think about the type of information you are sharing and choose the most appropriate method for communicating to help avoid issues that cause escalations.

Some of your stakeholders may not understand how they are involved with the project and may have special communication needs. Extra steps are required to properly engage them, and we'll cover this next.

Managing Stakeholder Expectations and Communication Needs

Managing stakeholder expectations concerns satisfying the needs of the stakeholders by managing communications with them, resolving issues, improving project performance by implementing requested changes, and managing concerns in anticipation of potential problems.

As the project manager, you are responsible for managing stakeholder expectations. By doing so, you will decrease the potential for project failure. Managing the expectations of your stakeholders will also increase the chance of meeting the project goals because issues are resolved in a timely manner, and disruptions during the project are limited.

Stakeholders need lots of communication in every form you can provide, and their communication preferences should be documented in the communication plan. If you are actively engaged with your stakeholders and interacting with them, providing project status, and resolving issues, your chances of a successful project are much greater than if you don't do these things. Communicating with stakeholders occurs throughout the project.

Let's look at some examples of stakeholder communication requirements. You can document these in the communication plan.

Frequency   Stakeholders may have differing requirements for project information, including the frequency with which they receive the information. Key stakeholders may require more frequent updates than others, so note the frequency in the communication plan.

Level of Report Detail   Like frequency, the level of detail stakeholders require will differ depending on who they are. For example, the project sponsor may need more details on the budget than most other project stakeholders. Stakeholders who represent a specific area of the business will want more detail about the tasks or risks associated with their own areas.

Types of Communication   Be certain to note the types of communication stakeholders need in the communication plan. Some will want every document you produce, whereas others may only be interested in updated status and schedules.

Confidentiality Constraints   You should pay close attention to sensitive or confidential information and who receives it. You wouldn't want to accidentally send a personnel write-up, for example, to everyone on the distribution list. Other confidential information may include contract details, financials, PII data, and company trade secrets.

Communication Styles   Stakeholders, like project team members, may have individual preferences for communication styles. Get to know your key stakeholders and ask them what method of communication they prefer, the frequency they want to receive it, and how they want you to update them on general project information versus critical or emergency type information.

Let's take another look at the communication plan with specific stakeholder needs in mind. Table 8.1 listed the following column headers in the communication plan:

- Stakeholder name
- Communication type
- Format of communication
- Distribution method
- Responsible person
- Frequency

You could add more columns to describe the level of report detail needed and perhaps use a designator such as high, medium, and low to see at a glance if an executive summary level of information will work or if you need to explain items in detail. Table 8.3 shows a sample communication plan with the additional information.

Remember that a stakeholder is anyone who has a vested interest in the outcome of a project. In previous chapters, I've identified some of the typical project stakeholders: project sponsor, functional managers, customers, project team members, and so on.

On large projects that cross multiple functional areas, you may have stakeholders who are not actively participating in the project or who do not fully understand their role. This can occur when large systems are being implemented or new products are being deployed across several geographic regions. Make certain you identify the key messages stakeholders want to know about, concerns the stakeholders may have about the project, and any other aspects of the project your stakeholders may want to know.

TABLE 8.3 Sample expanded communication plan

Stakeholder name	Communication type	Format of communication	Distribution method	Responsible person	Frequency	Level of detail	Confidential
Sponsor	Project status reports. Monthly executive status meeting.	Written and verbal	Email notification/ project repository	Project manager	Weekly status meetings, monthly executive meetings	H	No
Stakeholder A	Project plan, project status reports.	Written	Reports written and stored in project repository	Project manager	Weekly	M	No

Real World Scenario

Main Street Office Move

The project plan for the move is coming together. You're working on the communication plan and will obtain stakeholder approval once you meet with Emma. Here is what you know so far.

The following table shows a partial communication plan for the Main Street Office Move project:

Stakeholder name	Communication type	Format of communication	Method	Responsible person	Frequency	Level of detail	Confidential
Emma Sponsor	Project status reports, budget, schedule, moving company updates, issues, risk events, final project approval	Written and verbal	In-person project meetings, printed report, email, and phone	Project manager	Weekly	H	No
Jason IT	Project status reports, schedule, risk events, moving company updates	Written and verbal	Project meetings, in-person	Project manager, IT team members	Weekly	M	No
Juliette Communication	Project status reports, schedule, risk events, moving company updates	Written and verbal	In-person project meetings, email, or phone	Project manager, scheduler	Bi-weekly	H	No

There are several communication triggers that will create a need to inform Emma and other stakeholders of updates. You construct a triggers list and notification process, as shown here:

Trigger	Stakeholder	Reason	Method	Timing of notification
Project planning complete	All	Obtain sign-off.	Sign-off meeting	At completion of Planning phase
Project change	Emma and affected stakeholders	Obtain approval/ deferral of change.	Project meeting	Regularly scheduled change meeting
Risk register updates	Emma, Leah, Jason, Juliette	Update of risk events occurring, response plans put into action, or notification of new risks.	Special risk meeting, project meeting	Immediate and at regularly scheduled project meetings
Milestones	All	Completion, delay, or change to milestone.	Project meeting, special meeting if negative impacts/ occurrences	At regularly scheduled project meeting
Schedule changes	All	Notification of schedule change.	Project meeting, special meeting if negative impacts/ occurrences	Immediate to Emma, at regularly scheduled change meetings
Task initiation/ completion	Stakeholders responsible for task	Notification tasks are completed and make new task assignments.	Department meetings with functional team members	Daily to functional managers, regularly scheduled project meetings
Stakeholder changes	Emma, other stakeholders depending on the type of change	Discuss impacts/ consequences/ benefits of change.	Special meeting	Immediate to Emma, regularly scheduled change meetings, project meetings
Phase gate review	All	Discuss accomplishments/next steps.	Phase gate review meeting, project meeting	Phase gate review meetings
Resource changes	Emma, impacted stakeholders	Inform stakeholders of impacts, delays, or risks from resource changes.	Special meetings, project meetings	Immediate to Emma, special meetings, regularly scheduled project meetings

Summary

Most project managers spend the majority of their project management time in the act of communicating. Communication is performed using the sender-message-receiver model. Communications planning is a process where you determine who needs what types of communication, when, and in what format, and how that communication will be disseminated. The network communication model shows the lines of communication that exist between any number of project participants. Listening is another important communication skill for any project manager.

There are many methods of communicating, including meetings (which can take many forms such as in-person and virtual), email, fax, videoconferencing, voice conferencing, test messages, instant messages, face-to-face, printed media, and social media.

Factors that can influence communication methods include language barriers, time zone or geographical factors, technological factors, cultural differences, interorganizational and intraorganizational differences, and personal preferences. You'll want to build rapport and solid relationships with your team members so that you can overcome any of these factors that may be influencing communication.

Communication triggers are signs that you need to update stakeholders or share information. Communication triggers may include audits, project planning, change, risk register updates, milestones, schedule changes, task initiation/completion, stakeholder changes, phase gate reviews, business continuity response, incident response, and resource changes.

There are many meeting types that may occur on the project including: status meetings, kickoffs, focus groups, JAD sessions, demonstration/presentations, brainstorming, standups, backlog refinement, task setting, and steering committees.

You should spend time preparing for your meetings, including creating agendas and distributing them a few days prior to the meeting, outlining meeting roles, timeboxing agenda items and meetings, reviewing action items, creating meeting minutes (during the meeting), and following up.

Collaboration tools are easy for multiple people to use to create, edit, and share documents. Some of these tools include multi-authoring and editing software, file-sharing platforms, workflow and e-signature platforms, whiteboards, and a wiki knowledge base. Meeting tools can help in presenting information, arranging meeting times, and obtaining feedback from participants. These may include surveys/polling software, calendaring tools, print media, conferencing platforms, scheduling tools, version control tools, and time-tracking tools.

Project status reports inform the stakeholders on budget, schedule, change, risk, deliverables information, and more. Executives prefer to see project dashboards, which are typically no longer than one page and display status using a stoplight method of red-yellow-green. Charts can also be used for project reporting, including burndown, burnup, Kanban boards, Scrum boards, and task boards.

When creating and managing project communications, you'll want to keep several things in mind, including document security, document integrity, and archiving procedures.

Stakeholders sometimes have their own needs in regard to communication requirements, such as frequency of communication, level of report detail, types of communication, and confidentiality constraints. It's also important to tailor your communication style to the preferences of your stakeholders.

Exam Essentials

Describe the importance of communication planning.   Communication planning is the key to project success. It involves determining who needs information, what type, when, in what format, and the frequency of the communication and documenting this in the communication plan.

Describe communication methods.   Communication methods include meetings, email, fax, instant messaging, videoconferencing, voice conferencing, face-to-face, SMS or text messages, distribution of printed media, and social media.

Be able to name the types of meetings on agile teams.   Types of meetings include daily standups, iteration review, backlog refinement, and retrospective.

Name the common communication triggers on any project.   Common communication triggers include audits, project planning, project change, risk register updates, milestones, schedule changes, task initiation/completion, stakeholder changes, gate reviews, business continuity response, incident response, and resource changes.

Describe the factors influencing communication methods.   Factors include language barriers, time zones/geographical factors, technological factors, cultural differences, interorganizational differences, intraorganizational differences, personal preferences, rapport building/relationship building, tailoring of the method based on content of message, criticality factors, and specific stakeholder communication requirements.

Be able to name several communication triggers.   Triggers include audits, project planning, project change, risk register updates, milestones, schedule changes, task initiation/completion, stakeholder changes, phase gate reviews, business continuity response, incident response, and resource changes.

Be able to describe the three meeting types and examples of each.   Collaborative meeting types include workshops, focus groups, JAD sessions, and brainstorming.

Informative meeting types include demonstrations/presentations, standups, and project status.

Decisive meeting types include backlog refinement, task setting, sprint planning meeting, and project steering committees.

Be able to describe the elements required to prepare for meetings.   These elements include creating agendas, determining meeting roles, timeboxing agenda items and meetings, reviewing action items, preparing meeting minutes, and following up.

Be able to name collaboration tools for project communications.   Collaboration tools include multi-authoring and editing software, file-sharing platforms, workflow and e-signature platforms, whiteboards, and a wiki knowledge base.

Name some common meeting tools that assist with preparing, presenting, and obtaining feedback for meetings.   Common meeting tools include real-time surveys and polling, calendaring tools, print media, conferencing platforms, project management scheduling tools, version control tools, and time-tracking tools.

Name three ways to present project status information.   These ways are the project status report, the project dashboard, and charts. Project dashboards are the preferred method for executives.

Be able to describe the difference between a burndown and burnup chart.   A burndown chart shows the remaining work of the iteration. A burnup chart starts at zero and shows the work completed during the iteration along with all of the work of the project.

Name the three elements of maintaining communication records.   Elements of maintaining communication records are security, integrity, and archiving.

Name stakeholder needs regarding communication requirements.   Stakeholder needs include frequency of communication, level of report detail, types of communication, and confidentiality constraints. Make certain to tailor your communication style to the stakeholders' preference.

Key Terms

Before you take the exam, be certain you are familiar with the following terms:

action item	joint application development (JAD)
asynchronous communication	lines of communication
backlog refinement	message
basic communication model	phase gate review
burnup chart	receiver
communication platforms	retrospective
communication triggers	reviews

daily standup

formal communications

informal communications

sender

synchronous communication

wiki knowledge base

Review Questions

1. Why should you spend time developing a solid communication plan? (Choose three.)
   A. To set performance goals
   B. To set aside time for your own needs
   C. To keep vendors informed
   D. To understand where the blame lies when something goes wrong
   E. To keep stakeholders updated on your progress
   F. To keep team members informed of project progress

2. Which person is responsible for understanding the information correctly and making certain they've received all the information?
   A. Sender
   B. Messenger
   C. Project manager
   D. Receiver

3. There are four participants in your upcoming meeting. How many lines of communication are there?
   A. 6
   B. 4
   C. 8
   D. 16

4. You are working on a project that is being implemented in a country different from your country of origin. You also have team members in several locations around the globe. You should consider all of the following specifically in regard to managing and communicating with team members in this situation except for which one?
   A. Time zones
   B. Cultural differences
   C. Gate reviews
   D. Language barriers

5. A JAD session is an example of which of the following meeting types?
   A. Informative
   B. Collaborative
   C. Demonstrative
   D. Decisive

6. Your project team is located in differing time zones. You need to hold a kickoff meeting, and you decide to use which communication method?

   A. Videoconferencing

   B. Email

   C. In-person meeting

   D. Voice conferencing

7. Which of the following are considered communication methods?

   A. Email

   B. Meetings

   C. Social media

   D. Distribution of printed media

   E. Text message

   F. Face-to-face

   G. All of the above

   H. A, B, C, E, and F

8. Communications planning is the process of which of the following?

   A. Scheduling a regular meeting for the project team

   B. Developing a distribution list for the stakeholders

   C. Identifying the people or groups that need information on your project

   D. Creating a template to report project status

9. Which type of meeting is used to discuss project status at certain points in the project, normally after a project phase is completed or after a milestone has been met? These meetings may also be used as go/no-go decision points.

   A. Retrospective

   B. Project status meeting

   C. Iteration reviews

   D. Phase gate reviews

10. You are a new project manager working in the PMO. Your project customer is the Finance department. The Finance department is uncooperative when working with the PMO. You have experienced some pushback from members of the finance team on following established project management processes, and they repeatedly go around you to team members and other stakeholders with project information. What factor of influence on communication does this represent?

    A. Cultural differences

    B. Personal preferences

    C. Interorganizational differences

    D. Intraorganizational differences

11. You are a project manager for a telecommunications company assigned to a project to deploy a new wireless network using a technology that does not have a proven track record. One of the key stakeholders introduces a change that could impact the schedule. Which of the following does this describe?

    A. Communication method

    B. Factor influencing communication

    C. Communication trigger

    D. Communication preferences

12. The basic communication model consists of which of the following elements? (Choose three.)

    A. Decoder

    B. Sender

    C. Transmission

    D. Listen

    E. Message

    F. Receiver

    G. Encrypt

13. You have a project employee who had an inappropriate outburst in a meeting. You need to coach this team member and let them know how to better handle a similar situation in the future. What should the project manager's next step be with this employee in this circumstance?

    A. Set up a face-to-face meeting with the employee.

    B. Email the employee and explain this is not appropriate behavior.

    C. Set up a meeting with the functional manager and the employee.

    D. Text message the employee and demand they stop this behavior.

14. All of the following are types of synchronous communication except for which one?

    A. Face-to-face

    B. Instant messaging

    C. Phone call

    D. Email

15. You engage in hallway conversations, emails, and phone calls with your team members. What is this considered?

    A. Communication triggers

    B. Factors that influence communication

    C. Communication requirements

    D. Informal communication

16. Your agile team is having a meeting to discuss upcoming user stories for the next sprint. They need to understand the context of the user stories and how they relate to each other and to the project as a whole. What type of meeting is this?

    A. Standup

    B. Review

    C. Backlog refinement

    D. Retrospective

17. You have an important message to deliver to stakeholders. Which of the following should you do?

    A. Write the message in an email and distribute it to those who need to know.

    B. Tailor the communication method based on the content of the message.

    C. Call an impromptu meeting.

    D. Set up a voice conference meeting.

18. You have a complex message to communicate to the project stakeholders. Which of the following are the best methods to use? (Choose two.)

    A. In-person meeting

    B. Email

    C. Instant message

    D. Voice conference

    E. Informal

    F. Written format

19. Frequency, level of report detail, types of communication, confidentiality constraints, and tailoring your communication style are examples of which of the following? (Choose two.)

    A. Rapport building/relationship building

    B. Elements of the communication plan

    C. Communication methods

    D. Stakeholder communication requirements

20. Interorganizational differences, personal preferences, rapport building/relationship building, and technological factors are examples of which of the following?

    A. Factors influencing communication methods

    B. Specific stakeholder communication requirements

    C. Communication triggers

    D. Determining the target audience and rationale

Chapter

9

Processing Change Requests

THE COMPTIA PROJECT + EXAM TOPICS COVERED IN THIS CHAPTER INCLUDE:

✓ **1.0 Project Management Concepts**

    ▪ 1.1 Explain the basic characteristics of a project and various methodologies and frameworks used in IT projects

    ▪ 1.3 Given a scenario, apply the change control process throughout the project life cycle

✓ **2.0 Project Life Cycle Phases**

    ▪ 2.4 Given a scenario, perform activities during the project execution phase

✓ **3.0 Tools and Documentation**

    ▪ 3.1 Given a scenario, use the appropriate tools throughout the project life cycle

✓ **4.0 Basics of IT and Governance**

    ▪ 4.5 Explain operational change control processes during an IT project

The Executing phase of the project entails performing the work required to produce the deliverables and continually monitoring the results to make certain they meet the specifications according to the project plan. If deviations from the plan occur, corrective actions need to be taken to get the plan back on track. Executing involves a lot of activities, and we'll look at them in this chapter.

Deviations from the project plan can be warnings that changes may be required or have already occurred. You will experience requests for changes during the project that may come in the form of changes to deliverables or scope, to timelines, to budgets, in resource assignments, and more. Organizational changes such as reorganizations, or mergers and acquisitions, can bring about changes to the project, and so can operational changes involving IT hardware or software. A sound change control process will help you and the team deal with these requests effectively, and I'll talk in depth about those processes in this chapter.

We will circle back to agile projects at the end of this chapter and discuss agile project management methodologies and frameworks. Let's get started with a review of the Executing phase activities.

Executing Phase Activities

Executing is the phase where the work of the project takes place. All of the hard work you've done up to this point in creating the project management plan, including the scope statement, schedule, risk register, and more, will help ensure project success. The project management plan is your roadmap for success. It details deliverables, work packages, and schedules, among other things, and will also serve as a guide for determining whether changes should be approved or deferred.

There are several activities you will engage in during the Executing phase according to the CompTIA exam objectives:

- Execute tasks according to the project management plan.
- Implement organizational change management.
- Manage vendors.
- Conduct project meetings and updates.
- Report on and track project performance.
- Update the project budget.

- Update the project timeline.
- Manage conflict.
- Coordinate phase gate review meetings.

We have covered a few of these topics in previous chapters, including conducting project meetings, project reporting, managing conflict, and coordinating phase gate reviews. We will review the other Executing topics and more in this chapter. Let's start with a review of the project management plan.

Reviewing the Project Management Plan

Throughout this book, we've looked at the documents that make up the project management plan, such as the scope baseline, the cost baseline, and the schedule baseline. All these documents make up the project management plan, which is the final, approved plan that you'll use throughout the remainder of the project to measure project progress and, ultimately, project success. The key components of the project management plan include the following documents:

- Scope baseline
- Schedule baseline
- Communication plan
- Resource plan
- Procurement plan
- Budget baseline
- Quality plan
- Risk plan

This completed plan serves as the baseline for project progress. You will execute tasks according to the plan and use it to determine whether the project is on track or whether you need to take action to get the work in alignment with the plan. The project management plan is also referred to when a change is requested. It helps determine whether a change has occurred and to determine whether a requested change is aligned with the overall goals and objectives of the project.

The project management plan is also used as a communication tool for the sponsor, stakeholders, and members of the management team to review and gauge progress throughout the project. As such, it's a good idea to obtain sign-off from the sponsor and key stakeholders on the final plan. This helps assure a common understanding of the objectives for the project, the budget, and the timeline and will ideally prevent misunderstandings once the work of the project begins. It will also help serve as a baseline when the change requests start rolling in and stakeholders want "one more little feature" that may or may not be in keeping with the scope of the project. The project management plan should be updated whenever a change request is approved. Keep this plan within arm's reach because you'll be using it throughout the remainder of the project.

After-the-Fact Plan

I once was involved on a large project where the project management plan was being created as the project work was being performed. This resulted in a scenario where the project manager, the project team members, and other stakeholders did not have a plan to guide execution of the project, nor did they know what could or should be changed as the requests came in.

As you can imagine, confusion was rampant, and to no one's surprise, the project was quickly off track.

A project management plan is not a reflection of what has already occurred; it is a plan for future work that will meet the goals and objectives of the project. It will be used to determine whether the project was performed within the constraints (time, scope, cost), to determine whether the milestones were completed, and to validate change requests.

Managing Vendors

Managing vendors involves monitoring their performance and ensuring that all the requirements of the procurement agreement (this is usually the work order or contract) are met. You will verify compliance with the project objectives by measuring and monitoring deliverables, enforcing the rules of engagement, and verifying and approving the final deliverables. Monitoring vendors to verify that you are meeting the project objectives is closely linked with other project management processes. For example, you'll manage vendor relationships, monitor the progress of the contract, execute plans, track costs, measure outputs, approve changes, take corrective action, and report on status, just as you do when using internal resources for the project. Monitoring vendors and procurement activities is your responsibility as the project manager no matter whether you are using waterfall or agile methodologies to manage the work of the project.

 As the project manager, you need to manage stakeholder expectations regarding project goals for all projects, whether you are using vendors or performing the work in-house. This includes identifying key deliverables and measuring and monitoring them to ensure compliance with objectives.

You should conduct vendor performance reviews on a periodic basis to examine the seller's performance on the contract to date. Performance reviews can be done at the end of an iteration, when a key deliverable is completed, at the end of the project, or any other predetermined time periods. Vendor reviews examine the contract terms and seller performance for elements such as the following:

- Meeting scope requirements
- Meeting quality standards
- Staying within project budgets
- Meeting the project schedule

Performance reviews can be performed using inspections or audits. Inspections involve physically examining or inspecting the work. This may be performed by the buyer or a designated third party. Inspections may occur during the work of the project as well as at the completion of the work. If your project involves implementing software, test scenarios such as user acceptance testing will take the place of inspections. This test is just as it sounds. The users will perform various tests, based on the traceability requirements matrix, to determine if the software performs as required. We will talk more about testing methodologies in Chapter 10, "Managing Quality and Closing Out the Project."

Audits consist of reviews of vendor activities to determine whether they are meeting the right needs and whether the activities are being performed correctly and according to standards. Audits might also examine the procurement processes to determine areas of improvement and to identify flawed processes or procedures.

The point of a review is to determine if the seller is succeeding at meeting scope, quality, cost, and schedule requirements. If the seller is not in compliance, action must be taken to either get them back into compliance or terminate the contract. You'll use the contract statement of work and the terms of the contract to determine performance compliance.

Procurement audits might be used by either the buyer or the vendor, or by both, as an opportunity for improvement. It's a good idea to document what you learned during the audits as lessons learned—including the successes and failures that occurred. Doing so allows you to improve other procurement processes currently underway on this project or other projects. It also gives you the opportunity to improve the process for future projects.

Contract Change Control

Depending on the size of the organization, administering the contract or other procurement agreement might fall to someone in the procurement department. This doesn't mean you're off the hook as the project manager. It's still your responsibility to oversee the process and make sure the project objectives are being met. You'll be the one monitoring the performance of the vendor and informing them when and if performance is lacking. You'll also monitor the procurement agreement's financial conditions. For example, the seller should be paid in a timely manner when they've satisfactorily met the conditions of the agreement, and it will be up to you to let the procurement department know it's okay to pay the vendor. You may have to terminate the contract when the vendor violates the terms or doesn't meet the agreed-on deliverables. If the procurement department has this responsibility, you'll have to document the situation and provide this to the procurement department so that they can enforce or terminate the contract.

 Buyers and sellers are equally responsible for monitoring the contract. Each has a vested interest in ensuring that the other party is living up to their contractual obligations and that their own legal rights are protected.

Approved change requests for contracts should be processed through the contract change control system. The *contract change control system* documents how to submit changes, establishes the approval process, and outlines authorization approval levels for changes. Because a contract is a legal document, changes require the agreement of all parties, and therefore a formal procedure must be established to process and authorize (or deny) changes. The contract change control system includes the change request description, a unique identifier, the requestor, the disposition of the change, and approvers. Depending on the complexity of the project, you may need to record other information in the system or categorize changes such as scope or schedule changes.

Claims administration involves documenting, monitoring, and managing contested changes to the contract. Changes that cannot be agreed on are called *contested changes*. Contested changes usually involve a disagreement about the compensation to the vendor for implementing the change. You might believe the change is not significant enough to justify additional compensation, whereas the vendor believes they'll lose money by implementing the change free of charge. Contested changes are also known as *disputes*, *claims*, or *appeals*. These can be settled directly between the parties themselves, through the court system, or by a process called arbitration. *Arbitration* involves bringing all parties to the table with a disinterested third party who is not a participant in the contract to try to reach an agreement. The purpose of arbitration is to reach an agreement without having to go to court. Arbitration is a form of alternative dispute resolution (ADR) and could be a named tool in the contract for resolving disputes. Reaching a negotiated settlement through the aid of ADR techniques is the most favorable way to resolve the dispute.

Paying Vendors

Vendors submit seller invoices requesting payment for goods and services that have been delivered. *Seller invoices* should describe the work that was completed or the materials that were delivered and should include any supporting documentation necessary to describe what was delivered. The contract should state what type of supporting documentation is needed with the invoice. The organization might have a dedicated department, such as accounts payable, that handles vendor payments, or it might fall to the project manager. In either case, follow the policies and procedures the organization has established regarding vendor payments and make sure the payments themselves adhere to the contract terms.

Implementing Change Control Systems

Changes come about for many reasons, and most projects experience change during the project life cycle. Here are some common causes of project changes:

- Timeline change
- Funding change
- Risk events
- Requirements change
- Quality change
- Resource change
- Scope change

These change requests might come from the project sponsor, stakeholders, team members, vendors, and others. You'll want to understand the factors that bring about change, such as those listed here, and how a proposed change might impact the project if it's implemented.

The most important aspect of change in terms of project management is having a robust change control system in place to deal with the requests. *Change control systems* are documented procedures that describe how the deliverables of the project are controlled, changed, and approved. They also describe and manage the documentation required to request and track the changes and the updates to the project management plan.

The key to avoiding chaos is to manage change in an organized fashion with an integrated change control system that looks at the impact of any change across all aspects of the project plan. Changes, no matter how small, have an impact on the triple constraints (time, cost, or scope), and they may also impact quality. Not having a process to create and receive the change requests, analyze the impacts of the change, and determine whether it's worth the extra time, money, and so on to implement is a recipe for project failure.

In my experience, the three biggest project killers are a lack of adequate planning, poor risk planning, and inadequate change control processes. As the project manager, you have control over all three of these activities.

There are several aspects to an effective change management system that we'll look at throughout this section:

- Create and submit change requests.
- Identify and document the change request in the change request log.
- Conduct a preliminary review.
- Perform impact assessments.
- Document change recommendations.
- Determine decision-makers.

- Escalate to the change control board (CCB).
- Document status of the change request decision in the change control log.
- Communicating change status.
- Update the project plan.
- Implement the change.
- Validate the change and perform a quality check.
- Coordinate and communicate with the appropriate stakeholders.

Create and Submit the Change Request

After the project management plan is approved, all change requests must be submitted through the change control system. The processes and procedures for change control should be documented and easily accessible by stakeholders and team members. The process should describe where to obtain a form for a change request, where change requests are submitted for consideration and to whom, and a communication process for keeping the requestor apprised of the status.

A change request could be submitted by anyone working on or associated with the project. Change requests should always be in writing. This means you'll need to devise a template for stakeholders and others to document the change request, the reason the change is needed, and what will happen if the change is not made. You could include a place for other information on the form that you think will help the review committee determine whether the change should be made. For example, other information could include potential for additional profits, increased marketability, improved efficiencies, improved productivity, social awareness or benefits, and so on.

The change request is like a mini-business case that describes the justification, alternatives, and impacts of the change. Typically, the person requesting the change presents the request to the change control board.

Beware! Stakeholders are notorious for asking for changes verbally even though there is a change control process in place. Spend time at the kickoff meeting explaining to everyone where to find the forms and how to follow the process. Make it a point that only change requests that come in via the process will be considered. Verbal requests and drive-bys to the project team will not be accepted.

Documenting Changes in the Change Control Log and Conducting a Preliminary Review

A number of things happen once the change request is submitted. First, it should be assigned an identifying number for tracking purposes. Then, it should be recorded in the change request log. This log is easy to construct in a spreadsheet file. Table 9.1 shows a sample change request log.

TABLE 9.1   Change request log

ID	Date	Description	Requestor	Status	Disposition	Implementation or close date
01	11/11	Add a drop-down box on the entry screen.	Nora Smith	Submitted to review committee	Approved	11/13
02	11/14	Implement a virtual tape library for backups.	Brett Whatley	For review on 11/25		

You could add other columns to this spreadsheet for tracking purposes, depending on the needs of your project. For example, you might want to add the date of the committee's decision, implementation status, and columns to track costs and hours expended to implement the change. Reviewing the change control log should be a regular agenda item at your project status meetings.

After the change request is recorded in the tracking log, the next step is to conduct a preliminary review. The change request should be reviewed by the project team, subject matter experts, and other key stakeholders to determine the viability of the change, to perform an estimate of how long it will take to implement the change, and to determine the impacts the change may have on other aspects of the project. For example, a change in scope could be simple to implement or it could dramatically change the overall project. The project team should document the findings of the preliminary assessment, being careful to detail how the change request may affect the project, and then conduct an impact assessment, which we'll look at next.

Conducting Impact Assessments

Impact assessments are typically evaluated by the subject matter experts working on the area of the project that the change impacts, along with input from the project manager. The following questions are a good place to start the analysis process:

- Should the change be implemented?
- What's the cost to the project in terms of project constraints: cost, time, scope, and quality?
- Will the benefits gained by making the change increase or decrease the chances of project completion?
- What is the value and effectiveness of this change?
- Is there potential for increased or decreased risk as a result of this change?
- Does this change impact other areas of the project?
- Does the project team have the skills and ability to implement the change?

After answering these basic questions, the expert should then analyze the specific elements of the change request, such as additional equipment needs, resource hours, costs, skills or expertise needed to work on the change, and quality impacts. You can use some of the same cost and resource estimating techniques we discussed in previous chapters such as analogous estimates and three-point estimates to determine estimates for change requests.

The project manager will also analyze the scope baseline, schedule, budget, and resource allocation to determine what impacts will occur as a result of the change. This information is documented (a template comes in handy here as well) and then presented to the review committee, typically called a change control board, for approval or rejection.

Evaluating the impacts of the change request may include a *regression plan*. You can think of this as the ability to *reverse changes* or back out the changes and revert to the previous state. Information technology projects often have a *rollback plan* (or reverse changes plan). If the change does not perform as expected, you can go back to the previously known, working state.

 Regression plans, reverse changes, and rollback plans are three names for the same idea, which is the ability to roll back to the last known good state.

Keep in mind there is always an opportunity cost involved when analyzing change. When you ask your subject matter experts to stop working on their tasks to examine the impacts of the change request, their work on the project comes to a stop. This trade-off can be difficult to balance sometimes. There isn't a hard and fast rule on this. You'll have to keep an eye on the progress of the project work and the number of requests coming in. I sometimes track the number of hours spent by the team on change request analysis and report this to the stakeholders during our project status meetings. It helps them to be aware of the potential impact to the project if the change requests get out of hand, and if you have a savvy stakeholder group, they'll begin to self-discipline themselves and curtail frivolous requests.

Documenting Change Recommendations

So far, you've documented the change request in the change control log, and performed a preliminary assessment and an impact analysis. The PMO may have a template available for you to use to record the assessment and impact analysis findings. If not, I recommend creating a form to record this information. Note the change request ID number, title, and brief description on the assessment and analysis form, and keep this information on the project repository. Don't forget to ensure document security and integrity by limiting access to the information to only those who need to know, and/or as outlined in the security policy. It's a good idea to add a column to the change control log to document where the assessment and analysis findings are located so that all information associated with the change is in one place.

Determining Decision-Makers

After the change requests are evaluated and assessed for impacts, someone needs to make the decision whether to go forward with the change, defer it, or deny it. The decision-makers should be selected early on during the project Planning phase and documented in the change management plan. The change management plan describes the change control process, including how to submit a change request and where to find the forms, the decision-makers and their authority level, and the function of the change control board. This plan should be developed in collaboration with the project sponsor and key stakeholders. It should be created and documented well before the work of the project begins. You don't want to have a situation where an urgent change is needed, and no one knows who has the authority to approve or deny the request.

Decision-makers may include the project manager, project sponsor, key stakeholders, or other subject matter experts. The authority levels of decision-makers may depend on factors such as cost, timeline, and resource assignments. For example, perhaps the project manager has the authority to decide on change requests with costs up to $5,000, or those that have less than a 5 percent impact on the project timeline, and so on. Authority levels for each decision-maker should be documented in the change control plan.

Managing the Change Control Board

In many organizations, a *change control board* (CCB) is established to review all change requests and approve, deny, or defer the request. CCB members might include stakeholders, managers, subject matter experts, project team members, and others who might not have any connection to the project at hand. Some organizations have permanent CCBs that are staffed by full-time employees dedicated to managing change for the entire organization, not just project change. You might want to consider establishing a CCB for your project if the organization does not have one.

A basic CCB assigns approval authority equally among the key stakeholders on the project. Complex projects or projects that impact one business area more than others may require approval authority weighted toward that business unit. For example, let's say you're implementing a new recruitment software program for the human resources department. A change request is submitted that has to do with the recruitment business process and primarily affects the human resources department. In this case, the human resources stakeholder should have more say in the decision on the change request than other stakeholders.

Typically, the board meets at regularly scheduled intervals. Change requests and the impact analysis are given to the board for review, and they have the authority to approve, deny, or delay the requests. You should note their decision on the change request log shown in Table 9.1.

It's important to establish separate procedures for emergency changes. This should include a description and definition of an emergency, the authority level of the project manager in this situation, and the process for reporting the change after it's implemented. That way, when emergencies arise, the preestablished procedures allow the project manager to implement the change on the spot. This always requires follow-up with the CCB and completion of a formal change request, even though it's after the fact.

> In many organizations, the project sponsor is required to approve changes that impact scope, budget, time, or quality if the estimates surpass a certain limit. It's always good practice to inform your sponsor of major changes to scope, budget, time, or quality or any change that has the potential to increase risk. Check with your organization to learn the process for approvals.

Documenting Approval Status in the Change Control Log

As I've stated previously, stakeholders sometimes have short memories. I don't fault them for this. They have a vested interest in their projects and want their business units to function efficiently and effectively. They often see change requests as must-haves in order to achieve those efficiencies. As the project progresses, the memory lapse may come in the form of "I thought we had funding for that," or "I thought we agreed this change was needed," or "I thought this was already included in the requirements." This is when all the documentation we've talked about throughout this book, and in this chapter, comes into play. If you've followed the planning processes, the requirements are documented and signed off, the schedule has been agreed to and signed off, and the budget has been agreed to and signed off. You don't want to have an "I told you so" attitude here, but a gentle review of these documents can help the stakeholder remember what was agreed to during the Planning phase. This can help prevent scope creep and a nonstop flow of change requests.

You'll also want to document the final decision regarding the change request in the change control log. You'll recall that there is a column in the example in Table 9.1 showing the disposition of the change. Further details about the decision can be documented on the analysis and impact assessment form we talked about earlier, or your PMO template. The form or template should have a place to document the reasons for the decision, whether the change was approved or denied, who made the decision, and the date.

Communicating Change Status

The next step in the change control process is to communicate the status of the change. This can be done during a project status review meeting, during a CCB meeting, or during a special meeting called to discuss the change. You'll want to provide the documentation supporting the change decisions to the stakeholders and send it out ahead of the meeting. Most change discussions can occur at the regularly scheduled project status meeting. There should be a standing agenda item to discuss change requests, along with risk status, issue status, and other project information at the status meeting. Questions may arise about the decision, especially if the change request was contentious. For example, the change may have negative consequences for one business unit and yet benefit another. Make certain that your subject matter experts are on hand at the meeting to discuss the impacts of the change and the justification for the decision.

You'll need to keep the project sponsor and key stakeholders apprised of changes as well and communicate with them directly when there are contentious changes, when the process is being circumvented altogether, or when change requests hit the thresholds outlined in the change management plan. Don't hesitate to contact the project sponsor or other key stakeholders about major change requests that impact their areas. Also be aware of project team members who use the name of the sponsor or stakeholder as leverage, such as "I already discussed this with the project sponsor, and they agreed to the change." This is a case where you should reach out to the sponsor directly to confirm it, and gently remind them there is a standard process that should be followed for change requests.

Updating the Project Management Plan

Changes to the project will require updates to the affected project documents, including but not limited to the project scope statement, budget, schedule, risk register, and more.

Updating the project plan documents is an important step that is sometimes ignored. If your project has an extended timeline, the changes you've made could be long forgotten in the future if they are not documented. Multiple project managers may come and go, and without a record of the change, you could be putting a future project manager, the project, and the organization at risk. Another key reason for updating the project documents is to maintain an accurate record of the project. Remember that you can use these documents as a starting point on future projects. If you review and understand the changes that occurred on past projects while planning your next one, it may help you avoid problems.

Be certain to practice version control when updating project documents. This way, you'll know that you are always working with the latest document. For example, if the schedule has undergone a change previously and now a new request is submitted that will impact the schedule, you'll want to make sure you are updating the latest version of the schedule. Many project management software programs and electronic document and records management programs will automatically perform version control for you. If your organization has not implemented this feature, you can accomplish version control in a couple of ways. Include the version number in your document name, such as "Schedule_v1," or the date and time, "Schedule_2023-02-16."

Implementing the Change

When a change request is approved, you will need to implement the change. This may require timeline changes, resource changes, or additional funds. Depending on the complexity of the change, you may need to coordinate activities with the project team and schedule the change at an appropriate time. If the change will come at a later stage in the project, make certain to perform the risk processes because a change could introduce the potential for new risks. You'll need to identify the new risks, log them on the risk register, determine their risk score, and develop response plans for them if appropriate.

Validating the Change and Perform a Quality Check

Once the change is implemented, you'll need to validate that the change was made and that it met the requirements of the change request. You'll check the quality of the change to assure it was performed accurately and completely. If there are problems, you may need to implement your rollback plan and reverse the changes and then evaluate why the change did not function as planned.

Communicating Change Deployment

Change deployment should be communicated to the sponsor, stakeholders, and project team members. They'll be interested to know when the change was kicked off, to hear about progress on the change, and to know when it is fully implemented, along with the status of the change validation. One of the most effective ways to share this information is at the project status meeting.

Other Change Requests

The types of changes others may ask for are limitless. Changes most often affect project scope, schedules, and/or budgets. In addition to these changes, change requests may also take the form of *corrective actions*, *preventive actions*, or *defect repairs*. These usually come about from monitoring the actual project work results. Let's take a look at a brief description of each of these:

Corrective Actions Corrective actions bring the work of the project into alignment with the project management plan.

Preventive Actions Preventive actions are implemented to help reduce the probability of a negative risk event.

Defect Repairs Defect repairs either correct or replace components that are substandard or malfunctioning.

Project Change Management

The CompTIA exam objectives point out that project change is different than product change. *Product change* involves a change to the product of the project such as an application, a physical product, or a service. Change requests should be processed as described in the previous section. The change request should be written, submitted, and analyzed, and decisions should be made about the request. The description section in this case should contain detail about what part of the application or product should be changed and how. You could also note success criteria to determine and validate if the change works as planned.

> If a vendor is building the product, you'll follow the contract change control process to make changes. Product changes always require project changes.

For example, a change to the functionality of an application (the product in this case) is a scope change. The requirements are impacted because the business team no longer wants the functionality to perform as originally documented. This means you'll need to update the scope statement to reflect the change. Scope changes often bring about schedule changes. Adding scope will likely take more time, which will increase the project timeline. Eliminating scope may reduce the timeline, or it may not. If the schedule is changed, it should be updated. Scope changes may also impact the project budget and require more (or less) funds. I think you get the idea. Keep in mind that no matter the type of change, be it product or project, the requests should all follow the same change control process.

> Excessive changes to scope can cause irreparable damage to the product and the project. Scope creep comes about by not controlling change requests or by allowing changes to occur without following the change control process. Managing scope creep is an important activity for the project manager and you should monitor it closely.

Implementing Organizational Change

Scope, schedule, and cost are not the only changes that may impact the project. Organizational change can have a significant impact on the project. *Organizational change* involves transforming processes, systems, organizational structure, personnel, products, applications, or other significant aspects of the organization. We'll look at types of organizational change and how to implement organizational change in this section.

Types of Organizational Change

Organizational change may include reorganization of the company's departments and personnel, new executive leadership, new business models, implementing new systems, and more. Let's look at some examples of organizational change you'll need to know for the exam.

Business Merger/Acquisition   Changes that come in the form of mergers or acquisitions can lead to project changes or sometimes project cancelations. For the exam, it's important to understand the difference between a *merger* and an *acquisition*. A merger is when two companies come together to perform business as one organization. Once the merger is complete, they are one entity. An acquisition is when one business takes over another. The organization performing the takeover has the power and authority and becomes the decision-maker for both organizations. Mergers or acquisitions could change the overall objectives and goals of the project.

Business Demerger/Split   A *demerger* or *split* is the opposite of a merger or acquisition. The organizations that merged or were acquired decide to break into separate entities. A demerger or split is also likely to change the overall goals of the project or perhaps cause its cancellation.

Business Process Change   *Business process changes* typically occur within the organization. An example of a business process change is automating a process that was previously performed manually. It may also include implementing a new ERP or EDRMS, which in turn will change existing business processes. Business process changes may also come about because of new legislation, regulations, and industry standards.

Internal Reorganization   A *reorganization* can impact the resources assigned to and working on your project. This could potentially delay the schedule, especially if the resources originally planned for the project activities are no longer available. You'll need time to negotiate resource availability with the new managers.

Relocation   A *relocation* involves a physical move of the organization, or parts of the organization that may impact your project. There could be resources (both physical and human) assigned to the project that are targeted for relocation. This means their work time will be interrupted to perform move activities and they won't be available to work on project activities.

Outsourcing   *Outsourcing* occurs when an organization uses external resources to perform business processes and tasks. Outsourcing usually involves hiring outside companies to perform business functions or tasks such as payroll, information technology, security, and janitorial services. Outsourcing project team members by bringing in consultants to help with the work can alter the make-up of the team. You should watch for team cohesiveness when there are outside members and be certain to nip conflicts before they arise.

Implementing Organizational Change

Implementing organizational change is not for the faint of heart. If your organization is facing a significant change such as a merger or acquisition, or an enterprisewide change to organizational structure, I strongly recommend hiring experts in this field to help you through the change. There are many consulting firms that specialize in organizational change, and they will design and plan the entire process and help you successfully implement the change. They will guide the executives regarding communicating the message and gaining buy-in from staff members.

Changes on a smaller scale, such as establishing a new business process or implementing a new system, should also follow a solid organizational change process. It's critical that employees know a change is coming before it happens, while it happens, and after it happens. As you can imagine, this involves a significant amount of communication, which is one of the steps outlined in the CompTIA exam objectives. I've added a couple of my own here as well. The steps for managing organizational change include the following:

Define the change.   The changes should be defined clearly and in precise terms so that there is no confusion or misunderstanding by the team. The definition should be as detailed as needed to describe the change elements. Organizational changes usually have specific outcomes or goals. Perhaps the organization wants to improve efficiency or reduce waste. The goals that help define the change outcomes are best stated using the acronym SMART.

The S stands for specific, meaning goals should be specific and clear. Maybe your organization wants to implement a new ERP system and they have set this as the goal. However, this isn't specific. The goal is better stated this way: "We will implement a new ERP system with financial, human resource, and procurement functionality."

The M means the goal should be measurable. Let's say the goal involves implementing a new system to reduce time wasted on workflow processes for employee expense reimbursement. Today it takes employees 14 days on average to be reimbursed for travel expenses. The new system is expected to cut this average in half and employees will be reimbursed within 7 days of submitting expenses. The goal could be that you will reduce reimbursement time in half, or you will reduce reimbursement time from 14 days to 7 days. The idea is that you have a way to measure the outcome.

The A stands for attainable and means the goal should be something the organization can achieve. If you want to put a rocket on the moon but you are not in the rocket building business, this probably isn't an attainable goal.

The R means realistic. This is similar to attainable but not exactly the same. Realistic means the goal is something the organization can accomplish. Perhaps the organization wants to consolidate and relocate employees from across the country to one location. This is attainable, but maybe not realistic. You could lose hundreds of valuable employees, or perhaps the business is such that each location needs to be embedded in the local culture so it wouldn't be realistic to consolidate locations.

The T stands for time bound. For example, if you're implementing a new process or a new software system, you can state this part of the goals this way: "The new ERP system will go live on May 1, 2025."

Communicate that the change is coming.   Communication is the key to success for the project and for changes. Communicating the change can occur at meetings, in video-conferences, and in an email, among other ways. Organizational change communication should start well before the change is implemented. Perhaps begin with brown bag lunch sessions, posters, meetings, and other events to provide as much information as possible about the change, to let employees know how the change will impact them and the organization, and to hold a question-and-answer period during the session. Make certain to use a communication channel that is appropriate given the severity or impact of the change. Remember that it's generally better to deliver bad news in person rather than during a teleconference or via memo.

Analyze impacts and responses.   Impact assessments and responses apply to organizational change as well as project change. The impacts and responses of the organizational change should be examined by the team and or reported to the executives sponsoring the change, depending on their significance. You might use SWOT analysis, surveys, and polling; examine challenges; perform gap analysis; hold focus groups; and other methods to analyze the impacts of organizational change.

Conduct training.   Training is critical for project success and for organizational change success. For example, if you are implementing a new customer service software system but your employees don't know how to use it, they won't be able to address customer inquiries. There are countless examples where training may be required, such as implementing new systems, implementing new business processes, and explaining new organizational structures. Training should be required for all personnel who are impacted by the change.

Ensure adoption over time.   It's always good practice to follow up after a change has been implemented to ensure people are adhering to the new systems, processes, and so on. This is also an opportunity to discover pain points they may be experiencing because of the change. For example, perhaps the training sessions were delivered too early in the project, and they've forgotten some of the information. You could recommend additional training or refresher courses to help ensure adoption.

Communicate during and after the change.   You have been busy communicating the change is coming, but it's also important to communicate the change is happening. You can use any number of communication tools and methods to share the information; the important thing is to let the team know it's in the works and to provide status of the change along the way. Consider reporting on what phase or stage the change is in, any impacts to the implementation date, how it's proceeding, and the anticipated completion date. After the change is completed, you'll want to communicate again. If you underwent a significant organizational change or implemented a system that impacted most of the employees in the organization, you could host a completion party or similar gathering to celebrate the change.

Document the change.   I know I have been remiss in talking about both communicating and documenting information throughout this book. Only kidding. Of course, you'll want to document the change, its impacts, how the organization responded to the change, and so on. You can use this document as an artifact for historical purposes and refer to it when similar changes may come about in the future.

Create new knowledge bases.   Changes may create the need for new knowledge bases. For example, implementing a new software system should also involve creating a knowledge base where users can access frequently asked questions and help topics regarding the system functionality. New processes that employees must follow may require knowledge bases as well so that they can reference instructions about the process, who to contact, which forms to fill out, and more.

Create new processes.   Creating new processes may involve implementing a new system or simply creating a new form and workflow. There are thousands of ways new processes may come about. Creating new processes does bring about change, so make certain to communicate, provide training, and follow the other procedures outlined in this section.

Operational Change Control on an IT Project

Operational change control is the last change control topic we'll cover. Information technology departments manage infrastructure, software, cloud implementations, and more. As a normal course of business, these systems require changes, maintenance, patching, and so on. You'll want to have an operational change control process in place to manage IT-driven change. We'll look at several aspects of operational change control on an IT project next.

IT Infrastructure Control

IT infrastructure control involves managing changes to elements of the IT environment such as servers, routers, firmware, and software updates. The change control process should include schedules, notifications to users, and change control meetings.

Maintenance schedules are typically set as standard dates and times on a periodic basis that allows the IT team to perform maintenance activities such as updating firmware, performing security patching, tuning, and many other actions. A maintenance schedule might be set for every month, every quarter, or whatever time period the IT team needs to maintain the infrastructure.

Customer notifications about the change should occur in writing as well as at the change meeting. Many organizations use a change advisory board (CAB) or a change control board (CCB) to communicate upcoming changes. These meetings can be set at intervals that work for the IT team and the business users. The CAB meeting covers all the changes we'll talk about in this section, including hardware, software, and cloud changes. The CAB meeting can be held on a weekly or bi-weekly basis to inform users about the upcoming changes that are scheduled for later in the month. The users are given the opportunity to discuss impacts the proposed changes may have to the business and to ensure the date the work will be performed does not interfere with other business priorities. For example, if the IT team schedules a change for a Monday evening but the organization has convened a special board meeting on the following Tuesday, you'll likely want to move the change to Tuesday evening. Changes can introduce possible work disruptions and downtime, and you wouldn't want to be troubleshooting what went wrong with a change while the CEO is expecting to present an important update to the board.

After the CAB meeting, make certain to publish the meeting minutes. You might send them using email or post them to the CAB site so that users can reference the changes, the date of the change, and so on.

Rollback plans should be in place in case the change does not go as planned. Rollback plans allow you to restore to the last known good state. This means the business users can continue performing their work tasks. When changes go wrong and you don't have a rollback plan, you could have dozens, hundreds, or thousands of business users unable to work, which in turn costs the organization money paying idle employees, not to mention lost revenue during the downtime. If the rollback plan is implemented, the IT team will need to troubleshoot what went wrong with the change and reschedule for a future date.

Validation checks are the last step in the infrastructure change control process. This check may take the form of testing, visual inspection, or other activities to ensure the change was implemented appropriately and that the change has the intended effect. We will talk more in depth about testing in Chapter 10.

Software Change Control

Software changes typically involve an update or change to the software functionality, and requests might be submitted by end users as well as IT staff. Changes to functionality should follow the process defined in the "Implementing Change Control Systems" section of this chapter. The request should include a requirements definition that outlines the change and its expected outcomes. As described earlier in this chapter, you should also perform an impact assessment and a risk assessment that analyzes the change.

Software development generally involves three environments: development, beta-staging, and production. The development environment is where the code is written. The *beta-staging environment* is where the code is tested, and production is where the code resides that allows end users to access the system. Software changes follow the same process. First, the code changes are written in the development environment. Then, production data is copied to the beta-staging environment so that the test environment replicates production as closely as possible. Using production data in the beta-staging environment ensures that the changes behave in much the same way they will once they are released into the production environment. Next, the code changes are deployed from development to the beta-staging environment and rigorously tested. Once testing is complete and validated, the requestor approves the changes (in writing). Then notifications should be sent to end users about the coming change, including the date the changes will take effect and information on how to access training. And finally, the change is released to production.

Software changes that involve security patching or routine updates could follow the same process as outlined in the previous section describing infrastructure changes. Don't forget to create a rollback plan for software changes as well.

Other IT Change Processes

There are two other IT change processes highlighted in the CompTIA exam objectives that you need to know for the exam. The first is the difference between cloud changes and on-premises change control. We've already talked about on-premises change control throughout this chapter. However, keep in mind that many of the processes outlined here can apply to cloud changes as well.

Most cloud providers have well-documented processes for change control. Changes are usually scheduled and managed by the provider at consistent intervals such as quarterly or semi-annually. Consumers don't have much say about when the changes will occur. Cloud providers typically give their customers sufficient notice of the changes along with documentation describing the upcoming changes. Your team should perform testing after the changes are made to ensure there are no adverse reactions. You also need to initiate communication to end users and provide notifications about the change and how to access training or get help if needed.

Continuous integration is a type of software development methodology that helps improve the quality of code and the pace of delivery. Programming changes, configuration changes, bug fixes, and more are made and checked into a central repository for code changes. The system will then kick off automated build and test processes to ensure the change doesn't have unintended impacts to the overall system, and it ensures the change itself is sound. The idea is that changes can be introduced in small segments on a frequent basis. This makes errors easier to find and changes get delivered faster. Large changes involve complex testing, which can take weeks or months, and they have the potential to impact the entire system. Continuous integration reduces the potential for the entire system going down and disrupting end users' work while delivering quality changes more frequently.

Agile Frameworks

Framework is a term that describes an agile methodology. I have primarily used the word *methodology* throughout this book, but you could substitute the word *framework* as well. Agile frameworks consist of standardized processes. The team may want to tailor their own version of agile to meet their needs using parts of multiple agile methodologies. For example, they may want to use the team structure and roles associated with Scrum along with the daily standups, reviews, and retrospectives, but use a Kanban board to display work in process to control workflow. While executing the work, they might use pair programming, an XP methodology, to ensure quality and speed of delivery. Infinite possibilities exist for the team to tailor agile processes. If the team is new to agile, it's best to stick with one framework until they have learned how it works and have had some hands-on experience using it. Once they are proficient at it, loosen up a bit and allow them the flexibility to tailor the process to match their needs.

We've discussed several of agile frameworks throughout this book, including these:

- Scrum

- Kanban

- Scrumban

- Lean

- Kaizen

- eXtreme Programming (XP)

- Feature-Driven Development (FDD)

- Dynamic Systems Development Method (DSDM)

- Agile Unified Process (AUP)

- Hybrid

- PRINCE2

 The team does not need to use an established, predefined agile frame-work such as Scrum or Kanban. They may develop their own agile meth-odology as long as it follows the principles of the *Agile Manifesto*.

Scaling Frameworks

Agile practices work best with small teams. But what happens when you have a large project that can't be accomplished using only three to nine team members? This is where scaling agile frameworks comes into play. This approach involves simply taking agile and scaling it to the enterprise. For example, you may have a large project that requires a couple of dozen people to produce the software code needed by the project deadline. You could use several agile teams to accomplish this goal, where each team has their own set of objectives and requirements. Together, they are all working toward the overarching goal of completing the project. The teams may reside in different locations, but it's important that each individual team be collocated if possible. We'll look at the most popular scaling frameworks used in organizations today next.

Scrum of Scrums

Scrum of Scrums is an agile framework whereby two or more Scrum teams are assembled (each team consisting of three–nine members each) who work on the same project and, together, make up one large Scrum team. Each Scrum team focuses on a portion of the project work and uses the standard Scrum practices of defining their own backlog, con-ducting a sprint planning meeting, working the sprint, performing reviews, and holding retrospectives. Typically, one team member from each Scrum team meets daily with rep-resentatives of other Scrum teams to discuss and coordinate progress, work on removing obstacles from the project, and discuss any future impediments that may impair the work of the collective team. This is a Scrum of Scrums and is similar to a daily standup. These meetings may not always occur daily but should occur at least two times per week. The goal is to optimize the team's efficiency and ensure there are no obstacles or impediments to prevent progress. It also ensures the Scrum team is coordinating the work across the individual teams.

Scaled Agile Framework (SAFe)

Scaled Agile Framework (SAFe) involves implementing agile practices at an organizational or an enterprise level. SAFe uses a single Scrum team, and they all share the same backlog, they collaborate with all team members, and the team is self-organized and self-managed. SAFe has several principles that are focused on using systems thinking, taking an economic view, decentralizing decision-making, tapping into the intrinsic motivation of workers, and more. SAFe has an interactive knowledge base consisting of technical guidance, knowledge, and information about agile. It also contains information about the organization.

Disciplined Agile (DA)

Disciplined Agile (DA) is a framework that combines several agile best practices to help the organization transform to agile methodologies. It's a tailoring approach that combines the best of the more popular agile methodologies to fit the organization's needs. It includes information from functional areas such as finance, HR, and the PMO to help you make decisions and organize around the goals of the organization. The guiding principles of DA all center on delighting the customer by meeting, or better yet, exceeding their expectations.

This section wraps up our discussion of agile frameworks. Next we'll take a look at the PRINCE2 approach to project management.

Projects in Control (PRINCE2)

As you learned in Chapter 4, "Planning the Project," PRINCE2 stands for PRojects IN Controlled Environments. This is a project management methodology that divides up projects into small stages that are logically organized. PRINCE2 is a predictive or waterfall approach to project management. When using this methodology, you will define a project plan early in the project that will be used to manage the project in stages, step-by-step, and to keep it in control throughout the project life cycle. PRINCE2 can be used for any size project in any industry.

The primary roles in the PRINCE2 methodology include the executive (like the project sponsor), project manager, team manager, and project board. The project manager's role is the same as we've discussed throughout this book. The team manager is responsible for managing the team performing the work of the project and ensuring work products are delivered on time. The project board consists of the project executive and representatives from the business units who will use the product of the project and those who can provide subject matter expertise.

PRINCE2 has seven guiding principles and its own set of processes or phases. We'll take a look at these next.

- Continually justifying the business need for the project throughout the project
- Learning from previous projects and learning from experience
- Defining roles and responsibilities for all team members and outlining expectations
- Managing the work of the project in stages
- Managing exceptions to scope, schedule, and budget by the project board
- Focusing on the quality of the deliverables and ensuring quality criteria is outlined and used to determine if the deliverables are satisfactory
- Tailoring the processes to the project

The phases or stages as they are known in the PRINCE2 methodology are similar to others we've discussed throughout this book. They include the following:

Start Up or Request Stage   This is where a brief overview of the project is presented to the board. A determination is made regarding the feasibility of the project. Once approved, a business case should be written.

Initiating   Initiating defines the goals of the project and documents the project plan. The project management plan must include scope, time, cost, risk, benefits, and quality plans. This is used to monitor the work of the project as it progresses.

Directing   The project board authorizes the project to begin and oversees the work of the project as it proceeds. The board also approves the initiation of the next stage of a project, makes decisions throughout the project life cycle, and authorizes project closure when the project is completed.

Controlling   During this phase work is assigned to the team, the work is checked for quality, and progress is reported to the project board. Issues are managed and changes are implemented when needed to keep the project on track.

Delivering   In this phase, the quality of the deliverables is reviewed and validated to ensure they meet expectations. The project board approves deliverables.

Stage Boundaries   The board reviews each stage of the project to ensure the project is adhering to the plan and is meeting quality standards. This stage provides for a go/no-go to proceed to the next stage. The project manager documents lessons learned in this stage, updates are made to the project management plan, and planning for the next phase begins. Stage boundaries are performed at the end of each stage before proceeding to the next.

Closing   This is achieved when all the objectives are met and stakeholders are satisfied. The project board will review the overall project and lessons learned, and the product of the project is turned over to the customer. Once the project manager performs closing activities, they will request that the board close the project.

⊕ **Real World Scenario**

Main Street Office Move

You've implemented a change control process and established a CCB. The first change request came from Jason in IT. After meetings with the cloud provider, he discovered that more storage space will be needed than originally planned. This resulted in a change request for $50,000 to cover the costs to configure the additional space and the first-year subscription fees. This will exceed the project budget. You decide to meet with Emma before the CCB meeting to describe the situation and determine whether there is enough contingency funding to cover this cost (should the change request be approved by the CCB) or whether there are available funds elsewhere in the organization to fund this change. You tell Emma that the cost to relocate the fleet cars and the total cost for furniture is coming in below projections, so these are areas that may help fund this change request.

Jason presents the change request at the next CCB, and it is approved. Emma also made funding available from the contingency reserve if the costs exceed the savings expected from the furniture purchase and fleet move.

Jason has also submitted operational change requests for the cutover to the cloud services provider. There will be extensive testing performed during and after the migration, and business users will need to test their data to ensure everything is in order. The IT team has been using the Scrum methodology and the iterations are going as planned. Some of the data interfaces will change once the migration is complete and the Scrum teams are working on the programming changes to make this happen. The IT team has developed rollback plans for the migration and will be working round the clock during the move weekend to ensure a smooth transition.

Other project activities are well underway, and some offices are packed and ready to go. Some fleet cars are already moved to the new garage. You have implemented daily standup meetings for the non-IT work of the project. You have participated in a few of the daily standups with the Scrum team and saw the benefit of identifying issues and discussing progress daily. During a recent standup, a few minor issues were brought up by the team. They were discussed and resolved almost immediately. If they had not been discussed at the standup, the issues could have caused problems or potential delays.

Summary

The Executing phase of the project entails performing the work required to produce the deliverables and continually monitoring the results to make certain they meet the specifications according to the project plan. Deviations from the project plan can be warnings that changes may be required or have already occurred.

Managing vendors involves monitoring their performance to ensure the requirements of the procurement agreement are met. The project manager will measure and monitor deliverables, enforce the rules of engagement, and verify the final approvals. Vendor reviews entail examining the contract terms and the seller performance for elements such as meeting requirements, quality standards, staying with budget, and meeting the project schedule. Use a contract change control system to process contract changes.

Changes come about for many reasons and may also take the form of corrective actions, preventive actions, and defect repairs. An integrated change control system manages change requests, determines the global impacts of a change, and updates all impacted portions of the project plan when a change is made. Typically, a change control board is established to review and either approve, deny, or defer change requests. Integrated change control looks at the overall impact of change and manages updates across all elements of the project plan. Scope change control includes understanding the impact of a scope change, taking appropriate action, and managing a process to review and approve or reject requests for scope changes. Product change management involves changes to the product of the project whereas project change management involves changes to the project processes.

Organizational changes can bring about impacts to your projects as well as the organization itself. Internal reorganizations, mergers and acquisitions, and outsourcing can all bring about changes to the project. Organizational change includes the following steps: define the change, communicate the change, analyze impacts, training, ensure adoption over time, communicate during and after the change, document the change, create new knowledge bases, and create new processes.

Operational change control concerns managing the change process for IT projects and tasks and involves hardware, software, and other IT related changes. IT infrastructure control involves managing changes to the elements of the IT environment. Software development and software changes are created using three environments, the development environment, beta-staging environment, and production.

Agile frameworks are standardized processes teams can use to manage the work of the project. Two of the most commonly used frameworks are Scrum and Kanban. Agile scaling frameworks are used for large projects. This involves using an agile approach and scaling it to the enterprise. Some examples include Scrum of Scrums, Scaled Agile Framework (SAFe), and Disciplined Agile (DA). PRINCE2 is a methodology consisting of seven guiding principles, and it has its own set of processes for managing a project.

Exam Essentials

Describe the project management plan. The project management plan is the final, approved, documented plan that's used in the Executing phase to measure project progress.

Be able to describe vendor performance reviews. They are conducted on a periodic basis to examine the seller's performance to date. Vendor reviews examine scope, quality, budget, schedule, and more. They can be performed using inspections or audits.

Describe the elements of a change control process.   The elements of a change control process include creating and submitting change requests, identifying and documenting the change, conducting a preliminary review, performing impact assessments, documenting change recommendations, determining decision-makers, escalating to the CCB, documenting changes in the change control log, updating the project plan, implementing the change, validating the change, and coordinating and communicating with stakeholders.

Explain the purpose of a CCB.   The change control board reviews, approves, denies, or delays change requests.

Be able to name the types of organizational change.   Organizational change involves transforming processes, systems, organizational structure, personnel, products, applications, and more. The types of organizational change include business merger, acquisition, demerger, split, business process change, internal reorganization, relocation, and outsourcing.

Describe the process steps for organizational change.   The steps define the change, communicate, analyze impacts and responses, training, ensuring adoption over time, communicating during and after the change, documenting the change, creating new knowledge bases, and creating new processes.

Be able to describe operational change control on IT projects.   This involves infrastructure control for managing elements of the IT environment, including hardware, software, and cloud updates.

Be able to describe the three environments on IT projects.   The three environments are development, beta-staging, and production. Development is where code is written, beta-staging is the testing environment, and production is where the live program or application resides.

Describe the agile scaling framework including three examples.   This involves taking agile methodologies and scaling them to the enterprise. Examples include Scrum of Scrums, SAFe, and Disciplined Agile.

Name the seven guiding principles of PRINCE2.   The seven guiding principles are justifying the business need for the project throughout the project life cycle, learning from experience, defining roles and responsibilities, managing work in stages, managing exceptions, focusing on quality, and tailoring the processes.

Key Terms

acquisition

arbitration

beta-staging environment

IT infrastructure control

merger

operational change

business process changes

change control board

change control systems

claims administration

contested changes

continuous integration

contract change control system

corrective actions

defect repairs

demerger

Disciplined Agile (DA)

impact assessments

organizational change

outsourcing

preventive actions

product change

regression plan

relocation

reorganization

reverse changes

rollback plan

Scaled Agile Framework (SAFe)

Scrum of Scrums

seller invoices

split

Review Questions

1. You are a project manager for a project developing a new software application. You have just learned that one of your programmers is adding several new features to one of the deliverables. What is the best action to take?

   A. Make any needed adjustments to the schedule and cost baseline and tell the programmer that any future changes must be approved by you.

   B. Request that the programmer remove the coding for the new features because they are outside the boundaries of the original scope statement.

   C. Contact the appropriate functional manager and request a replacement for this programmer.

   D. Determine the source of the request for the new features and put this change through the change control process to determine the impact of the changes and obtain formal approval to change the scope.

2. Which of the following is not a type of change?

   A. Corrective actions

   B. Defect repairs

   C. Performance corrections

   D. Preventive actions

3. This entity is responsible for reviewing change requests, reviewing the analysis of the impact of the change, and determining whether the change is approved, denied, or deferred.

   A. CTB

   B. CCB

   C. CRB

   D. TRB

4. Which of the following should be established as part of the change control system in the event the change control board cannot meet in a timely manner?

   A. Emergency change request procedures

   B. Procedures for analyzing the impacts of change and preestablished criteria for determining which changes can be implemented

   C. Process for documenting the change in the change request log

   D. Coordination and communication with stakeholders

5. After a change request is submitted, all of the following steps occur prior to being reviewed by the change control board except for which one?

   A. The change request is recorded in the change log.

   B. Analysis of the impacts of the change is performed.

   C. Specific elements of the project, such as additional equipment needs, resource hours, quality impacts, and more, are analyzed.

   D. Update the appropriate project management planning document to reflect the change.

6. Stakeholders have come to you to tell you they want to change the scope. Before agreeing to the change, what things should you do? (Choose two.)

    A. Determine which project constraint (time, budget, quality) is most important to stakeholders.

    B. Discuss the proposed scope change with the sponsor.

    C. Ask team members what they think about the scope change.

    D. Define alternatives and trade-offs that you can offer the stakeholders.

    E. Implement the change.

7. You have just received the latest status updates from the team. Based on the progress to date, system testing is projected to take three weeks longer than planned. If this happens, user acceptance testing will have to start three weeks late, and the project will not complete on the planned finish date. The customer scheduled the user acceptance testing participants weeks in advance. What is the best course of action?

    A. Explain to the test team that the system test must end on the scheduled date, and they are accountable for the accuracy of the testing results.

    B. Meet with the test team to determine the cause of the delay. If you determine that there are not enough testers to complete all of the scenarios in the time allotted, work with the sponsor to secure additional testers to complete the system test as planned.

    C. Submit the change request to the CCB and, if it's approved, baseline the schedule again.

    D. Escalate the issue of the system test delay to the sponsor and let them decide what action to take.

8. Your company is implementing a significant change in staffing. Some departments are being consolidated, others are being eliminated, and some new ones are being created. Which of the following are true regarding this change? (Choose two.)

    A. This is an operational change.

    B. You should have a rollback plan in place in case the changes do not go as planned and employees need time to adjust to the new structure.

    C. You should ensure adoption of the change over time.

    D. New knowledge bases should be created for information and frequently asked questions about the change.

    E. This is an infrastructure change.

9. Your project is in danger of being canceled because of an organizational change. Despite the protests of your executive manager, several of the department managers in your old company have been laid off and replaced by the new organization's management team. Which of the following options does this scenario describe?

    A. Your company has experienced a demerger from another organization.

    B. Your company has been merged with another organization.

    C. Your company has been acquired by another organization.

    D. Your company has split from another organization.

10. Your company has implemented a new ERP system. This is a type of change that might require all of the following except which one?

   A. Training

   B. Ensuring adoption over time

   C. Creating new processes

   D. Updating the project management plan

11. You are in the Executing phase of your project implementing a new CRMS. The business expert (one of the key stakeholders on the project) has requested a change to the workflow process in the system for customer escalations. All of the following are true regarding this change except for which one?

   A. The change should be documented and submitted in writing.

   B. This is a project management change.

   C. Analysis of the impacts of the change should be performed before going to the CCB.

   D. The change should be logged in the change control log.

12. What is the final, approved, documented plan that is used throughout the Executing phase to measure project progress and to help analyze change requests?

   A. Project management plan

   B. Schedule baseline

   C. Scope baseline

   D. Cost baseline

13. You are in the Executing phase of your project and are working with a vendor who is responsible for implementing configuration changes to your cloud-based system. You need to review their activities and determine if they are being performed correctly, according to the contract statement of work. Which two actions might you use to make this determination? (Choose two.)

   A. Inspections

   B. Preventive actions

   C. Corrective actions

   D. Audits

   E. Defect repairs

14. Your vendor is contesting a recent change request. They believe they implemented the change as requested; the project team believes the change is not functioning as required. Which of the following documents, monitors, and manages these types of contested changes?

   A. Contested change control

   B. Contract change control system

   C. Claims administration

   D. Compensation administration

15. You know that the project management plan consists of several project documents and, once approved, serves as the baseline for the project. All of the following are true regarding the project management plan except which one?

A. It's used during the Executing phase to determine whether the project is on track.

B. It's used during the procurement processes to negotiate with the vendor.

C. It is a communication tool.

D. It's used when changes are requested to determine whether the change is in keeping with the original goals and objectives of the project.

16. The project team is performing testing on some of the work of the project. The testing does not appear to be lining up with the project management plan. Which of the following is required to get the project back on track?

A. Defect repair

B. Integrated change

C. Preventive action

D. Corrective action

17. You have conducted several successful agile projects and the organization is interested in scaling agile principles for a large project that is set to kick off in a few months. The organization wants to tailor an approach that will be best for them, and your executive sponsor has emphasized the importance of incorporating human resources principles when tailoring the agile process. Which agile framework does this describe?

A. PRINCE2

B. Scrum of Scrums

C. SAFe

D. DA

18. This waterfall methodology divides projects into specific stages such as startup, directing, and delivery.

A. Scrum of Scrums

B. PRINCE2

C. DA

D. SAFe

19. You have recommended using an agile methodology for a project the organization is ready to move to the Executing phase. This is a large, complex project and will require more than one agile team. You decide to use a methodology whereby each agile team will consist of three to nine members, they will all work on the same project but will have their own backlog to work from, and you will hold a daily standup with all the teams whereby one representative from each team will join the collective standup meeting. What methodology is this describing?

A. DA

B. PRINCE2

C. Scrum of Scrums

D. SAFe

20. You have recommended using an agile methodology for a project the organization is ready to move to the Executing phase. This is a large, complex project and will require one, large agile team. You decide to use a methodology whereby all team members reside on the same team and work from the same backlog. Team members will collaborate with each other, and the team is self-organized and self-directed. What methodology is this describing?

A. Scrum of Scrums

B. SAFe

C. PRINCE2

D. DA

Chapter

10

Managing Quality and Closing Out the Project

THE COMPTIA PROJECT+ EXAM TOPICS COVERED IN THIS CHAPTER INCLUDE:

✓ **1.0 Project Management Concepts**

   ▪ 1.4 Given a scenario, perform risk management activities

   ▪ 1.5 Given a scenario, perform issue management activities

   ▪ 1.7 Compare and contrast quality management concepts and performance management concepts

✓ **2.0 Project Life Cycle Phases**

   ▪ 2.3 Given a scenario, perform activities during the project planning phase

   ▪ 2.5 Explain the importance of activities performed during the closing phase

✓ **3.0 Tools and Documentation**

   ▪ 3.1 Given a scenario, use the appropriate tools throughout the project life cycle

   ▪ 3.3 Given a scenario, analyze quality and performance charts to inform project decisions

We'll examine the last of the Executing phase activities in this chapter and end with the Closing phase. We'll start with quality control, which monitors the project deliverables against the project requirements and the quality baseline to ensure that the project is delivering according to plan. We'll discuss testing techniques in this section as well.

Next we'll look at how to perform issue management activities and how issues relate to other aspects of the project. We'll look at a refresher on KPIs and cost and schedule variances as they relate to project verification and validation.

Lastly, we'll look at closing out the project, including creating a release plan and post-implementation support and warranties.

Controlling Quality

Quality is one of the common constraints all projects share, but it doesn't always receive the same amount of focus as scope, budget, or time constraints. Lack of quality management can have as many adverse impacts to the project as ignoring controls for cost, budget, or schedules may have. Quality control is the process of reviewing project results and determining whether they comply with the standards documented in the quality management plan and making any appropriate changes to remove the causes of unacceptable quality when the standards are not met. The quality management plan discussed is the foundation for the specific activities used to perform quality control. The quality activities, the procedures used to complete the quality activities, and the resources required are documented in the quality management plan.

Quality control is performed throughout the project. As I've mentioned in earlier chapters, milestones are often included in the project schedule to mark the completion of a project phase or major deliverable. Quality control is used to determine compliance with a minimum standard so that the milestones and deliverables can be validated and accepted.

We'll look at some of the quality activities you can perform to measure quality next.

Inspecting and Testing

We talked about inspections in Chapter 9, "Processing Change Requests," in terms of verifying vendor deliverables. Inspection is also used for quality control purposes. *Inspection* is an activity that involves examining, measuring, or testing work results to determine whether they conform to the quality standards and quality plan. Inspection may occur at intervals throughout the project, at the end of a project phase, or when the work is completed. When inspection occurs at any point in the project, a decision is made whether to accept or reject the work. When the work is rejected, it may have to go back through the process for rework.

Some costs associated with inspection are rework, labor costs, material costs, and potential loss of customers.

Inspection may involve taking measurements or using metrics to compare results to the plan. When measurements fall within a specified range, they are called *tolerable results*. For example, the requirement might state that the measurements must be within plus or minus 2 inches. Any work result that falls within this range is tolerable and would be accepted. *Attribute sampling* is another inspection technique. This method determines whether the results are conforming or nonconforming to the requirements. Conforming results meet the requirements and are accepted; nonconforming results do not. This is also sometimes known as a *pass/fail* or *go/no-go* decision.

Whether you use inspection or attribute sampling for the project will depend on the type of project you're working on. Inspection can be costly and time-consuming. Perhaps your project involves producing a new product that requires the production of hundreds of parts. It wouldn't be cost effective to test each and every part, so instead you could perform inspection or attribute sampling on every *x* number of parts to determine conformity.

Inspection for information technology projects involves testing. *Testing* is used as a form of inspection to tell you where problems may exist within the code. Here are several types of testing that can occur on software projects:

Smoke Testing   *Smoke testing* is a high-level test designed to identify simple failures that could jeopardize the software program or prevent it from being released to production. These tests typically look at the most critical functions of the program and expose issues and problems early in the coding process.

Unit Testing   *Unit testing* is performed on individual modules or units of source code. Each unit of code is tested as they're written to verify they operate properly. On an agile project, the testing would occur within the iteration to confirm the code functions as planned.

Integration Testing   *Integration testing* involves combining software modules and testing them as a group. This may also involve testing programs or modules that need to interact with one another. An integration test typically occurs after unit testing is completed. The integration test will group modules together that have been unit-tested previously and perform a series of tests to determine whether the modules are delivering the right results.

End-to-End Testing   *End-to-end testing* is a system-level test that is just as it sounds. This test involves using the software from start to end (and everything in between) to ensure the application is working correctly. This may include actions such as logging in, performing the functions for each of the roles and responsibilities in the program, and following all the impacts through to ensure they deliver the expected features or functionality. This test typically occurs after integration testing, and after all the code is written.

Regression Testing   *Regression testing* is performed after changes are made to the code, when software configurations are modified, or after maintenance activities are performed on the hardware the code resides on. Regression testing ensures that the software works the same way it did prior to the change or maintenance activity. Regression tests help to maintain product quality and ensure agile teams can maintain cadence in producing deliverables.

Stress Testing   *Stress testing* involves testing software for dependability and stability under heavy load conditions, typically more than the system will ever experience in production. This testing examines processing and error handling capabilities to ensure the system performs well and doesn't shut down or crash under these conditions.

Performance Testing   *Performance testing* is like stress testing in that the software is tested under different load scenarios. This testing examines how the software performs and is not intended to find defects in the code. It may uncover issues related to bottlenecks, slow responses, slow loading times, poor usage of memory, improper software configuration settings that cause performance to drag, and more.

User Acceptance Testing   *User acceptance testing (UAT)* testing is performed by the people who will be the end users of the system, along with other subject matter experts. They test features, functionality, calculations, and so on, to assure the system meets the requirements laid out in the scope statement.

Prevention is different from inspection. Inspection occurs after the work is complete (or at certain points during the process). Prevention keeps errors from occurring in the first place. It always costs less to prevent problems than to find them later and have to fix them.

Inspection tells you where problems exist and gives you the opportunity to correct them, but there's generally a cost associated with the fix. Prevention keeps mistakes from occurring or reaching the customer, and it's usually less costly, less time-consuming, and more efficient to correct errors before they reach the customer.

Using Quality Charts

Performance charts are used in quality control to measure and verify quality and to help inform project decisions. We'll look at several examples next. Don't forget you can also use these charts along with inspection and attribute sampling.

Histogram   A *histogram* displays the frequency distributions of variable data. It looks like a bar chart, and it's easy to create and understand. The data might include temperature, length, time, mileage, weight, distance, and so on. For example, let's say you are measuring the chemical levels of a certain segment on the production line. Your team takes measurements six times per day for 10 days. The ideal range is 2 to 4 parts per million. The histogram in Figure 10.1 shows the frequency of measurements and their distribution.

FIGURE 10.1   Histogram chart

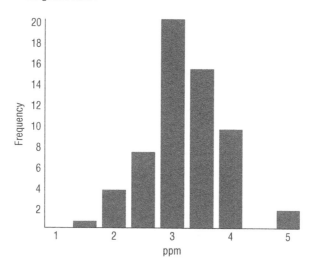

Pareto Diagram   A *Pareto diagram* is used to rank the importance of a problem based on its frequency of occurrence over time. This diagram is based on the Pareto principle, which is more commonly referred to as the *80/20 rule*. The Pareto principle is named after Vilfredo Pareto, an Italian sociologist and economist, who observed that 80 percent of the wealth in Italy was held by 20 percent of the population. This principle has been applied to many disciplines since Pareto first discovered it. Applying the principle to quality control means that the majority of the project defects are caused by a small set of problems. A Pareto diagram helps isolate what the major problems are so that you can take actions that will have the greatest impact. A bar graph is used to display problems in decreasing order of occurrence so that priorities for improvement can be established.

The purpose of a Pareto diagram is twofold:

- It displays the relative importance of the defects.

- It directs the improvement efforts to those areas that will have the biggest impact.

Let's take a look at how this works. A Pareto diagram typically starts with a table that lists information regarding the frequency of the defects or failures uncovered during testing. Table 10.1 shows the frequency of failure for items A–E, the number of occurrences, the percent of defects that this item represents, and a cumulative percent.

TABLE 10.1 Frequency of failures

Item	Defect frequency	Percent of defects	Cumulative percent
A	800	.33	.33
B	700	.29	.62
C	400	.17	.79
D	300	.13	.92
E	200	.08	1.0

With this data in hand, you can create a Pareto diagram, as shown in Figure 10.2. The bars are ordered from left to right based on frequency. The bars depict the defect numbers, and the cumulative percentages are plotted using the circles. By looking at the data in Figure 10.2, you can see that the most significant problems you want to focus on are A and B. Fixing these two items will resolve more than half the defects.

FIGURE 10.2 Pareto diagram

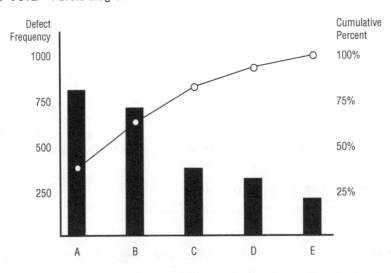

Control Charts   A *control chart* measures and displays the variance of several samples of the same process over time. It is most commonly used in manufacturing. A control chart is based on a mean, an upper control limit, and a lower control limit. The upper control limit is the point beyond which preventing additional defects becomes cost prohibitive. The lower level is the limit at which the customer or end user will reject the product because of the defects. The goal is to stay in the middle area (the mean), where the best product for the lowest cost is obtained. Figure 10.3 shows an example of a control chart.

FIGURE 10.3   Control chart

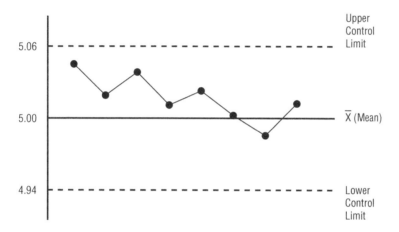

Statistical Sampling   If you have numerous work results that require inspection or testing, you may decide to use *statistical sampling*, where you gather a subset of all the applicable work results and randomly select a small number for testing or examination. The results for this subset represent the whole. Statistical sampling can be very cost effective, especially in projects where multiple versions of the same product are produced.

Flowcharting   *Flowcharts* are diagrams that show the logical steps that must be performed in order to accomplish an objective. They can also show how the individual elements of a system interrelate. Flowcharting can be an effective tool during quality control to help determine how the problem occurred.

Run Charts   *Run charts* are used to show variations in the process over time or to show trends (such as improvements or the lack of improvements) in the process. They are similar to control charts in that they plot the result of a process over time, although a run chart does not depict acceptable limits. Differences in results will occur because there is no such thing as a perfect process. When processes are considered in control, differences in results might occur because of common causes of variances. You can observe positive (or negative) change with a run chart as well. For example, let's say your organization is releasing a new product. They might plot the dollar amount of sales of the new product over a time period. Figure 10.4 shows a sample of this data.

FIGURE 10.4 Run chart

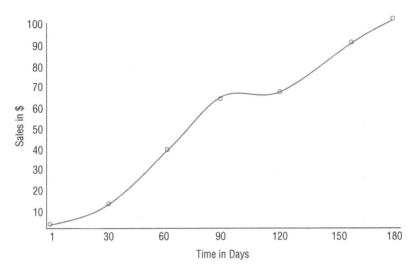

Ishikawa Diagram   An Ishikawa diagram is also known as a *cause-and-effect diagram*, which shows the relationship between the effects of problems and their causes. This diagram depicts every potential cause and subcause of a problem and the effect that each proposed solution will have on the problem. This diagram is also called a *fishbone diagram*, and it's named after its developer, Kaoru Ishikawa. Figure 10.5 shows a sample cause-and-effect diagram.

FIGURE 10.5   Fishbone diagram

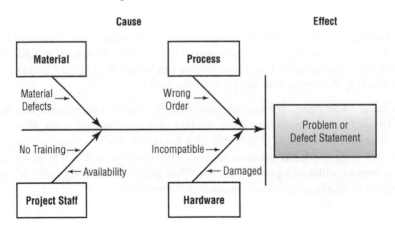

Decision Tree   *Decision trees* are diagrams that show the sequence of interrelated decisions and the expected results of choosing one alternative over the other. Typically, more than one choice or option is available when you're faced with a decision or, in this case, potential outcomes from a risk event. The available choices are depicted in tree form starting at the left, with the risk decision branching out to the right with possible outcomes. Decision trees are often used for risk events associated with time or cost.

Figure 10.6 shows a sample decision tree using expected monetary value (EMV) of a risk event as one of its inputs.

FIGURE 10.6   Decision tree

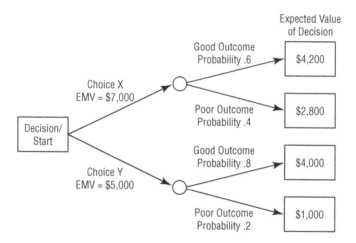

The EMV of the decision is a result of the probability of the risk event multiplied by the impact for two or more potential outcomes and then summing their results. The squares in this figure represent decisions to be made, and the circles represent the points where risk events might occur.

The decision with an expected value of $7,000 is the correct decision to make because the resulting outcome has the greatest value.

Scatter Diagram   A *scatter diagram* plots two numerical variables on a chart to determine whether there is a correlation between them. Scatter diagrams, also known as correlation charts, display the relationship between these two elements as points on a graph. The closer these variables are to each other, the closer the variables are related. This relationship is typically analyzed to prove or disprove cause-and-effect relationships. As an example, maybe your scatter diagram plots the ability of your employees to perform a certain task. The length of time (in months) they have performed this task is plotted as the independent variable on the x-axis, and the accuracy they achieve in performing this task, which is expressed as a score—the dependent variable—is plotted on the y-axis. The scatter diagram can help you determine whether cause-and-effect (in this case, increased experience over time versus accuracy) can be proved. Scatter diagrams can also help you look for and analyze root causes of problems. Figure 10.7 shows a sample scatter diagram.

FIGURE 10.7 Scatter diagram

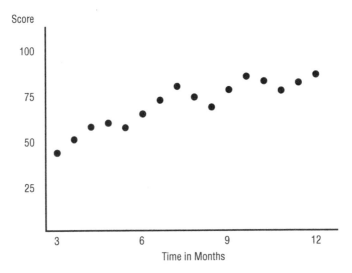

Common Causes of Variances

Variance measurements are a common theme when it comes to quality control. *Common causes of variances* come about as a result of circumstances that are relatively common to the process you're using and are easily controlled at the operational level. Three types of variances make up the common causes of variances that you should be familiar with.

Random Variances   Random variances might be normal, depending on the processes you're using to produce the product or service of the project, but they occur as the name implies—at random.

Known or Predictable Variances   Known or predictable variances are variances that you know exist in the process because of particular characteristics of the product, service, or result you are processing. These are generally unique to a particular application.

Variances That Are Always Present in the Process   The process itself will have inherent variability that may be caused by human mistakes, machine variations or malfunctions, the environment, and other factors, which are known as variances always present in the process. These variances generally exist across all applications of the process.

Common cause variances that do not fall within the acceptable range are difficult to correct and usually require a reorganization of the process. This has the potential for significant impact, and decisions to change the process always require management approval.

Once the results you obtain from testing or other quality techniques are completed, you'll use them to determine whether any action should be taken to correct poor quality. We'll look at the actions needed to correct poor quality next.

Taking Action on Quality Control

As you measure quality activities, you need to make decisions on the appropriate course of action based on the results received. Any action taken to resolve quality problems has trade-offs, so you will need to involve other stakeholders in the decision process. The most common actions taken because of quality activities are rework, process adjustments, and acceptance.

Rework

Rework is action that is taken to correct a defect that was discovered while performing quality control. Rework is as it sounds—performing work already completed in order to correct an error.

Rework sounds like the ideal solution to any quality problem that is found. If you discover a problem, you should fix it, right? In an ideal world with no time and budget constraints, that would be true, but rework often impacts both the project schedule and the budget. The time to complete the deliverable will be longer than estimated because of the time it takes to fix the problem, and the people doing the rework will be billing additional hours to your project.

A decision on rework is often tied to the severity of the defect and its impact on the ability of the end user to use the product. Your client, sponsor, and other impacted stakeholders need to be involved in rework decisions.

Process Adjustments

Changing a process can have a ripple effect throughout the rest of the project. Unless it is very clear that a process change is contained to a small work group or a few team members with no downstream effects, it is best to use the change control process to analyze the impacts of a process change and obtain formal approval before making any changes.

Acceptance

Acceptance is the decision to agree to any defects that are found as a result of quality testing. Acceptance is a common action based on the analysis of the severity and frequency of the defects uncovered during testing. For example, some commercially available software products are released for sale to the public with known defects that will be fixed with an upgrade later. Meeting the publicized release date for the product is more important than fixing defects; in other words, the schedule takes priority over quality. The overall impact of accepting a defect should be analyzed and communicated to project stakeholders. You should obtain stakeholder sign-off to accept defects.

Quality control takes different forms depending on the industry you're working in, the type of project, and whether the end goal of the project is a tangible product, a service, or a result of some other type. Quality is often impacted by one of the triple constraints (budget, schedule, scope), so careful attention should be paid to these processes throughout the course of any project.

Managing Issues

Issues are items that occur that could impact the project or delay or prevent the completion of deliverables. Issue management involves monitoring and managing issues to prevent, reduce, or mitigate adverse effects to the project. There is a strong tie between issues, risks, and changes. Risks are potential future events that are analyzed to determine their probability of occurring and the impact to the project if they happen. Once a risk event manifests, it becomes an issue and should be managed as such. Changes may cause issues, and issues can bring about changes to the project. No matter how or why the issues come up, they should be assigned to owners and logged in the issue log, and resolutions plans should be developed and executed to mitigate their impacts. We'll examine the steps involved in managing issues next.

Remember that a risk is a *potential future event* that can bring about positive or negative consequences to the project. An issue is something that has already occurred. Once a negative risk occurs, it becomes an issue and should be recorded in the issue log.

Roles and Responsibilities

Issues, like risks, should be assigned to an issue owner. It is the owner's responsibility to monitor the issue, implement the resolution plan, report on the issue and its impacts, and document relevant information about the issue and its resolution.

An escalation path should be established so that the appropriate stakeholders are notified about the issue. Escalation could be based on dollar impacts, scope, schedule, or other elements the project team or sponsor has developed.

Issue Tracking

Issues should be captured in an *issue log*. Common elements in an issue log are as follows:

- Identification number for tracking
- Date the issue was recorded

- Description of the issue
- Name of the person who reported the issue
- Name of the person who owns the issue and will follow through to resolution
- Priority ranking
- Urgency
- Resolution plan
- Status of the issue
- Resolution date

Be aware that an issue log that is not carefully managed can turn into an unwieldy monster, with new issues added weekly and nothing getting resolved. As you review the issue log with the project team, you want to ensure the person who has been assigned to resolve the issue is working toward closure. Sometimes project issues will remain open for weeks or even months, especially if you consider "we are still working on this one" an acceptable progress report. The status should always include both a plan for resolution and a target date to resolve the issue. If no progress is made, perhaps the responsible party needs assistance or does not really understand the issue. It may also require escalation to the sponsor to obtain help in overcoming roadblocks.

Although the goal is to assign all issues and resolve them as quickly as possible, in some instances you need to prioritize issues and have them worked on in priority order. If multiple issues require the same team member or group, review the impact of each issue to the project and establish a priority list.

Resolution Plan

The resolution plan describes the actions to take to mitigate the impacts of the issue. The resolution plan is based on several factors, according to the CompTIA exam objectives. First is the prioritization of the issue, which is recorded in the issue log. Determining the priority involves several factors:

- Issue severity
- Impact to the project
- Urgency of the issue
- Scope of the impact to the organization
- Issue escalation

Issue severity can be determined using the same techniques we talked about for risk analysis. Routine projects may use a simple scale such as *high-medium-low* or may involve quantitative techniques. Root cause analysis is especially useful in determining the severity of the impact to the project. You'll recall that root cause analysis involves looking for the reasons or causes that brought about the issue and then eliminating or reducing them. It's not uncommon to examine symptoms of the issue (or risk) rather than looking at the deep-level, root cause. For example, you start sneezing, one after another, and realize you need to take some action to stop the sneezing. However, sneezing is the symptom. You need to understand the underlying cause of the sneezing so that you can take the right actions to stop it. This is the same for issues. Go deeper than the symptoms to determine the root cause and deal with it, rather than the symptoms.

Urgency will help determine the actions to take to resolve the issue and how quickly you need to implement the plan. As you examine the root cause of the issue, urgency is usually straightforward. For example, if you discover a flood in the server room, it should be addressed immediately by shutting off the water until you can find out where the water is coming from and fix the issue.

The scope of the impact to the organization will also help determine the urgency and actions needed to mitigate the issue. If the scope of the impact is minor in nature, such as a 3 percent impact to the budget, the action plan will be different than it will for an issue that causes a 10 percent impact to the budget. You as the project manager should spend some time early in the project determining the criteria for urgency, impacts to the organization, and escalation of issues. We talked about escalation a little earlier in this chapter. Make certain to work with the sponsor and key stakeholders to determine these criteria and document them in an issue management plan.

Resolution Techniques

Issue resolution can involve some of the same techniques we discussed for risks such as exploit, transfer, avoid, and accept. Don't forget that contingency budgets come in handy for issues as well. The project manager may execute contingency funds, or if the issue is larger than the project manager's authority, you'll need to have the sponsor execute management reserves.

Work-arounds are another issue resolution technique whereby you go around the issue itself and take some action to address it, at least for now. Work-arounds are often temporary fixes or may only partially resolve the issue, but they can be used to hold off significant impacts until the team has time to examine the root cause and implement a permanent fix.

Outcome Documentation

After the issue is resolved, the issue owner needs to document the outcomes. They should document the actions taken to resolve the problem; describe whether the issue was resolved; list what impacts occurred as a result of the resolution, if any; document whether changes were required because of the issue; list cost and schedule impacts; and so on.

Action Items

Action items are not the same as issues, but they are often lumped together. *Action items* are tasks that come about, usually at a project status meeting, that require follow-up or resolution. They are typically about the project but don't have a direct impact on the work of the project. For example, a stakeholder may ask how much money was spent on the previous work order with the project vendor. This action item is recorded on the action item log, and its results are reported at the next status meeting. Action items can take many forms, such as requests for additional information, to prepare a briefing on a specific topic, to contact someone in the procurement department about an upcoming bid, and so on.

Action items are also captured in a log and reported on at the project status meeting. Action item logs include the following elements:

- Identification number

- Date the action was recorded

- Action item description

- Action item owner

- Progress or resolution to the action item

- Closed date

Using Performance Measures

The Executing phase focuses on performing the work of the project and monitoring and measuring project performance to identify variances from the project management plan. During this phase, you will collect project data, analyze it, and report on it. The data you'll report on might include information concerning project quality, costs, scope, project schedules, procurement, and risk, and it can be presented in the form of status reports, progress measurements such as key performance indicators, or forecasts.

The project management plan contains the project management baseline data (typically cost, schedule, and scope baselines), which you'll use to monitor and compare performance measurements against. Typically, you'll establish performance metrics when developing the plan and then measure them once the work of the project has started. Performance metrics and any deviations from the project management plan should be reported to the stakeholders at the project status meetings.

Key Performance Indicators

I introduced key performance indicators (KPIs) in Chapter 4, "Planning the Project." You'll recall that a KPI is a measurable value that shows whether the project is reaching its intended goals. KPIs are a performance metric that's used extensively in the Executing phase.

KPIs should be measurable and applicable to the project. For example, perhaps you have KPIs regarding project costs, project management processes, vendor performance, and so on. Almost any element of the project you want to measure can become a KPI. Here are some more specific examples:

- Project costs must not exceed more than 5% of the budgeted cost baseline.

- Quality standards will meet or exceed industry standards by no more than +/–.03 standard deviations.

- Increase the number of page visits to the new website by 10% over 6 months.

- Increase shared links on social media sites by 15% over the next 12 months.

- Increase the number of bookings using self-service check-in to 70% over the next two years.

 The important thing to note is that KPIs must be measurable, and they should be communicated to the project team and stakeholders.

If you see that KPIs are not being met or you are finding issues and risks escalating out of control, you need to communicate with your project sponsor. No one likes bad news, but you'll be much better off if you present the facts as soon as you know them. Too many project managers try to ignore problems and hope that the project will turn around eventually—that rarely happens. If you're in doubt, talk with your project sponsor so that they can intervene and help before it's too late.

 **Real World Scenario**

A Phased Delay

A fellow project manager I know had an early project experience that involved a new system application that was being developed for customer care representatives from two recently merged companies. Although the requirements and all of the major deliverables referenced one system, each company had separate back-end systems that needed to interface with the new customer care system. Unfortunately, this piece of information was not discovered until the work of the project started. So, the development team had twice the application interface work to do than was originally planned.

Everyone on the team knew there was no way that the project would be completed as scheduled. The development team provided a revised estimate that showed project completion six months later than the original schedule. Both the development manager and the project manager were afraid to go to the sponsor with this news, so they reported at the next project status meeting there would be a two-week delay and hoped for a miracle. Unfortunately, a miracle didn't occur, so they reported there would be another two-week delay. At this point, the sponsor started asking a lot of questions, and the project manager had to admit that the best estimates of the additional work indicated a six-month delay. The sponsor was furious that she had not been told the truth from the beginning, and it ruined the credibility of the project manager. In fact, a new project manager was named shortly after this incident.

Balanced Scorecard

A *balanced scorecard* is a performance management tool used to measure the activities and processes a business uses to meet its strategic goals. It's a way to determine whether the performance of the organization is measuring up to its goals. The balanced scorecard measures elements such as financial goals, business processes, innovation, the customer experience, and customer satisfaction. Typically, the balanced scorecard methodology focuses on strategic areas of the business and monitors a small number of important data elements. Balanced scorecard measures are usually communicated throughout the organization and, in my experience, are also tied to individual performance reviews. Comparing the project results to the balanced scorecard will help determine whether the project is on track to fulfill the organization's strategic goals. You'll recall from all the way back in the early chapters of this book that all projects should tie to the organization's strategic goals, and if they don't, they shouldn't be taken on.

Key Objectives and Results

Key objectives and key results are another performance metric you can use to determine whether the project is on track. Objectives, like goals, should be specific, measurable, attainable, realistic, and time bound. These elements are recorded in the project management plan, and as the objectives are met, you can measure them against the criteria to determine if they are satisfactory.

The requirements traceability matrix can help with these measures as well. You'll recall that the matrix documents the requirements, their expected outcomes, and how the requirements (or results) will be tested. Testing, performance measurements, examining, inspecting, and auditing are all valid techniques to determine whether key objectives and results are satisfactory.

Cost and Schedule Performance

Cost and schedule performance measures are used to determine whether the project is adhering to the budget and the schedule. We discussed cost and schedule variance techniques in Chapter 7, "Defining the Project Budget and Risk Plans."

As a refresher, cost variance tells you whether your costs are higher than budgeted (with a resulting negative number) or lower than budgeted (with a resulting positive number). It measures the actual performance to date against what's been spent.

Schedule variance compares an activity's actual progress to date to the estimated progress and is represented in terms of cost. It tells you whether the schedule is ahead of or behind what was planned for this period. This formula is most helpful when you've used the critical path methodology to build the project schedule.

Cost performance index measures the value of the work completed at the measurement date against the actual cost. It is the most critical of all the earned value measurements because it tells you the cost efficiency for the work completed to date or at the completion of the project.

Schedule performance index measures the progress to date against the progress that was planned. This formula should be used in conjunction with an analysis of the critical path activities to determine whether the project will finish ahead of or behind schedule.

Project Endings

You've finally made it to the end of the project. The Closing process is the last phase of the project management life cycle, and it's the most often overlooked. However, there are a few key activities you'll want to complete in the Closing phase. Before diving into those activities, let's look at the characteristics of closing and the reasons projects come to an end.

Characteristics of Closing

A few characteristics are common to all projects during the Closing phase. You've already completed the majority of the work of the project—if not all of the work—so the probability of not finishing the project is low. Risk is also low in this phase because the work is completed. There's little chance that a risk would occur at the end that would derail the project. Stakeholders have the least amount of influence during the Closing processes, whereas project managers have the greatest amount of influence. Costs are significantly lower during this phase because the majority of the project work and spending has already occurred.

All projects eventually come to an end, and there are several types of project endings I'll cover next.

Types of Project Endings

We all usually think of a project coming to an end when all the deliverables are completed. Ideally, this is what you'll experience most of the time. There are several reasons that a project might end, including but not limited to these:

- They are completed successfully.
- They evolve into ongoing operations and no longer exist as projects.
- Their budgets are slashed.
- The project resources are redirected to other activities or projects.
- The customer goes out of business or is merged with another entity.
- They are canceled prior to completion.

I've worked on many projects that ended in cancellation. This can occur for any number of reasons: project sponsors move on to other assignments, budgets are cut, new management comes into power and changes direction, vendors don't perform as anticipated, and many more. The important thing to remember about cancellation is that all the steps of project closeout should be performed when a project is canceled so that the records are archived and the reasons for cancellation are documented.

All the reasons for project endings I just listed, including cancellation, are incorporated into four formal types of project endings:

- Addition
- Starvation
- Integration
- Extinction

Addition

Projects that evolve into ongoing operations are considered projects that end because of *addition*; in other words, they become their own ongoing business unit or the product or result of the project transitions into an existing business unit before the project is completed.

Starvation

When resources are cut off from the project or are no longer provided to the project, it's starved prior to completing all the requirements, and you're left with an unfinished project on your hands. *Starvation* can happen for any number of reasons:

- Resources are diverted to other projects, leaving you with no funds or human capital to complete the current project.
- The customer reduces or cancels an order.
- The project budget is reduced.
- A key resource quits.

Resource starving can include cutting back or withholding human resources, equipment and supplies, or money. In any case, if you're not getting the people, equipment, or money you need to complete the project, it's going to starve and probably end abruptly.

Integration

Integration occurs when the resources of the project—people, equipment, and supplies—are distributed to other areas in the organization or are assigned to other projects. Starvation withholds or cuts back on resources, whereas integration redirects resources to other projects or other areas of the business.

The difference between starvation and integration is that starvation is the result of staffing, funding, or other resource cuts, whereas integration is the result of reassignment or redeployment of the resources.

Extinction

This is the best kind of project end because *extinction* means the project has been completed and accepted by the stakeholders. As such, it no longer exists because it had a definite end date, the goals of the project were achieved, and the project was closed out.

> Sometimes, closing out a project is like finishing a great book. You just don't want it to end. The team is working at peak performance, deliverables are checked off at record pace, and camaraderie is high. If you practice good project management techniques and keep the communication channels open, many of your projects can fall into this category.

Now that you've determined the reason for your project ending, it's time to examine the steps in project closeout and obtain formal written acceptance of the project.

Steps in Closing Out a Project

Project closeout involves accepting the final product or service of the project and then turning it over to the organization. Closing out a project involves several steps:

- Verification and validation of deliverables
- Obtaining formal sign-off
- Developing a transition plan and operational handoff
- Removing access
- Releasing project resources
- Closing out contracts
- Archiving documentation
- Conducting lessons learned and project evaluation
- Project closure meeting
- Project closeout report
- Rewards and celebration
- Postimplementation support and warranty period

We'll look at each of these steps next.

Verification and Validation of Deliverables

Verification and validation of deliverables occurs as the deliverables are completed and again at the end of the project. The verification process ensures the deliverables meet the requirements of the project. Verification and validation can be performed by using testing, inspection, performance measures, and more. If you are working with a vendor, make certain the contract spells out how validation and verification of the deliverables will occur.

Obtaining Sign-Off

Obtaining formal written sign-off and acceptance of the project is the primary focus of the Closing phase.

Documenting formal acceptance is important because it signals the official closure of the project, and it is your proof that the project was completed satisfactorily. Formal acceptance includes distributing notice of the acceptance of the project results to the stakeholders. Ideally, obtaining sign-off should be a formality. If you've involved the sponsor and stakeholders in the verification and validation of the deliverables during the Executing phase, it should be easy to obtain sign-off on the project because they have been informed all along and approved deliverables as they were completed. It's always good practice to perform a final verification of the project as a whole once all the deliverables are complete.

The sponsor is the person who has the authority to end the project and/or accept the final outcome of the project. In cases where you are working on a project that involves an external customer, the sponsor typically is the customer.

Developing a Transition Plan and Operational Handoff

A transition plan consists of several elements, including user documentation for the product, operational training plans, go-live dates, special skills needed to operate or use the product, maintenance items and costs for the future, ongoing licensing costs, warranty periods, and other important information the new owner must know to care for (or use) the product of the project.

After delivering the documentation to the new owner, set up a meeting—or a series of meetings, depending on the complexity of the project—with the department or people who will be responsible for the ongoing upkeep of the product you're turning over so that you can answer questions and gain assurance they understand the product.

Training is an important component of transition. Structure the training for the system or product so that it occurs closer to the go-live, or handoff date. I've seen failed training programs many times because they happen too early in the project. People receive training and think they understand, only to find months later once the system is implemented that they need training again because too much time has gone by between training and using the system. Ongoing training should be included when appropriate in the transition plan as well. Once end users become familiar with the basic functions of a software system, for example, they will need to learn more complex functions until they master the system. Ongoing training can provide the appropriate training at the right intervals of time to allow them to grow and learn.

Operational handoffs occur by physically delivering the product of the project to the department or personnel who will be using the product. In the case of software systems, moving the system into production is an operational handoff that allows end users to begin using the system.

Keep your audience in mind when writing the transition plan, training, and associated documentation. Internal and external audiences will have different needs and require different levels of detail.

Removing Access

Throughout this book, we've discussed different levels of security and how to ensure only those who need to know have access to information. Once the project is complete, it's time to review and then remove or revoke access for project team members who no longer have a need to know.

Releasing Team Members

Releasing team members or other resources may occur once or several times throughout the project. Projects that are divided into phases will likely release team members at the end of each phase. Other times, team members are brought on for one specific activity and are released when that activity is completed. No matter when the team members are released, you'll want to keep the functional managers or other project managers informed as you get closer to project completion so that they have time to adequately plan for the return of their employees. This gives the other managers the ability to start planning activities and scheduling activity dates for their employee.

Team members may become anxious about their status on the project, especially if they see people rolling off at different times. Make certain to explain to all team members that as various deliverables are completed, project staff who have completed their assignments are released. This is a normal ebb and flow on a project. Provide your team members with as much information as you can on anticipated release dates, so they are prepared a few weeks ahead of time. This will help to decrease anxiety and give them the opportunity to reengage with their functional manager on upcoming assignments.

Be sure to perform a final performance appraisal when releasing team members from the project. If you work in a functional organization, you should coordinate this with the employee's functional manager and make certain your review is included as part of their final, annual review.

Closing Out the Contract

Closing out the contract is the process of completing and settling the terms of the contract and documenting acceptance. This process determines whether the work described in the procurement documentation or contract was completed accurately and satisfactorily.

Procurement documents might have specific terms or conditions for completion and closeout. You should be aware of these terms or conditions so that project closure isn't held up because you missed an important detail. If you are not administering the procurement yourself, be certain to ask your procurement department whether there are any special conditions that you should know about so that your project team doesn't inadvertently delay contract or project closure.

The procurement department needs to provide the vendor with formal written notice that the deliverables have been accepted and the contract has been completed. This letter will be based on your approval of the work.

You should retain a copy of the completed contracts to include in the project archives, which I'll discuss next.

Archiving Documentation

Archiving documentation is where project records and documents are collected and archived, including the project-planning documents, change logs, issue logs, schedule baseline, budget, lessons learned, and more. You'll also collect and archive documentation showing that the project is completed and that the transfer of the product of the project to the organization (or department responsible for ongoing maintenance and support) has occurred.

You'll need to perform a final reconciliation of the project budget before archiving this document. You must ensure that the budget accounts are closed out and that all the funds are either dispersed or released back to the organization.

You have created a lot of documents over the course of your project, particularly in the Planning phase. The purpose for archiving those documents is twofold. First, it's to show you have completed the work of the project and that you can produce sign-offs, and other legal documents, should the need arise. The second primary benefit of archiving the project documentation is that it can be used to help you or other project managers on future projects. Your planning documents can be a reference for cost and time estimates or used as templates for planning similar projects in the future.

Check with your project management office (PMO) to determine whether they have a centralized project archive such as an intranet site or wiki pages for the project documents. They will tell you what the guidelines are for documentation and how to file, organize, and store it.

If you don't have a PMO, you'll need to create your own archiving solution. Check with your organization regarding standards compliance and document retention policies. For example, the organization may require all documents to be numbered or named in a certain fashion. Part of your archiving process will include the retention period. Your organization may have guidelines regarding when certain types of documents can be destroyed or what information must be retained. There are also laws regarding retaining some types of documents, so make certain you are familiar with them when creating your archiving site.

Documenting Lessons Learned and Project Evaluation

A *lessons learned* review session should be conducted at the conclusion of the project or shortly before. The size and complexity of the project will help you decide whether you need to hold one or more review meetings. You'll want to include all key project team members, the project sponsor, and the key stakeholders at a minimum.

The purpose for this review is to obtain feedback from the stakeholders and project team members to assess the good and the not-so-good aspects of the project. During this meeting, you'll evaluate each phase of the project to determine the things that went right and the things that could be improved. You should also conduct an overall evaluation of the project during this session.

Lessons learned describe the successes and failures of the project. As an example, lessons learned document the reasons why specific corrective actions were taken, their outcomes, the causes of performance variances, unplanned risks that occurred, mistakes that were made and could have been avoided, processes that worked exceptionally well, and so on.

Documenting lessons learned gives you the opportunity to improve the overall quality of your project management processes on the next project and benefits projects currently underway.

Lessons learned help you assess what went wrong and why, not so you can point fingers but to improve performance on the next project by avoiding the pitfalls you encountered on this one. It also helps you determine what went right so that you can repeat these processes on the next project. Lessons learned review involves analyzing the strengths and weaknesses of the project management process, the project team, and, if you dare, the project manager's performance.

Unfortunately, sometimes projects do fail. You can learn lessons from failed projects as well as from successful projects, and you should document this information for future reference. Most project managers, however, do not document lessons learned. The reason for this is that employees don't want to admit to making mistakes or learning from mistakes made during the project. And they do not want their name associated with failed projects or even with mishaps on successful projects.

You and your management team will have to work to create an atmosphere of trust and assurance that lessons learned are not reasons for punishing employees but are learning opportunities that benefit all those associated with the project. Lessons learned allow you to carry knowledge gained on this project to other projects you'll work on going forward. They'll also prevent repeat mistakes in the future if you take the time to review the project documents and lessons learned prior to undertaking your new project.

Lessons learned can be the most valuable information you'll take away from a project. We can all learn from our experiences, and what better way to have even more success on your next project than to review a similar past project's lessons learned document? But lessons learned will be there only if you document them now.

The following is a partial list of the areas you should review in the lesson learned session. This is by no means a complete list but should give you a good starting point. You should document everything you learn in these sessions. Lessons learned are included with all the other project documentation and go into the project archive when completed.

- Review each process phase (Discovery/Concept, Initiating, Planning, Executing, and Closing).
- Review the performance of the project team.
- Examine vendor performance.
- Examine sponsor and key stakeholder involvement.
- Review the effectiveness of the risk response plans.
- Document risks that occurred that were not identified during the project.
- Evaluate the estimating techniques used for costs and resources.
- Evaluate the project budget versus actual performance.
- Review the schedule performance, critical path, and schedule control.
- Review the effectiveness of the change management process.

 **Real World Scenario**

Involving Project Team Members in Lessons Learned

Although you can evaluate the various components of the project on your own using the project management plan and the project results, to get a more comprehensive lessons learned review, you should involve the stakeholders and the team members.

One way to organize a project review session is to make the session interactive. Let the participants know in advance which aspects of the project the review will focus on and ask them to be prepared to contribute input on both what went well and what did not. You could also distribute some questions ahead of the meeting for them to consider. One question you'll always want to ask is, "If you could change one thing about this project, what would it be?"

You should always set ground rules before you start. You want to stress that the purpose of this session is not to assign blame but to assess the project so that both this team and other project teams can learn from your experience.

Prepare the meeting room in advance with easel paper listing all the areas of the project you want to cover and provide each team member with a pad of sticky notes. For each topic, ask the team members to post one positive occurrence and one negative. Each negative comment needs a plan for improvement. If they encounter this situation on a future project, what would they do differently?

Requiring a plan for improvement serves two purposes: it engages the team members and stakeholders in the review by making them part of the problem-solving process, and it helps keep under control those few team members who may only want to whine. However, this is not the time or place to complain.

When you have concluded the session, collect all the notes and use them as input for your written report.

Lessons learned don't have to wait for the end of the project. You can conduct lessons learned or feedback sessions throughout the project and document them for inclusion in the final report. Consider a lessons learned session at the end of each project phase, when major milestones are met, or other appropriate times throughout the project. Don't forget to hold a final lessons learned meeting at the end of the project. Review all of the information collected in the prior sessions and perform an overall project evaluation of the good and the bad.

Project Closure Meeting

The project closure meeting is held to officially announce the end of the project. You may review all of the information we've discussed in this section at that meeting, including lessons learned. You'll also deliver the project closeout report at the meeting. We'll look at this next.

Project Closeout Report

A final project closeout report needs to be prepared and distributed to all the project stakeholders. This is the final status report for the project and should include at least the following:

- Recap of the original goals and objectives of the project
- Statement of project acceptance or rejection (and the reasons for rejection)
- Summary of project costs
- Summary of project schedule
- Lessons learned and historical data

This report is usually prepared after the lessons learned review meeting so that lessons learned and other historical data can be included in the report. You'll distribute this to the stakeholders after they have accepted and signed off on the project, typically at the project closure meeting.

Rewards and Celebrations

It's a great idea to hold a celebration at the conclusion of a successful project. The team has worked hard to satisfy the stakeholder requirements, and you should officially recognize their efforts and thank them for their participation. Any number of ideas come to mind here—a party, a trip to a ball game, pizza and sodas at lunchtime. Even if you don't have funds for a formal celebration, your heartfelt "thank you" can go a long way in showing your appreciation for a job well done.

A celebration helps team members formally recognize the end of the project and bring closure to the work they've done. It also encourages them to remember what they've learned and to start thinking about how their experiences will benefit them and the organization during the next project.

Postimplementation Support and Warranty Period

Project closeout kicks off the beginning of the postimplementation support or warranty period. Sometimes project managers or vendors will warranty their work for a certain time after completing the project. For example, newly developed software programs might be warranted from bugs for 90-day time frame from the date of implementation or the date of acceptance. Typically, in the case of software projects, bugs are fixed for free during the warranty period. Watch out because users will try to squeeze new requirements into the "bug" category mold, so be at the ready to explain the difference between a defect and new functionality. If you offer a warranty, it's critical that the warranty spells out exactly what is covered and what is not and when the warranty period expires.

 **Real World Scenario**

Main Street Office Move: Project Closure

Since the beginning of this project, you have held regularly scheduled status meetings with the stakeholders and used a mix of daily standup meetings and regular status meetings with the project team members. It seemed to work well, and you will use daily standups on future projects. It seemed that issues raised during the standup meetings were more easily addressed and resolved sooner than issues that waited for a formal review meeting.

Your status meetings addressed the work completed in the previous period, the work expected to be completed in the current period, and a review of issues and action items. You were diligent in keeping an issue log and action item log up-to-date and current so that by the time the moving day came, all items were resolved. There was an issue that arose during the move itself. You documented this and discussed it at the last status meeting held in the new office.

The cutover to the IaaS provider was successful, but there was an issue when the organization's data was temporarily unavailable for testing. Jason had to work with the IaaS provider to get the issue resolved to allow enough time for testing before employees showed up for work in the new year. The team used smoke testing, end-to-end testing, and user acceptance testing to verify that all the systems running on the cloud infrastructure performed as they should.

Once you settle into the new offices, you hold a lessons learned review meeting with the team members and stakeholders. At the rate your company is growing, you anticipate another move within three to five years. The lessons learned from this project will help improve the process next time. You also retain the issue log with the lessons learned because some of the issues could be addressed in the next project plan and ideally avoided in the future.

Summary

This chapter covered a lot of ground, starting with quality control. Quality control is the process of reviewing project results and determining whether they comply with the standards documented in the quality management plan and making any appropriate changes to remove the causes of unacceptable quality when the standards are not met. Inspecting and testing, audits, and quality charts are all methods of measuring quality. There are several types of tests used in technology projects: smoke, unit, integration, end-to-end, regression, stress, performance, and user acceptance testing.

Quality charts are a valuable project management tool. Histograms are a type of bar chart that displays data distributed over time. They are easy to construct and understand. A Pareto chart is a histogram that rank-orders the most important data by their frequency over time. A control chart measures and shows variances of several samples of the same process over time. Statistical sampling is a process of examining a subset of work results that represent the whole. Flowcharts show the logical steps that must be performed to achieve an objective. A run chart displays data observed or collected over time as plots on a line. Fishbone charts are also called Ishikawa diagrams and are a cause-and-effect diagram. Decision trees are diagrams that show the sequence of interrelated decisions and the expected results of choosing one alternative over the other. A scatter diagram plots two numerical variables on a chart to determine whether there is a correlation between them. The closer these variables are to each other, the closer the variables are related to each other. This relationship is typically analyzed to prove or disprove cause-and-effect relationships. Scatter diagrams are also known as correlation charts.

Issues are items that occur that could impact the project. Risks become issues once they happen. Issue management involves defining roles and responsibilities, issue tracking, developing resolution plans, and documenting the outcomes. The issue log should be regularly updated to reflect new issues and to document the status of ongoing issues. The issue log should be reviewed at the status meetings. Action item lists should also be updated and reviewed at the status meetings.

Performance measures include key performance indicators (KPIs), which are a measurable value that shows whether the project is reaching its intended goals. KPIs should be measurable and applicable to the project. Balanced scorecards are a performance management tool used to determine whether the organizational goals are being achieved. Key objectives and results may also be used as performance measures. Cost and schedule performance measures are used to determine if the budget and schedule are on track. These include cost and schedule variance, and cost and schedule performance index measures.

Project closeout should be performed when the project ends or when it's killed or canceled. The Closing process group is the most often skipped on projects because project managers and team members are anxious to move on to their next assignments. It's important to take the time to perform the steps in the Closing process phase so that you can obtain sign-off on the project, turn over the product to the organization, release project resources, close out the contract, document lessons learned, and create a final project report.

Four types of project endings encompass many of the reasons a project comes to an end. They are addition, starvation, integration, and extinction.

Closing out contracts involves completing and settling the terms of the contract and documenting its acceptance. Product verification occurs here that determines whether the work was completed accurately and satisfactorily.

Administrative closure activities involve gathering and centralizing all the project documents and archiving them.

Perhaps the most important element of project closure is obtaining feedback from stakeholders in the form of the lessons learned document. This entails identifying where things went wrong, what things went well, and the alternatives you considered during the course of the project. Lessons learned are an extremely useful reference for future projects regarding what worked and what didn't, for estimating techniques, for establishing templates, and more.

The project closeout report is distributed to the stakeholders and includes several elements, including the project's goal, the statement of acceptance, a summary of costs and schedule data, and lessons learned data.

Exam Essentials

Be able to name the purpose for controlling quality.   Quality control involves monitoring work results to determine whether they comply with the standards set in the quality management plan.

Name the types of testing performed on technology projects.   The types are smoke, unit, integration, end-to-end, regression, stress, performance, and user acceptance testing.

Be able to explain a histogram. A histogram displays data distributed over time. It is a type of bar chart.

Be able to explain a fishbone diagram. A fishbone diagram is a cause-and-effect diagram, also known as an Ishikawa diagram.

Be able to explain a Pareto chart. A Pareto chart is a histogram that rank-orders data by frequency over time.

Be able to explain a run chart. A run chart displays data as plots on a timeline.

Be able to explain a control chart. Control charts measure and display the variance of several samples of the same process over time.

Be able to explain a decision tree. Decision trees are diagrams that show the sequence of interrelated decisions and the expected results of choosing one alternative over the other.

Be able to explain a scatter diagram. A scatter diagram displays the relationship between two numerical variables and determines whether they are related to each other. It can also be used to prove or disprove cause-and-effect relationships. Scatter diagrams are also known as correlation charts.

Name the three common causes of variance. These are random variances, known or predictable variances, and variances that are always present in the process.

Name three actions that you can take when quality is not as expected. Three actions are rework, process adjustments, and acceptance.

Be able to describe an issue. An issue is something that could impact the project or delay the completion of deliverables. Risks become issues once they occur.

Be able to describe the issue log. The issue log is where information about issues are logged and may include an identification number, description, priority ranking, resolution plan, and other information.

Name the performance measurement tools that can be used for quality assessments. They are key performance indicators (KPIs), balanced scorecards, key objectives and results, and cost and schedule performance measures.

Name the four reasons for project endings. They are addition, starvation, integration, and extinction.

Understand the steps involved in closing a project. The steps are verification and validation of deliverables, obtaining sign-off, transition plan creation, revoking access, releasing project resources, closing out contracts, archiving documents, lessons learned, closure meeting, closeout report, celebration, and postimplementation support and warranty period.

Explain the purpose of obtaining formal customer or stakeholder sign-off. The formal sign-off documents that the customer accepts the project work and that the project meets the defined requirements. It also signals the official closure of the project and the transfer of the final product of the project to the organization.

Describe lessons learned.   Lessons learned describe the successes and failures of the project.

Key Terms

Before you take the exam, be certain you are familiar with the following terms:

acceptance	Pareto diagram
action items	performance testing
addition	prevention
balanced scorecard	regression testing
cause-and-effect diagram	rework
common causes of variances	run charts
control chart	smoke testing
decision trees	starvation
end-to-end testing	statistical sampling
extinction	stress testing
flowcharts	testing
integration	unit testing
integration testing	user acceptance testing (UAT)
lessons learned	

Review Questions

1. You are working on a project that was proceeding well until a manufacturing glitch occurred that requires corrective action. It turns out the glitch was an unintentional enhancement to the product, and the marketing people are enthused about its potential. The corrective action is canceled, and you continue to produce the product with the newly discovered enhancement. As the project manager, you know that a variance has occurred. Which of the following is not true?

    A. Common causes of variance are situations that are unique and not easily controlled at the operational level.

    B. Random variances, known or predictable variances, and variances that are always present in the process are known as common causes of variance.

    C. Inspection determines whether measurements fall within tolerable results.

    D. Scatter diagrams display the relationships between an independent and a dependent variable to show variations in the process over time.

2. You have just left a meeting with the project sponsor where you were advised that your project has been canceled because of budget cuts. You have called the project team together to fill them in and to review the remaining activities to close out the project. Several of your team members question the benefit of doing a lessons learned review on a project that has been canceled. What should your response be?

    A. Advise the team that part of the review time will be spent on documenting the failure of the lack of clear requirements from the customer.

    B. Tell the team they need to do this to be able to stay on the project payroll another week while they look for a new assignment.

    C. Inform the team that a final report is a requirement from the PMO, regardless of how the project ends.

    D. Explain that there is value both to the team and for future projects in analyzing the phases of the project that have been completed to date to document what went right, what went wrong, and what you would change.

3. You have just left a meeting with the project sponsor where you were advised that your project has been canceled because of budget cuts. You have called the project team together to fill them in and to review the remaining activities to close out the project. Which of the following describes the type of project ending this project experienced?

    A. Extinction

    B. Starvation

    C. Addition

    D. Integration

4. Which of the following measurement tools are used to measure operational or performance goals for projects?

A. KPIs

B. Key objectives

C. Balanced scorecard

D. Key results

E. All of the above

5. Which of the following is the "best" type of project ending?

A. Extinction

B. Addition

C. Integration

D. Starvation

6. What is the primary purpose of a formal sign-off at the conclusion of the project work?

A. The sign-off allows the project manager to start a new assignment.

B. The sign-off means the project team is no longer accountable for the product of the project.

C. The sign-off is the trigger for releasing team members back to their functional organization.

D. The sign-off indicates that the project meets the documented requirements and the customer has accepted the project deliverables.

7. Which of the following charts is a type of histogram?

A. Scatter diagram

B. Fishbone

C. Pareto chart

D. Run chart

8. What is the focus of the lessons learned report?

A. The report should cover both the positive and negative aspects of the project, with suggestions for improvement.

B. The report should primarily summarize the results of the project schedule, the budget, and any approved scope changes.

C. The report should focus on the project deliverables and any issues that were created by the customer.

D. The report should cover what went well during the project and should determine which team member or business unit was responsible for failures or issues.

9. Your project concerns writing a new software app to track physical activity such as running, biking, and walking, including time spent on the activity, heart rate, and speeds. You've performed some preliminary testing and discovered some changes need to be made to the code. Once the changes are made, you'll test again to ensure the app is working as expected, starting with logging in, tracking each activity, and measuring each criterion for accuracy. What type of testing does this question describe?

    A. Regression

    B. End-to-end

    C. Unit

    D. User acceptance

10. You are in the Monitoring and Controlling phase of the project. Several problems have come to light, and you want to know what the causes of the problems are that are generating the effect. You hold a brainstorming meeting with key team members and plot the cause and effect scenarios on this type of chart.

    A. Pareto chart

    B. Histogram

    C. Fishbone diagram

    D. Scatter diagram

11. This document records items that usually arise during a status meeting. They concern the project but do not generally impact the project work directly. This document contains a description, an owner, and status, among other items.

    A. Status report

    B. Action items log

    C. Issue log

    D. Meeting minutes

12. Your team is working on some configuration and coding changes to your human resource software program. The coding changes have just started, and you want to perform a test that will identify simple failures and look at the most critical functions of the program before proceeding. What type of test does this describe?

    A. Unit

    B. Integration

    C. Smoke

    D. Performance

13. Your project evolved over time into an ongoing operation. What type of project ending is this?

    A. The project ending is because of extinction.

    B. The project ending is because of starvation.

    C. The project ending is because of integration.

    D. The project ending is because of addition.

14. Which of the following charts are cause-and-effect diagrams or used to determine if there is a cause-and-effect correlation between two numerical variables? (Choose two.)

   A. Pareto chart

   B. Ishikawa diagram

   C. Run chart

   D. Scatter diagram

   E. Histogram

15. This document is produced at the end of the project and reports the final project outcomes.

   A. Lessons learned

   B. Status report

   C. Project close report

   D. Postmortem analysis

16. You're a project manager for a large project. You're in the middle of the Executing phase. The project sponsor has decided to cancel the project because of unexpected cost overruns and resource shortages. What are your next steps? (Choose two.)

   A. Change vendors to obtain a lower bid for hardware and software components.

   B. Prepare project closure documents.

   C. Perform a lessons learned analysis and release resources.

   D. Ask the sponsor to allow you to redesign the project with fewer deliverables.

   E. Ask the stakeholders to speak to the sponsor.

17. You are at the end of the project and need to obtain final sign-off and create the project closure report. According to CompTIA, before obtaining sign off, what should you do?

   A. Inspect the deliverables.

   B. Perform verification and validation of the product of the project.

   C. Test the product of the project.

   D. Audit the deliverables.

18. All of the following are true regarding the release of team members except for which one?

   A. Team members are released after lessons learned are documented.

   B. The project manager should perform a final performance appraisal for team members when they're released from the project.

   C. The project manager should inform the functional managers well in advance of the team members' release date.

   D. The project manager should communicate with the team members about their upcoming release date.

19. Your project has experienced some setbacks, and your stakeholders are not happy with progress. A hurricane wiped out one of your vendor's warehouses, and you are scrambling for parts. The hurricane was unexpected and unusual for that area. You work with the vendor and your procurement department to find other suppliers who may have the parts you need. Which of the following is the best option given this scenario?

    A. Cancel the project.

    B. This is a risk that has come about, and you should implement the response plan.

    C. This is an issue that should be recorded and tracked in the issue log.

    D. This is a KPI that the vendor has not met.

20. Who is responsible for authorizing the closure of the project?

    A. Stakeholders

    B. Project manager

    C. Executive team members

    D. Sponsor

Appendix

Answers to Review Questions

Chapter 1: Introducing the Project

1. C, E. A project creates a unique product, service, or result and has defined start and finish dates. Interrelated activities or processes repeated multiple times are not projects because they don't have start and finish dates, and they don't produce unique results. Option D outlines some of the reasons a project might come about.

2. B. Options A, C, and D describe a project.

3. D. A program is a group of related projects that can benefit from coordinated project management. Life cycles are the various stages a project goes through, and process groups consist of Discovery/Concept, Initiating, Planning, Executing, and Closing.

4. A, C. Portfolios consist of programs, subportfolios, and independent projects that are not necessarily related to one another. An organization could have any number of portfolios.

5. B. The life cycle phases of project management according to CompTIA are Discovery/Concept, Initiating, Planning, Executing, and Closing. The *PMBOK® Guide* calls these process groups and they are as follows: Initiating, Planning, Executing, Monitoring and Controlling, and Closing.

6. A. A request to develop a product for use by an internal department is an organizational need. Market demands are driven by the needs of the market, legal requirements come about because of rules or regulations that must be complied with, and technological advances come about due to changes or advancements in technology. This question describes purchasing and implementing a new system for the organization but doesn't imply the technology itself is new or advanced.

7. E. The business case analysis may include the feasibility study but should always include the justification for the project, alignment to the strategic plan, benefits and rewards (using financial analysis), alternative solutions, and more.

8. C, D. Artifacts, also known as historical information, include any documents, physical elements, evidence, or information associated with past projects.

9. A. The discounted cash flow technique compares the total value of each year's expected cash inflow to today's dollar. IRR calculates the internal rate of return, NPV determines the net present value, and cost-benefit analysis determines the cost of the project versus the benefits received.

10. B, C. This is the formula for ROI. ROI does not take time periods into account, so you'll need to annualize the returns for comparison purposes.

11. C. Money received today is worth more than the same amount of money received in the future due to the time value of money. Inflation and other factors will erode the value of money over time.

12. F. The alternative solutions section should contain the information in all the options.

13. D. Payback period is a technique that calculates the expected cash inflows over time to determine how many periods it will take to recover the original investment. In this case, our

initial investment is $850,000. Subtract year 1 inflows from this to see what's remaining. This leaves us with a $350,000 balance. If you annualize year 2 returns of $700,000, you get approximately $58,343 per month. It will take six months of inflows at $58,343 to recoup the $350,000.

14. D. The next best step to take in this situation is to perform a feasibility study. Feasibility studies are typically undertaken for projects that are risky, projects that are new to the organization, or projects that are highly complex. Projects of significant risk to the organization shouldn't be taken to the selection committee without having a feasibility study first. Writing the project plan doesn't make sense at this point because you don't know if the project will be approved to move forward yet. You also can't reject the project because there isn't enough information to determine whether it should be rejected until the feasibility study is completed.

15. A, C. Preexisting contracts are active contracts in place at the organization. You could use an existing contract to bring these resources on board. Likewise, prequalified vendors will help speed the process. You can go directly to this list and choose a vendor who has the resource type you need at the price they stated.

16. G. All of the options are types of project selection methods.

17. A. This is known as predetermined clients. These are partners who have been prequalified to work with the software platform you are implementing.

18. C. NPV is calculated by subtracting the total of the expected cash inflows stated in today's dollars from the initial investment. In this question, the initial investment is higher than the cash flows, so the resulting NPV is less than 0, and the project should be rejected. Discounted cash flows tell you the value of the cash flows in today's dollars.

19. D, E. Validating a project requires writing the business case and identifying and analyzing the stakeholders.

20. A, B, F. Current state versus future state examines the impact of changes on the future state of the organization. First, however, you need to understand the current state and document the process using diagrams or other techniques, to understand what the future state may look like. This is also known as "as is—to be," which is a type of performance analysis.

Chapter 2: Understanding IT Fundamentals

1. B. Project managers can spend up to 90 percent of their time communicating. The other skills listed here are important as well, but the clue in this question is the 90 percent figure that relates to the amount of time project managers may spend communicating.

2. C. Negotiating involves obtaining mutually acceptable agreements with individuals or groups. Leadership involves imparting a vision and motivating others to achieve the goal. Problem solving involves working together to reach a solution. Communicating involves exchanging information.

3. D. PII stands for personally identifiable information and is not part of ESG. ESG stands for environmental, social, and governance.

4. C. A customer relationship management (CRM) system is one that is used by companies to interact with their customers.

5. B. This question states the company is looking to decommission their on-premises data center consisting of servers, databases, and applications. Data centers consist of infrastructure; therefore IaaS is the correct option. Infrastructure as a service allows the cloud consumer to provision servers, storage, networking, operating systems, and other computing resources on demand. With IaaS, companies have the ability to stand up servers, operating systems, networking hardware, databases, and applications that mirror (or even improve on) the current data center environment.

6. A. Data entered into a database system is structured data that is organized in a meaningful way. Unstructured data is a blob of data that has not yet been organized with any meaning in mind. Flat data is a term that is often used to describe data that's entered into spreadsheets.

7. B, E. Sensitive personally identifiable information is stand-alone data that by itself can identify an individual. Options A, C, and D are linkable data and, if combined with PII, will become SPII.

8. B. Linkable data such as zip code, date of birth, and more become sensitive personally identifiable information when it is linked to a PII element.

9. A. The Health Insurance Portability and Accountability Act (HIPAA) concerns the electronic protected health information (ePHI) of patients. A patient might be talking with a customer service representative about their prescriptions. This is protected information that someone else should not overhear.

10. C. A wide area network (WAN) is a style of networking that is able to connect various campuses spread across locations within a city.

11. A. The presentation layer collects and displays the information the user needs to interact with the system.

12. C. A common word that is used to generically refer to a company's computing resources is called "the enterprise." Thus, when architecting a system that brings various corporate functionality together, an enterprise resource planning (ERP) system is often chosen.

13. A, C. When users are working with a document, the contents of the document are stored in the computer's RAM. When the user saves what they are working on, a copy of the document is saved to the hard drive or to a NAS, the cloud, or some other form of storage. This person could not find their document because they did not save it to the hard drive and the working copy was only stored in RAM.

14. B. A data warehouse is a collection of data for the purpose of helping stakeholders make sense out of the data for the purpose of analysis and decision-making. Data in a data warehouse may include internal as well as external data resources.

15. D. IT is responsible for documenting the corporate computing resources.

16. C. This type of cloud environment is called software as a service (SaaS) and provides a platform to develop and/or host software applications.

17. B. In the multitenant model, cloud providers can offer their computing resources to multiple customers. This is called resource pooling.

18. D. In the United States the National Institute of Standards and Technology (NIST) publishes the rules for personally identifiable information.

19. D. Random access memory is a type of primary storage.

20. D. According to NIST, there are three levels of impact that can affect the organization when a breach occurs: low, medium, or high impacts.

Chapter 3: Creating the Project Charter

1. C. The Initiating phase is the second phase in the project management life cycle. This is where the project charter that authorizes the project to begin is created and published.

2. A. The project sponsor is responsible for authorizing the project to begin and is the person who signs the project charter.

3. B, C. A stakeholder register includes the stakeholder name, department, contact information, role on the project, needs, concerns, interests, level of involvement on the project, level of influence over the project, and notes for your own reference. A stakeholder register is an artifact. The question does not mention that project objectives, timelines, budgets, or any other information is included, which rules out options D and E.

4. B. Zoe is a SME. She is also considered a developer/engineer, which is not an option for this question.

5. D. Zack is an IT architect. Testers ensure the code works as designed. Developers write programming code, and end users are the ones who use the program to perform business functions once it's written.

6. C, E. Ravi is both an end user and a subject matter expert. Options A, B, and D describe IT team members. The question hints at his business unit, which is not IT.

7. D. The preliminary scope statement's primary purpose is to document the objectives and the business problem you're trying to solve. The primary purpose of the project charter is to authorize the project to begin.

8. C, D, F. The PMO provides standards and practices for the organization, including tools, templates, and governance processes.

9. B, C, E. The project sponsor/champion approves funding, approves the project charter, markets the project benefits, removes roadblocks, and defines the business justification for the project.

10. A. The project manager should take the time to define the problem or need generating the project request and document this in the high-level scope definition. It could be that the business case was not well-defined, but the reason for that is also because the problem or need was not well-defined.

11. B, D, F, G. The project baseline includes the approved schedule, cost, scope, and quality plans and documents and is approved by the project sponsor. The project baseline is then used to measure performance as the project progresses. You can refer back to the project baseline at any time to determine whether you are on schedule, within scope, and within budget, and to determine whether the quality standards are on target.

12. C. The project charter formally approves the project and authorizes work to begin. The project schedule and cost estimates are developed later in the Planning process.

13. A. After the project charter is signed and approved, you should hold a kickoff meeting with key stakeholders and key team members to discuss the goals of the project.

14. C. A records management system manages records according to the life cycle of records and the processes defined by the records management plan.

15. D. A power/interest grid is a quadrant grid with power on one axis and interest on the other.

16. B, D. An access control system restricts access to systems, data, functions, and more. You should implement the principle of least privilege to guard against cyberattacks.

17. C. Milestones are major events in a project that are used to measure progress. They may also mark when key deliverables are completed and approved. Milestones are also used as check-points during the project to determine whether the project is on time and on schedule.

18. C, D. The project charter does not include a high-level cost–benefit analysis, or the equip-ment and resources needed for the project. The business case is where the cost–benefit anal-ysis is documented.

19. B. Assumptions are things believed to be true. In this case, you have not verified Greg's avail-ability and are assuming the functional manager will agree to assign him to the project.

20. D. Constraints restrict or dictate the actions of the project team and may take the form of budget, resources, schedules, or other limitations. Situations believed to be true are assumptions.

Chapter 4: Planning the Project

1. C. The key components of scope planning are the scope management plan, scope statement, and work breakdown structure. The project charter is created during initiation.

2. A. The scope statement serves as a basis for understanding the work of the project and for future decision-making.

3. B, C, D. The sections of a scope statement are project description, key deliverables, success and acceptance criteria, exclusions, time and cost estimates, assumptions, and constraints.

4. E. All of the options describe and provide examples of influences.

5. B. Scope creep involves changing the product or project scope without regard to impacts to the schedule, budget, and/or resources. KPIs are key performance indicators that help you incrementally monitor project performance.

6. A, C, E. They are budget, scope, and time, all of which impact quality.

7. A. This is an example of acceptance criteria for the user story.

8. A, C, D. Option B describes the waterfall, or predictive, process.

9. C. The seven wastes are associated with Kaizen, a lean methodology.

10. E, F. Scrum and Kanban are considered pull systems because user stories are moved from one point in the process to the next, thereby freeing up space to pull other user stories from the backlog.

11. B. Extreme Programming (XP) strongly encourages collocation of team members. Refactoring reduces duplication and eliminates poor code.

12. A, C, D. The agile methodologies require close contact with the stakeholders, and this provides continuous feedback to the project team throughout the project. In a waterfall approach, stakeholders typically have a lot of contact and involvement with the team at the beginning of the project, and this involvement tapers off toward the end of the project. Option E also describes an agile methodology approach. Waterfall, or predictive, methodologies do not have iterative reviews, and changes are rigorously controlled and managed.

13. B, C. The *Agile Manifesto* focuses on value to the customer, not in measuring processes or the quality of deliverables. Success is measured in incremental steps.

14. C. This describes a hybrid development life cycle. Early on, requirements might be gathered in detail, and as the project progresses, the team reverts to an agile approach to deliver functionality incrementally.

15. A, D. The minimum viable product is a component of work, or a task, that's been broken down into the lowest tangible feature, function, or result possible. The product owner is responsible for determining if the requirements have been met. The project team does not manage or prioritize the backlog; the product owner does. The Scrum master is a facilitator. Team members do not report to the Scrum master, and they do not assign tasks to team members. The Scrum team is self-directed.

16. D. All of the options are true regarding the minimum viable product.

17. B, C, E. The project scope statement further elaborates the project deliverables and documents the product scope description, acceptance criteria, and project exclusions. It serves as a basis for future project decisions. It is an agreement between the project team and customer on the precise work of the project. This question describes a hybrid approach, so you could use either a project scope statement or a product backlog to compile user stories, which are the deliverables and requirements for the project. Options A and D describe the scope management plan.

18. A. The requirements traceability matrix links requirements to their origin and traces them throughout the project. Option B is partially true but does not include the business need of the project, assumptions, or constraints. Requirements documents do not have to be formal or complex. Option C refers to the project scope statement, not the requirements. Option D describes a requirements management plan, not the requirements document.

19. C. The solutions architect may assist the business analyst in requirements gathering to understand the needs and to be able to relay this information, in technical terms, to the team.

20. B. DevOps and DevSecOps combines the operations, development, and security team (in the case of DevSecOps) to deliver projects faster and encourage collaboration and communication among the team members.

Chapter 5: Creating the Project Schedule

1. D. A WBS is a deliverables-oriented hierarchy that defines the work of the project and can be used on projects of any size or complexity.

2. B. Decomposition breaks the major deliverables down into smaller, more manageable units of work that can be used to estimate cost and time and perform resource planning.

3. A. The lowest level of a WBS is the work package. The number of levels will vary by project and complexity.

4. D. The scope management plan, not the WBS, describes how the deliverables will be validated.

5. D. The code of accounts identifier is a unique number assigned to each component of the WBS. It is documented in the WBS dictionary and is tied to the chart of accounts.

6. C. The first level of the WBS is the project name, in this case ABC Product Launch. The second level of the WBS represents major project deliverables, project phases, or subprojects. If the project has phases or subprojects, these are listed at the second level, with deliverables listed at the third level. Since the question asks about phase II of the project and option C is project phases, this is the correct second-level entry for the WBS.

7. B. The critical path is the longest path on the project. The tasks have zero float because the critical path controls the project end date. Using critical path, you can determine which tasks can start late or go longer than planned without impacting the project end date.

8. A. A requirement such as weather conditions or a specific season that drives the scheduling of a task is an example of an external dependency.

9. D. Analogous estimating is also called top-down estimating. It is used early in the project when there is not enough detail to do a detailed estimate.

10. B. There is a finish-to-start dependency relationship between Activity A and Activity B. You do not have enough information to determine whether the dependency between the two activities is mandatory, discretionary, or external or if they are critical path activities.

11. A. Duration compression involves either crashing the schedule by adding more resources or creating a fast track by working activities in parallel that would normally be done in sequence.

12. C. Float time is the length of time a task may be started late or the additional duration a task may take without impacting the project completion date. The early start and late start dates are the same, and the early finish and late start finish dates are the same.

13. C. The total workday duration is 8 days. The first day counts as one full day.

14. A. Agile release planning is the best option for the project described. Release planning breaks a large project into releases, similar to phases, that can be accomplished using either Kanban or Scrum, or other agile methodologies to complete. Option B describes Kanban with the exception of the last part of the sentence. Kanban is capacity-based, not time-based. Option C describes Scrum but it is time-based, not capacity-based. Epics are placeholders, large user stories, or descriptions of features or functionality for the project. These modules or releases could be considered epics; however, epics are not a method of planning or implementing the project. They are placeholders for big ideas.

15. B. If you didn't know the quantity and rate, option C or D would be acceptable. In this case, you'd use the parametric estimating technique because you do know the quantity and rate; 30 hours times 4 miles is a total duration of 120 hours.

16. D. Milestone charts list the major deliverables, key events, or project phases and show the scheduled and actual completion dates of each milestone. They may include other information, but that information would not be displayed as bar charts.

17. B, C. Velocity is used to determine how long it will take to complete the work of the iteration. It measures the speed the team progresses, not capacity as stated in Option A. In this case, it will take seven iterations to complete the work (165 story points / 24 story points per iteration). The remaining work for each of the seven iterations can be tracked on a burndown chart. Kanban boards display work based on capacity and this questions is asking about velocity, or speed of work.

18. D. A Kanban board is capacity-based and a Scrum board is time-bound. Both Kanban and Scrum boards are known as on-demand scheduling, and both may use rolling wave planning and progressive elaboration.

19. C, D. Options C and D describe iterative scheduling. Options A and B describe on-demand scheduling or pull-based scheduling.

20. B. This question describes the sprint planning meeting. The product owner does not determine the project timeline—the team determines this with assistance from the Scrum master. An agile team is self-directed, and they will determine the tools and techniques that will work best to break down tasks and determine estimates. This question does not describe a large project conducive to release planning.

Chapter 6: Resource Planning and Management

1. A. When a new team member is introduced on the project, the team development stage starts again at the forming stage, no matter which stage the team was in before.

2. A. Time and materials contracts are a cross between fixed-price and cost-reimbursable contracts. They assign a unit rate for work, but the total cost isn't known until the work is complete.

3. C, E. This situation describes varying work styles, which are a common cause of conflict. An interproject resource contention is where resources are working on multiple projects and there are scheduling issues. Low-quality resources lack skills or abilities. The negotiating conflict technique often uses a third party to help the two conflicting sides reach a resolution.

4. B. The stages of team development are forming, storming, norming, performing, and adjourning. Collaborating is a conflict-resolution technique.

5. D. The key problem with a projectized organization is that there may not be a new project in place at the conclusion of the one team members were released from. This leaves specialists "sitting on the bench" with no work to do and is costly to the organization. It's an advantage to a projectized organization to work on projects. Costs aren't necessarily any higher in this type of organization than others. Costs will depend on the type of project you're working on, not the organizational structure. And the project managers have control over who works on the projects in a project-based organization.

6. D. The smoothing conflict resolution technique is temporary, and one of its symptoms is emphasizing the areas of agreement and keeping the real issue buried.

7. A. Weighted scoring models weigh various criteria from the RFP and SOW, which allows you to score each vendor on each of the criteria and determine an overall score for each vendor.

8. D. Cost-reimbursable contracts are the riskiest for buyers since the buyer is responsible for reimbursing the seller on the costs of producing the goods or services.

9. D. To address the issue, you need to understand what is behind the system engineer's current behavior. He may have been given additional work that you are not aware of, or he may misunderstand the project goals, to name just a couple of possibilities. The situation cannot be ignored, no matter how valuable the person is, and it should be handled in private.

10. A, C, E. A RACI is a matrix-based chart that shows resources (or business units) responsible for project tasks. It stands for responsible, accountable, consulted, and informed. Accountable does mean this resource approves the work, but the A in RACI stands for accountable.

11. D. Rewards and recognition do not have to involve money, and many times they may include rewards such as a thank-you, a letter to the functional manager, a public mention of the accomplishment at a team meeting, and so on.

12. A. This question refers to a resource shortage. You have one resource that's needed for two tasks. Resource allocation is assigning the resource with the right skills and abilities to the task. Interproject dependencies rely on one project finishing before the next can start, and shared resources are typically resources that are shared among departments or between the functional manager and the project manager.

13. B, E. A matrix organization can be structured as a strong, weak, or balanced matrix. Employees are assigned to projects by their functional managers, and the project tasks are assigned to them by the project manager. The project manager has the majority of power in a projectized organization.

14. C. The RACI chart acronym stands for responsible, accountable, consulted, and informed. The person accountable also is an approver of the work.

15. A, B. Whenever a new team member is introduced, the team development stage reverts to the forming stage and progresses through all the stages once again with the new team member.

16. B, C, E. The resources this question describes are core resources because they are required for the entire project. Option D describes the team size for an agile development methodology. The question does not state what development methodology the project team is using, so there is not enough information to know if option D is correct. A waterfall project may have dozens of team members.

17. E. The WBS is too detailed to review at a project kickoff meeting and is better handled during a meeting with project team members only.

18. D. Smoothing is lose-lose technique, forcing is win-lose, confronting is win-win, and avoiding is lose-lose.

19. B. Benched resources are costly to an organization. These are resources who are not currently assigned to project tasks and are typically between projects. This generally occurs in a projectized organization.

20. C. An organization breakdown structure shows work by the department or work unit responsible for completing the work packages. A resource breakdown structure shows the types of resources needed and the work packages. A project organization chart shows the hierarchy of the project team members, and an organization chart shows the hierarchy of the reporting structure within an organization.

Chapter 7: Defining the Project Budget and Risk Plans

1. B, C. This question describes a digital security policy. Multifactor authentication uses at least two forms of verification of identity at the sign-in process.

2. C. Registered products are those that have been trademarked and registered with the U.S. Patent and Trademark office.

3. E.. All of the options are true. You may still decide to refuse to answer after viewing their badge, as option C describes. You should always verify the identity of the person asking for personally identifiable information (PII).

4. D, F. The labor, $75/hour, times 10 trees is $750. This is the parametric method of estimating because you are multiplying the quantity times the rate. Analogous estimating involves using estimates from similar projects, and three-point estimates use the average of three estimates.

5. B. A work effort estimate or person-hour estimate is used to develop the cost estimates. This is the amount of time it will take to complete the task from beginning to end without accounting for work breaks, holidays, and so on. Duration estimates account for holidays, work breaks, and so on. Bottom-up estimates are estimates for individual components of work that are rolled up into the overall estimate, and parametric estimates are usually derived by multiplying quantity by rate.

6. C. A contingency fund is an amount allocated to cover the cost of possible adverse events, and the project manager generally has the ability to use this fund. The project manager does not usually have the authority to spend money from the management reserve. The chart of accounts is a description of the accounts listed in the accounting ledger, and the cost baseline is the total expected cost for the project.

7. C. Bottom-up estimates start at the work package level of the WBS. Each work package on the WBS for the first phase of the project is summed to come up with an overall estimate for this phase. Historical data would be useful if you were using the analogous estimating technique. The chart of accounts doesn't help at all with this exercise, and the scope statement will give you an understanding of what's detailed on the WBS, but it won't help with estimating.

8. B. Bottom-up estimates are the most accurate estimates, and analogous estimates are the least accurate. Estimates based on expert judgment are analogous estimates. Parametric estimates are only as accurate as the data you're using for the parametric model.

9. C. The cost baseline is approved by the project sponsor, not the project manager.

10. D, G, H. Three-point estimates are the average of the most likely, optimistic, and pessimistic estimates.

11. C. The burn rate is typically calculated using the cost performance index (CPI). This tells you the efficiency or benefits of the money spent at any point in the project.

12. D. Transfer is a risk strategy that transfers the consequences of the risk to another party.

13. A. SWOT stands for strengths, weaknesses, opportunities, and threats. Examining the project from each of these perspectives helps you identify risks. The other options are cost performance measurements.

14. A, B, C. During the early stages of risk planning, a risk register typically has a risk identification number, a description of the risk, the probability and impact of the risk event, risk score, and risk owner. Your risk register could also contain the risk trigger and other pertinent information about the risk.

15. D. The risk strategy of accepting a risk involves dealing with the consequences when they occur. You don't prepare a risk response plan for risks you plan to accept.

16. B. The difference between what you planned to spend and what was actually spent is known as a budget variance.

17. A. Risk triggers are symptoms or signs that a risk event is about to occur.

18. C. Sharing is a positive risk strategy. The negative risk strategies are avoid, transfer, mitigate, and accept.

19. A. When project costs are displayed graphically over time, they represent an S curve. This is because spending starts out slowly on the project, picks up speed during the middle of the project, and tapers off at the end.

20. C, F. The risk score is calculated by multiplying the probability by the impact. Probability is the likelihood a risk event will occur. It is expressed as a number from 0.0 to 1.0. Impact is the consequence of the risk event if it occurs and is expressed as a range of numbers or costs determined by the team, the PMO, or the organization.

Chapter 8: Communicating the Plan

1. C, E, F. A communication plan is developed to determine who needs communication, when, and in what format, and the frequency of the communications. Once the plan is developed, it's used to update stakeholders, team members, vendors, and others who need information on the project.

2. D. In the sender-message-receiver model, the receiver is responsible for understanding the information correctly and making certain they've received all the information.

3. A. There are four participants in the meeting and six lines of communication. The formula for this is 4 (4 − 1) ÷ 2 = 6.

4. C. Gate reviews are meetings held to discuss status and determine if the project should move forward. Language barriers, cultural differences, and others are factors that influence communication methods.

5. B. Joint application development sessions are a type of collaborative meeting where the focus is developing requirements for the system or application the team is developing.

6. A. One of the purposes of a kickoff meeting is to introduce team members to one another. Videoconferencing would be the best choice so that team members can see one another during introductions as well as hear the project goals and so on.

7. G. All of the options are considered communication methods. You should tailor the method of communication to the audience.

8. C. Communications planning is the process of identifying who needs to receive information on the project, what information they need, and how they will get that information.

9. D. This question describes phase gate reviews. Reviews and retrospectives are meetings held on agile projects. The iteration review is held at the end of the sprint to review the work accomplished to date. The retrospective is held after the review meeting and involves all cross-functional team members. It reviews overall progress to date, changes, ideas for improvements, and more. Project status meetings are intended to review the status of the project and are held at regular intervals such as weekly or monthly. They are not go/no-go decision points.

10. D. Intraorganizational differences affect different departments across the organization. This question states you work for the PMO and the Finance department is uncooperative, meaning you have two departments involved in the difference.

11. C. A stakeholder change is an example of a communication trigger.

12. B, E, F. The basic communication model is the sender-message-receiver model.

13. A. A face-to-face meeting with the employee is the best method of communicating when you need to discuss sensitive information. If the employee refuses to change their behaviour, the next step might be meeting with the functional manager. However, you should always try to resolve the problem first with just the employee.

14. D. Synchronous communication happens in real time. Emails are a form of asynchronous communication.

15. D. Informal communications include email, hallway conversations, and phone calls. They are typically unplanned and casual in nature.

16. C. Backlog refinements are conducted midway to a few days before the end of the current sprint.

17. B. The first step is to tailor the communication method based on the content of the message. There isn't enough information in the question to determine the content of the message, so we don't know which method is best to use.

18. A, F. Complex information is best delivered in a written format and then explained at an in-person meeting so the stakeholders can ask questions and you are able to determine if their body language indicates they understand.

19. B, D. These are all stakeholder communication requirements and should be recorded in the communication plan.

20. A. The question describes factors that influence communication.

Chapter 9: Processing Change Requests

1. D. The customer or a stakeholder may have requested the new features. If these are required features that were omitted from the original scope statement, you need to analyze the impact to the project and obtain approval for the change. If you just make adjustments to the budget and schedule without any analysis, not only do you risk being late and over budget, but there may be impacts to other areas of the plan or risks associated with this change. Removing the new features may add cost and time to the schedule as well as create a potentially hostile relationship with the customer. Unless this is a situation where the programmer has repeatedly changed scope outside of the approval process, requesting a replacement resource is not an appropriate response.

2. C. Corrective actions, defect repairs, and preventive actions are all types of change.

3. B. The change request board (CCB) is responsible for reviewing and approving, denying, or deferring change requests. The CCB is also sometimes known as the change advisory board (CAB).

4. A. Emergency change request procedures should be documented so that changes that must be made on an emergency basis prior to the next CCB meeting can be made. All changes should be documented and reported at the next CCB meeting.

5. D. After options A–C are conducted, the change request and analysis are given to the CCB to make a decision. The appropriate project planning document is not updated until the CCB makes a decision regarding the disposition of the change request.

6. A, D. Determining the constraint that stakeholders think is driving the project will help you determine the kinds of trade-offs or alternatives you can propose to lessen the effect of the proposed scope change.

7. C. The correct action to take in this situation is to submit the change request to the CCB. If it is approved, it will require that you re-baseline the schedule to reflect the new dates.

8. C, D. This is an organizational change. Organizational change involves transforming processes, systems, organizations, and more and requires communication, analysis, training, ensuring adoption over time, documenting the change, and creating new knowledge bases and new processes. Rollback plans are used for infrastructure changes.

9. C. An acquisition gives power to the organization that is taking over. In this scenario, your old company has experienced some layoffs and managers from the new organization have taken over. This describes an acquisition.

10. D. This is an organizational change. Updating the project management plan would come about as a result of a project management change, not an organizational change.

11. B. This is a product change, not a project management change. Product changes almost always result in a project management change, but the question is describing the product change.

12. A. The project management plan is the documented plan that's used to monitor the work of the project throughout the Executing phase and to analyze change requests.

13. A, D. Audits consist of reviews of vendor activities to determine whether they are meeting the right needs and whether the activities are being performed correctly and according to standards. Inspections involve physically inspecting the results to determine if they meet the requirements or standards set out in the SOW.

14. C. Claims administration involves documenting, monitoring, and managing contested changes to the contract. Contested changes usually involve a disagreement about the compensation to the vendor for implementing the change. You might believe the change is not significant enough to justify additional compensation.

15. B. The project management plan serves as the baseline for project progress and is used throughout the Executing phase to determine whether the project is on track. It is used to help evaluate changes against the original goals and objectives of the project and serves as a communication tool.

16. D. Corrective actions bring the work of the project into alignment with the project management plan. Preventive actions help reduce the probability of a negative risk event. Defect repairs correct or replace components that are not functional. Integrated change control manages change requests and their global impacts to the project and the organization.

17. D. This question describes Disciplined Agile.

18. B. PRINCE2 divides projects into stages, and stage boundaries are performed at the end of each stage before proceeding to the next.

19. C. This question describes Scrum of Scrums. This methodology uses more than one Scrum team who each work from their own backlog.

20. B. This question describes Scaled Agile Framework. It uses one large Scrum team. Scrum of Scrums uses multiple Scrum teams, PRINCE2 uses stages to manage the work, and Disciplined Agile is a way to tailor agile methodologies for the team.

Chapter 10: Managing Quality and Closing Out the Project

1. A. Common causes of variance are situations that are common to the process you're using and are easily controlled at the operational level.

2. D. There is valuable information to be gained from a review of any project, even projects that do not complete. The assessment should focus on those phases of the project that did finish, as well as a look at whether anything could have been done differently to make the project a success. The purpose of lessons learned is not to assign blame, even for projects that are canceled.

3. B. Starvation is a project ending caused by resources being cut off from the project. Extinction occurs when the project work is completed and is accepted by the stakeholders. Addition occurs when projects evolve into ongoing operations, and integration occurs when resources are distributed to other areas of the organization.

4. A. KPIs are used to measure any element of the project or operational areas of the business to determine whether goals are being achieved. A balanced scorecard is used to determine whether organizational goals are being met.

5. A. Extinction occurs when the project work is completed and is accepted by the stakeholders. This is the best type of project ending. Starvation is a project ending caused by resources being cut off from the project. Addition occurs when projects evolve into ongoing operations, and integration occurs when resources are distributed to other areas of the organization.

6. D. A sign-off is the formal acceptance of the project's final product, service, or result. Its primary purpose is the customer's acceptance of the product of the project. Team members are released after sign-off, but this isn't the primary purpose of a formal sign-off. Both the project manager and the project team members may continue to be involved in the project until all closure activities are complete.

7. C. A Pareto diagram is a type of histogram that measures the frequency of occurrences of data elements in rank order over time.

8. A. Both the successes and failures of a project need to be documented in the lessons learned report. Successes will provide blueprints to follow on future projects, and failures will alert teams on what to avoid. A good lessons learned document covers all aspects of the project from all participants. It should include all project information, not just schedule, budget, and changes, and it should never place blame for the things that went wrong.

9. B. Regression testing is performed after changes are made to the code, but this question is specific about testing for all modules starting at logon, which indicates an end-to-end test is in order. Unit testing is the testing of one module or one unit of code, such as the biking feature, and user acceptance testing is performed by the end users of the product.

10. C. The fishbone diagram is a cause-and-effect diagram and is also known as an Ishikawa diagram. Brainstorming sessions are a great way to construct this chart and determine what causes are impeding your results.

11. B. Action items generally arise during the status meetings. They should be documented in an action item list. They are assigned an identification number, a description, and an owner, and their status is recorded and reviewed at status meetings. Issues generally impact the project work directly and may impede progress or bring about a risk. Action items are usually "to dos" or questions that must be answered regarding the project.

12. C. A smoke test is a high-level test designed to identify simple failures that could jeopardize the software program or prevent it from being released to production. These tests typically look at the most critical functions of the program and expose issues and problems early in the coding process.

13. D. Extinction occurs when the project comes to an end as planned. Starvation occurs when resources are cut off from the project. Integration occurs when the resources on the project are reassigned to other projects or activities. Addition occurs when the project evolves into ongoing operations.

14. B, D. Fishbone diagrams are cause-and-effect diagrams. Scatter diagrams are used to determine whether there is a correlation between cause and effect.

15. C. The project close report is produced at the end of the project, and it serves as the final status report. It summarizes the project goals, costs, schedule, lessons learned, and historical data.

16. B, C. If you have a sponsor who opts to cancel the project, you will still perform project closing procedures. During this process, you'll assemble the closure documents, perform a lessons learned analysis, and release any resources working on the project.

17. B. You need to verify and validate that the product of the project meets the requirements set out in the statement of work and/or contract documents. All of the other options are ways to perform verification and validation.

18. A. Team members can be released prior to the lessons learned session. If your team members are leaving the organization or are located at a different geographical location, you could perform a lessons learned session with them before they leave, or you could include them in the final lessons learned session using videoconferencing or similar technology.

19. C. This question describes an issue that has occurred on the project that will likely impede progress. You will record this issue in the issue log and report regularly on its status. Option B is not true given this question because the hurricane was unlikely and unusual so the team would probably not have documented this as a risk. Once a risk occurs, it becomes an issue.

20. D. The sponsor is the one who signs off on the closure documents. As the project manager, you create the documentation and provide supporting artifacts to demonstrate that all deliverables have been successfully completed.

Index

A

acceptance, 373–374
access control, 92, 99
access requirement, 92–93
acquisition of resources, 204
action item, 306–307, 376–377
activity list, 162
actual cost (AC), 257
addition project ending, 381
after-the-fact plan, 332
agenda, 305–306
agile methodology
    agile release planning, 182–183
    Agile Unified Process (AUP/AgileUP), 133
    backlog refinement within, 296
    burndown chart within, 178–179
    daily standups within, 295
    Disciplined Agile (DA), 351
    dynamic systems development method
        (DSDM), 132–133
    estimating techniques within, 177–178
    Extreme Programming (XP), 130–132
    feature-driven development (FDD), 132
    frameworks for, 349–351, 354
    hybrid, 133–134
    iteration review within, 296
    Kaizen, 129–130
    Kanban, 127–129
    Kanban board, 180–181
    Lean, 129–130
    overview of, 126–127, 144, 186
    retrospective meeting within, 296
    Scaled Agile Framework (SAFe), 351
    scaling frameworks for, 350–351
    scheduling techniques using, 177–183
    scope determination on, 138–139
    Scrum, 127
    Scrum board, 181–182
    Scrum of Scrums, 350–351
    Scrumban, 129
    selecting, 136–138
    story points within, 179–180
    team members for, 139–140, 144, 206
    velocity within, 179–180
agile release planning, 182–183
agile team, communication on, 294–297
Agile Unified Process (AUP/AgileUP), 133

alternative dispute resolution (ADR), 334
analogous estimating (top-down estimating),
    165–166, 245–246
anything as a service (XaaS), 54
appeal, 334
application tier, 47
approval, 90, 118, 175–176
arbitration, 334
architect, IT, 78
archiving, 314–315, 385
artifacts, 21–22, 26, 75
assumption, 88, 113, 142
asynchronous communication, 288
attribute sampling, 365
audit, 299, 333
avoiding, as conflict management, 217

B

background check, 243
backlog refinement meeting, 304
backup procedure, 315
balanced scorecard, 379
basic communication model, 285
benched resources, 203
benefits, determination of, 14–21
beta-staging environment, 348
bidder conference, 223
bottom-up estimating, 166, 246–248, 250
brainstorming, 80, 217, 261–262, 304
branding restriction, 241
breach of confidentiality, 43–44
budget burndown chart, 255–256
budget/budgeting
    as constraint, 114
    contingency reserve within, 252–253
    cost baseline within, 253–254
    creating, 250–254
    defined, 60–61
    expenditure tracking and reporting
        within, 254–260
    management of, 75
    management reserve within, 253
    overview of, 273
    within project charter, 88
    sample of, 252
buffer (contingency reserves), 172, 252–253

building SDLC phase, 125
burn rate, 255, 260
burndown chart, 311–312
burnup chart, 312–313
business analyst, 76, 98
business case, 6, 13–14
business continuity response, 300
business demerger/split, 344
business merger/acquisition, 343–344
business process change, 344
business requirement, 119–120

C

calendaring tool, 309
capital expense (CapEx), 251
capital resources, 201
Cascading Style Sheet (CSS), 60
cash flow techniques, 17–21
cause-and-effect diagram (Ishikawa diagram),
    370, 390
cease-and-desist letter, 228
celebration, 389
central programming unit (CPU), 48
champion, 74
change advisory board (CAB), 347
change control board (CCB), 339–340, 347, 354
change control system, 335–342
change log, 50
change request, 116, 335
chart, 311–313
charter, project, 85–90, 98
claims administration, 334
classification of records, 91
clients, predetermined, 23
closeout report, 388
closeout report, project, 388, 391
Closing phase
    characteristics of, 380
    controlling quality within, 364–374
    defined, 26
    overview of, 10, 391
    project endings overview, 380–382
    steps for, 382–389
closure meeting, project, 388
Cloud+, 55
cloud computing, 51, 63
Cloud Essentials, 55
cloud service model, 51–55, 64
code of account, 156
collaborating, 217, 307–308, 321
communication
    on agile team, 294–297
    on agile teams, 294–297
    archiving within, 314–315

asynchronous, 288
for audits, 299
backlog refinement as, 296
basic communication model, 285
for business continuity response, 300
of change deployment, 342, 345–346
of change status, 340–341
channels for, 313
collaboration tools for, 307–309
conflicts regarding, 215
controlling, 315–316
cultural differences regarding, 297–298
daily standups as, 295
decoding, 286
document integrity within, 314
document security within, 314
effective *versus* efficient, 287
email as, 289–290
escalating, 315–316
face-to-face meetings as, 290–291
factors influencing, 297–299, 321
fax as, 290
file-sharing platform for, 308
formal, 293
forms of, 288–289
for incident response, 300
informal, 293
information exchanging within,
    285–287
instant messaging as, 290
iteration review as, 296
lines of, 286–287
listening, 287
meetings as, 289
message within, 285
methods of, 288–297, 321
for milestones, 300
multi-authoring and editing software
    for, 307–308
overcommunication, 294
overview of, 321
for phase gate reviews, 300
planning, 284–287, 292–293, 318, 321
platforms for, 307
printed media as, 291
for project changes, 299
of project manager, 35–36
for project planning, 299
with project team members, 293–294
receiver within, 285
records of, 313–315
for resource changes, 301
retrospective, 296
for risk register updates, 300
for schedule changes, 300
scheduled meetings as, 292
sender within, 285

short message service (SMS) as, 291
social media as, 291
for stakeholder changes, 300
stakeholder expectations and, 316–317, 322
synchronous, 288
for task initiation/completion, 300
technology barriers regarding, 298
time zones regarding, 297
transmitting, 286
triggers for, 299–302, 321
verbal, 289
video and voice conferencing as, 290
whiteboard for, 308
wiki knowledge base for, 308
workflow and e-signature platforms for, 308
written, 289
community cloud, 54–55
compliance, 40–45, 63
compromising, as conflict management, 217
computing service, 46–47, 63
conferencing platforms, 309
confidentiality, breach of, 43–44
conflict, 215
conflict management, 215–219, 231
connectivity, 47–48
constrained optimization models, 24
constraint, 88–89, 113–117, 143, 215
constraint reprioritization, 116
content management system (CMS), 59–60, 64
contingency reserve (buffers), 172, 252–253
continuous integration, 349
contract, 23, 226–227, 333–334, 384–385, 391
contract change control system, 334
control chart, 369, 390
copyright, 241–242
core team member, 207
corrective action, 342
cost baseline, 250, 253–254, 273
cost estimate
    analogous estimating (top-down estimating),
        165–166, 245–246
    bottom-up estimating, 246–248, 250
    example of, 142
    within life cycles, 135
    overview of, 245–250, 273
    parametric estimating, 246
    within scope statement, 112–113
    techniques for, 245–249
    three-point estimates, 248–249
    tips for, 249–250
cost of capital, 18
cost performance index (CPI), 258–259, 379–380
cost plus award fee (CPAF), 227
cost plus fixed fee contract (CPFF), 226
cost plus incentive fee contract (CPIF), 226
cost plus percentage of cost (CPPC), 227
cost variance (CV), 257–258, 379

cost-benefit analysis, 15
cost-reimbursable contract, 226
crashing, 173, 186
critical path, 171
critical path method (CPM), 170–172, 186
critical success factor, 112
cube, stakeholder, 83
culture, communication considerations
        regarding, 297–298
current state, future state *versus*, 21
customer, 73
customer relationship management (CRM),
        56–57, 64

D

daily standup, 295
dashboard, 311
data classification, 244, 273
data confidentiality, 40–44, 63
data security, 244
data tier, 47
data warehouse, 49–50, 63
database, 57–59
decision model, 24
decision tree, 371
decision-maker, within change control systems, 339
decoding, 286
dedicated resources, 202–203
defect repair, 342
defects waste, 130
defining SDLC phase, 125
deliverables
    as constraint, 114
    example of, 142
    overview of, 143
    within project charter, 87
    within scope statement, 112
    verification and validation of, 382–383
    within work breakdown structure
        (WBS), 155–156
demerger/split, 344
demonstration/presentation, 304
dependencies, 162–163
deploying SDLC phase, 125
designing SDLC phase, 125
developer/engineer, 78
development life cycle, 125, 144
DevOps, 124
digital security, 243–244, 273
Disciplined Agile (DA), 351
discounted cash flow, 18–19
Discovery/Concept Preparation phase
    benefits and rewards determination
        within, 14–21

business case creation within, 13–14
cash flow techniques within, 17–21
defined, 25–26
examining existing artifacts within, 21–23
financial and performance analysis
    within, 15–17
overview of, 6
project origin within, 11–13
project selecting within, 13–14
stakeholders within, 13, 14
discretionary dependency, 162
dispute, 334
document integrity, 314
document security, 314
documentation, 50, 63, 376, 385
duration, of tasks, 165
duration compression, 172–173, 186
dynamic systems development method
    (DSDM), 132–133

E

earned value (EV), 257
earned value management (EVM), 256–260
Eiffel, Gustave, 17
80/20 rule, 367
electronic document and record management
    system (EDRMS), 59, 64
email, 289–290
end user, 73
end-to-end testing, 365–366
engineer/developer, 78
enterprise resource planning (ERP) system,
    56, 64, 80
environment, as constraint, 115
environmental, social, and governance (ESG)
    factors, 38–39, 62
epic, 177
equipment, procurement planning for, 221
escalating communications, 315–316
estimate to complete (ETC) formula, 260
estimating, techniques for, 165–166
exclusions from scope, 112, 142
Executing phase
    activities within, 330–331
    agile frameworks within, 349–351
    change control system implementation
        within, 335–342
    defined, 26
    managing issues within, 374–377
    operational change control on an IT project
        within, 347–349
    organizational change implementation
        within, 343–347

overview of, 9, 353–354
performance measure usage within, 377–380
project change management within, 342–343
project management plan review
    within, 331–332
Projects in Control (PRINCE2), 122,
    124, 351–352
quality control within, 364–374
vendor management within, 332–334, 354
expenditure reporting, 255, 260
expenditure tracking and reporting, 254–260
expert judgment, 25, 166
external dependency, 163
external resources, 202
extinction project ending, 382
Extreme Programming (XP), 130–132, 144

F

face-to-face meeting, 290–291
fast tracking, 173, 186
fax, 290
feasibility study, 14, 123
feature-driven development (FDD), 132
feedback, 213, 391
file-sharing platform, 308
financial accounting, 60–61
financial analysis, 15–17
finish-to-finish (FF) relationship, 163
finish-to-start (FS) relationship, 163
fishbone diagram, 370, 390
fixed-price contract, 226
float time, 170–171
flowcharting, 369, 390
focus group, 303
follow-up, meeting, 307
force majeure, 262
forcing, as conflict management, 217
formal communication, 293
forming, teams, 211
framework, 349
functional organization, 196–198
functional requirement, 120, 121
functional/extended team member, 207
future state, current state *versus*, 21

G

Gantt chart, 170, 186
gap analysis, 207–208
go/no-go decision, 365
governance gate, 176–177

H

hardware decommissioning, 205
Health Insurance Portability and Accountability
    Act (HIPPA), 42
histogram, 366–367, 390
human resources, 201
hybrid cloud, 55
hybrid methodology, 133–134, 160
Hypertext Markup Language (HTML), 60

I

impact, 263
impact analysis, 263–264
impact assessment, 337–338
incident response, 300
influence, as constraint, 116
informal communication, 293
information security, 240–244
information technology (IT)
    cloud models of, 51–55
    defined, 46
    financial systems within, 60–62
    infrastructure control, 347–348
    infrastructure of, 46–50
    overview of, 46, 63
    security policies for, 240–242
    software for, 55–60
    standards within, 45
    team, 78–79, 98
infrastructure, 46–50
infrastructure as a service (IaaS), 53
Initiating Phase
    kickoff meeting within, 93–95, 99,
        219–220, 303
    overview of, 6, 72, 98–99
    preliminary scope statement creation
        within, 83–85
    project charter creation within, 85–90
    records management plan creation
        within, 90–91
    stakeholder assessment within, 80–83
    stakeholder identification within, 72–80
inspecting, for quality control, 364–366
instant messaging, 290
integration project ending, 381
integration testing, 365
internal dependency, 163
internal rate of return (IRR), 20
internal resources, 202
interproject dependency, 203–204
interproject resource contention, 203–204
interrupting, 287
Ishikawa diagram (cause-and-effect diagram),
    370, 390

issue
    action items for, 376–377
    defined, 374
    managing, 374–377
    outcome documentation for, 376
    overview of, 390–391
    resolution plan for, 375–376
    resolution techniques for, 376
    tracking, 374–375
iteration review, 296
iterative approach, 5, 178
iterative process, 110

J

joint application development (JAD)
    meetings, 303–304

K

Kaizen, 129–130
Kanban, 127–129, 140, 144
Kanban board, 180–181
key performance indicator (KPI), 111–112,
    377–378, 391
kickoff meeting, 93–95, 99, 219–220, 303
knowledge base, for organizational
    change, 346–347

L

language, communication considerations
    regarding, 297
Lean, 129–130
legal requirement, 12, 44
lessons learned review, 385–388
letter of intent, 228
life cycle, 122–123, 134–135, 144, 204–206
lines of communication, 286–287
linkable data, 41–42
listening, 287
local area network (LAN), 47–48
logical relationship, 163, 186
low-quality resources, 202

M

maintenance, of resources, 204
maintenance agreement, 228
make-or-buy analysis, 220
management, 117, 206–215, 374

management reserve, 253
mandatory dependency, 162
Manifesto for Agile Software Development, 126
master service agreement (MSA) contract, 227
matrix organization, 198–200
matrix-based chart, 209–210
meeting
    action items within, 306–307
    agendas for, 305–306
    backlog refinement, 304
    brainstorming, 304
    calendaring tools for, 309
    collaborative, 303–304, 321
    as communication, 289
    conferencing platforms for, 309
    decisive, 304–305
    demonstrations/presentations, 304
    focus groups, 303
    follow-ups for, 307
    informative, 304
    joint application development (JAD), 303–304
    kickoff, 93–95, 99, 219–220, 303
    minutes for, 307
    overview of, 321
    preparing for, 305–307, 321
    print media for, 309
    project closure, 388
    project management scheduling tools
        for, 309–310
    project status, 302–303
    real-time surveys and polling for, 309
    roles within, 306
    scheduled *versus* impromptu, 292
    standup, 304
    steering committee, 304–305
    task setting, 304
    timeboxing for, 306
    time-tracking tools for, 310
    tools for, 309–310
    types of, 302–305
    version control tools for, 310
    workshops, 303
memorandum of understanding (MOU), 228
message, 285
milestone, 87, 168, 186, 300
minimum viable product (MVP), 139, 144
minutes, meeting, 307
Monte Carlo analysis, 266
motion waste, 130
multi-authoring and editing software, 307–308
multifactor authentication (MFA), 243–244
multitiered architecture, 47, 63

N

need, understanding, 84–85
needs assessment, 204

need-to-know basis, 244
negotiation, 36–37
net present value (NPV), 19
network attached storage (NAS), 49
network diagram, 164
networking, 47–48, 63
"The NIST Definition of Cloud Computing," 51
nondisclosure agreement (NDA), 228
nonfunctional requirement, 120–121
norming, teams, 211

O

objective, 84, 86, 111, 379
on-demand scheduling, 180
operational change control, 347–348, 349
operational expense (OpEx), 251
operational handoff, 383–384
operational security, 243
operations, 4
order of magnitude estimate, 112–113
organization breakdown structure (OBS), 209
organizational change, 343–347, 354
organizational chart, 208–209
organizational management, 37
organizational structure, 196–201, 230
outsourcing, 344
overproduction waste, 130
overview of, 60–62

P

pair programming, 131
parametric estimating, 166, 246
Pareto diagram, 367–368, 390
pass/fail decision, 365
payback period, 16–17
peformance measurement baseline, 159
performance analysis, 15–17
performance index, 258–259
performance measure, 377–380, 391
performance review, 333
performance testing, 366
performing, teams, 211
personal health information/protected health
    information (PHI), 42–43, 63, 244
personally identifiable information (PII),
    40–42, 63, 244
personnel management
    gap analysis for, 207–208
    matrix-based charts for, 209–210
    organizational charts within, 208–209
    overview of, 206
    position descriptions within, 208–209
    roles and responsibilities within, 208

team building and management
    within, 211–212
team composition within, 206
team member selection within, 206–208
team performance monitoring within, 212–216
trust building within, 212
phase, 125
phase gate review, 300
physical resources, 201
physical security, 242
planned value (PV), 257
planning, within life cycles, 135
Planning phase
    agile methodologies within, 126–138
    agile team members within, 139–140
    defined, 26, 108–109
    feasibility study within, 123
    overview of, 7–9, 108, 143–144
    project methodology determining
        within, 122–125
    requirement documentation within, 119–122
    scope determination on agile projects, 138–139
    scope management plan documenting
        within, 109–110
    scope statement writing within, 110–118
    solutions design determination within, 140–141
    waterfall methodology within, 125–126
planning SDLC phase, 125
platform, communication, 307
platform as a service (PaaS), 52
PMBOK® Guide, 5
points of escalation, 269
political influence, 25
polling, 309
portfolio, 3, 25
postimplementation support, 389
power/interest grid, 82
precedence diagramming method (PDM), 164
predecessor activity, 163
predetermined client, 23
predictive methodology, 125–126
preexisting contract, 23
preliminary review, 337
preliminary scope statement, 83–85
prequalified vendor list, 22–23
presentation tier, 47
presentation/demonstration, 304
prevention, 366
preventive action, 342
primary storage, 48, 63
principle of least privilege, 92
printed media, 291, 309
priority, 122
privacy, 40–45, 63
privacy regulations, 44
private cloud, 54
probability, 263, 273

probability and impact matrix, 263–264
problem solving, 36
process adjustment, 373
process diagram, 119–120
processing waste, 130
procurement audit, 333
procurement document, 385
procurement planning
    contract types within, 226–227
    equipment and, 221
    make-or-buy analysis, 220
    overview of, 220–221, 231
    staff augmentation for, 221
    statement of work (SOW) within, 221–222
    vendor selection criteria within, 223–226
    vendor solicitation within, 222–223
    vendor-related documents within, 228
product backlog, 138
product description, 111
product manager, 111
product owner, 138–139, 140
product schedule
    critical path method (CPM), 170–172
    developing, 167–177
    duration compression, 172–173
    Gantt chart, 170
    milestones within, 168
    Program Evaluation and Review Technique
        (PERT), 169, 170
    resource loading, 173–175
product scope, 111
program, defined, 3, 25
Program Evaluation and Review Technique
    (PERT), 169, 170
program manager, 77–78
project
    cancellation of, 380–381
    defining, 2–5, 25
    identifying, 2–3
    information reporting for, 310–316
    life cycle phases of, 5–10, 25–26, 122–123,
        134–135, 144
    objectives for, 111, 141
    operations and, 4
    planning, communication for, 299
    programs and portfolios regarding, 3–4
    reason or purpose, 3
    scope, 108
    within scope statement, 111
    selecting, 13–14
    selection methods, 23–25, 24, 25
    sponsor, 74, 98
    stakeholder staisfaction of, 3
    status, 310–316, 321
    status meeting, 302–303
    temporary, 3
    unique, 3

project baseline, 74
project budget
   contingency reserve within, 252–253
   cost baseline within, 253–254
   creating, 250–254
   expenditure tracking and reporting
      within, 254–260
   management reserve within, 253
   overview of, 273
   sample of, 252
project change, 299, 342–343
project charter, 85–90, 98
project closeout report, 388, 391
project closure meeting, 388
project description, 87
project ending, 380–382
project evaluation, 385–388
project management
   compliance and privacy considerations
      regarding, 40–45
   defined, 4, 25
   documents regarding, 8–9
   environmental, social, and governance (ESG)
      factors regarding, 38–39
   factors influencing activities of, 38–45
   legal and regulatory impacts within, 44
   phases of, 123
   privacy regulations within, 44
   scheduling tools for, 309–310
   software for, 175
project management office (PMO),
   77
project management plan, 108, 109, 159–160,
   331–332, 341
project manager (PM)
   communication role of, 35–36
   defined, 4, 62, 98
   in functional organization, 197
   leadership role of, 35
   in matrix organization, 199
   negotiation role of, 36–37
   organizational management by, 37
   overview of, 75–76
   problem solving role of, 36
   in projectized organization, 200
   role of, 34–37
   time management by, 37
project methodology, 122–125
project organization chart, 208–209, 231
project schedule
   agile methodology scheduling techniques
      for, 177–183
   approval of, 175–176
   burndown chart for, 178–179
   governance gates for, 176–177
   overview of, 186
   project management plan within, 159–160

quality gates within, 176
   resource assigning within, 164
   schedule baseline, 175–176
   schedule planning within, 160–161
   software for, 175
   task defining within, 161–162
   task duration determination within, 165–167
   task sequencing within, 162–164
   work breakdown structure within, 154–158
project team, 75, 293–294
projectized organization, 200–201
Projects in Control (PRINCE2), 124, 144, 351–352
prototype, 127
public cloud, 55
pull system, 128–129
pull-based scheduling, 180
purchase order (PO), 227

Q

qualitative analysis, 265, 273
quality assurance (QA), 78, 115
quality control
   acceptance within, 373–374
   charts for, 366–372, 390
   inspecting and testing within, 364–366
   overview of, 364, 390
   process adjustments within, 373
   rework, 373
   taking action regarding, 373–374
   variance causes within, 372–373
quality gates, 176
quantitative analysis, 266, 273

R

RACI chart, 210, 231
random access memory (RAM), 48
rapid elasticity, 52, 63
read-only memory (ROM), 48
Real World Scenario
   Assessing the Impact of Regulations and Legal
      Requirements, 12
   The Bathroom Remodel Project, 167
   The Data Center Upgrade, 22
   The Enterprise Resource Planning
      Implementation, 61, 80
   The Geographically Dispersed Team, 298–299
   Kickoff for Remote Team Members, 219–220
   Lessons Learned, 387–388
   Main Street Office Move, 62, 95–97, 141–143,
      183–185, 229–230, 270–272, 319–320,
      353, 389–390

Negotiating with the Business Unit, 36–37
New Wine, 45
A Phased Delay, 378
Planning a School Building Repair, 88
Project Management 101, 215
The Road Trip, 268
Sample Scope Statement, 117–118
real-time surveys, 309
receiver, 285
record, 90
records management plan, 90–91
records management system, 91, 99
refactoring, 131
register, stakeholder, 79
registered trademark, 241
regression plan, 338
regression testing, 366
regulations, 12, 44
relational database (RDBMS), 58–59
relocation, 344
remote access, 243–244
remote resources, 202
reorganization, 344
request for bid (RFB), 222–223
request for information (RFI), 222–223
request for proposal (RFP), 222–223
request for quote (RFQ), 222–223
requirement
    business, 119–120
    as constraint, 115
    document for, 119–122
    functional, 120, 121
    within life cycles, 135
    nonfunctional, 120–121
    overview of, 143
    priority for, 122
    process diagram for, 119–120
    within project charter, 87
    traceability matrix, 121–122
resolution plan, 375–376
resource breakdown structure (RBS), 209
resource calendar, 164
resource changes, communication for, 301
resource leveling, 174, 175, 186
resource loading, 173–175
resource pooling, 51, 63
resource smoothing, 174, 175, 186
resources
    allocation of, 230
    assigning, 164
    benched, 203
    capital, 201
    as constraint, 115
    end-of-life software, 205
    hardware decommissioning of, 205
    human, 201

internal *versus* external, 202
interproject dependencies and, 203–204
interproject resource contention and, 203–204
life cycle of, 204–206
low-quality, 202
maintenance of, 204
in matrix organization, 199
overallocation of, 203, 230
overview of, 230
physical, 201
rates for, 247
remote, 202
shared *versus* dedicated, 202–203
shortages of, 203
successor planning for, 205–206
responsibility assigned matrix (RAM), 209
retention schedule, 91
retrospective meeting, 296
return on investment (ROI), 20
reverse resource allocation scheduling, 175
reward, 14–21, 389
rework, 373
risk, 75, 89, 135, 261, 374
risk identification, 261–263
risk owner, 269
risk planning
    defined, 261
    impact analysis within, 263–264
    overview of, 260–261, 273
    qualitative analysis within, 265
    quantitative analysis within, 266
    risk analysis within, 263–267, 273
    risk identification within, 261–263
    risk monitoring within, 270
    risk response preparation within, 267–269, 273
    situational/scenario analysis within, 266–267
    strengths, weaknesses, opportunities, and
        threats (SWOT) analysis within, 262–263
risk register, 262, 300
risk response plan, 262
risk trigger, 269
rollback plan, 338, 348
run chart, 369–370, 390

S

SaaS (software as a service), 52
salience model, for stakeholders, 83
Scaled Agile Framework (SAFe), 351
scatter diagram, 371–372, 390
schedule, 75, 115, 135, 160–161, 300
schedule baseline, 175–176
schedule performance index (SPI), 259, 380
schedule variance, 258, 379

scope
    as constraint, 114
    defined, 75, 108
    determination on agile projects, 138–139
    excessive changes to, 343
    within security policy, 241
scope baseline, 158
scope creep, 109, 116
scope management plan, 108, 109–110
scope statement, 108, 110–118, 143
scoring model, 15–16
Scrum, 127, 139–140, 144, 179–180, 186
Scrum board, 181–182
Scrum master, 140, 178
Scrum of Scrums, 350–351
Scrumban, 129
secondary storage, 49, 63
security clearance, 243
security policy, 240–244, 272–273
seller invoices, 334
sender, 285
senior management team, 75
sensitive personally identifiable data elements
    (SPII), 40, 63
sequencing, 162
service level agreement (SLA), 228
shared resources, 202–203
short message service (SMS), 291
sign-off, 383
simulation techniques, 266
situational/scenario analysis, 266–267
SMART goals, 345
smoke testing, 365
smoothing, as conflict management, 217
social media, 291
soft logic, 162
soft skill, 34
software, 55–60, 64, 205
software as a service (SaaS), 52
software change control, 348
software development life cycle (SDLC), 125, 144
software development project, 127
solicitation, vendor, 222–223
solutions architect, 140–141, 144
solutions design, 140–141
split/demerger, 344
sponsor, project, 74, 98
sponsors, as constraint, 117
sprint planning meeting, 177–178
sprints, 127, 177–178
staff augmentation, 221
stakeholder
    within agile teams, 140
    analyzing/assessing, 14, 80–83, 98
    business analyst as, 76
    categorization of, 81–82
    change status communication to, 340–341

    communication for, 300, 316–317, 322
    as constraint, 117
    cubes for, 83
    customer as, 73
    data ownership by, 205
    defined, 13, 72, 73, 98
    end user as, 73
    enterprise resource planning (ERP)
        system for, 80
    expertise of, 73
    identifying, 14, 73, 98
    interviewing, 81
    IT team as, 78–79
    within life cycles, 135
    negotiation with, 73
    power/interest grid for, 82
    program manager as, 77–78
    project management office (PMO) as, 77
    project manager as, 75–76
    project sponsor as, 74
    register for, 79
    responsibilities of, 72–80
    roles of, 72–80
    salience model for, 83
    senior management team as, 76
    subject matter expert (SME) as, 76–77
standup meetings, 304
start-to-finish (SF) relationship, 163
start-to-start (SS) relationship, 163
starvation project ending, 381
statement of work (SOW), 221–222
statistical sampling, 369, 390
status reports, 310–311
steering committee meeting, 304–305
storage, 48–49, 63
storage area network (SANs), 49
storage waste, 130
storming, teams, 211
story card, 131
story point, 179–180
strengths, weaknesses, opportunities, and threats
    (SWOT) analysis, 262–263
stress testing, 366
structured data, 57
subject matter expert (SME), 37, 76–77
success criteria, 89–90, 111–112
synchronous communication, 288

T

task, 161–164, 165–167
task board, 181–182
task initiation/completion, 300
task list, 162
task setting meeting, 304

team
  adjourning, 211
  building of, 211–212
  communication with, 293–294
  composition of, 206
  core members of, 207
  disgruntled members within, 218–219
  disputes within, 218
  expectations for, 213
  functional/extended members of, 207
  gap analysis for, 207–208
  management of, 211–212
  overview of, 231
  performance monitoring of, 212–216
  releasing members of, 384
  remote, 219–220
  rewards for, 214–215, 231
  roles and responsibilities within, 208
  selecting members for, 206–208
  training for, 215
  trust building within, 212
  work styles within, 215
terms of reference (TOR), 227
test-driven development, 131
testers, IT, 78
testing, for quality control, 364–366
testing SDLC phase, 125
three-point estimate, 248–249
time and materials (T&M) contract, 227
time estimate, 112–113, 142
time management, 37
time zone, 297
timeboxing, 306
time-tracking tools, for meeting, 310
tolerable result, 365
top-down estimating (analogous estimating), 165–166, 245–246
traceability matrix, 121–122
training, 215, 346, 383
transition plan, 383–384
transmitting, communication, 286
transportation waste, 130

unit testing, 365
unstructured data, 58
user acceptance testing (UAT), 366
user stories, 138, 177, 186

V

validation check, 348
variances, within quality control, 372–373
velocity, 179–180
vendor, 223–226, 228, 332–334, 354
vendor list, prequalified, 23
vendor solitiation, 222–223
verbal communication, 289
version control tools, 310
video and voice conferencing, 290

W

waiting waste, 130
warranty, 228, 389
waterfall methodology, 125–126, 160, 206
weighted average, 169
whiteboard, 308
wide area network (WAN), 47–48
wiki knowledge base, 308
wine, 45
wired network, 47
wireless network, 47
work breakdown structure (WBS), 108, 154–158, 185–186
work effort, 246
work package level, 155
work-around, 376
Workday, 23
workflow and e-signature platform, 308
workshop, 303
written communication, 289

U

Ultimate Kronos Group, 54
unit price contract, 227

X

XaaS (anything as a service), 54

Online Test Bank

To help you study for your CompTIA Project+ certification exam, register to gain one year of FREE access after activation to the online interactive test bank—included with your purchase of this book! All of the chapter review and practice questions in this book are included in the online test bank so you can study in a timed and graded setting.

Register and Access the Online Test Bank

To register your book and get access to the online test bank, follow these steps:

1. Go to www.wiley.com/go/sybextestprep
2. Select your book from the list.
3. Complete the required registration information, including answering the security verification to prove book ownership. You will be emailed a pin code.
4. Follow the directions in the email or go to www.wiley.com/go/sybextestprep.
5. Find your book on that page and click the "Register or Login" link with it. Then enter the pin code you received and click the "Activate PIN" button.
6. On the Create an Account or Login page, enter your username and password, and click Login or, if you don't have an account already, create a new account.
7. At this point, you should be in the test bank site with your new test bank listed at the top of the page. If you do not see it there, please refresh the page or log out and log back in.

SYBEX®
A Wiley Brand